18th Conference on Natural Language Processing/Konferenz zur Verarbeitung naturlicher Sprache (KONVENS 2022)

Potsdam, Germany
12-15 September 2022

ISBN: 978-1-7138-6763-0

Printed from e-media with permission by:

Curran Associates, Inc.
57 Morehouse Lane
Red Hook, NY 12571

Some format issues inherent in the e-media version may also appear in this print version.

Printed with permission by Curran Associates, Inc. (2023)

For permission requests, please contact the Association for Computational Linguistics at the address below.

Association for Computational Linguistics
209 N. Eighth Street
Stroudsburg, Pennsylvania 18360

Phone: 1-570-476-8006
Fax: 1-570-476-0860

acl@aclweb.org

Additional copies of this publication are available from:

Curran Associates, Inc.
57 Morehouse Lane
Red Hook, NY 12571 USA
Phone: 845-758-0400
Fax: 845-758-2633
Email: curran@proceedings.com
Web: www.proceedings.com

Table of Contents

Data Augmentation for Intent Classification of German Conversational Agents in the Finance Domain 1
Sophie Rentschler, Martin Riedl, Christian Stab and Martin Rückert

MONAPipe: Modes of Narration and Attribution Pipeline for German Computational Literary Studies and Language Analysis in spaCy 8
Tillmann Dönicke, Florian Barth, Hanna Varachkina and Caroline Sporleder

Lemma Hunting: Automatic Spelling Normalization for CMC Corpora 16
Eckhard Bick

DocSCAN: Unsupervised Text Classification via Learning from Neighbors 21
Dominik Stammbach and Elliott Ash

Modelling Cultural and Socio-Economic Dimensions of Political Bias in German Tweets 29
Aishwarya Anegundi, Konstantin Schulz, Christian Rauh and Georg Rehm

Adapting GermaNet for the Semantic Web 41
Claus Zinn, Marie Hinrichs and Erhard Hinrichs

Assessing the Linguistic Complexity of German Abitur Texts from 1963–2013 48
Noemi Kapusta, Marco Müller, Matilda Schauf, Isabell Siem and Stefanie Dipper

Measuring Faithfulness of Abstractive Summaries 63
Tim Fischer, Steffen Remus and Chris Biemann

Sentiment Analysis on Twitter for the Major German Parties during the 2021 German Federal Election 74
Thomas Schmidt, Jakob Fehle, Maximilian Weissenbacher, Jonathan Richter, Philipp Gottschalk and Christian Wolff

Do gender neutral affixes naturally reduce gender bias in static word embeddings? 88
Jonas Wagner and Sina Zarrieß

Improved Open Source Automatic Subtitling for Lecture Videos 98
Robert Geislinger, Benjamin Milde and Chris Biemann

Constructing a Derivational Morphology Resource with Transformer Morpheme Segmentation 104
Łukasz Knigawka

Improved Opinion Role Labelling in Parliamentary Debates 110
Laura Bamberg, Ines Rehbein and Simone Paolo Ponzetto

ABSINTH : A small world approach to word sense induction 121
Victor Zimmermann and Maja Hoffmann

This isn't the bias you're looking for: Implicit causality, names and gender in German language models 129
Sina Zarrieß, Hannes Gröner, Torgrim Solstad and Oliver Bott

Evaluation of Automatic Speech Recognition for Conversational Speech in Dutch, English, and German: What Goes Missing? 135
Alianda Lopez, Andreas Liesenfeld and Mark Dingemanse

Semantic Role Labeling for Sentiment Inference: A Case Study 144
Manfred Klenner and Anne Göhring

Building an Extremely Low Resource Language to High Resource Language Machine Translation System from Scratch 150
Flammie A Pirinen and Linda Wiechetek

More Like This: Semantic Retrieval with Linguistic Information 156
Steffen Remus, Saba Anwar, Gregor Wiedemann, Fynn Petersen-Frey, Seid Muhie Yimam and Chris Biemann

TopicShoal: Scaling Partisanship Using Semantic Search 167
Sami Diaf and Ulrich Fritsche

Bye, Bye, Maintenance Work? Using Model Cloning to Approximate the Behavior of Legacy Tools 175
Piush Aggarwal and Torsten Zesch

Proceedings of the 18th Conference on Natural Language Processing/Konferenz zur Verarbeitung natürlicher Sprache (KONVENS 2022)

12-15 September, 2022
University of Potsdam
Potsdam, Germany

Introduction

The papers of these proceedings have been presented at the 18th edition of KONVENS (Konferenz zur Verarbeitung natürlicher Sprache/Conference on Natural Language Processing). KONVENS is a conference series on computational linguistics established in 1992 that was held biennially until 2018 and has been held annually since. KONVENS is organized under the auspices of the German Society for Computational Linguistics and Language Technology, the Special Interest Group on Computational Linguistics of the German Linguistic Society, the Austrian Society for Artificial Intelligence and SwissText.

The 18th KONVENS took place on-site from September 12 to September 15, 2022 at University of Potsdam. The KONVENS main conference was accompanied by a workshop, a shared task (GermEval), two tutorials and a 'PhD Day'. In addition, this year's edition hosted a career networking event. In total these proceedings contain 21 papers (10 long, 11 short).
Many thanks to all who submitted their work to KONVENS and to our board of reviewers for supporting us greatly with evaluating the submissions. Moreover we would like to thank University of Potsdam for providing the conference rooms, all people involved in organisation, and our sponsors. Without their support KONVENS 2022 would not have been possible.

Robin Schaefer
Xiaoyu Bai
Manfred Stede
Torsten Zesch

People

Local Organization

Mohammad Yeghaneh Abkenar, Xiaoyu Bai, Annemarie Friedrich (GSCL), Freya Hewett, René Knaebel, Robin Schaefer, Manfred Stede

Program Chairs

Xiaoyu Bai, Robin Schaefer, Manfred Stede, Torsten Zesch

Program Committee

Adrien Barbaresi, Maria Berger, Marcel Bollmann, Peter Bourgonje, Ernst Buchberger, Berthold Crysmann, Stefanie Dipper, Stephanie Evert, Jana Götze, Anke Holler, Roman Klinger, Valia Kordoni, Brigitte Krenn, Udo Kruschwitz, Ekaterina Lapshinova-Koltunski, Katja Markert, Alexander Mehler, Clemens Neudecker, Rainer Osswald, Simon Ostermann, Simone Paolo Ponzetto, Ines Rehbein, Georg Rehm, Josef Ruppenhofer, Felix Sasaki, Roland Schäfer, Tatjana Scheffler, Yves Scherrer, David Schlangen, Helmut Schmid, Gerold Schneider, Roman Schneider, Sabine Schulte im Walde, Maria Skeppstedt, Manfred Stede, Henning Wachsmuth, Magdalena Wolska, Sina Zarrieß, Torsten Zesch, Heike Zinsmeister

Satellite Events

2nd Workshop on Computational Linguistics for Political Text Analysis
Organizers: Ines Rehbein, Christopher Klamm, Simone Ponzetto, Gabriella Lapesa

Text Complexity DE Challenge 2022 (GermEval)
Organizers: Salar Mohtaj, Babak Naderi, Sebastian Möller

Text to talk: foundations of interactive language modeling for conversational AI and talking robots (Tutorial)
Organizers: Andreas Liesenfeld, Ada Lopez, Mark Dingemanse

Retico – An Introduction to Building Incremental Dialogue Systems in Python (Tutorial)
Organizers: Thilo Michael, Maike Paetzel-Prüsmann, Jana Götze, David Schlangen

PhD Day
Organized by local organizers

Invited Talks

Malvina Nissim: In Other Words. Models and Evaluation for Text Style Transfer

Whenever we write about something, we make a choice (consciously or not) on how we do it. For example, I can write about a series I watched while I was COVID-bound at home like this: 'I viewed it and I believe it is a high quality program.' but also like this: 'I've watched it and it is AWESOME!!!!'. The content is (approximately) the same, but the style I've used is different: informal in the second formulation, much more formal in the first one. In the larger field of Natural Language Generation, text style transfer is, broadly put, the task of converting a text of one style (for example informal) into another (for example formal) while preserving its content. How can models be best trained for this task? What can be expected of a system performing text style transfer? And what does it mean to do it well, especially given the broad range of rewriting possibilities? In this talk I will present various strategies to model the task of style transfer under different conditions and I will discuss insights from both human and automatic evaluations. Chiefly, through the analysis of both modelling and evaluation and through engagement with audience, I will also reflect on the nature, the definition, and the the future of the task itself.

Henning Wachsmuth: Generation of Subjective Language. Chances and Risks

Research on natural language generation has made tremendous advances in the last years, due to powerful neural language models, such as BART, T5, and GPT-3. While generation technologies have been studied extensively for fact-oriented applications such as machine translation and customer service chatbots, they are recently also employed increasingly for creating and modifying subjective language – from the encoding of human beliefs in newly produced text to the debiasing of corpora and the transfer of subjective style characteristics of human-written texts. This bring up the question whether there are generation tasks that we should refrain from doing research on, due to the ethical issues they may entail. In this talk, I will give an overview of recent research on the generation of subjective language and present selected approaches in detail, covering the areas of computational argumentation, media framing, and social bias mitigation. On this basis, I will discuss both the chances for humans and society emerging from respective generation technologies and the ethical risks that come with their application. The interaction of chances and risks defines a red line that, I argue, should not be crossed without important reasons.

Proceedings of the 18th Conference on Natural Language Processing (KONVENS 2022)

Data Augmentation for Intent Classification of German Conversational Agents in the Finance Domain

Sophie Rentschler, Martin Riedl, Christian Stab, Martin Rückert
Diamant Software GmbH, KI Kompetenzzentrum
Robert-Bosch-Str. 7, 64293 Darmstadt
{s.rentschler,m.riedl,c.stab,m.rueckert}@diamant-software.de

Abstract

In this paper, we focus on improving the intent recognition for a conversational agent. For languages other than English, labeled data needed for training is often limited. Limitations rise even more when moving to specific domains. Here, our goal is to improve the intent recognition for a German conversational agent deployed in the financial sector. We treat this problem as a classification task. Using several augmentation techniques we expand the seed data used for training and compare the performance of the intent classifier. Applying a backtranslation approach using a commercial Machine Translation (MT) engine yields significant improvement ($p < 0.01$) over a baseline system.

1 Introduction

Conversational agents are becoming ubiquitous as lots of companies employ such agents for supporting and extending their services. Based on the applied domain, their languages – specifically, their vocabulary – constantly expand depending on the range of their services as well as the domain they are applied in. Machine learning methods are mainly used to teach conversational agents to react to user requests, called *intents*. For recognizing the intent, usually a *natural language understanding* (NLU) component is used.

In order to train the NLU, for each intent various user utterances are required to understand the user and to discriminate between different intents. Due to the efforts required to manually create sufficient amounts of training data, we investigate if augmentation methods for enriching the training data helps to improve the performance.

In this paper, we tackle various research questions: Is it beneficial to add noise to the data by randomly replacing words or do we really need to have "human"-readable paraphrases? Also, we will investigate which methods are suitable for automatic paraphrase generation for intents. Most of the previous paraphrasing approaches for dialogue agents focus on training data from the open domain (e.g. booking a hotel, booking a table in a restaurant, calling the police) written in English (Kumar et al., 2019; Quan and Xiong, 2019). In this paper, we research the applicability of augmentation approaches for German for the finance domain.

We present results for a manually created dataset for the finance domain. Using paraphrasing methods to augment training data used for machine learning differs from the typical paraphrasing scenario. Whereas for e.g. text simplification the goal is to generate sentences that can be read by humans, here our goal is to teach the machine learning method to be more robust against textual variations when understanding natural language.
In order to extend the data we use methods based on lexical resources (PPDB (Ganitkevitch et al., 2013), GermaNet (Hamp and Feldweg, 1997)), embeddings and contextual embeddings (BERT (Devlin et al., 2019)) as well as backtranslation using an out-of-the-box machine translation (MT) system. Based on our experiments we achieve significant improvements using backtranslation.

2 Related Work

In recent years, deep learning techniques have become popular to tackle intent classification (Mesnil et al., 2013). This line of work has been continued by combining different tasks of the NLU component into one model (Goo et al., 2018; Haihong et al., 2019). Sequence-to-sequence models have been leveraged to bootstrap intent classification in new features (Jolly et al., 2020). Yet, sufficiently large training datasets are required for such approaches.

Several proposals have been made to resolve the lack of training data for this task and avoid costly generation of suitable datasets by hand. Machine translation (MT) can be used if seed data already exists (Gaspers et al., 2018). Furthermore, exploiting backtranslation techniques, commonly used in MT to overcome shortage of parallel data has become popular for automatic paraphrase generation (Mallinson et al., 2017). Using similar languages for back and forth translation has been proven useful for MT (Hajic, 2000). Whereas backtranslation originates from MT (Sennrich et al., 2016), it recently has been applied to augment data for other tasks such as hate speech detection and transfer learning (Beddiar et al., 2021; Subedi et al., 2021).

Machine Learning tasks are fairly robust to noise in text as long as the corpus is large. Agarwal et al. (2007) report only slight degradation of the system when adding 70% of noise to the text. When adding 40% of noise to the text the system almost performs on par with its competitor which was trained on clean text. Word order and syntactic information are elements which have proven to be mostly irrelevant for text classification[1]. Random word swaps and deletions which first and foremost harm syntax even prove to be helpful data augmentation techniques (Wei and Zou, 2019).

Following the pattern of paraphrase generation, external linguistic resources such as PPDB (Ganitkevitch and Callison-Burch, 2014) or WordNet (Miller, 1995) have been used for retrieval-based approaches (Zukerman and Raskutti, 2002; Babkin et al., 2017; Alva-Manchego et al., 2020). Zhang et al. (2017) established a sentence paraphrasing framework formulated as an encoder-decoder problem. In more recent years, contextualized embeddings were introduced and became the center of attention. BERT (Devlin et al., 2019), ELMo (Peters et al., 2018) and GPT-2 (Radford et al., 2019) have not only been used for paraphrase generation but also for paraphrase candidate ranking (Zhou et al., 2019).

3 Data Augmentation Methods

We use the Rasa framework (Bocklisch et al., 2017) to setup a task-oriented conversational agent. It structures dialogues into two components, namely *Core* and *Natural Language Understanding* (NLU). The Core component takes care of the dialogue management whereas the NLU component performs the entire processing of the text, e.g. tokenization, identification of entities, dependency parsing and classification of intent types. Here, we focus on a basic NLU pipeline including tokenization, intent classification and entity recognition. We aim to improve the task of intent classification by enhancing our training data using augmentation techniques for this task.

Here, we present the augmentation methods we apply in order to enhance the data used to train an intent classifier.

For the resource- and embedding-based approaches we paraphrase one word per intent phrase. We mask words which convey unique information in order to ensure domain-specific words are excluded from paraphrasing. Furthermore, we restrict paraphrasing to words belonging to the categories *verb* and *adverb* for these methods so crucial words remain unchanged. Results (translated to English) of the augmentation methods can be found in Table 1.

PPDB: The multilingual PPDB (Ganitkevitch and Callison-Burch, 2014) is a resource built on bilingual parallel corpora aimed to capture paraphrases. We use the German part of the PPDB for replacing single tokens using the n best-scored words.

GermaNet: GermaNet (Hamp and Feldweg, 1997) is a manually crafted resource. Here, we replace a word by all other words in the same synset.

Embeddings: We consider skip-gram word2vec embeddings (Mikolov et al., 2013)[3]. We paraphrase lexemes' vocabularies using the n most similar words based on the cosine similarity. For this, we sort the vocabulary by cosine similarity and select the n most similar words in order to paraphrase intent samples.

Contextual Embeddings: BERT-based embeddings (Qiang et al., 2020) are used by feeding the intent phrase to the contextual embedding while masking the target word which we want to paraphrase. For replacing verbs and adverbs we proceed in the same manner as with the embeddings approach.

Machine Translation: We make use of the machine translation technique commonly used to over-

[1]We are aware that some machine learning methods are relying more on word ordering than others (e.g. sequence models like CRF or HMM), however, we assume that correctness is more relevant when generating text for humans rather than for machines.

[2]Since the PPDB does not only store lemmatized word forms or infinitives and the pivoting approach uses English as a reference language which is morphologically less complex than German, it groups morphological inflections into the same paraphrase cluster. This is the reason why we find morphological variations of the same verbs used as paraphrases.

[3]We use spaCy vectors which are part of the *de_core_news_md* model containing 276,087 words with vectors and 20,000 unique vectors trained on Wikipedia and OSCAR Common Crawl (Ortiz Suárez et al., 2019)

Augmentation method	**Original phrase**	**Augmented phrases**
GermaNet	Show the name of the company.	**Display** the name of the company. **Indicate** the name of the company. **Express** the name of the company.
PPDB	Show the name of the company.	**Shows** the name of the company.[2]
Embedding	Show the name of the company.	**Theatre** the name of the company. **View** the name of the company. **Spectacle** the name of the company.
BERT	Show the name of the company.	**Display** the name of the company. **Demonstrate** the name of the company. **Present** the name of the company.
Machine Translation	Show the name of the company.	**Give me** the name of the company. **Say** the name of the company. **Present** the **company's name**.

Table 1: Paraphrase examples. Underlined target words in the original phrase are replaced by the bold words in the augmented phrases.

come shortage of parallel data. Applying backtranslation, we first translate an intente phrase from a source language (i.e. German) into different target languages and then translate it back into the source language. Here, we use Google's commercial Cloud Translation API[4].

4 Evaluation

Baselines: To judge the performance of the paraphrasing methods we consider three baselines. Gold: The first baseline is represented by the performance without using any augmented data and solely train on the labeled training data.
Random: For the random baseline we replace verbs and adverbs with random words selected from the vocabular of the embeddings. For each training instance we replace one word at maximum.
Duplicate: For the duplicate baseline we add each utterance twice to the gold standard data. This baseline determines whether plainly adding data improves the classifier or more diverse data is needed to improve the system.

Dataset: We evaluate the methods on a manually created German finance dataset for the accounting domain. For the creation of the dataset several people wrote down utterances they would use in a given setting to retrieve information from the dialogue assistant. The dataset comprises 20 intents out of which 12 are exclusive to the finance domain. The remaining eight intents provide domain-independent dialogue elements such as greetings, continuation and abortion of dialogues or confirmation and rejection in selection processes. This data is not balanced across intents. On average, intents are represented by about 44 intent phrases. Examples (translated to English) are listed in Table 2.

Intent	**Phrases**
who	Who are you? Are you a bot? What's your task?
kpi-help	What KPIs do you know? Which KPIs can you report on? For which KPIs do you have information?
company-set	Let's continue with company XYZ. Change to company XYZ. Please proceed with company XYZ.

Table 2: Baseline dataset: intent phrase examples.

Experimental Setup. Our experiments are based on the Rasa framework[5] from which we use the DIET classifier (Bunk et al., 2020) to train an intent classifier. In this paper, we solely focus on the intent classification and disregard the entity recognition. We randomly split the training data into train, dev and test sets in the ratio of 80/10/10. As we observe high fluctuation in performance between data splittings, for each experiment we use 10 different random seeds to split the data in order to account for outliers which are caused by inconvenient data splittings (Søgaard et al., 2021). In the

[4] https://cloud.google.com/translate

[5] https://rasa.com/

Intents	Gold baseline	Random baseline	Duplicate baseline	BERT	PPDB	GermaNet	Embedding	Top 3 translations NL + IT + FR
affirm	0.6153	0.0047	0.0927	-0.0601	0.0673	-0.0638	0.0402	0.0617
answer-date	0.9153	0.0551	0.0396	-0.0152	0.0469	0.0416	-0.0036	0.0665
answer-taxonomy	0.8222	-0.0440	-0.1451	-0.1166	-0.0773	-0.0097	-0.0504	-0.0707
cancel	0.5503	-0.1979	-0.0044	-0.0540	0.0548	-0.0716	0.0042	0.1521
company-ask-for	0.8951	0.0215	-0.0054	0.0117	0.0326	0.0315	0.0223	0.0470
company-set	0.9452	-0.0406	-0.0212	-0.0167	-0.0110	0.0038	-0.0095	0.0060
compare-kpis	0.9626	-0.0292	-0.0023	-0.0353	0.0087	0.0130	-0.0184	0.0297
customer-overview	0.9382	-0.0340	-0.0131	-0.0009	0.0116	-0.0044	-0.0046	0.0002
greet	0.9139	-0.0231	-0.0678	-0.0012	0.0107	-0.0664	0.0093	-0.0066
kpi	0.9692	-0.0173	-0.0185	-0.0232	0.0000	0.0028	-0.0051	0.0011
kpi-help	0.9344	-0.0179	-0.0018	0.0161	0.0043	0.0268	0.0148	0.0310
op-note-get	0.9001	-0.0440	-0.0446	-0.0420	-0.0069	-0.0203	-0.0386	0.0042
op-note-set	0.8980	-0.0688	-0.0279	-0.0546	-0.0030	-0.0194	-0.0188	0.0203
out-of-scope	0.8676	-0.0169	0.0037	-0.0073	0.0178	-0.0077	0.0008	0.0078
query-op-all-customers	0.9517	-0.0453	-0.0222	-0.0148	-0.0082	-0.0202	-0.0090	-0.0077
query-op-single-customer	0.9524	-0.0708	-0.0300	-0.0102	-0.0048	-0.0148	-0.0240	0.0000
reject	0.5105	-0.1650	-0.0500	-0.1095	0.0879	0.0534	0.0543	0.0895
tell-a-joke	0.9333	-0.0143	-0.0082	-0.0970	-0.0454	-0.0870	-0.0187	0.0667
thx	0.7719	-0.0278	-0.2228	-0.0695	-0.0195	-0.0824	-0.1548	0.0305
who	0.4941	0.0363	0.1224	0.0505	0.1759	0.1150	0.0445	0.1891
macro avg	**0.8371**	**-0.0370**	**-0.0213**	**-0.0325**	**0.0171**	**-0.0090**	**-0.0082**	**0.0359**

Table 3: Report of the F1 scores of the intent classification for the accounting datatset for all paraphrasing approaches.

following, we report scores averaged across these 10 data splittings.

5 Results

Our results for the accounting dataset are reported in Table 3. We show the macro F1 score for the gold baseline and present the delta scores between the augmentation methods and the gold baseline.

The random and duplicate baselines perform inferior to the gold baseline whereas the random baseline works slightly better than the duplicate baseline. We find these differences to be significant[6]. This confirms that the system does not benefit from neither adding pure noise to the training data nor adding data which does not enhance variance in phrasing the same content and benefits overfitting to the training data.

This is in line with the finding that quantity does not beat quality: Augmentation approaches generating the most data (random baseline (+342 intent phrases) and embedding-based approach (+283 intent phrases) vs. BERT (+121 intent phrases) and top 3 translations (+129 intent phrases)) do not necessarily perform best. Indeed, all of these approaches perform inferior to the baseline.

Overall, we observe that using PPDB for augmenting improves the system and we achieve significant improvements with the backtranslation approach ($p = 0.006$). For this approach we tested seven different target languages to extract paraphrases for the source sentence (see results in Table 4). In order to investigate whether the system benefits from an even larger data we combined the backtranslations from different languages. Indeed, the system performs best when combining backtranslations from the top three performing languages (Dutch, Italian and French). However, the improvements are only marginal in comparison to using solely augmentations based on the Dutch translation (0.8715 vs 0.8730).

Whereas we only show the average across ten different data splittings in Table 3 we observe considerable fluctuation in performance across data splittings for a specific group of intents: Both intents which are represented by only a few samples in the training set and intents which tend to have a fixed list of expression (e.g. greet, cancel, reject, thanks, affirm) seem highly susceptible to the random seed used when splitting the data (e.g. the gold baseline F1 score for intent *reject* ranges from 0.0 to 0.89 depending on the data splitting). Here, data augmentation does not eliminate this phenomenon and the splitting of the keywords is mainly responsible for the performance. In contrast, largest performance boost using augmentation methods are on average achieved for these intents (see intents *who* and *reject*), yet dependence on the data splitting

[6]p=0.04 for random baseline and p=0.008 for duplicate baseline using the Wilcoxon signed-rank test.

remains. This suggests that (1) as long as important keywords are present in the given data splitting augmentation methods are specifically beneficial for these intents and that (2) the methods presented cannot make up for missing keywords.

Unexpectedly, the BERT-based approach works worst among all other augmentation methods while its macro average is comparable to the random baseline. In particular, intents *reject* and *answer-taxonomy* suffer from this approach. e.g. the intent *answer-taxonomy* is mostly misclassified as intent *kpi*.

Pivot system	**Macro average F1**	**Increase over gold baseline**
English	0.8572	2.40%
Spanish	0.8468	1.16%
French	0.8630	3.10%
Italian	0.8611	2.87%
Hindi	0.8442	0.85%
Chinese	0.8441	0.84%
Dutch	0.8715	4.11%
All combined	0.8428	0.68%
Top 3	**0.8730**	**4.29%**

Table 4: Results for all languages tested with the MT approach.

Overall, the backtranslation approach outperforms the gold baseline and all other augmentation approaches. However, it is striking that macro averages drop considerably for Chinese and Hindi compared to the rest of the languages. Specifically, for intents *query-op-all-customers* and *query-op-single-customer* the performance drops significantly compared to the baselines. This drop is interlinked as *query-op-all-customers* is misclassified as *query-op-single-customer* and vice versa. Here, again, the intents are very similar and the augmentation does not help the classifier to discriminate the intents. This pattern resembles the behaviour described above: data representing these intents are similar. Paraphrasing this data leads to an overlap causing confusion between the two intents.

The best scores are achieved when combining the outcomes of the three best backtranslation systems. We observe that *answer-taxonomy* is an outlier for this approach as performance decreases by about seven percentage points. Again, this intent is mostly confused with intent *kpi*. However, without exception this intent gets inferior with any of the paraphrasing methods. As expected for the MT approach, the more similar the target language is to the source language (here, German) the more suitable the emerging paraphrases are and thus, the more the classifier benefits from them. This seems apparent comparing Chinese or Hindi scores with the Dutch scores.

6 Conclusion

In this paper, we present several augmentation methods to extend our training data to train a classifier for intent classification. Our best methods achieve significant improvements for the classification task while being easy to implement and not requiring lots of computational resources. We mainly face two limitations regarding the proposed approaches: (1) When we try to build up on lacking data (e.g. missing key words in the original dataset) our methods fail to fill this gap. (2) In case intents are very similar, augmentation approaches seem to rather confuse the classifier than enhance differences which leads to miss-classifications.

References

Sumeet Agarwal, Shantanu Godbole, Diwakar Punjani, and Shourya Roy. 2007. How much noise is too much: A study in automatic text classification. In *Seventh IEEE International Conference on Data Mining (ICDM 2007)*, pages 3–12. IEEE.

Fernando Alva-Manchego, Carolina Scarton, and Lucia Specia. 2020. Data-driven sentence simplification: Survey and benchmark. *Computational Linguistics*, pages 135–187.

Petr Babkin, Md Faisal Mahbub Chowdhury, Alfio Gliozzo, Martin Hirzel, and Avraham Shinnar. 2017. Bootstrapping chatbots for novel domains. In *Workshop at Neural Information Processing Systems on Learning with Limited Labeled Data*.

Djamila Romaissa Beddiar, Md Saroar Jahan, and Mourad Oussalah. 2021. Data expansion using back translation and paraphrasing for hate speech detection. *Online Social Networks and Media*, 24:100153.

Tom Bocklisch, Joey Faulkner, Nick Pawlowski, and Alan Nichol. 2017. Rasa: Open source language understanding and dialogue management. abs/1712.05181.

Tanja Bunk, Daksh Varshneya, Vladimir Vlasov, and Alan Nichol. 2020. Diet: Lightweight language understanding for dialogue systems. *arXiv preprint arXiv:2004.09936*.

Jacob Devlin, Ming-Wei Chang, Kenton Lee, and Kristina Toutanova. 2019. Bert: Pre-training of deep bidirectional transformers for language understanding. In *Proceedings of the 2019 Conference of the North American Chapter of the Association for Computational Linguistics: Human Language Technologies, Volume 1 (Long and Short Papers)*, pages 4171–4186.

Juri Ganitkevitch and Chris Callison-Burch. 2014. The multilingual paraphrase database. In *Language Resources and Evaluation Conference*, pages 4276–4283.

Juri Ganitkevitch, Benjamin Van Durme, and Chris Callison-Burch. 2013. PPDB: The paraphrase database. In *Proceedings of the 2013 Conference of the North American Chapter of the Association for Computational Linguistics: Human Language Technologies*, pages 758–764.

Judith Gaspers, Penny Karanasou, and Rajen Chatterjee. 2018. Selecting machine-translated data for quick bootstrapping of a natural language understanding system. In *Proceedings of the 2018 Conference of the North American Chapter of the Association for Computational Linguistics: Human Language Technologies, Volume 3 (Industry Papers)*, pages 137–144.

Chih-Wen Goo, Guang Gao, Yun-Kai Hsu, Chih-Li Huo, Tsung-Chieh Chen, Keng-Wei Hsu, and Yun-Nung Chen. 2018. Slot-gated modeling for joint slot filling and intent prediction. In *Proceedings of the 2018 Conference of the North American Chapter of the Association for Computational Linguistics: Human Language Technologies, Volume 2 (Short Papers)*, pages 753–757.

E Haihong, Peiqing Niu, Zhongfu Chen, and Meina Song. 2019. A novel bi-directional interrelated model for joint intent detection and slot filling. In *Proceedings of the 57th Annual Meeting of the Association for Computational Linguistics*, pages 5467–5471.

Jan Hajic. 2000. Machine translation of very close languages. In *Sixth Applied Natural Language Processing Conference*, pages 7–12.

Birgit Hamp and Helmut Feldweg. 1997. Germanet-a lexical-semantic net for german. In *Automatic information extraction and building of lexical semantic resources for NLP applications*.

Shailza Jolly, Tobias Falke, Caglar Tirkaz, and Daniil Sorokin. 2020. Data-efficient paraphrase generation to bootstrap intent classification and slot labeling for new features in task-oriented dialog systems. In *Proceedings of the 28th International Conference on Computational Linguistics: Industry Track*, pages 10–20.

Ashutosh Kumar, Satwik Bhattamishra, Manik Bhandari, and Partha Talukdar. 2019. Submodular optimization-based diverse paraphrasing and its effectiveness in data augmentation. In *Proceedings of the 2019 Conference of the North American Chapter of the Association for Computational Linguistics: Human Language Technologies, Volume 1 (Long and Short Papers)*, pages 3609–3619.

Jonathan Mallinson, Rico Sennrich, and Mirella Lapata. 2017. Paraphrasing revisited with neural machine translation. In *Proceedings of the 15th Conference of the European Chapter of the Association for Computational Linguistics: Volume 1, Long Papers*, pages 881–893.

Grégoire Mesnil, Xiaodong He, Li Deng, and Yoshua Bengio. 2013. Investigation of recurrent-neural-network architectures and learning methods for spoken language understanding. In *Interspeech*, pages 3771–3775.

Tomas Mikolov, Kai Chen, Greg Corrado, and Jeffrey Dean. 2013. Efficient estimation of word representations in vector space. *arXiv preprint arXiv:1301.3781*.

George A Miller. 1995. Wordnet: a lexical database for english. *Communications of the ACM*, pages 39–41.

Pedro Javier Ortiz Suárez, Benoît Sagot, and Laurent Romary. 2019. Asynchronous pipelines for processing huge corpora on medium to low resource infrastructures. Proceedings of the Workshop on Challenges in the Management of Large Corpora, pages 9–16.

Matthew E Peters, Mark Neumann, Mohit Iyyer, Matt Gardner, Christopher Clark, Kenton Lee, and Luke Zettlemoyer. 2018. Deep contextualized word representations. In *Proceedings of NAACL-HLT*, pages 2227–2237.

Jipeng Qiang, Yun Li, Yi Zhu, Yunhao Yuan, and Xindong Wu. 2020. Lexical simplification with pretrained encoders. In *Proceedings of the AAAI Conference on Artificial Intelligence*, volume 34, pages 8649–8656.

Jun Quan and Deyi Xiong. 2019. Effective data augmentation approaches to end-to-end task-oriented dialogue. In *2019 International Conference on Asian Language Processing*, pages 47–52.

Alec Radford, Jeffrey Wu, Rewon Child, David Luan, Dario Amodei, and Ilya Sutskever. 2019. Language models are unsupervised multitask learners.

Rico Sennrich, Barry Haddow, and Alexandra Birch. 2016. Improving neural machine translation models with monolingual data. In *Proceedings of the 54th Annual Meeting of the Association for Computational Linguistics (Volume 1: Long Papers)*, pages 86–96.

Anders Søgaard, Sebastian Ebert, Jasmijn Bastings, and Katja Filippova. 2021. We need to talk about random splits. In *Proceedings of the 16th Conference of the European Chapter of the Association for Computational Linguistics: Main Volume*, pages 1823–1832.

Ishan Mani Subedi, Maninder Singh, Vijayalakshmi Ramasamy, and Gursimran Singh Walia. 2021. Application of back-translation: a transfer learning approach to identify ambiguous software requirements. In *Proceedings of the 2021 ACM Southeast Conference*, pages 130–137.

Jason Wei and Kai Zou. 2019. EDA: Easy data augmentation techniques for boosting performance on text classification tasks. In *Proceedings of the 2019 Conference on Empirical Methods in Natural Language Processing and the 9th International Joint Conference on Natural Language Processing (EMNLP-IJCNLP)*, pages 6382–6388, Hong Kong, China. Association for Computational Linguistics.

Chi Zhang, Shagan Sah, Thang Nguyen, Dheeraj Peri, Alexander Loui, Carl Salvaggio, and Raymond Ptucha. 2017. Semantic sentence embeddings for paraphrasing and text summarization. In *2017 IEEE Global Conference on Signal and Information Processing*, pages 705–709.

Wangchunshu Zhou, Tao Ge, Ke Xu, Furu Wei, and Ming Zhou. 2019. Bert-based lexical substitution. In *Proceedings of the 57th Annual Meeting of the Association for Computational Linguistics*, pages 3368–3373.

Ingrid Zukerman and Bhavani Raskutti. 2002. Lexical query paraphrasing for document retrieval. In *Proceedings of the 19th International Conference on Computational Linguistics*, page 1–7.

Proceedings of the 18th Conference on Natural Language Processing (KONVENS 2022)

MONAPipe: Modes of Narration and Attribution Pipeline for German Computational Literary Studies and Language Analysis in spaCy

Tillmann Dönicke[1], Florian Barth[1], Hanna Varachkina[2], Caroline Sporleder[1]
[1]Göttingen Centre for Digital Humanities, [2]Department of German Philology
University of Göttingen
{tillmann.doenicke@,florian.barth@,hanna.varachkina@stud.,caroline.sporleder@cs.}
uni-goettingen.de

Abstract

MONAPipe is a collection of pipeline components for the open-source Python library spaCy. The components perform a broad range of morphological, syntactic, semantic and pragmatic analyses for German texts and are mostly developed specifically for the literary domain. MONAPipe[1] combines implementations from various separate resources with new ones in one place, constituting a convenient tool for computational linguistics and literary studies.

1 Introduction

When working with text using computational methods, one has to follow a series of standard processing steps that are often combined into a pipeline for efficiency. Although the choice of the existing pipelines is large, there are only a view which focus on the literary domain (e.g. BookNLP[2]), from which to our knowledge none is usable for German. It is well known that literary texts have properties which pose challenges for natural language processing (NLP), such as non-standard orthography, long and complex sentences, long-distance coherence and possibly multi-layered narrative levels to name but a few. MONAPipe presents an extension of the spaCy pipeline which provides basic NLP components based on high-performance German models. Our custom pipeline consists of numerous components that can be divided into six categories: preprocessing, morphosyntactic analysis, semantic analysis, speech and coreference resolution, feature extraction and discourse units, narration and attribution. Some components are domain-independent (e.g. tense tagging), while others are specifically created to analyze fiction and literary concepts (e.g. literary comment).

[1]https://gitlab.gwdg.de/mona/pipy-public
[2]https://github.com/booknlp/booknlp

2 SpaCy

MONAPipe is developed for spaCy (v2.3[3]), which is an open-source software library for crosslinguistic natural language processing in Python. An input text is converted to a document object and then consecutively piped through a series of (built-in or custom) pipeline components which can be arranged by the user. The components enrich the document with information that can be attributed to the document, its tokens or spans (of tokens).

3 Pipeline Components

The main contribution of MONAPipe are new pipeline components for spaCy. Some of the components were developed from scratch whereas others are reimplementations or wrappers of existing tools. Table 1 provides an overview of the currently usable MONAPipe components, which we will discuss in the following.

3.1 Preprocessing

If one wants to process a text which is not already tokenized, one can use spaCy's built-in **Tokenizer**. Built-in follow-up components are a part-of-speech (POS) **Tagger** which assigns both German (Smith, 2003b, p. 12 f.) and universal (de Marneffe et al., 2021, p. 261) POS tags, a dictionary-based **Lemmatizer**, and a named entity recognizer (**NER**) that recognizes persons, locations, organizations and miscellaneous entities (Nothman et al., 2013).

Older texts commonly exhibit non-standard orthography, which can cause problems in follow-up language processing. We therefore provide a **Normalizer** that replaces every out-of-vocabulary word by its most frequent normalized form in the German Text Archive[4] (DTA), a collection of 4,160

[3]https://v2.spacy.io/usage
[4]https://www.deutschestextarchiv.de/download

Component	Type	Main Reference(s)
Preprocessing		
Tokenizer	B	spaCy
Tagger	B	spaCy
Lemmatizer	B	spaCy
NER	B	spaCy
Normalizer	I	this paper
Morphosyntactic Analysis		
Sentencizer	B/W	spaCy, NLTK
DependencyParser	B/I	spaCy, Dönicke (2020)
Clausizer	I	Dönicke (2020)
Analyzer	I	Altinok (2018), Dönicke (2020)
TenseTagger	I	Dönicke (2020)
Semantic Analysis		
TemponymTagger	R	Strötgen and Gertz (2010, 2015)
GermanetTagger	I	Hamp and Feldweg (1997), this paper
EmotionsTagger	I	Mohammad and Turney (2010), this paper
Speech and Coreference Resolution		
SpeechTagger	W/I	Brunner et al. (2020)
SpeakerExtractor	I	this paper
Coref	R	Krug et al. (2015), this paper
Feature Extraction and Discourse Units		
FeatureExtractor	I	Dönicke (2021), this paper
DiscourseSegmenter	I	Dönicke (2021)
Modes of Narration and Attribution		
EventTagger	W	Vauth et al. (2021)
AnnotationReader	I	this paper
CommentTagger	I	Weimer et al. (to appear)
GenTagger	I	Gödeke et al. (to appear)
EntityLinker	I	Barth et al. (2022)
AttributionTagger	I	Dönicke et al. (2022)

Table 1: Overview of MONAPipe components with origin (B: built-in in spaCy, R/I: re-/implemented by MONAPipe authors, W: wrapper for external tool). See text for more information.

texts (480M tokens) from 1600–1900. This approach correctly normalizes over 99.9% of tokens and types in the DTA. Original forms and character positions of tokens are preserved as attributes.

3.2 Morphosyntactic Analysis

The **Sentencizer** (i.e. sentence splitter) adds sentence spans to the document. Currently, one can use either a sentencizer from spaCy or NLTK[5].

The **DependencyParser** adds a dependency tree to each sentence. Which dependency scheme is used depends on the spaCy model, where the German model provided by spaCy produces trees in the TIGER scheme (Smith, 2003b). An alternative to TIGER is the Universal Dependencies (UD) scheme (de Marneffe et al., 2021). While some of our components function in either scheme, most do either require UD parses or function significantly better with them. We therefore recommend using MONAPipe with a UD-based spaCy model and use the model provided by Dönicke (2020).

Dönicke (2020) also provides a **Clausizer** that splits UD trees into clauses and adds clause spans to the document and its sentences, a morphological **Analyzer** based on DEMorphy (Altinok, 2018), and a **TenseTagger** that extracts grammatical features (finiteness, tense, mood, voice) and modal verbs like *müssen* 'must' from a clause's (potentially composite) verb. Dönicke (2020) reports accuracies of 93% for tense, 79% for mood, 94% for voice and 80% for modal verbs in the literary domain. We integrate these components into MONAPipe and make a small change in the handling of modal verbs, so that semi-modal verbs like *pflegen (zu)* 'use (to)' are properly recognized as modal verbs in according contexts (and not always treated as full verbs).[6]

3.3 Semantic Analysis

The **TemponymTagger** extracts and normalizes temporal expressions from a document. The component is a reimplementation of the HeidelTime[7] system (Strötgen and Gertz, 2010, 2015) and uses its resource files for German.

The **GermanetTagger** assigns Levin (1995)'s semantic categories to verbs and clauses (in case the verb is the root) and Hundsnurscher and Splett (1982)'s categories to adjectives, which are extracted from GermaNet (Hamp and Feldweg, 1997). Using the lemmas of verbs and adjectives, possible word senses (synsets) are identified and disambiguated using the synsets from the token's context.

The **EmotionsTagger** adds scores for sentiment (positive, negative) and basic emotions as defined by Ekman (1992) (anger, anticipation, disgust, fear, joy, sadness, surprise, trust) from the NRC Word-Emotion Association Lexicon[8] (Mohammad and Turney, 2010, 2013) to tokens.

3.4 Speech and Coreference Resolution

The **SpeechTagger** assigns scores for speech[9] types to tokens and clauses. We provide two im-

[5]https://www.nltk.org/

[6]For example, the semi-modal verb *use* is a full verb in *John used a lighter* and a modal verb in *John used to smoke*. We distinguish the two cases as follows: A semi-modal verb is a modal verb if it is accompanied by a subordinate verb and it is a full verb otherwise.

[7]https://github.com/HeidelTime/heideltime

[8]https://saifmohammad.com/WebPages/NRC-Emotion-Lexicon.htm

[9]We use the term "speech" for any speech, thought or writing representation in texts (cf. Brunner et al., 2020).

plementations of this component. The first one uses Brunner et al. (2020)'s Redewiedergabe tagger to predict token-wise scores for direct, indirect, free indirect and reported speech. It achieves 85% F1 for direct, 76% F1 for indirect, 60% F1 for reported and 59% F1 for free indirect speech for texts from the 19th to the 20th century (both fiction and non-fiction). The second, faster implementation simply labels tokens within quotation marks as direct speech (ignoring other speech types) and achieves 70% F1 on the same test set (since direct speech is not always marked by quotation marks in older texts). The clause-wise scores are calculated from the product of the token-wise scores.

The **SpeakerExtractor** then adds direct speech spans to the document and tries to identify speaker and addressee for each span. We use a small set of rules to identify a preceding/succeeding verbum dicendi first and then select its subject as speaker and object as addressee.

The development of our **Coref** (coreference) component was driven by the aim to resolve anaphoric pronouns and coreferent nominal phrases (NPs) in a text. We therefore consider all NPs as mentions (including pronouns[10], common NPs and named entities), which contrasts other works. For example, in DROC – a corpus of German novels – (Krug et al., 2018) only mentions of literary characters are annotated, and in ParCorFull – a parallel corpus of news and other domains – (Lapshinova-Koltunski et al., 2018) mentions can be non-nominal and the annotation of a generic NP depends on whether it is a common NP or a pronoun. The corpus with the most similar concept of mentions to ours is GerDraCor-Coref – a corpus of German dramatic texts – (Pagel and Reiter, 2020), although non-nominal mentions are also annotated in part of the corpus.

The Coref component is a UD-based reimplementation of Krug et al. (2015)'s rule-based system which consecutively executes 11 passes to find the antecedent of a mention. Since Krug et al. (2015)'s system was developed for DROC, we made some adjustments to handle a wider variety of NPs (passes 3, 5–7). We use the Extended Open Multilingual Wordnet[11] (Bond and Foster, 2013) to find synonyms in the semantic pass (pass 8) and

[10]We exclude indefinite, interrogative and expletive pronouns since they do not have antecedents. Possessive pronouns are de facto exclduded since they usually appear within a larger mention but we do not consider nested mentions.

[11]http://compling.hss.ntu.edu.sg/omw/summx.html

	Mentions	MUC	B^3	CEAFe	CoNLL
GerDraCor					
HotCoref	–	56.55	14.98	14.84	28.79
DramaCoref	60.00	42.54	19.87	18.97	27.12
full mentions	56.24	43.21	19.78	12.56	25.18
mention heads	70.25	58.20	29.18	15.04	34.14
NP heads	74.36	57.10	31.91	18.18	35.73
gold NP heads	97.03	68.22	39.91	33.97	47.37
DROC					
Schröder et al. (2021)	–	–	–	–	64.72
Krug (2020)	–	87.50	40.40	31.60	53.17
full mentions	38.25	30.67	11.92	3.99	15.53
mention heads	57.04	45.55	24.06	10.88	26.83
NP heads	61.97	50.78	29.60	12.28	30.89
gold NP heads	97.85	68.14	39.42	28.85	45.47
ParCorFull					
Pražák et al. (2021)[13]	–	–	–	–	55.40
full mentions	36.98	24.19	18.76	16.15	19.70
mention heads	41.04	26.68	21.63	18.12	22.14
NP heads	43.21	28.23	23.73	20.63	24.20
gold NP heads	96.99	62.67	68.04	57.58	62.76

Table 2: Coref evaluation on three corpora. The first numeric column shows the F1 for mention identification. MUC, B^3 and CEAFe are F1-based metrics for coreference resolution (cf. Moosavi and Strube, 2016). The CoNLL score is the average of the three.

the results from the SpeechTagger and SpeakerExtractor to resolve pronouns in direct speech (passes 10–11). We store coreference clusters in the same format as NeuralCoref[12], so that one can replace our Coref component by a (currently non-existent) German NeuralCoref model in the future without producing errors in follow-up components.

Despite contrasts to other works, we score our system on GerDraCor, DROC and ParCorFull (see Table 2) using the scorer from Moosavi et al. (2019) to get a rough impression on its performance and to compare it to previous works. We accede to Nedoluzhko et al. (2021) and consider an evaluation on mention heads in a cross-resource scenario as more meaningful than using full mentions, but show scores for full mentions for comparison. For example, mention identification scores 14% higher for mention heads than for full mentions on GerDraCor.[14] Since our system only links NPs, we also show the scores when (heads of) non-nominal mentions are excluded.[15] Our system achieves sim-

[12]https://github.com/huggingface/neuralcoref

[13]The performance of Pražák et al. (2021)'s system on ParCorFull is listed at https://github.com/ondfa/coref-multiling.

[14]One reason is that mentions in GerDraCor may include succeeding punctuation which is not the case for our mentions.

[15]According to the UD guidelines, we define a mention as nominal if its head has one of these relations: nsubj, obj, iobj, obl, vocative, expl, dislocated, nmod, appos, nummod.

ilar results to those of the recently tested systems HotCoref (Roesiger and Kuhn, 2016) and DramaCoref (Pagel and Reiter, 2021).[16] For DROC and ParCorFull, the F1 for mention identification suffers from a low precision, since we consider much more NPs to be mentions than those in the corpora, and our system performs much lower than the neural systems presented in Krug (2020, p. 173) and Schröder et al. (2021) for DROC[17] and Pražák et al. (2021) for ParCorFull. We therefore also provide the scores for evaluating on gold NPs only: the gold NPs in DROC are linked with a similar performance as those in GerDraCor, and even better in ParCorFull.

3.5 Feature Extraction and Discourse Units

The **FeatureExtractor** combines the information from previous components and some additional information in a (mostly) delexicalized functional grammar (DFG) structure. DFG structures combine rudiments of lexical functional grammar (LFG) and UD grammar and are created for each clause. We take over the basic set-up of Dönicke (2021), who includes grammatical features from the clause, the complex verb, NPs and discourse markers, and add separate levels for adjectives, articles and quantifiers. We further integrate all available semantic information, including GermaNet category and emotion (see Section 3.3), sentiment from SentiWS[18] (Remus et al., 2010), speech type (see Section 3.4) as well as overt quantifier type (using Dönicke et al. (2021)'s categories), and link pronominal anaphora to their antecedents. An example is shown in the appendix.

Dönicke (2021) uses the feature structures for discourse unit segmentation and we also integrate his German model as **DiscourseSegmenter**. The model achieved 92% F1 for German in the DISRPT 2021 Shared Task on Elementary Discourse Unit Segmentation (Zeldes et al., 2021) (4% lower than the best-performing, neural system).

3.6 Narration and Attribution

The **EventTagger** is a wrapper for the event-classification model from Vauth et al. (2021)[19], which classifies clauses into four event types: non-event, stative event, process event and change of state. The model was trained on works of literature and achieves accuracies of 84% for non-event, 75% for stative event, 79% for process event and 56% for change of state. Note that Vauth et al. (2021)'s event types are based on narrative theory (e.g. Schmid, 2014; Prince, 2012) but there are parallels to discourse/situation entity types (also known as clause-level aspect) from linguistic theory (e.g. Vendler, 1957; Smith, 2003a; Friedrich and Palmer, 2014), most importantly the distinction between dynamic and stative events, which is why we consider the EventTagger a useful component for both narratological and linguistic analyses.

MONAPipe further includes components for the automatic identification of narrative modes, which are especially useful for the analysis of fictional literature. The components were developed on the Modes of Narration and Attribution Corpus (MONACO) (Barth et al., 2021), a corpus of fictional texts from 1600 to 1950 which are annotated with narratological information. The annotations in MONACO are saved in a CoNLL-based format and the XML-based output format of the annotation tool CATMA[20]. We provide an **AnnotationReader** that can read CATMA files for the piped document and assigns the annotations to its tokens and clauses. In this way, predictions and annotations (e.g. gold annotations) can be directly accessed at an element of interest.

The term 'narrative mode' itself is a cover term for various stylistic devices that shape the narration of a story. Bonheim (1975) distinguishes four narrative modes: description (depiction of things in motion), report (depiction of things in motion), speech (utterances, thoughts etc. of characters), and comment. In comment, the narration pauses and additional information is provided, e.g. when the narrator interprets what just happened. A text example with all narrative modes is shown in Figure 1. Since report and description usually constitute the most part of a narrative text and speech can be identified by the SpeechTagger, we consider comment to be the most interesting narrative mode to automatically identify in a text.

The annotation guidelines in MONACO follow Chatman (1980) and distinguish three subtypes of comment: interpretation (of story elements), judgment/attitude (towards story elements), and metafictional comment (about the story or the narra-

[16]Like Pagel and Reiter (2021), we also randomly selected 80% of the texts in GerDraCor-Coref (1.2.1) as test set but chances are high that our test sets are not identical.

[17]We use the same 18 texts from DROC as test set.

[18]https://github.com/Liebeck/spacy-sentiws

[19]https://github.com/uhh-lt/event-classification

[20]https://catma.de/

[Dr. Johnson was well along in years]$_{\text{DESCRIPTION}}$ [when Boswell explained to him the solipsism of Bishop Berkeley, yet Johnson was still nimble enough to kick a pebble down the path and exclaim,]$_{\text{REPORT}}$ ['thus do I refute him, Sir!']$_{\text{SPEECH}}$ [His was the voice of common sense kicking logic out of the way.]$_{\text{COMMENT}}$

Figure 1: Example text with annotated narrative modes (Bonheim, 1975). Brackets mark annotation spans.

tion itself). The fourth subtype included by Chatman (1980), generalization (i.e. general truths that "reach beyond the world of the fictional work into the real universe", p. 243), is not treated as a subtype of comment in MONACO. Instead, generalization and non-fictionality are treated as separate modes with own subtypes.

Special difficulty when developing text-classification systems for narrative modes is posed by the fact that they can span arbitrarily long text passages and overlap with each other. Since 'passages' in MONACO are defined as sequences of clauses, one can approach the task as multi-class multi-label classification of clauses and address the reconnection of subsequent clauses with the same labels to passages in a postprocessing step.

The statistical **CommentTagger** of MONAPipe (described in Weimer et al. (to appear)) uses the features from Section 3.5. When tested on two held-out texts, the binary model achieves 59% F1, which we consider to be a good state of the art given the difficulties of the task and the literary domain. The multi-class model achieves 36% F1 for interpretation, 28% F1 for attitude and 48% for meta-fictional comment. Taggers for generalizing and non-fictional passages are still in development but MONAPipe also includes the current versions of a rule-based and a statistical **GenTagger** to recognize generalizations (described in Gödeke et al. (to appear)) as well as an **EntityLinker** (described in Barth et al. (2022)), which links named entities to Wikidata[21] entries and determines whether they are fictional or real entities.

MONACO also contains annotations for speaker attribution, i.e. whether the content of a clause is conveyed by a character, the narrator and/or the author of the text. In Dönicke et al. (2022), we trained a neural classifier on MONACO, which we also wrap in a spaCy component. The **AttributionTagger** and the SpeechTagger are indeed somewhat similar, e.g. free indirect speech is typically attributed to a character and the narrator. However, while the task of the SpeechTagger is to identify certain constructions, the AttributionTagger labels the supposed source of information (independently from preselected constructions). In Dönicke et al. (2022), the model achieves 84% accuracy on a held-out test set.

[21]https://www.wikidata.org/wiki/Wikidata:Main_Page

4 Other Features

Automatic saving/loading of intermediate results can be enabled to avoid unnecessary recomputation, which is especially useful for long texts.

We also include functions to 1) calculate inter-annotator agreement in terms of Fleiss's κ, Krippendorff's α and Mathet et al.'s γ after adding annotations to documents, and 2) compare annotations to automatically assigned labels in terms of accuracy, precision, recall and F1 or with a confusion matrix. Agreement and evaluation measures can be executed for tokens and clauses.

In addition, we developed a **CorpusReader** that reads metadata from the source files (TEI-XML) of our literary corpus and provides structured metadata, e.g. GND-identifiers[22] for a work's author, that can be accessed within the pipeline. Furthermore, we enrich existing metadata, e.g. we detect Wikidata entries for a literary work. These metadata is used in MONAPipe components such as the EntityLinker.

5 Conclusion and Future Work

MONAPipe is a custom spaCy pipeline that provides a set of tools for the linguistic and literary analysis of German texts. Many of its components do not have equivalents and present state of the art in the field of computational literary studies or show competitive results compared to the existing tools.

We plan to add further components for natural and narratological language processing as well as new versions of existing components, e.g. taggers for generalization and non-fictionality. The current coreference system is meant to be a make-shift implementation and we want to develop wrappers for other tools in the future. We also plan to upgrade MONAPipe from spaCy v2.x to v3.x.

[22]GND: Integrated Authority File, German for "Gemeinsame Normdatei", https://www.dnb.de/EN/Professionell/Standardisierung/GND/gnd_node.html.

References

Duygu Altinok. 2018. DEMorphy, German language morphological analyzer. arXiv:1803.00902.

Florian Barth, Tillmann Dönicke, Benjamin Gittel, Luisa Gödeke, Anna Mareike Weimer, Anke Holler, Caroline Sporleder, and Hanna Varachkina. 2021. MONACO: Modes of Narration and Attribution Corpus. https://gitlab.gwdg.de/mona/korpus-public.

Florian Barth, Hanna Varachkina, Tillmann Dönicke, and Luisa Gödeke. 2022. Levels of non-fictionality in fictional texts. In *Proceedings of the 18th Joint ACL - ISO Workshop on Interoperable Semantic Annotation within LREC2022*, pages 27–32, Marseille, France. European Language Resources Association.

Francis Bond and Ryan Foster. 2013. Linking and extending an open multilingual Wordnet. In *Proceedings of the 51st Annual Meeting of the Association for Computational Linguistics (Volume 1: Long Papers)*, pages 1352–1362, Sofia, Bulgaria. Association for Computational Linguistics.

Helmut Bonheim. 1975. Theory of narrative modes. *Semiotica*, 14(4):329–344.

Annelen Brunner, Ngoc Duyen Tanja Tu, Lukas Weimer, and Fotis Jannidis. 2020. To BERT or not to BERT – comparing contextual embeddings in a deep learning architecture for the automatic recognition of four types of speech, thought and writing representation. In *SwissText/KONVENS*.

Seymour Benjamin Chatman. 1980. *Story and Discourse: Narrative Structure in Fiction and Film*. Cornell paperbacks. Cornell University Press.

Tillmann Dönicke. 2020. Clause-level tense, mood, voice and modality tagging for German. In *Proceedings of the 19th International Workshop on Treebanks and Linguistic Theories*, pages 1–17, Düsseldorf, Germany. Association for Computational Linguistics.

Tillmann Dönicke. 2021. Delexicalised multilingual discourse segmentation for DISRPT 2021 and tense, mood, voice and modality tagging for 11 languages. In *Proceedings of the 2nd Shared Task on Discourse Relation Parsing and Treebanking (DISRPT 2021)*, pages 33–45, Punta Cana, Dominican Republic. Association for Computational Linguistics.

Tillmann Dönicke, Luisa Gödeke, and Hanna Varachkina. 2021. Annotating quantified phenomena in complex sentence structures using the example of generalising statements in literary texts. In *Proceedings of the 17th Joint ACL - ISO Workshop on Interoperable Semantic Annotation*, pages 20–32, Groningen, The Netherlands (online). Association for Computational Linguistics.

Tillmann Dönicke, Hanna Varachkina, Anna Mareike Weimer, Luisa Gödeke, Florian Barth, Benjamin Gittel, Anke Holler, and Caroline Sporleder. 2022. Modelling speaker attribution in narrative texts with biased and bias-adjustable neural networks. *Frontiers in Artificial Intelligence*, 4.

Paul Ekman. 1992. An argument for basic emotions. *Cognition & emotion*, 6(3-4):169–200.

Joseph L. Fleiss. 1971. Measuring nominal scale agreement among many raters. *Psychological bulletin*, 76(5):378.

Annemarie Friedrich and Alexis Palmer. 2014. Situation entity annotation. In *Proceedings of LAW VIII - The 8th Linguistic Annotation Workshop*, pages 149–158, Dublin, Ireland. Association for Computational Linguistics and Dublin City University.

Luisa Gödeke, Florian Barth, Tillmann Dönicke, Anna Mareike Weimer, Hanna Varachkina, Benjamin Gittel, Anke Holler, and Caroline Sporleder. to appear. Generalisierungen als literarisches Phänomen. Charakterisierung, Annotation und automatische Erkennung. *Zeitschrift für digitale Geisteswissenschaften*.

Birgit Hamp and Helmut Feldweg. 1997. Germanet-a lexical-semantic net for german. *Automatic Information Extraction and Building of Lexical Semantic Resources for NLP Applications*.

Klaus Krippendorff. 2018. *Content analysis: An introduction to its methodology*. Sage publications.

Markus Krug. 2020. *Techniques for the Automatic Extraction of Character Networks in German Historic Novels*. doctoral thesis, Universität Würzburg.

Markus Krug, Frank Puppe, Fotis Jannidis, Luisa Macharowsky, Isabella Reger, and Lukas Weimar. 2015. Rule-based coreference resolution in German historic novels. In *Proceedings of the Fourth Workshop on Computational Linguistics for Literature*, pages 98–104, Denver, Colorado, USA. Association for Computational Linguistics.

Markus Krug, Frank Puppe, Isabella Reger, Lukas Weimer, Luisa Macharowsky, Stephan Feldhaus, and Fotis Jannidis. 2018. Description of a Corpus of Character References in German Novels - DROC [Deutsches ROman Corpus]. DARIAH-DE Working Papers 27, Göttingen: DARIAH-DE. URN: urn:nbn:de:gbv:7-dariah-2018-2-9.

Ekaterina Lapshinova-Koltunski, Christian Hardmeier, and Pauline Krielke. 2018. ParCorFull: a parallel corpus annotated with full coreference. In *Proceedings of the Eleventh International Conference on Language Resources and Evaluation (LREC 2018)*, Miyazaki, Japan. European Language Resources Association (ELRA).

Beth Levin. 1995. English verb classes and alternations. *A preliminary Investigation*, 1.

Marie-Catherine de Marneffe, Christopher D. Manning, Joakim Nivre, and Daniel Zeman. 2021. Universal Dependencies. *Computational Linguistics*, 47(2):255–308.

Yann Mathet, Antoine Widlöcher, and Jean-Philippe Métivier. 2015. The unified and holistic method gamma (γ) for inter-annotator agreement measure and alignment. *Computational Linguistics*, 41(3):437–479.

Franz Hundsnurscher and Jochen Splett. 1982. *Semantik der Adjektive des Deutschen. Analyse der semantischen Relationen.*

Saif Mohammad and Peter Turney. 2010. Emotions evoked by common words and phrases: Using Mechanical Turk to create an emotion lexicon. In *Proceedings of the NAACL HLT 2010 Workshop on Computational Approaches to Analysis and Generation of Emotion in Text*, pages 26–34, Los Angeles, CA. Association for Computational Linguistics.

Saif Mohammad and Peter Turney. 2013. Crowdsourcing a word–emotion association lexicon. *Computational intelligence*, 29(3):436–465.

Nafise Sadat Moosavi, Leo Born, Massimo Poesio, and Michael Strube. 2019. Using automatically extracted minimum spans to disentangle coreference evaluation from boundary detection. In *Proceedings of the 57th Annual Meeting of the Association for Computational Linguistics*, pages 4168–4178, Florence, Italy. Association for Computational Linguistics.

Nafise Sadat Moosavi and Michael Strube. 2016. Which coreference evaluation metric do you trust? a proposal for a link-based entity aware metric. In *Proceedings of the 54th Annual Meeting of the Association for Computational Linguistics (Volume 1: Long Papers)*, pages 632–642, Berlin, Germany. Association for Computational Linguistics.

Anna Nedoluzhko, Michal Novák, Martin Popel, Zdeněk Žabokrtský, and Daniel Zeman. 2021. Is one head enough? mention heads in coreference annotations compared with UD-style heads. In *Proceedings of the Sixth International Conference on Dependency Linguistics (Depling, SyntaxFest 2021)*, pages 101–114, Sofia, Bulgaria. Association for Computational Linguistics.

Joel Nothman, Nicky Ringland, Will Radford, Tara Murphy, and James R. Curran. 2013. Learning multilingual named entity recognition from wikipedia. *Artificial Intelligence*, 194:151–175. Artificial Intelligence, Wikipedia and Semi-Structured Resources.

Janis Pagel and Nils Reiter. 2020. GerDraCor-coref: A coreference corpus for dramatic texts in German. In *Proceedings of the 12th Language Resources and Evaluation Conference*, pages 55–64, Marseille, France. European Language Resources Association.

Janis Pagel and Nils Reiter. 2021. DramaCoref: A hybrid coreference resolution system for German theater plays. In *Proceedings of the Fourth Workshop on Computational Models of Reference, Anaphora and Coreference*, pages 36–46, Punta Cana, Dominican Republic. Association for Computational Linguistics.

Ondřej Pražák, Miloslav Konopík, and Jakub Sido. 2021. Multilingual coreference resolution with harmonized annotations. In *Proceedings of the International Conference on Recent Advances in Natural Language Processing (RANLP 2021)*, pages 1119–1123, Held Online. INCOMA Ltd.

Gerald Prince. 2012. A grammar of stories. In *A Grammar of Stories*. De Gruyter Mouton.

Robert Remus, Uwe Quasthoff, and Gerhard Heyer. 2010. SentiWS - a publicly available German-language resource for sentiment analysis. In *Proceedings of the Seventh International Conference on Language Resources and Evaluation (LREC'10)*, Valletta, Malta. European Language Resources Association (ELRA).

Ina Roesiger and Jonas Kuhn. 2016. IMS HotCoref DE: A data-driven co-reference resolver for German. In *Proceedings of the Tenth International Conference on Language Resources and Evaluation (LREC'16)*, pages 155–160, Portorož, Slovenia. European Language Resources Association (ELRA).

Wolf Schmid. 2014. *Elemente der Narratologie*. de Gruyter.

Fynn Schröder, Hans Ole Hatzel, and Chris Biemann. 2021. Neural end-to-end coreference resolution for German in different domains. In *Proceedings of the 17th Conference on Natural Language Processing (KONVENS 2021)*, pages 170–181, Düsseldorf, Germany. KONVENS 2021 Organizers.

Carlota S. Smith. 2003a. *Modes of discourse: The local structure of texts*, volume 103. Cambridge University Press.

George Smith. 2003b. A brief introduction to the TIGER treebank. Technical report, Universität Potsdam.

Jannik Strötgen and Michael Gertz. 2010. HeidelTime: High quality rule-based extraction and normalization of temporal expressions. In *Proceedings of the 5th International Workshop on Semantic Evaluation*, pages 321–324, Uppsala, Sweden. Association for Computational Linguistics.

Jannik Strötgen and Michael Gertz. 2015. A baseline temporal tagger for all languages. In *Proceedings of the 2015 Conference on Empirical Methods in Natural Language Processing*, pages 541–547, Lisbon, Portugal. Association for Computational Linguistics.

Michael Vauth, Hans Ole Hatzel, Evelyn Gius, and Chris Biemann. 2021. Automated event annotation in literary texts. In *Proceedings of the Conference on Computational Humanities Research 2021 (CHR 2021)*, pages 333–345, Amsterdam, the Netherlands.

Zeno Vendler. 1957. Verbs and times. *The philosophical review*, 66(2):143–160.

Anna Mareike Weimer, Florian Barth, Tillmann Dönicke, Luisa Gödeke, Hanna Varachkina, Anke Holler, Caroline Sporleder, and Benjamin Gittel. to appear. The (in-)consistency of literary concepts – formalising, annotating and detecting literary comment. *Journal of Computational Literary Studies*.

Amir Zeldes, Yang Janet Liu, Mikel Iruskieta, Philippe Muller, Chloé Braud, and Sonia Badene. 2021. The DISRPT 2021 shared task on elementary discourse unit segmentation, connective detection, and relation classification. In *Proceedings of the 2nd Shared Task on Discourse Relation Parsing and Treebanking (DISRPT 2021)*, pages 1–12, Punta Cana, Dominican Republic. Association for Computational Linguistics.

A Appendices

Aber Peter kauft sich jeden Morgen einen schlechten Kaffee.
'But Peter buys himself a bad coffee every morning.'

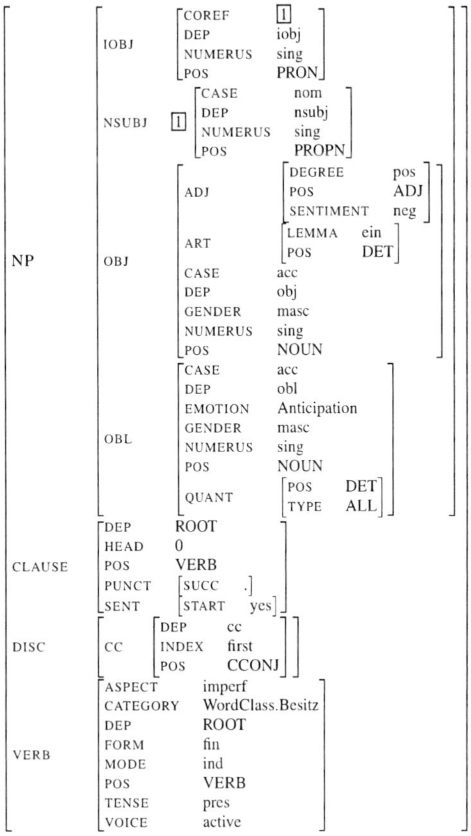

Figure 2: Sample DFG structure.

Acknowledgements

We thank all the researchers and developers who made their code and models publicly and freely accessible so that we could integrate them into MONAPipe. When using MONAPipe, you should reference all contributors of the components that you use (as listed in this paper or MONAPipe's project documentation).

We further thank the anonymous reviewers for their valuable comments. This work is funded by Volkswagen Foundation (Dönicke, Sporleder), and by the Deutsche Forschungsgemeinschaft (DFG, German Research Foundation) – 424264086 (Barth, Varachkina, Sporleder).

Proceedings of the 18th Conference on Natural Language Processing (KONVENS 2022)

Lemma Hunting: Automatic Spelling Normalization for CMC Corpora

Eckhard Bick

University of Southern Denmark

eckhard.bick@mail.dk

Abstract

This paper presents and evaluates a method for automatic orthographic normalization and the treatment of out-of-vocabulary words (OOV) in German social media data. The system uses a cascade of spellchecking operations including casing-, sound- and keyboard-based letter permutations, as well as letter context likelihoods, and combines partial and root spellchecking with compound analysis and heuristic inflection analysis in novel ways. The system also handles contractions, elisions and some tokenization errors. In addition, pattern-based recognition of foreign words and abbreviations is attempted, supported by jargon-informed lexicon expansion. Contextual Constraint Grammar (CG) disambiguation is used to resolve possible ambiguity. For Twitter data, F-scores of 87.3 and 77.1 were achieved for the identification and correct lemmatization, respectively, of German spelling errors and non-standard abbreviations. 77.6% of foreign words were recognized with 86.5% precision and 1/3 POS errors.

1 Introduction

Computer-mediated communication (CMC) is a notoriously difficult genre to annotate, an important issue being non-standard orthography and unusual word formation. For Social Media, in particular, Proisl (2018) and Beißwenger (2016) mention a host of problems such as out-of-vocabulary words (OOV), emoticons/emojis, interaction words (*lach* [laugh], *heul* [cry]), URL's and discourse links (hashtags and user id's), onomatopoeia, spelling variation and contractions, emphasis by upper-casing or letter repetition, as well as syntactic idiosyncrasies. In a corpus annotation scenario, all of these may lead to reduced lexicon coverage, affecting tagging performance. Thus, Neunerdt (2013) reports a drop in accuracy from 95.8% to 68% for OOV words, a problem he successfully tackled by adding a specialized web lexicon. But even with word additions and a correct (heuristic) POS assignment, a failure to group spelling variations, abbreviations and spelling errors under the same lemma negatively affects the possibility of corpus searches and statistics. In this paper, following Sidarenka et al. (2013), we suggest an automatic, spellchecking-like normalization process to address the problem, providing a common lemma for spelling variants and outright errors at the same time. For a language like German, compound analysis may also increase the search-accessibility of a corpus, and prevent false positive spelling corrections. The work presented here was performed on a large German Twitter and Facebook corpus compiled for the XPEROHS hate speech project (Baumgarten et al. 2019) and annotated with a multi-level Constraint Grammar (CG) parser (GerGram[1]). All examples in the paper are authentic exerpts from this corpus.

2 Systematic normalization

A relatively straightforward first step of

[1] https://visl.sdu.dk/de/parsing/automatic/

normalization concerns systematic variation, especially re-casing of lower-cased German nouns and of words written in all-uppercase for emphasis, both very common in our corpus. However, ignoring upper/lower case may lead to ambiguity between two German words or a foreign and a German word. This needs to be resolved contextually and is a possible source of errors.

Another case of systematic variation is gendering, which in German writing manifests as a female suffix, *-In* (sg.) or *-Innen* (pl.), attached to the (male/neutral) root with a variety of separators ('*', '_', '/' or '#') or with only the upper-case 'I' as a separator. For word classification and corpus search purposes all should be grouped under one lemma. Sometimes, this task borders on spellchecking or lexicography. Thus, our corpus contained examples of plural or adjective roots (*FreundeInnen* 'friends', *GrünInnen* 'Green Party-ists') and phonetic e-ellision (*RabaukInnen* - *Rabauke* 'brawler').

3 Spell-checking techniques

The second, and more challenging, step in normalization consists of spell-checking proper. In a text processor environment, a spell-checker offers a prioritized list of suggestions to be interactively processed by a human user. For automatic spell-checking, this is obviously not possible, so we only allowed suggestions with a Levenshtein distance of 1, meaning that the correction can be achieved by substituting, inserting or deleting a single letter. Again, contextual disambiguation may be necessary, because even at the Levenshtein-1 level, more than one correction may be possible. In our setup, disambiguation is an automatic side affect of ordinary CG disambiguation, triggered by differences in POS or inflection between the possible corrections.

To validate letter changes as legitimate corrections, we use a fullform dictionary with 1.23 million correct entries, consisting in part of a proof-read token list from non-CMC corpora, in part of fullform expansions arrived at by using German inflectional paradigms. The dictionary also contains 68907 error forms with their correction(s), also these consisting of manually sanctioned corpus examples and some paradigmatic expansion. The lexicalized error forms complement free spell-checking in two ways: First, in obvious cases, they can pre-empt the need for contextual disambiguation. Second, they represent a safe option for covering cases with higher Levenshtein-distance above 1.

Our spell-checking pipeline consists of a cascade of steps progressing from safe to unsafe. The first round mostly contains letter changes sanctioned by phonetic similarity, QWERTY keyboard layout or surrounding letters[2]. This module is run after ordinary lookup, inflectional analysis and prefix-/suffix-stripping, but before compound analysis. It performs the following checks:

- keyboard adjacency (e.g. *v/b, b/n*) or left-right confusion (e.g. *s/l*)
- phonetics, e.g. vowel lengthening markers (*i/ie/ih, versö(h)nlich*) and other grapheme ambiguity (*äu/eu*) or silent consonants (*ck/k, tz/z, ch/sch*)
- s-errors and pre-reform spelling (*ss/ß*)
- umlaut / diacritics (e.g. *u/ue/ü, a/ae/ä, o/oe/ö, e/é*)
- gemination errors and letter repetition (*Papkasse, Tannnte, gaaanz lang*)
- weak letter omission: *g(e)kauft, bedeuten(d)ste, pakistan(i)schen*
- extra letter: *Bein(e)ame, Freundin(g)*
- letter pair repetition: *Ahnen(en)reihe, digit(it)ale*
- letter swap: *turg->trug, gignen->gingen*

It is a specific trait of German that a large proportion of OOV words are ordinary

[2] In this module, change patterns may involve 2 changed letters, or unchanged letters, and in that sense, while safer, are not ordinary Levenshtein-1 spellchecks.

compounds[3]. Further spellchecking is therefore blocked if morphological analysis can identify a high-confidence compound split, based on lexicon support for both parts, as well as their length, POS and semantics.

When spell-checking is activated, it is carried out by a letter-permutation subroutine. The task of trying out all possible letter changes and comparing them to the lexicon is surprisingly complex: For the average 6-letter word there are 5 swaps, 6 deletions, 5 splits, 25 * 6 substitutions and 26 * 6 insertions, resulting in 322 look-ups. Many of these may match a real word and need to be prioritized. We use a letter-context frequency strategy[4] to address both the complexity and the prioritization issue. For this, we extracted letter quintuples from corpus data, counting space as a letter, too, and computed the letter likelihood for the three middle positions given their left and right letter neighbors in the quintuple. These data can be used to suggest the most likely substitution or insertion, rather than trying them all with no prioritization. The overall worth of a possible correction word is then computed as the product of its normalized corpus frequency and either a fixed "method prioritization constant" (for swaps and deletions) or the frequency of a given substitution or insertion relative to the embedding quintuple. Finally, the subroutine will return the correction operation with the highest value, considering only corrections that can be verified in the fullform lexicon.

In order to minimize false hits, the letter-permutation subroutine is first fed unknown word parts of partially recognized words, reserving full-word spellchecking as a last step. For this purpose, the system remembers "almost"-hits in the compound analysis of longer words, where a first or second part could be matched in the lexicon, but the remainder of the word (i.e. the potential other compound part) could not. In these cases, if both parts have a minimum length, the unknown part is spellchecked on its own:

pædophlie|verdächtig > pädophilieverdächtig
Voraussage|mögichkeit >Voraussagemöglichkeit

Failing this, the system looks up the last 5 letters in an endings/affix database, and spellchecks the remainder as a kind of artificial root. Only after this, as a last resort, fullform spellchecking is carried out. To avoid over-generation in the face of short word parts, letter deletions are not allowed for compound parts, and splitting is only allowed for full words.

4 Word splitting and fusion

A certain amount of spelling variation can not be addressed with the above techniques, because they concern tokenization. The most common problems were English-style splitting of noun compounds (e.g. *Terroristen Pack, Kanaken Gang*) and colloquial contractions of pronouns and short verbs (e.g. *machen wirs [=wir es] doch* ['let's do it'], *kannste [= kannst du]* ['can you']). We use lexical rules to split the contractions, maintaining the fullform on the first part and marking the split on both parts. For identifying split compounds (in particular, OOV compounds), contextual CG rules are necessary, implying a certain risk of error. Rather than creating a new, fused token, we mark the split on the first part, but maintain both as tokens in order to preserve the individual lemmas, as well as semantic and other tagging, for corpus searching purposes.

5 Abbreviations and foreign words

Abbreviations are at the same time a very frequent and a very variable feature of CMC data. Thus, neither casing nor the presence and

[3] Our corpus contained 10% compounds, of which 1/6 were OOV, i.e. found through live analysis. 2/3 of the OOV compounds were flagged as hight confidence. 17% of low-confidence compounds were really names or spelling errors.

[4] The size of the context window has to be balanced to avoid sparse-data problems, but in prinicple, a similar strategy could be used for entire words and word contexts of sufficient frequency (future work). Also, the list of correction possibilities could be passed on to CG disambiguation, exploiting the wider context of the sentence/utterance. However, while the latter technique worked well for ordinary, interactive spell-checking, it proved to be much less safe for cases where the context itself is also full of errors, orthographical creativity and OOV tokens, as is often the case in CMC data.

placement of dots can be trusted. For instance, *zB, zB., z.B., z.b.* all mean *zum Beispiel* ('for instance'). There is also great variation as to which letters (other than the first) are used to abbreviate single words (*vll, vllt, vlt = vielleicht* ('maybe'). Very typical are multi word expressions (MWEs) representing small utterances, e.g. *ka = keine Ahnung* ('no idea') or *kb = kein Bock* ('no desire to'), including many English ones, e.g. *WTF (what the fuck)* or *omg (oh my God).* Arguably, recognizing abbreviations is not a classical spellchecking, but either a lemmatization/normalization task (for *z.B.* and *vlt*) or a lexicalization task (*WTF, omg*) necessary for assigning a "syntactically harmless" word class such as adverb or interjection, but also to *prevent* spellchecking an abbreviation into a regular word (e.g. *omg* as *mg* or *Oma*). Foreign words need to be recognized for the same reason, also if they are not abbreviated, because a small change may make them look like a German word. The problem was addressed by pre-filtering input lines that looked English in their entirety, by matching certain letter patterns typical of English but not of German, and by adding some genre-typical words may to the lexicon.

6 Evaluation

We evaluated the performance of the normalizer tool on two chunks of tweets from a random day. The sample consisted of 5764 tokens containing 4761 words when excluding punctuation, web links and @-names. Of these, 6.5% were words in need of spelling correction and/or other lexical normalization[5] to support a correct reading[6]. Another 2.1% were non-name foreign[7] words also representing a recognition challenge. The system identified 82.5% of the spelling errors and non-standard abbreviations, and 77.6% of the foreign words as such. 66.8% of the former (79.9% of the recognized ones) were assigned the correct normalization/lemma. Of the unrecognized spelling errors, half were OOV, half were real word errors, e.g. *frage* not recognized as the noun *Frage,* but rather accepted as a possible (but wrong in-context) inflection form of the verb *fragen. 7.2%* of all words marked as spelling errors were false positives, mostly foreign words misread or, sometimes, miscorrected as German, e.g. *locker* (a German adjective, but in-context an English noun) or *freefall* (read as *Freifall*). These numbers translate into F-scores of 87.3 and 77.1 for the identification and correction of spelling errors, respectively (see Table 1).

	R	P	F[8]	ERR[9]
identification task	82.5	92.8	87.3	77.1
correction task	66.8	91.2	77.1	60.3
foreign word recog.	77.6	85.4	81.3	64.3

Table 1: Recall, precision, F-score (%), ERR

The ERR score for the correction task can in principle be compared to results obtained in the shared task for multilingual lexical normalization (MultiLexNorm) in the W-NUT workshop 2021 (van der Goot et al., 2021), where only the best system, ÚFAL (Samuel and Stracka, 2021), achieved a higher score (ERR=66.2) in the intrinsic evaluation. However, the data sets are not directly comparable, and differences in normalization principles and tokenization made it impossible to perform a true cross-evaluation within the scope of this paper[10].

Recognition of foreign words worked reasonably, but not as well as German normalization, considering that 1/3 of the recognized foreign words received a wrong POS. 7% of the non-name foreign words were tagged as proper nouns because they were in upper case. For foreign words, false positives were triggered by lower-case names or by some OOV

[5] The latter includes e.g. clitic-splitting and recognition of chat-style abbreviations and interjections, that would otherwise be OOV and/or get a wrong lemma or word class.

[6] A further 0.5% of minor errors were ignored, These were errors concerning hyphenation and inflection not causing POS changes or lemmatization errors.

[7] Counting foreign words occurring in German sentences. Six separate short sentences (4 English, 2 Spanish) with 5-6 words each, were not included here.

[8] F1-score, defined as 2*recall*precision/(recall+precision)

[9] Defined as ERR=(CF-FP)/(CF+FN), with CF=correctly found, FN=false negatives, FP=false positives

[10] Still, as a first step, a filter program was written to convert system output into the MultiLexNorm two-column format.

abbreviations without dot, e.g. *guna* (= *Gute Nacht* 'good night').

7 Conclusions and outlook

We have discussed a method for ameliorating the high OOV rate in German CMC data using automatic spellchecking, morphological analysis and letter pattern recognition. The system has been integrated with a CG disambiguator and parser, and used in the annotation of a 3-billion-word Twitter corpus with satisfactory results. Based on qualitative error analysis from the test run, real-word errors should also be addressed, in particular where lower-casing errors of real German words can be confused with other German words, foreign words or abbreviations. For this task, wider word context should be exploited, either statistically and/or through CG disambiguation of the most likely replacements.

References

Baumgarten, N.; Bick, E.; Geyer, K.; Iversen D. A.; Kleene, A.; Lindø, A. V.; Neitsch, J.; Niebuhr, O.; Nielsen, R.; Petersen, E. N. 2019. Towards Balance and Boundaries in Public Discourse: Expressing and Perceiving Online Hate Speech (XPEROHS). In: Mey, J., Holsting, A., Johannessen, C. (ed.): RASK - International Journal of Language and Communication. Vol. 50., pp. 87-108. University of Southern Denmark.

Beißwenger, M.; Bartsch, S.; Evert, S.;Würzner, K.-M. 2016. EmpiriST 2015: A shared task on the automatic linguistic annotation of computer-mediated communication and web corpora. In: Paul Cook et al. (ed.): Proceedings of the 10th Web as Corpus Workshop (WAC-X) and the EmpiriST Shared Task. pp. 44-56. Berlin: Association for Computational Linguistics.

Bick, E.; Didriksen, T. 2015. CG-3 – Beyond Classical Constraint Grammar. In: Beáta Megyesi: *Proceedings of NODALIDA 2015, May 11-13, 2015, Vilnius, Lithuania*. pp. 31-39. Linköping: LiU Electronic Press. ISBN 978-91-7519-098-3

Neunerdt, M., Trevisan, B.,Reyer, M., Mathar, R. Part-of-Speech Tagging for Social Media Texts. (2013). Language Processing and Knowledge in the Web. pp. 139-150. Springer

Proisl, T. SoMeWeTa: A Part-of-Speech Tagger for German Social Media and Web Texts. In: Proceedings of ELREC 2018. pp. 665-670

Samuel, D. and Straka, M. 2021. ÚFAL at Multi-LexNorm 2021: Improving multilingual lexical normalization by fine-tuning ByT5. In Proceedings of the 7th Workshop on Noisy User-generated Text (W-NUT 2021), Punta Cana, Dominican Republic. Association for Computational Linguistics.

Sidarenka, U., Scheffler, T., Stede, M. Rule-Based Normalization of German Twitter Messages. (2013). In: Proceedings of the GSCL Workshop: Verarbeitung und Annotation von Sprachdaten aus Genres internetbasierter Kommunikation.

van der Goot, R. et al. 2021. MultiLexNorm: A Shared Task on Multilingual Lexical Normalization. In: Proceedings of the Seventh Workshop on Noisy User-generated Text (W-NUT 2021). pp. 493–509, Online. Association for Computational Linguistics.

Proceedings of the 18th Conference on Natural Language Processing (KONVENS 2022)

DocSCAN: Unsupervised Text Classification via Learning from Neighbors

Dominik Stammbach
ETH Zurich
dominsta@ethz.ch

Elliott Ash
ETH Zurich
ashe@ethz.ch

Abstract

We introduce DocSCAN, a completely unsupervised text classification approach built on the *Semantic Clustering by Adopting Nearest-Neighbors* algorithm. For each document, we obtain semantically informative vectors from a large pre-trained language model. We find that similar documents have proximate vectors, so neighbors in the representation space tend to share topic labels. Our learnable clustering approach then uses pairs of neighboring datapoints as a weak learning signal to automatically learn topic assignments. On three different text classification benchmarks, we improve on various unsupervised baselines by a large margin.

1 Introduction

"What is this about?" is the starting question in human and machine reading of text documents. While this question would invite a variety of answers for documents in general, there is a large set of corpora for which each document can be labeled as belonging to a singular category or topic. Text classification is the task of automatically mapping texts into these categories. In the standard supervised setting (Vapnik, 2000), machine learning algorithms learn such a mapping from annotated examples. Annotating data is costly, however, and the resulting annotations are usually domain-specific. Unsupervised methods promise to reduce the number of labeled examples needed or to dispense with them altogether.

This paper builds on recent developments in the domain of unsupervised neighbor-based clustering of images, the SCAN algorithm: *Semantic Clustering by Adopting Nearest neighbors* (Van Gansbeke et al., 2020). We adapt the algorithm to text classification and report strong experimental results on three text classification benchmarks. The intuition behind SCAN is that images often share the same label, if their embeddings in some representation space are close to each other. Thus, we can leverage this regularity as a weakly supervised signal for training models. We encode a datapoint and its neighbors through a network where the output of the network is determined by a classification layer. The model learns that it should assign similar output probabilities to a datapoint and each of its neighbors. In the ideal case, model output is consistent and one-hot, i.e. the model confidently assigns the same label to two neighboring datapoints.

Deep Transformer networks have led to rapid improvements in text classification and other natural language processing (NLP) tasks (see e.g. Yang et al., 2019). We draw from such models to obtain task-agnostic contextualized language representations. We use SBERT embeddings (Reimers and Gurevych, 2019), which have proven performance in a variety of downstream tasks, such as retrieving semantically similar documents and text clustering. We show that in this semantic space, indeed neighboring documents tend to often share the same class label and we can use this proximity to build a dataset on which we apply our neighbor-based clustering objective. We find that training a model exploiting this regularity works well for text classification and outperforms a standard unsupervised baseline by a large margin. All code for DocSCAN can be found publicly available online.[1]

2 Related Work

Unsupervised learning methods are ubiquitous in natural language processing and text classification. For a more general overview, we refer to surveys discussing the topic in extensive details (see e.g. Feldman and Sanger, 2006; Grimmer and Stewart, 2013; Aggarwal and Zhai, 2012; Thangaraj

[1] https://github.com/dominiksinsaarland/DocSCAN

and Sivakami, 2018; Li et al., 2021). One common approach for text classification is to represent documents as vectors and then apply any clustering algorithm on the vectors (Aggarwal and Zhai, 2012; Allahyari et al., 2017). The resulting clusters can be interpreted as the text classification results. A popular choice is to use the k-means algorithm which learns cluster centroids that minimize the within-cluster sum of squared distances-to-centroids (see e.g. Jing et al., 2005; Guan et al., 2009; Balabantaray et al., 2015; Slamet et al., 2016; Song et al., 2016; Kwale, 2017). This methodology has also applications in social science research, where for example Demszky et al. (2019) classify tweets using this method. K-means can also be applied in an iterative manner (Rakib et al., 2020).

There exist more sophisticated methods for generating weak labels for unsupervised learning for text classification. However, most of these methods take into account some sort of domain knowledge or heuristically generated labels. For example, Ratner et al. (2017) generate a correlation-based aggregate of different labeling functions to generate proxy labels. Yu et al. (2020) create weak labels via heuristics, and Meng et al. (2020) use seed words (most importantly the label name) and infer the text category assignment from a masked language modeling task and seed word overlap for each category. DocSCAN is not subject to any of these dependencies. Similarly to k-means, we only need the number of topics present in a dataset. Hence, we think it is well suited to be compared against k-means.

3 Method

In this work, we build on the SCAN algorithm (Van Gansbeke et al., 2020). It is based on the intuition that a datapoint and its nearest neighbors in (some reasonable) representation space often share the same class label. The algorithm consists of three stages: (1) learn representations via a self-learning task, (2) mine nearest neighbors and fine-tune a network on the weak signal that two neighbors share the same label, and (3) confidence-based self-labeling of the training data (which is ommitted in this work[2]).

[2]The authors use heavily augmented images for the confidence-based self-labeling step. There is no straightforward translation of this approach to NLP. Tokens are discrete, symbolic characters, rather than the continuous quantities contained in pixels. We skip this step and leave exploration to future work.

Our adaptation DocSCAN to text classification works as follows. In Step 1, we need a document embedding method that serves as an analogue to SCAN's self-learning task for images. Textual Entailment (Dagan et al., 2005) is an interesting pretraining task yielding transferable knowledge and generic language representations, as already shown in (Conneau et al., 2018). Combining this pretraining task and large Transformer models, e.g., (Devlin et al., 2019) has led to SBERT (Reimers and Gurevych, 2019): A network of BERT models fine-tuned on the Stanford Natural Language Inference corpus (Bowman et al., 2015). SBERT yields embeddings for short documents with proven performance across domains and for a variety of tasks, such as semantic search and clustering. For a given corpus, we apply SBERT and get a 768-dimensional dense vector for each document.[3] We directly use the pre-trained SBERT model fine-tuned on top of the MPNet model[4] (Song et al., 2020), which yields the best[5] (on average) performing embeddings for 14 sentence embedding tasks and 6 semantic search tasks.

Step 2 is the mining of neighbors in the embedding space. We apply Faiss (Johnson et al., 2017) to get Euclidean distances between all embedded document vectors. The retrieved neighbors are the documents having the smallest Euclidean distance to a reference datapoint.

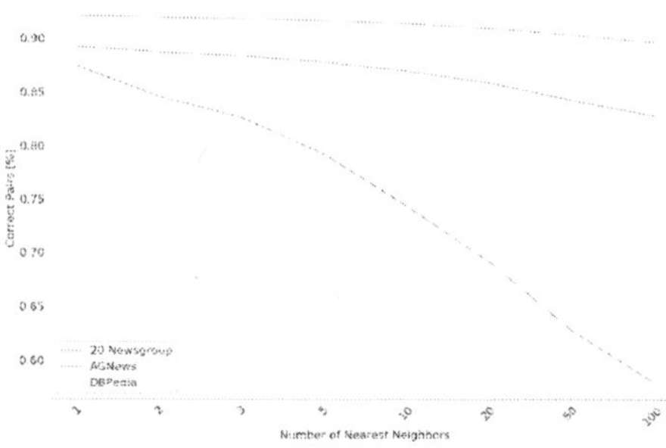

Figure 1: Accuracy of datapoint/neighbor pairs sharing the same label for different text classification benchmarks.

SCAN worked because images with proximate embeddings tended to share class labels. Is that

[3]We also experimented with other document representations. We discuss results in more detail in Appendix B

[4]The *all-mpnet-base-v2* model taken from `https://www.sbert.net/docs/pretrained_models.html`

[5]"best" embeddings at the time of submission of this work

the case with text? Figure 1 shows that the answer is yes: across three text classification benchmarks, neighboring document pairs do indeed often share the same label. The fraction of pairs sharing the same label at $k = 1$ is above 85% for all datasets examined. For $k = 5$, the resulting fraction of correct pairs (from all mined pairs) is still higher than 75% in all cases. Furthermore, these frequencies of correct pairs for $k = 5$ are often higher than the frequency of correct pairs reported for images in (Van Gansbeke et al., 2020).

Next, we describe the SCAN loss,

$$-\frac{1}{|\mathcal{D}|}\sum_{x\in\mathcal{D}}\sum_{k\in\mathcal{N}_x} log(f(x)\cdot f(k)) + \lambda\sum_{i\in\mathcal{C}} p_i log(p_i) \tag{1}$$

which can be broken down as follows. The first part of Eq. (1) is the consistency loss. Our model f (parametrized by a neural net) computes a label for a datapoint x from the dataset $\mathcal{D}$ and for each datapoint k in the set of the mined neighbors from x in $\mathcal{N}_x$. We then simply compute the dot product (denoted as $\cdot$) between the output distribution (normalized by a softmax function) for our datapoint x and its neighbor k. This dot product is maximized if both model outputs are one-hot with all probability mass on the same entry in the respective vectors. It is consistent because we want to assign the same label for a datapoint and all its neighbors. The second term is an auxiliary loss to obtain regularization via entropy (scaled by a weight λ), such that the model is encouraged to spread probability mass across all clusters $\mathcal{C}$ where p_i denotes the assigned probability of cluster i in $\mathcal{C}$ by the model. Without this entropy term, there exists a shortcut by collapsing all examples into one single cluster. The entropy term ensures that the distribution of class labels resulting from applying DocSCAN tends to be roughly uniform. Thus, it works best for text classification tasks where the number of examples per class is balanced as well.

To summarize: We use SBERT and embed every datapoint in a given text classification dataset. We then mine the five nearest neighbors for every datapoint. This yields our weakly supervised training set. We fine-tune networks on neighboring datapoints using the SCAN loss. At test time, we compute $f(x)$ for every datapoint x in the test set. We set the number of outcome classes equal to the numbers of classes in our considered datasets and use the hungarian matching algorithm (Kuhn and Yaw, 1955) to obtain the optimal cluster-to-label assignment.

4 Experiments

We apply DocSCAN on three widely used but diverse text classification benchmarks: The 20NewsGroup data (Lang, 1995), the AG's news corpus (Zhang et al., 2015), and lastly the DBPedia ontology dataset (Lehmann et al., 2015). We provide further dataset descriptions in Appendix Section A.

The main results are reported in Table 1. For all experiments, we report the mean accuracy over 10 runs on the test set (with different seeds and the 95% confidence interval). The columns correspond to the benchmark corpora. The rows correspond to the models, starting with a random baseline [1], two k-means baselines [2, 3] and the results obtained by DocSCAN in [4]. We also report a supervised learning baseline [5] and results taken from related literature in [6].

Row [1] provides a sensible lower-bound, row [5] analogously a supervised upper-bound for text classification performance. In the random draw [1], accuracy by construction converges to the average of the class proportions. The supervised model [5] is an SVM classifier applied to the same SBERT embeddings[6] which serve as inputs to the k-means baseline and to DocSCAN. Predictably, the supervised baseline obtains strong accuracy on these benchmark classification tasks.

The industry workhorse for clustering is k-means, an algorithm for learning cluster centroids that minimize the within-cluster sum of squared distances-to-centroids. When applied to TF-IDF-weighted bag-of-n-grams features [2], k-means improves over the results obtained in [1]. When applied to SBERT vectors [3], we see large improvements over all previous experiments. These results suggest that k means applied to reasonable document embeddings already yields satisfactory results for text classification. Second, they corroborate what we already saw in Figure 1, that neighbors in SBERT representation space contain information about text topic classes.

So what does DocSCAN add? We fine-tune a classification layer using the SBERT embeddings with the SCAN objective (Eq. 1) and $k = 5$ neighbors. We observe unambiguous and significant improvements over the already strong k-means base-

[6]We also trained the SVM classifier with TF-IDF representations and obtained similar results for all experiments.

Experiment	20 News	AG news	DBPedia
[1] Random Baseline	7.0 ±0.0	26.1 ±0.3	7.7 ±0.0
[2] TF-IDF + k-means	32.6 ±1.1	49.5 ±6.3	47.6 ±3.0
[3] SBERT embeddings + k-means	54.2 ±1.6	69.2 ±7.3	76.9 ±4.3
[4] DocSCAN	**59.4** ±1.9	**84.1** ±2.6	**84.6** ±3.8
[5] SBERT embeddings + SVM	82.7	92.1	98.7
6] Related Literature	58.2	84.52 ±0.50	91.1

Table 1: Test-set accuracy by benchmark dataset (columns) and classifier (rows). Cell values give the mean over 10 runs with 95% confidence interval. Note that the results reported from the related literature in the last row might not be directly comparable to our method due to different experimental setups. The 20 News results are taken from (Chu et al., 2021), the AG news results from (Rakib et al., 2020), and the DBPedia results from (Meng et al., 2020).

line in all three datasets (as we can judge from the 95% confidence intervals). The smallest improvements (over 5% points) are made on the 20 News dataset, containing 20 classes. The largest improvement gains are observed for AG news with 4 classes, suggesting that DocSCAN above all works best for text classification tasks with a lower number of classes. Surprisingly, we do not find that the improvements correlate with the accuracy of neighboring pairs sharing the same label (see Figure 1), but rather with the numbers of classes in the dataset (see Table 2). In the case of the AG news data with only a few different classes, we find that DocSCAN approaches the performance of a supervised baseline using the same input features.

Finally, in [6] we show results from related literature on unsupervised text classification. We find that DocSCAN performs comparable to other completely unsupervised methods. We find that DocSCAN obtains the best results for the 20 News dataset, comparable results in the case of AG news data and slightly worse results than the related literature on the DBPedia data. However, we note that DocSCAN is a simple method consisting of only $hidden\_dim * num\_classes$ parameters, that is exactly one classification layer which is fine-tuned in a completely unsupervised manner using the SCAN loss. Whereas the results for DBPedia from (Meng et al., 2020) are obtained by fine-tuning whole language models using domain knowledge (seed words).

We show and discuss ablation experiments for DocSCAN in Appendix B. Specifically, we conduct experiments regarding the various hyperparameters of the algorithm and find that it is robust to such choices. Furthermore, we find that DocSCAN outperforms a k-means baseline over different input features in all settings. Given the findings derived from these experiments, we recommend default hyperparameters for applying DocSCAN.

5 Conclusion

In this work, we introduced DocSCAN for unsupervised text classification. Analogous to the recognizable object content of images, we find that a document and its close neighbors in embedding space often share the same class in terms of the topical content. We show that this consistency can be used as a weak signal for fine-tuning text classifier models in an unsupervised fashion. We start with SBERT embeddings and fine-tune DocSCAN on three text classification benchmarks. We outperform a random baseline and two k-means baselines by a large margin. We discuss the influence of hyper-parameters and input features for DocSCAN and recommend default parameters which we have observed to work well across our main results.

As with images, unsupervised learning with SCAN can be used for text classification. However, the method may not work as generically, and should for example be limited to text classification in cases of balanced datasets (given that we use an entropy loss as an auxiliary objective). Still, this work points to the promise of further exploration of unsupervised methods using embedding geometry.

References

Charu C. Aggarwal and ChengXiang Zhai. 2012. *A Survey of Text Clustering Algorithms*, pages 77–128. Springer US, Boston, MA.

Mehdi Allahyari, Seyedamin Pouriyeh, Mehdi Assefi, Saied Safaei, Elizabeth D. Trippe, Juan B. Gutierrez, and Krys Kochut. 2017. A brief survey of text mining: Classification, clustering and extraction techniques.

Ricardo A. Baeza-Yates and Berthier A. Ribeiro-Neto. 1999. *Modern Information Retrieval*. ACM Press / Addison-Wesley.

Rakesh Chandra Balabantaray, Chandrali Sarma, and Monica Jha. 2015. Document clustering using k-means and k-medoids.

Samuel R. Bowman, Gabor Angeli, Christopher Potts, and Christopher D. Manning. 2015. A large annotated corpus for learning natural language inference. In *Proceedings of the 2015 Conference on Empirical Methods in Natural Language Processing (EMNLP)*. Association for Computational Linguistics.

Daniel Cer, Yinfei Yang, Sheng-yi Kong, Nan Hua, Nicole Limtiaco, Rhomni St. John, Noah Constant, Mario Guajardo-Cespedes, Steve Yuan, Chris Tar, Brian Strope, and Ray Kurzweil. 2018. Universal sentence encoder for English. In *Proceedings of the 2018 Conference on Empirical Methods in Natural Language Processing: System Demonstrations*, pages 169–174, Brussels, Belgium. Association for Computational Linguistics.

Zewei Chu, Karl Stratos, and Kevin Gimpel. 2021. Unsupervised label refinement improves dataless text classification. In *Findings of the Association for Computational Linguistics: ACL-IJCNLP 2021*, pages 4165–4178, Online. Association for Computational Linguistics.

Alexis Conneau, Douwe Kiela, Holger Schwenk, Loic Barrault, and Antoine Bordes. 2018. Supervised learning of universal sentence representations from natural language inference data.

Ido Dagan, Oren Glickman, and Bernardo Magnini. 2005. The pascal recognising textual entailment challenge. In *Proceedings of the First International Conference on Machine Learning Challenges: Evaluating Predictive Uncertainty Visual Object Classification, and Recognizing Textual Entailment*, MLCW'05, page 177–190, Berlin, Heidelberg. Springer-Verlag.

Dorottya Demszky, Nikhil Garg, Rob Voigt, James Zou, Matthew Gentzkow, Jesse Shapiro, and Dan Jurafsky. 2019. Analyzing polarization in social media: Method and application to tweets on 21 mass shootings.

Jacob Devlin, Ming-Wei Chang, Kenton Lee, and Kristina Toutanova. 2019. Bert: Pre-training of deep bidirectional transformers for language understanding.

Ronen Feldman and James Sanger. 2006. *Text Mining Handbook: Advanced Approaches in Analyzing Unstructured Data*. Cambridge University Press, USA.

Justin Grimmer and Brandon M Stewart. 2013. Text as data: The promise and pitfalls of automatic content analysis methods for political texts. *Political Analysis*, page mps028.

Hu Guan, Jingyu Zhou, and Minyi Guo. 2009. A class-feature-centroid classifier for text categorization. In *Proceedings of the 18th International Conference on World Wide Web*, WWW '09, page 201–210, New York, NY, USA. Association for Computing Machinery.

Liping Jing, Michael K. Ng, Jun Xu, and Joshua Zhexue Huang. 2005. Subspace clustering of text documents with feature weighting k-means algorithm. In *Advances in Knowledge Discovery and Data Mining*, pages 802–812, Berlin, Heidelberg. Springer Berlin Heidelberg.

Jeff Johnson, Matthijs Douze, and Hervé Jégou. 2017. Billion-scale similarity search with gpus.

Diederik P. Kingma and Jimmy Ba. 2014. Adam: A method for stochastic optimization. Cite arxiv:1412.6980Comment: Published as a conference paper at the 3rd International Conference for Learning Representations, San Diego, 2015.

H. W. Kuhn and Bryn Yaw. 1955. The hungarian method for the assignment problem. *Naval Res. Logist. Quart*, pages 83–97.

Francis Musembi Kwale. 2017. A critical review of k means text clustering algorithms. *International Journal of Advanced Research in Computer Science*, 4(9):27–34.

Ken Lang. 1995. Newsweeder: Learning to filter netnews. In *Proceedings of the Twelfth International Conference on Machine Learning*, pages 331–339.

Jens Lehmann, Robert Isele, Max Jakob, Anja Jentzsch, Dimitris Kontokostas, Pablo N. Mendes, Sebastian Hellmann, Mohamed Morsey, Patrick van Kleef, Sören Auer, and Christian Bizer. 2015. DBpedia - a large-scale, multilingual knowledge base extracted from wikipedia. *Semantic Web Journal*, 6(2):167–195.

Qian Li, Hao Peng, Jianxin Li, Congying Xia, Renyu Yang, Lichao Sun, Philip S. Yu, and Lifang He. 2021. A survey on text classification: From shallow to deep learning.

Yu Meng, Yunyi Zhang, Jiaxin Huang, Chenyan Xiong, Heng Ji, Chao Zhang, and Jiawei Han. 2020. Text classification using label names only: A language model self-training approach. In *Proceedings of the 2020 Conference on Empirical Methods in Natural Language Processing (EMNLP)*, pages 9006–9017, Online. Association for Computational Linguistics.

Jeffrey Pennington, Richard Socher, and Christopher Manning. 2014. Glove: Global vectors for word representation. In *Proceedings of the 2014 Conference on Empirical Methods in Natural Language Processing (EMNLP)*, pages 1532–1543, Doha, Qatar. Association for Computational Linguistics.

Md Rashadul Hasan Rakib, Norbert Zeh, Magdalena Jankowska, and Evangelos Milios. 2020. Enhancement of short text clustering by iterative classification. In *Natural Language Processing and Information Systems*, pages 105–117, Cham. Springer International Publishing.

Alexander Ratner, Stephen H. Bach, Henry Ehrenberg, Jason Fries, Sen Wu, and Christopher Ré. 2017. Snorkel. *Proceedings of the VLDB Endowment*, 11(3):269–282.

Nils Reimers and Iryna Gurevych. 2019. Sentence-bert: Sentence embeddings using siamese bert-networks.

Cepy Slamet, Ali Rahman, Muhammad Ali Ramdhani, and Wahyudin Darmalaksana. 2016. Clustering the verses of the holy qur'an using k-means algorithm.

Jia Song, Xianglin Huang, Sijun Qin, and Qing Song. 2016. A bi-directional sampling based on k-means method for imbalance text classification. In *2016 IEEE/ACIS 15th International Conference on Computer and Information Science (ICIS)*, pages 1–5.

Kaitao Song, Xu Tan, Tao Qin, Jianfeng Lu, and Tie-Yan Liu. 2020. Mpnet: Masked and permuted pre-training for language understanding.

M. Thangaraj and M Sivakami. 2018. Text classification techniques: A literature review. *Interdisciplinary Journal of Information, Knowledge, and Management*, 13:117–135.

Wouter Van Gansbeke, Simon Vandenhende, Stamatios Georgoulis, Marc Proesmans, and Luc Van Gool. 2020. Scan: Learning to classify images without labels. In *Proceedings of the European Conference on Computer Vision*.

Vladimir Vapnik. 2000. *The Nature of Statistical Learning Theory*. Springer: New York.

Zhilin Yang, Zihang Dai, Yiming Yang, Jaime Carbonell, Russ R Salakhutdinov, and Quoc V Le. 2019. Xlnet: Generalized autoregressive pretraining for language understanding. In *Advances in Neural Information Processing Systems*, volume 32, pages 5753–5763. Curran Associates, Inc.

Yue Yu, Simiao Zuo, Haoming Jiang, Wendi Ren, Tuo Zhao, and Chao Zhang. 2020. Fine-tuning pre-trained language model with weak supervision: A contrastive-regularized self-training approach.

Xiang Zhang, Junbo Zhao, and Yann LeCun. 2015. Character-level convolutional networks for text classification. In *Advances in Neural Information Processing Systems*, volume 28, pages 649–657. Curran Associates, Inc.

A Dataset Statistics

Dataset	# Examples	# Classes	Avg. Length	Example
20News	11'314	20	248	[...] I Have a Sound Blaster ver 1.5 When I try to install driver ver 1.5 (driver that comes with window 3.1) [...]
AG's Corpus	120'000	4	31	Wall St. Bears Claw Back Into the Black (Reuters) Reuters - Short-sellers, Wall Street's dwindling band of ultra-cynics, are seeing green again.
DBPedia	560'000	14	46	Abbott of Farnham E D Abbott Limited was a British coachbuilding business based in Farnham Surrey trading under that name from 1929. A major part of their output was under sub-contract to motor vehicle manufacturers. Their business closed in 1972.

Table 2: Dataset Statistics

We apply DocSCAN to three diverse datasets widely used in unsupervised text classification: (1) The 20NewsGroup data contains text from UseNet discussion groups (20 classes). (2) The AG's news corpus (Zhang et al., 2015), which consists of the title and description field of news articles (4 classes). And lastly the DBPedia ontology dataset (Lehmann et al., 2015) which includes titles and abstracts of Wikipedia articles (14 classes).

In Table 2, we show the numbers of training examples, number of classes, the average document length and one text example from each dataset. We selected these datasets because they are established standard datasets for unsupervised text classification. The three datasets vary in domain, number of classes, and text lengths. But they have all in common that the number of examples per class are roughly balanced, hence DocSCAN is well suited to tackle these datasets.

B Ablation Experiments

In Table 3, we report how DocSCAN performs under various different hyper-parameters which possibly could affect the performance of the algorithm. In the two last columns, we report the mean accuracy of 10 runs (and the 95% confidence interval) on the AG news and DBPedia training datasets. As common practice in unsupervised learning, we cluster the dataset and then report evaluation metrics on the training set itself (whereas in the main results, we discuss the performance on the test sets of the respective datasets).

We investigate the number of neighbors considered (A), the weight of the entropy loss (B), batch sizes (C), dropout (D) and number of epochs (E). To optimize the SCAN loss, we use Adam (Kingma and Ba, 2014) with default parameters in all experiments. DocSCAN runs somewhat stable across different choices of these hyperparameters, yielding similar results which all outperform the k-means baseline by a large margin. The two worst performances are achieved if we either set the entropy weight too low ($\lambda = 1$) or do not consider enough neighboring pairs ($k = 2$). The influence of all other hyperparameters seems limited. We recommend using the default parameters reported in the first row. The main results in Table 1 were obtained using this set of hyperparameters.

We also investigate whether the success of DocSCAN for text classification stems from the chosen document embeddings. For this, we consider a number of different input features for the algorithm and run DocSCAN with these features, holding everything else constant. We show results in Table 4. We report the mean performance of 10 runs and the 95% confidence interval on the AG news training set.

We run several document embedding techniques, starting with the TF-IDF-weighted bag-of-n-grams (Baeza-Yates and Ribeiro-Neto, 1999). Second, we consider the averaged GloVe embeddings of all words in a document (Pennington et al., 2014), Universal Sentence Encoder (USE) embeddings (Cer et al., 2018) and lastly the performance of DocSCAN using SBERT embeddings (Reimers and Gurevych, 2019). We observe again that DocSCAN performs better than k-means in every setting. However, the performance gap for different features varies. For example, we observe best k-means performance using USE embeddings, whereas the best DocSCAN performance is achieved via SBERT embeddings. Also, TF-IDF + k-means yields rather mixed results, whereas TF-IDF + DocSCAN performs more than 20%

	Neighbors	Entropy Weight	Batch Size	Dropout	Epochs	Accuracy AG news	Accuracy DBPedia
DocSCAN	5	2	128	0.1	5	83.2 ±3.8	85.8 ±3.5
(A)	2					77.5 ±6.7	83.1 ±5.1
	3					78.4 ±5.5	85.3 ±3.0
	10					82.4 ±5.6	86.1 ±3.5
(B)		1				75.8 ±5.3	80.3 ±2.8
		4				80.4 ±3.5	86.7 ±2.8
(C)			64			82.4 ±5.0	87.5 ±4.2
			256			81.3 ±4.3	84.6 ±4.1
(D)				0		81.9 ±3.7	86.1 ±4.4
				0.33		80.3 ±3.9	86.8 ±2.6
(E)					3	79.4 ±5.3	84.2 ±4.4
					10	81.5 ±3.4	84.7 ±3.7
k-means						66.2 ±8.2	77.1 ±4.9

Table 3: Ablation Studies for DocSCAN Hyper-parameters (results reported on the AG news and DBPedia training set, cell values give the mean over 10 runs with 95% confidence interval).

points better. In light of these results, we recommend to use SBERT embeddings if considering applying DocSCAN to other work.

Features	k-means	DocSCAN
TF-IDF	53.9 ±4.1	76.8 ±4.3
avg. GloVe	55.4 ±3.6	59.3 ±0.3
USE Embeddings	74.4 ±8.3	79.1 ±8.6
SBERT	66.2 ±8.2	83.2 ±3.8

Table 4: Ablation Studies for Different Input Features (results reported on the AG news training set, cell values give the mean over 10 runs with 95% confidence interval).

Proceedings of the 18th Conference on Natural Language Processing (KONVENS 2022)

Modelling Cultural and Socio-Economic Dimensions of Political Bias in German Tweets

Aishwarya Anegundi[1] and **Konstantin Schulz**[1] and **Christian Rauh**[2] and **Georg Rehm**[1]
[1] Deutsches Forschungszentrum für Künstliche Intelligenz GmbH (DFKI), Berlin, Germany
aishwarya.anegundi@dfki.de, konstantin.schulz@dfki.de, georg.rehm@dfki.de
[2] Wissenschaftszentrum Berlin für Sozialforschung (WZB), Berlin, Germany
christian.rauh@wzb.eu

Abstract

We introduce a new bi-dimensional classification scheme for political bias. In particular, we collaborate with political scientists and identify two important aspects: cultural and socio-economic positions. Using a dataset of tweets by German politicians, we show that the new scheme draws more distinctive boundaries that are easier to model for machine learning classifiers (F1 scores: 0.92 and 0.86), compared to one-dimensional approaches. We investigate the validity by applying the new classifiers to the whole dataset, including previously unseen data from other parties. Additional experiments highlight the importance of dataset size and balance, as well as the superior performance of transformer language models as opposed to older methods. Finally, an extensive error analysis confirms our hypothesis that lexical overlap, in combination with high attention values, is a reliable empirical predictor of misclassification for political bias.

1 Introduction

Political radicalization is linked to a society's sense of insecurity (Bartoszewicz, 2016). Such a feeling may arise especially in times of crisis, such as financial crashes, large migration movements, or pandemics. In this setting, citizens' trust in a country's government or into the political system more generally can decline quickly (Easton, 1975; Dostal, 2015), leading to further radicalization.

The effects of such a development are visible not only in terms of elections (Funke et al., 2016; Recuero et al., 2020) and media coverage (Bender et al., 2021), but also in general public political discourse and corresponding language use: Politically biased texts tend to exhibit a wording that is different from their neutral counterparts (Krestel et al., 2012; Fairbanks et al., 2018). At times, this lexical deviation is hard to detect because the texts are positioned in seemingly neutral environments like technological or scientific sections of a newspaper (Kang and Yang, 2022). Furthermore, there are additional factors beyond wording: The filtering and selection of information to be presented in a given spot is a bias in its own right, but can directly affect or reflect political discourse: Presenting quotes by famous hyperpartisan politicians often serves as a subtle disguise for an author's own political motives (Fan et al., 2019). Besides, the media coverage of political parties or crime-related ethnical aspects is indicative of the current government, the popularity of specific parties (Lazaridou and Krestel, 2016) and the trust in the executive's impartiality (Pfeiffer et al., 2018).

By training language models on such tendentious texts, we tend to reproduce and spread their bias (Bender et al., 2021), even if the resulting models are used in rather neutral contexts (Liu et al., 2021). Since political bias (PB) is closely related to credibility (Su et al., 2020; Vargas et al., 2020; Aksenov et al., 2021; DeVerna et al., 2021; Saltz et al., 2021) and trustworthiness (Viviani and Pasi, 2017), such language models will suffer from reduced acceptance and utility unless we can reasonably detect and decrease their bias. The same applies to traditional media content: There is no way to holistically analyze media credibility without considering the PB of respective outlets. Thus, we make the following contributions:

- We introduce a new classification scheme for PB adapted to recent insights of political science.
- Using the Polly corpus (De Smedt and Jaki, 2018), a dataset of German tweets, we train and evaluate transformer-based classifiers with our new scheme. Polly corpus does not provide the labels with respect to political dimension; instead provides a political party

label. Although there are large annotated datasets incorporating fine-grained schemes for parliament speeches and interviews (Blätte and Blessing, 2018; Rauh and Schwalbach, 2020), there are none for social media such as Twitter. Hence we use party affiliations as a proxy for the dimensions. We represent the extremes of cultural dimension with political parties *Grüne* and *AfD* and the extremes of socio-economic dimension with *Die Linke* and *FDP*.

- Using the classifiers, we test four hypotheses:
  1. The current one-dimensional schemes are overly simplistic models of PB. Integrating socio-economic and cultural dimensions of political conflict is more effective for classifying PB.
  2. Adding more data and balancing the dataset leads to better PB classification results.
  3. Misclassified texts often exhibit lexical overlap with the opposing end of the respective dimension.
  4. In misclassified texts, words from the opposing end of the respective dimension receive high attention from the transformer model.

We make our source code[1] and models[2] publicly available. In the following, we describe our conceptual model of PB, the annotations in the dataset and the architecture of our classifiers, as well as their training and the corresponding evaluation.

2 Related Work

Previous machine learning approaches to PB detection have mostly conceptualized it as binary text classification: Given an input text, the algorithm assigns a label indicating the presence or absence of PB. Similarly, the binary choice can also be used to model the direction of bias on continuous scales (Iyyer et al., 2014; Fairbanks et al., 2018; Liu et al., 2021), moving the desired outputs closer to seminal applications of text-based ideological scaling in the political sciences (Laver et al., 2003; Slapin and Proksch, 2008; Rheault and Cochrane, 2020; Sältzer, 2022).

[1] https://github.com/konstantinschulz/political-bias-classification

[2] https://live.european-language-grid.eu/catalogue/tool-service/18689

As in many cases of language modeling, binary decisions are easy to set up and learn. On the downside, they do not properly reflect all nuances of complex concepts like PB. That is why some approaches use more fine-grained classification schemes: They extend the left-right spectrum to incorporate more intermediate positions (Aksenov et al., 2021) or reuse datasets that originally proceeded this way (Fairbanks et al., 2018). Such advanced schemes may be more accurate than the simple binary models, but are also harder to annotate. In cases where this kind of data does not yet exist, many researchers fall back to using other documented phenomena as proxies for PB: Preference of specific political parties (Krestel et al., 2012; Kang and Yang, 2022), membership in such parties (Iyyer et al., 2014) and social interactions of the authors on Twitter (Li and Goldwasser, 2019) are prominent examples in that regard.

All in all, existing computational approaches to PB detection are still mostly one-dimensional, thereby reducing the political conflict to a single 'left-right' dimension. In political science, however, there is a growing agreement that political conflict is at least two-dimensional. The conventional left-right dimension comprising of socio-economic preferences regarding the relative power of markets and the state is increasingly complemented by a separate 'cultural' dimension of political conflict (Hooghe et al., 2002; Kriesi et al., 2008; Bornschier, 2010; Zürn and de Wilde, 2016; Lengfeld and Dilger, 2018). This dimension captures disagreements on culturally 'liberal' versus 'conservative' value orientations, compounding political stances on the openness of borders, migration, minority protection, environmentalism, or gender and sexuality questions. This two-dimensional structure has been shown to map onto political competition among partisan elites (Kriesi et al., 2008) and is also reflected in attitudes and vote intentions of citizens (Lucassen and Lubbers, 2012; Lengfeld and Dilger, 2018; Norris and Inglehart, 2019).

3 Methodology

This section discusses our conceptual model of PB, and different ways of classifying PB, followed by methods used to explain cases of misclassification.

Conceptual Model: To provide a more sophisticated model of PB, we follow recent insights from the field of political science and abandon the overly simple one-dimensional perspective. Instead, we use a two-dimensional approach aimed at capturing both socio-economic and cultural conflict lines. Unfortunately, to our knowledge, there is no dataset of German texts with readily available aggregate annotations on these two dimensions. Therefore, we use party affiliation as a proxy for the two dimensions. The intuition is that certain political parties in Germany represent the extremes on each of the two separate dimensions. This assumption is consistent with extant party-classification schemes in the political sciences (Polk and Rovny, 2017; Volkens et al., 2021) and is a common makeshift solution in PB classification suffering from annotation scarcity.

Domain and Register: We build on previous work analyzing social media because this forum of public discourse is known to be associated with PB (Badjatiya et al., 2019; Li and Goldwasser, 2019; Recuero et al., 2020) and corresponding disinformation (Gallotti et al., 2020; Keller et al., 2020; Sharma et al., 2020; Zhou et al., 2020; DeVerna et al., 2021; Mattern et al., 2021; Weinzierl and Harabagiu, 2021). This decision has important consequences for our trained classifiers: They will be well-adjusted to the short, rather colloquial texts on social media, but may fail when confronted with more formal registers and longer texts. The key challenge here is domain divergence (Kashyap et al., 2021), which we cannot reliably address without having access to multiple comparable datasets. Considering the political science work on correspondences between social media communication and parliamentary behavior of politicians (Silva and Proksch, 2021; Sältzer, 2022), one step into this direction would be the application of our classifiers to German parliamentary speeches (similar to the approach by Krestel et al., 2012). In that case, the domain would still be political, but the register drastically differs. We plan to evaluate this setup in future studies.

Classification: As a baseline, we chose to encode the tweets using FastText embeddings (Bojanowski et al., 2017) and train traditional machine learning (ML) models. FastText embeddings are learned with a method built on top of the continuous skip-gram model (Mikolov et al., 2013) overcoming the limitation of assigning a different vector for every word of the vocabulary by considering sub-word information. Hence, FastText embeddings perform better for morphologically rich languages like German and are suitable for our classification problem. We obtain the FastText embeddings for each word in the tweet, average them and feed them into ML models. We train different classifiers based on Random Forests (Breiman, 2001), Logistic Regression (Cox, 1958), Multi-Layer Perceptrons (MLP, Ramchoun et al., 2016), and Support Vector Machines (SVM, Cortes and Vapnik, 1995) with a linear kernel. Random Forest is an ensemble classification algorithm whose output is based on predictions of several decision trees constructed at training time. The Logistic Regression algorithm classifies a data point by computing log-odds on the linear combination of independent variables. MLP is a simple feed-forward neural network trained with backpropagation. SVMs construct a hyperplane in a high-dimensional space separating the two classes. The location of the data points on either side of the hyperplane determines their class.

FastText embeddings only incorporate distributional semantic relations between words but fail to consider the context of a word in a sentence, such as word order. We use transfer learning from pre-trained language models such as GBERT (Chan et al., 2020) to overcome this limitation. We chose GBERT-base model for our classification task due to the limited amount of data. GBERT has the same architecture as BERT (Devlin et al., 2019), but it is pre-trained on a large German corpus and has achieved impressive performance on various natural language processing tasks. The architecture of BERT is based on the multi-layer bidirectional transformer encoder with a multi-head attention mechanism (Vaswani et al., 2017). The base version consists of 12 layers, a hidden size of 768, and 12 attention heads, making up $110M$ parameters.

Error Analysis: For the error analysis, we are mainly interested to find out how well the model can learn the data distribution. Hence, we analyze attention scores (hypothesis 4) as an approximation of token importance (Wiegreffe and Pinter, 2019; Tutek and Šnajder, 2020), in combination with association scores (hypothesis 3) derived from the dataset. To identify the most important words associated with a particular class, we use a custom **word importance** WI metric which includes Pointwise Mutual Information (PMI) and Term Frequency–Inverse Document Frequency (TF-IDF), weighted by relative word frequency. Both measures have been shown to be useful approximations of association strength (Bouma, 2009; Krestel et al.,

2012; Fan et al., 2019). The distance between association scores for different classes gives higher scores to the words frequent in one class and infrequent in the opposite class. Normalizing by relative word frequency helps us avoid high scores for words with rare occurrences. The formula is

$$WI(c,w) = (\alpha(c,w) - \alpha(\hat{c},w)) \cdot f(c,w) \quad (1)$$

where $\hat{c}$ is the opposing class, α is either PMI or TF-IDF and $f(c,w)$ is the relative frequency of w within class c. We create two vocabularies for each class consisting of important words, one identified with the WI metric using PMI as α (PMI vocabulary) and the other using TF-IDF as α (TF-IDF vocabulary). Furthermore, we compute attention scores for each word in the tweet, summing up the attention scores for all sub-tokens forming the word. We average the attention score over all the attention heads across all the layers.

To verify hypothesis 3, we analyze the percentage of confusing words in each tweet. A word is confusing if $WI(c,w) - WI(\hat{c},w)$ is positive, indicating that the word is more important in the opposite end of the dimension. We analyze the amount of tweets above a certain threshold percentage of confusing words and examine how this number changes for varying minima. We compare the ratio of wrong and correct predictions for each threshold to confirm the hypothesis. Further, to verify the hypothesis 4, we rank the confusing words according to the magnitude of $WI(c,w) - WI(\hat{c},w)$ and check if the topmost confusing words receive the highest attention from the model. Again, we compare the ratio of false and correct predictions to confirm the hypothesis. We repeat the process for the vocabularies in both dimensions.

4 Experiments

Dataset: We trained our classification models on a subset of the Polly corpus (De Smedt and Jaki, 2018). The corpus focuses on the 2017 German Federal Election and consists of 125K tweets collected from August 2017 to December 2017. It comprises seven subgroups denoting tweets by fans, by politicians, about politicians, containing the phrase *ist ein* ("is a"), hate speech, emojis, and random tweets. In our study, we used the subset containing tweets by politicians also denoted as "By-Party" currently in their Google Sheet[3]. Each tweet in the By-Party subset also provides metadata such as likes, timestamps, names of the politicians, and their associated political parties. The By-Party subset has about 14.2K tweets from seven different parties: CDU, CSU, SPD, Die Linke, Die Grünen, FDP, and AfD. With respect to gender, it contains tweets from 13 female and 22 male politicians selected based on their popularity.

Following extant party-classification schemes in the political sciences (Polk and Rovny, 2017; Volkens et al., 2021) we exploit the following party labels. For the dimension capturing conflict between culturally liberal and conservative stances, we consider tweets from Die Grünen (the rather cosmopolitan German Green party) and the Alternative für Deutschland (AfD, a populist far-right party) as representations of the most extreme stances. We anchor the socio-economic left-right dimension on tweets from Die Linke (a far-left party) and the FDP (taking market-liberal stances). This results in about 4.5K tweets for each dimension. The data distribution for the socio-economic dimension is $1.96k$ tweets for Die Linke and $2.52k$ tweets for FDP (Die Linke = 43.82%, FDP = 56.7%). Similarly, the distribution for the cultural dimension is $2.16k$ tweets for Die Grünen and $2.4k$ tweets for AfD (Die Grünen = 47.33%, AfD = 52.66%). Given the limited data points, we split the collection of tweets into train and test data at a 90:10 ratio. We then preprocess the tweets to remove mentions, URLs and the retweet string "RT @mention". While we retain the emoticons for the classification using the BERT model, we remove them for the FastText embeddings because FastText does not contain meaningful embeddings for them. We always downsample the majority class to achieve class balancing before training the model.

Baseline Model: For our classification task, we download the 300-dimensional pre-trained vectors for the German language[4], provided by Facebook[5] to initialize the FastText model using the Gensim library[6]. We normalize and tokenize the tweets using the ICU-Tokenizer[7]. To obtain the final embedding, we average the FastText word embeddings of each token in the tweet. The resulting vectors are used to train the ML classifiers with the scikit-learn library.

[3]https://docs.google.com/spreadsheets/d/1c5peNMjt24U0FcEMSj8gD_JjzumqXTWbPWa_yb2nNt0/edit. URLs were all last accessed on 2022-06-09.

[4]https://dl.fbaipublicfiles.com/fasttext/vectors-wiki/wiki.de.zip

[5]https://fasttext.cc/docs/en/pretrained-vectors.html

[6]https://radimrehurek.com/gensim/models/fasttext.html

[7]https://github.com/mingruimingrui/ICU-tokenizer

The Random Forest classifier is trained with the Gini criterion with 100 trees as estimators. The MLP classifier comprises 12 layers and is trained with the Adam optimizer, ReLU activation and early stopping. We use a linear kernel for the SVM classifier and Stochastic Average Gradient solver for the Logistic Regression.

GBERT Model: We fine-tune the GBERT-base model on the Polly By-Party subcorpus using the HuggingFace transformers library[8]. Before fine-tuning, we tokenize the tweets using the AutoTokenizer for GBERT from the same library. The GBERT model encodes the tweets, and these encodings are fed into an output feed-forward network, followed by a softmax layer. This is achieved by using the AutoModelForSequenceClassification class from the transformers library. We train the model with the AdamW optimizer, with a learning rate of 5e-5 and a batch size of 8 for five epochs.

5 Results

Classification: Tables 1 and 2 show the accuracy, micro-averaged precision, recall and F1 scores for different classification models over cultural and socio-economic dimensions. We use micro-averaging for the evaluation to be consistent with our additional experiments on class imbalance (see below). GBERT-base performs best for both dimensions, although the performance is much higher for the cultural dimension with 92% accuracy than for the socio-economic dimension with 86%. The better performance of GBERT in comparison to ML algorithms can be explained by the fact that GBERT has been pre-trained on large German text corpora. Besides, it takes into consideration the context of a word in both directions. Its large number of parameters enables it to model a complex underlying function. All the ML algorithms perform the same, more or less, and the varying model sizes can explain the slight differences. In contrast, the GBERT model trained on a traditional left-right dimension with Die Linke on the left end and AfD on the right end of the spectrum as proxies has an accuracy of 87.02% (micro F1 = 86.4%). Hence, deviating from the traditional one-dimensional approach leads to higher classification performance, supporting our hypothesis 1.

Table 3 shows the results of the GBERT model trained with reduced data for balanced and unbalanced scenarios. For both dimensions, the model's performance reduces when trained with half the data, supporting hypothesis 2. We can see that the majority class (FDP) is easier to classify for the socio-economic dimension. Hence, the accuracy drops after balancing. Meanwhile, for the cultural dimension, both classes are equally hard to classify, and increasing the relative importance of the minority class (Die Grünen) through balancing leads to a slight increase of overall accuracy. We hypothesize that, after the balancing intervention, the model uses a larger share of its weights and biases to model the (former) minority class, which increases the performance for that class.

Application: We apply the two trained classifiers to the whole dataset (see Figure 1). Each tweet gets a cultural and a socio-economic score. The score for a specific party is the average of all its associated tweets. We observe that, as expected, the four proxy parties (AfD, FDP, Die Grünen, Die Linke) are close to the respective extreme of the dimension that they represent. Interestingly, these proxy parties form two pairs: The distance from the Left to the Green party is smaller than to the liberal or conservative party. The same goes for the liberal party, which has a small distance to the conservative party, as opposed to the Left or Green. Finally, we note that most parties are situated in the lower left quadrant (open, socialist), while the remaining two occupy outlier places (liberal and/or conservative). This could be an indication of political isolation. However, the dataset is a sample of just a few dozen politicians with a moderate bias regarding the distribution of gender, and possibly age or other important factors. Thus, our results

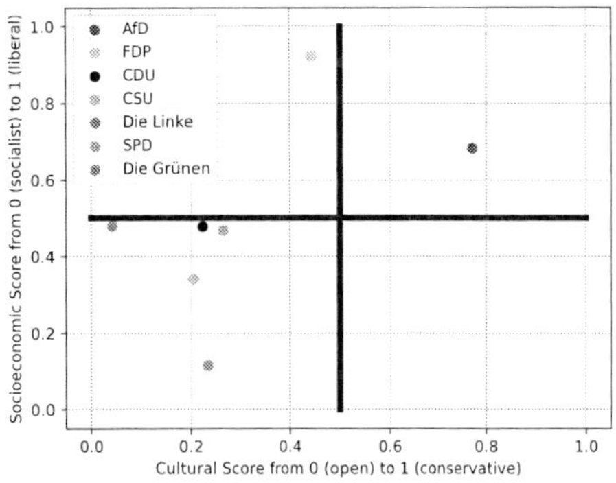

Figure 1: Cultural and Socio-economic Scores of German Political Parties

[8] https://huggingface.co/bert-base-german-cased

are not necessarily representative of each party as a whole. Instead, they can serve as general tendency that needs to be investigated more thoroughly in future studies.

TF-IDF Vocabulary: Figures 2 and 3 show the percentage of tweets consisting of a minimum number of confusing words (threshold) for the TF-IDF vocabulary. For the cultural dimension (Figure 2), we can infer that, on average, 10.6% more tweets meeting the threshold are misclassified, compared to the correct predictions. Although not consistent over all the thresholds, we see similar behavior (Figure 3) for the socio-economic dimension, between the 10% and 35% thresholds, with 1.3% more tweets meeting the threshold and being misclassified, compared to the correct predictions on average. Furthermore, misclassified tweets make up a larger share of the dataset (+19.3%) compared to the correctly classified ones, with at least one confusing word receiving the highest attention for the cultural dimension (Figure 4). We see a different behavior when we consider only a few of the top confusing words up to a minimum of 30%, after which the trend reverses. The same trend emerges for the socio-economic dimension (see Appendix A) when we consider at least the top 25% of confusing words. The behavior is not as strong as in the cultural dimension, with only 2% of wrong predictions consisting of a confusing word receiving highest attention in comparison to 1.5% for the correct predictions. Some lexical examples of commonly confused words in a TF-IDF vocabulary are as in Table 6.

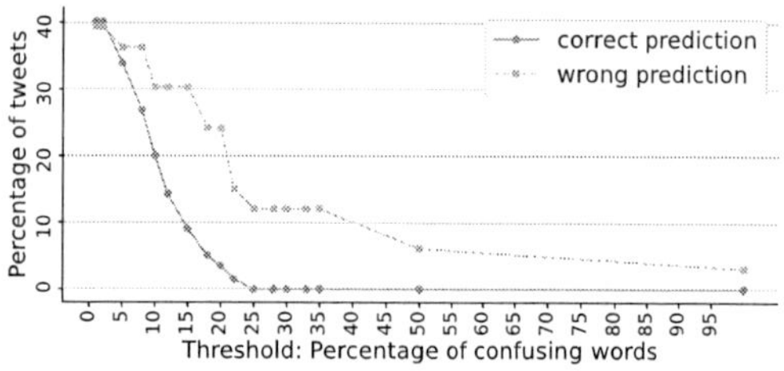

Figure 2: Percentage of wrong predictions and correct predictions for varying thresholds of confusing words computed using the TF-IDF vocabulary for the cultural dimension.

PMI Vocabulary: Analogous to our analysis using TF-IDF, we also observe the variation in the percentage of wrong and correct predictions for the PMI vocabulary. For the cultural dimension (Appendix A), at any given threshold, the percentage of misclassified tweets meeting the threshold exceeds the correctly classified tweets by 11.6% on average. For the socio-economic dimension, we observe the same trend up to the 28% threshold, with wrong predictions meeting the threshold exceeding the correct predictions by 5.31% on average. Also, similar to the TF-IDF vocabulary, on average, 12.7% more misclassified tweets than correct ones in the cultural dimension includes at least one confusing word that receives the highest attention (Figure 5). We observed the same trend when considering only a few of the top confusing words. The behavior is not so evident for the socio-economic dimension, with wrong predictions constituting only 2% more than correct predictions on average. The trend reverses when we consider more than 55% of the top confusing words (Appendix A). For lexical examples of commonly confused words in a PMI vocabulary see Table 6.

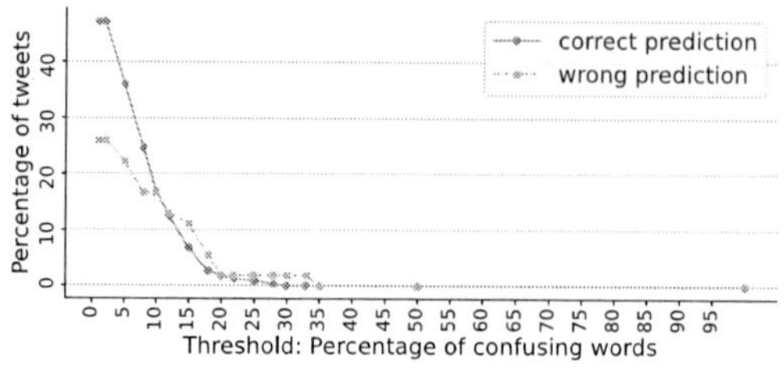

Figure 3: Percentage of wrong predictions and correct predictions for varying thresholds of confusing words computed using the TF-IDF vocabulary for the socio-economic dimension.

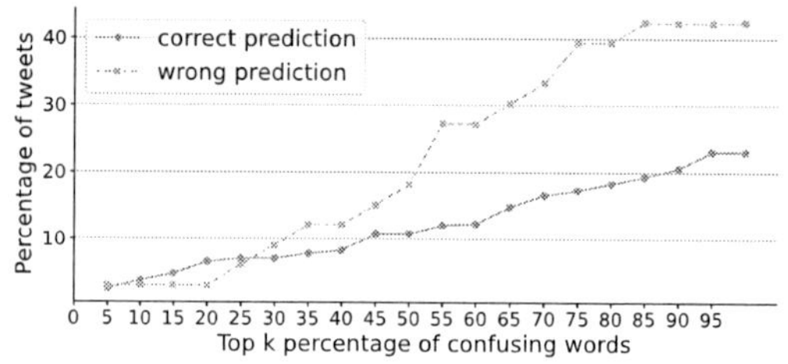

Figure 4: Percentage of tweets consisting of a confusing word receiving the highest attention from the model for the cultural dimension with the TF-IDF vocabulary.

For both TF-IDF vocabulary and PMI vocabulary, hypothesis 3 holds for the cultural dimension over all the thresholds. In contrast, hypothesis 4 is confirmed with a larger margin for the PMI vocabulary compared to the TF-IDF vocabulary (Figures 4 and 5). For the socio-economic dimension, hy-

Model	Accuracy	Precision	Recall	F1
GBERT-base	**0.92**	**0.93**	**0.92**	**0.92**
Logistic Regression	0.80	0.81	0.80	0.80
SVM	0.83	0.83	0.83	0.83
Random Forests	0.81	0.81	0.81	0.81
MLP	0.82	0.82	0.82	0.82

Table 1: Comparative evaluation of classification: GBERT-base with ML classifiers for the cultural dimension (Die Grünen vs. AfD) on Polly test data.

Model	Accuracy	Precision	Recall	F1
GBERT-base	**0.86**	**0.89**	**0.83**	**0.86**
Logistic Regression	0.68	0.68	0.68	0.67
SVM	0.71	0.71	0.71	0.71
Random Forests	0.73	0.73	0.73	0.73
MLP	0.70	0.70	0.70	0.69

Table 2: Comparative evaluation of classification: GBERT-base with ML classifiers for the socio-economic dimension (Die Linke vs. FDP) on Polly test data.

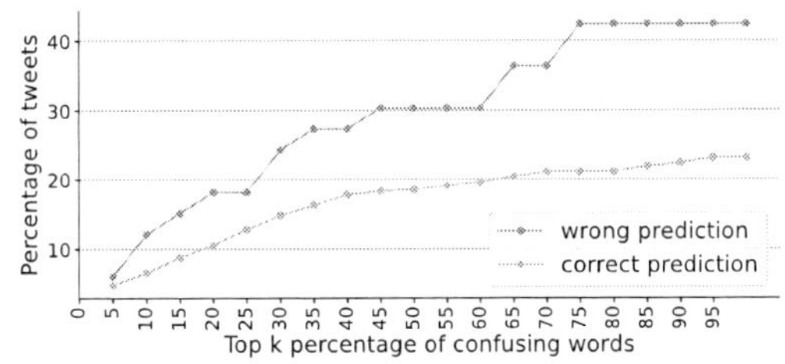

Figure 5: Percentage of tweets consisting of a confusing word receiving the highest attention from the model for the cultural dimension with the PMI vocabulary.

pothesis 3 holds over a specific range of thresholds only, although the distinction is more explicit in the PMI vocabulary than in the TF-IDF vocabulary. Similarly, the PMI vocabulary shows a clearer difference between wrong and correct predictions for hypothesis 4 than the TF-IDF vocabulary. Furthermore, hypothesis 4 holds when we consider more confusing words for the TF-IDF vocabulary in contrast to fewer confusing words in the case of the PMI vocabulary for the socio-economic dimension (Appendix A).

6 Conclusions

We have shown that PB can be reliably analyzed in two dimensions. In particular, we follow recent insights from political science and abandon one-dimensional scales like 'left vs. right'. Instead, we use separate dimensions for cultural and socio-economic conflict lines to model different aspects of PB. Due to a lack of appropriately annotated datasets for this new scheme, we use party affiliation as a proxy for the dimensions: The German political parties *Grüne* and *AfD* represent different extremes of the cultural dimension, while *Die Linke* and *FDP* span up the socio-economic conflict line. We use GBERT to train separate binary classifiers for tweets by each of those parties' members, showing that the cultural distinction is easier to model in our setup. In both cases, the deep learning approach is superior to other ML baselines like SVM or Random Forests.

We conduct additional experiments to explain classification errors. The classifiers struggle when many words from the opposing political spectrum are used and receive high attention by the transformer model. This is particularly true for the cultural dimension, but only partially for the socio-economic cleavage. We hypothesize that, in the latter case, the language use of the different parties is more similar to each other, blurring the lexical boundaries and thus reducing the risk of classification errors based solely on the presence of specific words. This may be related to a long-standing political science debate on position- vs. salience-based party competition (Dolezal et al., 2014): in the former perspective, parties compete with different stances on the same topics, which would mean that they share a high number of words. In the latter perspective, parties compete by emphasizing different topics, which should be related to greater lexical diversity across tweets from different parties.

Dimension	Data Distribution (%)			F1		Accuracy
socio-economic		Die Linke	FDP	Die Linke	FDP	
	unbalanced	43.82	56.7	0.825	0.861	0.845
	balanced	50	50	0.841	0.833	0.837
cultural		Die Grünen	AfD	Die Grünen	AfD	
	unbalanced	47.33	52.66	0.884	0.894	0.889
	balanced	50	50	0.898	0.897	0.897

Table 3: Evaluation of the GBERT model trained on only half of the Polly train data. For each dimension, we see the model's performance in balanced and unbalanced setups indicated by per-class F1 score and overall accuracy. The two classes for each dimension are the two extremes of the dimension represented by political parties.

In terms of future work, we plan to evaluate our classifiers on other datasets of political language, such as extant collections of German parliamentary speeches (Blätte and Blessing, 2018; Rauh and Schwalbach, 2020). Besides, we need to empirically explore possible reasons for the different classification performance in our two dimensions. Furthermore, creating new annotations specifically for our proposed model of PB would enable researchers to train classifiers with a higher construct validity. Finally, while our bi-dimensional scheme for PB detection is better than the single-dimensional scheme, exploring other dimensions is worthwhile following new political science research.

Acknowledgments

The research presented in this paper is funded by the German Federal Ministry of Education and Research (BMBF) through the project PANQURA (grant no. 03COV03E).

References

Dmitrii Aksenov, Peter Bourgonje, Karolina Zaczynska, Malte Ostendorff, Julian Moreno-Schneider, and Georg Rehm. 2021. Fine-grained Classification of Political Bias in German News: A Data Set and Initial Experiments. In *Proceedings of the 5th Workshop on Online Abuse and Harms (WOAH 2021)*, pages 121–131, Online. Association for Computational Linguistics.

Pinkesh Badjatiya, Manish Gupta, and Vasudeva Varma. 2019. Stereotypical Bias Removal for Hate Speech Detection Task using Knowledge-based Generalizations. *The World Wide Web Conference on - WWW '19*, pages 49–59.

Monika Gabriela Bartoszewicz. 2016. Festung Europa: Securitization of migration and radicalization of European Societies. *Acta Universitatis Carolinae Studia Territorialia*, 16(2):11–37.

Emily M Bender, Timnit Gebru, Angelina McMillan-Major, and Shmargaret Shmitchell. 2021. On the Dangers of Stochastic Parrots: Can Language Models Be Too Big?. In *Proceedings of the 2021 ACM Conference on Fairness, Accountability, and Transparency*, pages 610–623.

Andreas Blätte and Andre Blessing. 2018. The GermaParl Corpus of Parliamentary Protocols - ACL Anthology. In *Proceedings of the Eleventh International Conference on Language Resources and Evaluation*, Miyazaki, Japan. European Language Resources Association (ELRA).

Piotr Bojanowski, Edouard Grave, Armand Joulin, and Tomas Mikolov. 2017. Enriching word vectors with subword information. *Transactions of the Association for Computational Linguistics*, 5:135–146.

Simon Bornschier. 2010. *Cleavage Politics and the Populist Right: The New Cultural Conflict in Western Europe*. Temple University Press.

Gerlof Bouma. 2009. Normalized (pointwise) mutual information in collocation extraction. *Proceedings of GSCL*, pages 31–40.

Leo Breiman. 2001. Random forests. *Machine Learning*, 45(1):5–32.

Branden Chan, Stefan Schweter, and Timo Möller. 2020. German's next language model. In *Proceedings of the 28th International Conference on Computational Linguistics*, pages 6788–6796, Barcelona, Spain (Online). International Committee on Computational Linguistics.

C. Cortes and V. Vapnik. 1995. Support vector networks. *Machine Learning*, 20:273–297.

David R. Cox. 1958. The regression analysis of binary sequences (with discussion). *J Roy Stat Soc B*, 20:215–242.

Tom De Smedt and Sylvia Jaki. 2018. The Polly corpus: Online political debate in Germany. In *Proceedings of the 6th Conference on Computer-Mediated Communication (CMC) and Social Media Corpora (CMC-corpora 2018)*, pages 33–36, Antwerp.

Matthew R DeVerna, Francesco Pierri, Bao Tran Truong, John Bollenbacher, David Axelrod, Niklas Loynes, Christopher Torres-Lugo, Kai-Cheng Yang, Filippo Menczer, and John Bryden. 2021. CoVaxxy: A collection of English-language Twitter posts about COVID-19 vaccines. In *Proceedings of the Fifteenth International AAAI Conference on Web and Social Media (ICWSM 2021)*, pages 992–999, Virtual. AAAI.

Jacob Devlin, Ming-Wei Chang, Kenton Lee, and Kristina Toutanova. 2019. BERT: Pre-training of deep bidirectional transformers for language understanding. In *Proceedings of the 2019 Conference of the North American Chapter of the Association for Computational Linguistics: Human Language Technologies, Volume 1 (Long and Short Papers)*, pages 4171–4186, Minneapolis, Minnesota. Association for Computational Linguistics.

Martin Dolezal, Laurenz Ennser-Jedenastik, Wolfgang C. Müller, and Anna Katharina Winkler. 2014. How parties compete for votes: A test of saliency theory. *European Journal of Political Research*, 53(1):57–76. _eprint: https://onlinelibrary.wiley.com/doi/pdf/10.1111/1475-6765.12017.

Jörg Michael Dostal. 2015. The Pegida movement and German political culture: Is right-wing populism here to stay? *The Political Quarterly*, 86(4):523–531.

David Easton. 1975. A Re-Assessment of the Concept of Political Support. *British Journal of Political Science*, 5(4):435–457.

James Fairbanks, Natalie Fitch, Nathan Knauf, and Erica Briscoe. 2018. Credibility assessment in the news: Do we need to read? In *Proc. of the MIS2 Workshop Held in Conjunction with 11th Int'l Conf. on Web Search and Data Mining*, pages 1–8, Marina Del Rey. ACM.

Lisa Fan, Marshall White, Eva Sharma, Ruisi Su, Prafulla Kumar Choubey, Ruihong Huang, and Lu Wang. 2019. In plain sight: Media bias through the lens of factual reporting. *arXiv preprint arXiv:1909.02670*.

Manuel Funke, Moritz Schularick, and Christoph Trebesch. 2016. Going to extremes: Politics after financial crises, 1870–2014. *European Economic Review*, 88:227–260.

Riccardo Gallotti, Francesco Valle, Nicola Castaldo, Pierluigi Sacco, and Manlio De Domenico. 2020. Assessing the risks of 'infodemics' in response to COVID-19 epidemics. *Nature Human Behaviour*, 4(12):1285–1293.

Liesbet Hooghe, Gary Marks, and Carole J. Wilson. 2002. Does Left/Right Structure Party Positions on European Integration? *Comparative Political Studies*, 35(8):965–989. Publisher: SAGE Publications Inc.

Mohit Iyyer, Peter Enns, Jordan Boyd-Graber, and Philip Resnik. 2014. Political ideology detection using recursive neural networks. In *Proceedings of the 52nd Annual Meeting of the Association for Computational Linguistics (Volume 1: Long Papers)*, pages 1113–1122.

Hyungsuc Kang and Janghoon Yang. 2022. Quantifying perceived political bias of newspapers through a document classification technique. *Journal of Quantitative Linguistics*, 29(2):127–150.

Abhinav Ramesh Kashyap, Devamanyu Hazarika, Min-Yen Kan, and Roger Zimmermann. 2021. Domain Divergences: A Survey and Empirical Analysis. *arXiv:2010.12198 [cs]*.

Franziska B Keller, David Schoch, Sebastian Stier, and JungHwan Yang. 2020. Political astroturfing on Twitter: How to coordinate a disinformation campaign. *Political Communication*, 37(2):256–280.

Ralf Krestel, Alex Wall, and Wolfgang Nejdl. 2012. Treehugger or Petrolhead? Identifying bias by comparing online news articles with political speeches. In *Proceedings of the 21st International Conference on World Wide Web*, pages 547–548.

Hanspeter Kriesi, Edgar Grande, Romain Lachat, Martin Dolezal, Simon Bornschier, and Timotheos Frey. 2008. *West European Politics in the Age of Globalization*. Cambridge University Press, Cambridge.

Michael Laver, Kenneth Benoit, and John Garry. 2003. Extracting Policy Positions from Political Texts Using Words as Data. *The American Political Science Review*, 97(2):311–331.

Konstantina Lazaridou and Ralf Krestel. 2016. Identifying political bias in news articles. *Bulletin of the IEEE TCDL*, 12(2).

Holger Lengfeld and Clara Dilger. 2018. Kulturelle und ökonomische Bedrohung. Eine Analyse der Ursachen der Parteiidentifikation mit der „Alternative für Deutschland" mit dem Sozio-oekonomischen Panel 2016: Cultural and Economic Threats. A Causal Analysis of the Party Identification with the "Alternative for Germany" (AfD) using the German Socio-Economic Panel 2016. *Zeitschrift für Soziologie*, 47(3):181–199.

Chang Li and Dan Goldwasser. 2019. Encoding social information with graph convolutional networks for political perspective detection in news media. In *Proceedings of the 57th Annual Meeting of the Association for Computational Linguistics*, pages 2594–2604.

Ruibo Liu, Chenyan Jia, Jason Wei, Guangxuan Xu, Lili Wang, and Soroush Vosoughi. 2021. Mitigating Political Bias in Language Models through Reinforced Calibration. *Proceedings of the AAAI Conference on Artificial Intelligence*, 35(17):14857–14866.

Geertje Lucassen and Marcel Lubbers. 2012. Who fears what? Explaining far-right-wing preference in Europe by distinguishing perceived cultural and economic ethnic threats. *Comparative Political Studies*, 45(5):547–574.

Justus Mattern, Yu Qiao, Elma Kerz, Daniel Wiechmann, and Markus Strohmaier. 2021. FANG-COVID: A New Large-Scale Benchmark Dataset for Fake News Detection in German. In *Proceedings of the Fourth Workshop on Fact Extraction and VERification (FEVER)*, pages 78–91, Dominican Republic. Association for Computational Linguistics.

Tomas Mikolov, Ilya Sutskever, Kai Chen, Greg Corrado, and Jeffrey Dean. 2013. Distributed representations of words and phrases and their compositionality. In *Proceedings of the 26th International Conference on Neural Information Processing Systems - Volume 2*, NIPS'13, page 3111–3119, Red Hook, NY, USA. Curran Associates Inc.

Pippa Norris and Ronald Inglehart. 2019. *Cultural Backlash: Trump, Brexit, and Authoritarian Populism.* Cambridge University Press. Google-Books-ID: I8aGDwAAQBAJ.

Christian Pfeiffer, Dirk Baier, and Sören Kliem. 2018. Zur Entwicklung der Gewalt in Deutschland. Schwerpunkte: Jugendliche und Flüchtlinge als Täter und Opfer. Zentrale Befunde eines Gutachtens im Auftrag des Bundesministeriums für Familie, Senioren, Frauen und Jugend (BMFSFJ). Technical report, Zürcher Hochschule für Angewandte Wissenschaften, Zürich.

Jonathan Polk and Jan Rovny. 2017. Anti-Elite/Establishment Rhetoric and Party Positioning on European Integration. *Chinese Political Science Review*, pages 1–16.

Hassan Ramchoun, Youssef Ghanou, Mohamed Ettaouil, and Mohammed Amine Janati Idrissi. 2016. Multilayer perceptron: Architecture optimization and training. *International Journal of Interactive Multimedia and Artificial Intelligence*, 4(1):26–30.

Christian Rauh and Jan Schwalbach. 2020. The ParlSpeech V2 data set: Full-text corpora of 6.3 million parliamentary speeches in the key legislative chambers of nine representative democracies.

Raquel Recuero, Felipe Bonow Soares, and Anatoliy Gruzd. 2020. Hyperpartisanship, disinformation and political conversations on Twitter: The Brazilian presidential election of 2018. In *Proceedings of the International AAAI Conference on Web and Social Media*, volume 14, pages 569–578.

Ludovic Rheault and Christopher Cochrane. 2020. Word Embeddings for the Analysis of Ideological Placement in Parliamentary Corpora. *Political Analysis*, 28(1):112–133. Publisher: Cambridge University Press.

Emily Saltz, Soubhik Barari, Claire Leibowicz, and Claire Wardle. 2021. Misinformation interventions are common, divisive, and poorly understood. *Harvard Kennedy School Misinformation Review*, 2(5):1–25.

Karishma Sharma, Sungyong Seo, Chuizheng Meng, Sirisha Rambhatla, and Yan Liu. 2020. Covid-19 on social media: Analyzing misinformation in twitter conversations. *arXiv preprint arXiv:2003.12309*.

Bruno Castanho Silva and Sven-Oliver Proksch. 2021. Politicians unleashed? Political communication on Twitter and in parliament in Western Europe. *Political Science Research and Methods*, pages 1–17. Publisher: Cambridge University Press.

Jonathan Slapin and Sven-Oliver Proksch. 2008. A Scaling Model for Estimating Time-Series Party Positions from Texts. *American Journal of Political Science*, 52(3):705–722.

Qi Su, Mingyu Wan, Xiaoqian Liu, and Chu-Ren Huang. 2020. Motivations, Methods and Metrics of Misinformation Detection: An NLP Perspective. *Natural Language Processing Research*, 1(1-2):1–13.

Marius Sältzer. 2022. Finding the bird's wings: Dimensions of factional conflict on Twitter. *Party Politics*, 28(1):61–70. Publisher: SAGE Publications Ltd.

Martin Tutek and Jan Šnajder. 2020. Staying True to Your Word: (How) Can Attention Become Explanation? *arXiv preprint arXiv:2005.09379*.

Luis Vargas, Patrick Emami, and Patrick Traynor. 2020. On the detection of disinformation campaign activity with network analysis. In *Proceedings of the 2020 ACM SIGSAC Conference on Cloud Computing Security Workshop*, pages 133–146, Virtual. ACM.

Ashish Vaswani, Noam Shazeer, Niki Parmar, Jakob Uszkoreit, Llion Jones, Aidan N Gomez, Łukasz Kaiser, and Illia Polosukhin. 2017. Attention is all you need. In *Advances in Neural Information Processing Systems*, pages 5998–6008.

Marco Viviani and Gabriella Pasi. 2017. Credibility in social media: Opinions, news, and health information—a survey. *Wiley interdisciplinary reviews: Data mining and knowledge discovery*, 7(5):e1209.

Andrea Volkens, Tobias Burst, Werner Krause, Pola Lehmann, Theres Matthieß, Sven Regel, Bernhard Weßels, Lisa Zehnter, and Wissenschaftszentrum Berlin Für Sozialforschung (WZB). 2021. Manifesto Project Dataset. Type: dataset.

Maxwell A. Weinzierl and Sanda M. Harabagiu. 2021. Automatic Detection of COVID-19 Vaccine Misinformation with Graph Link Prediction. *arXiv:2108.02314 [cs]*.

Sarah Wiegreffe and Yuval Pinter. 2019. Attention is not not explanation. *arXiv preprint arXiv:1908.04626*.

Xinyi Zhou, Apurva Mulay, Emilio Ferrara, and Reza Zafarani. 2020. ReCOVery: A Multimodal Repository for COVID-19 News Credibility Research. In *Proceedings of the 29th ACM International Conference on Information & Knowledge Management*, pages 3205–3212, Virtual Event Ireland. ACM.

Michael Zürn and Pieter de Wilde. 2016. Debating globalization: cosmopolitanism and communitarianism as political ideologies. *Journal of Political Ideologies*, 21(3):280–301.

A Detailed Results

In this section, we provide additional plots and information that further strengthen the discussions provided in the main paper.

A.1 Error Analysis

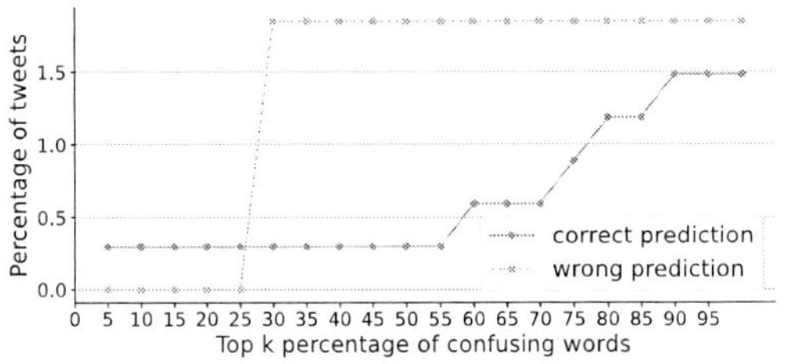

Figure 6: Percentage of tweets consisting of a confusing word receiving the highest attention from the model for the socio-economic dimension with the TF-IDF vocabulary.

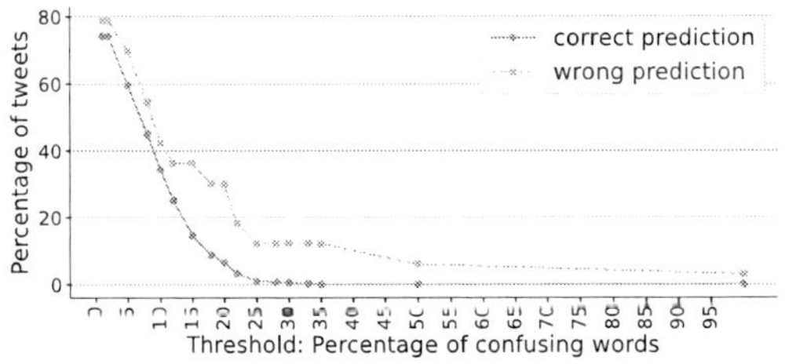

Figure 7: Percentage of wrong predictions and correct predictions with varying thresholds of confusing words computed using the PMI vocabulary for the cultural dimension.

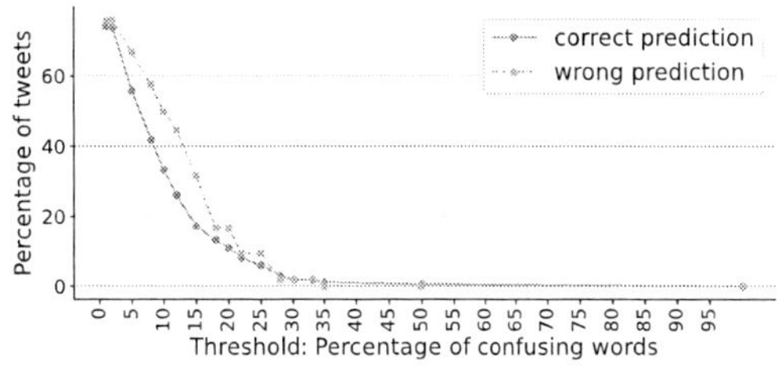

Figure 8: Percentage of wrong predictions and correct predictions with varying thresholds of confusing words computed using the PMI vocabulary for the socio-economic dimension.

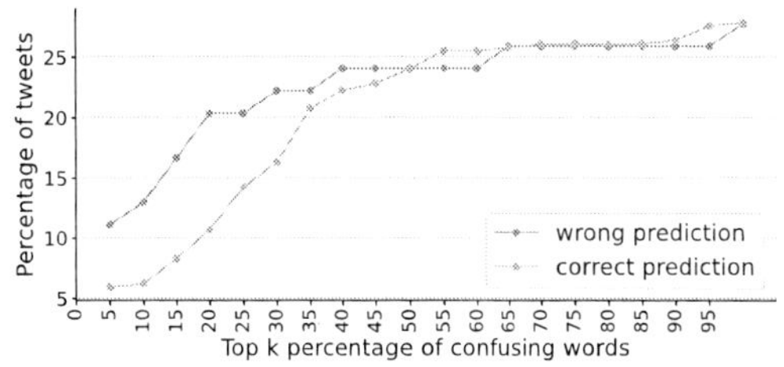

Figure 9: Percentage of tweets consisting of a confusing word receiving the highest attention from the model for the socio-economic dimension with the PMI vocabulary.

Die Linke	FDP	Die Grünen	AfD
btw17	cl	darumgruen	afd
heute	tl	darumgrün	traudichdeutschland
linke	btw17	btw17	btw17
mehr	denkenwirneu	get	merkel
merkel	fdp	heute	mehr
spd	jamaika	mehr	zeit
menschen	beer	katrin	wer
cdu	heute	geht	fdp
müssen	mal	klimaschutz	eu
soziale	mehr	jamaika	morgen

Table 4: Top 10 important words based on WI with TF-IDF as α.

Die Linke	FDP	Die Grünen	AfD
linke	fdp	klimaschutz	afd
soziale	netzdg	kohleausstieg	traudichdeutschland
merkel	cl	sondierungen	dr
btw17	tl	bdk17	merkel
gerechtigkeit	sondierung	sondierung	guten
cdu	kurdistan	umwelt	bitte
spd	freut	jamaika	grenzen
arbeit	denkenwirneu	zukunft	spitzenkandidatin
menschen	digitalisierung	grün	bundestag
rente	trendwende	klima	zeit

Table 5: Top 10 important words based on WI with PMI as α.

TF-IDF as α		PMI as α	
Cultural	**Socio-Economic**	**Cultural**	**Socio-Economic**
zeit	mal	btw17	btw17
statt	bt	mehr	mal
fdp	geht	statt	mehr
mal	ab	zeit	müssen
berlin	dank	mal	warum
merkel	klar	gibt	jamaika
ganz	besser	jamaika	menschen
immer	genau	fdp	eu
politik	interview	politik	wohl
warum	bildung	merkel	brauchen

Table 6: Examples of some commonly confused words for each dimension.

Proceedings of the 18th Conference on Natural Language Processing (KONVENS 2022)

Adapting GermaNet for the Semantic Web

Claus Zinn
Department of Linguistics
University of Tuebingen
Germany
claus.zinn
@uni-tuebingen.de

Marie Hinrichs
Department of Linguistics
University of Tuebingen
Germany
marie.hinrichs
@uni-tuebingen.de

Erhard Hinrichs
Department of Linguistics
University of Tuebingen
Germany
erhard.hinrichs
@uni-tuebingen.de

Abstract

GermaNet[1] (Hamp and Feldweg, 1997) is a lexical-semantic net that relates German nouns, verbs, and adjectives semantically. For this purpose, it groups lexical units that express the same concept into *synsets* and it defines semantic relations between them. GermaNet has been developed since 1997, and its most recent edition contains over 200,000 lexical units and about 160,000 synsets. The GermaNet resource is of high quality as all its entries have been manually entered with great care. GermaNet has been linked with the *InterLingual Index* and with *Wiktionary*, and it is our goal to increase such linkage with other resources such as the *Leipzig Corpora Collection* and the *DWDS-Wörterbuch.* For this purpose, GermaNet is converted to RDF, a format that facilitates the interlinking of data sources significantly.

1 Introduction

GermaNet is a rich lexical resource that describes German vocabulary as a light-weight ontology. While GermaNet has been inspired by the Princeton Wordnet, the German resource deviates from it by a number of design decisions aimed to better represent the German language, *e.g.*, by giving an adequate account of German compounds. The creation of GermaNet started in 1997 and it has been maintained and extended ever since. The latest version of GermaNet (release 17.0, April 2022) offers about 205,000 lexical units and nearly 160,000 synsets. It defines 173,742 conceptual relations between synsets, and 12,204 lexical relations between lexical units; the number of segmented compounds is 115,366. GermaNet already has some substantial linking to external data sources such as 28,564 pointers to the interlingual index and 29,546 links to Wiktionary.

[1] https://uni-tuebingen.de/en/142806

GermaNet data is stored in a relational database from which an XML-based serialisation can be generated. Although the database is part of the yearly GermaNet releases, its main purpose is to serve as a reliable way to store and manage continuous and simultaneous updates by the GermaNet team. The XML representation, which is stored in several XML files, gives programmers easy access to the data, as Java and Python libraries are available to read and access all information. However, it is not practical, nor intended, to extract information about synsets and their lexical entries from the XML representation using a text editor. In this paper, we describe how we map GermaNet's XML-based format to RDF, the standard format for data interchange in the Semantic Web. The new format gives users a compact, human-readable representation, as all information about a synset (or a lexical unit) is directly attached to it. The RDF format also makes it possible to easily link such information with external knowledge sources such as Babelnet, Wikidata, DWDS, or the Leipzig Corpus Collection.

2 Background

2.1 GermaNet

In many ways, GermaNet's XML serialisation reflects its original database-centered representation of database tables. With 23 files for nouns, 15 files for verbs, and 16 files for adjectives, the information on synsets is spread over 54 synset files. The names of these 54 files encode the word category and the semantic class of the synsets they contain. For instance, all nouns related to humans are given in the XML file *nomen.Mensch.xml*.

In addition, there are three XML files to encode the wiktionary links for nouns, verbs, and adjectives, respectively. Also, there is an XML file to encode the entries for the interlingual index and

```
<synset id="s50724" category="nomen" class="Tier">
 <lexUnit id="l71792" sense="1" source="core" namedEntity="no" artificial="no" styleMarking="no">
  <orthForm>Eisbär</orthForm>
  <compound>
   <modifier category="Nomen">Eis</modifier>
   <head>Bär</head>
  </compound>
 </lexUnit>
 <lexUnit id="l199681" sense="1" source="core" namedEntity="no" artificial="no" styleMarking="no">
  <orthForm>Polarbär</orthForm>
  <compound>
   <modifier category="Adjektiv">polar</modifier>
   <head>Bär</head>
  </compound>
 </lexUnit>
</synset>
```

Figure 1: Lexical units *Eisbär* and *Polarbär* in XML

another file to encode the conceptual and lexical relations. Each type of XML file is accompanied by a DTD file that defines the syntactic validity of their content.

In the remainder of this section, we describe how each type of information is described in XML. Fig. 1 depicts the lexical entries *Eisbär* and *Polarbär* (taken from the file *nomen.Tier.xml*), both sharing the same meaning, and therefore, they are part of the same synset. Each synset has a unique identifier (here, *s50724*), a category (*nomen*), and a class (*Tier*), naming the part of speech (noun) and the semantic class (animal) of its members. A synset consists of one or more lexical units. Each unit has an orthographic form, and if applicable, a child tagged *compound*, which defines its head and its modifiers. A lexical unit also comes with a number of attributes, for instance, information about whether it represents a named entity or whether it is stylistically marked.[2]

A separate file (*gn_relations.xml*) specifies lexical relations between lexical units and conceptual relations between synsets. For our synset *s50724*, we find the following entry, a conceptual relation:

```
<con_rel name="has_hypernym"
         from="s50724"
         to="s50721"
         dir="revert"
         inv="has_hyponym" />
```

The representation reads as follows: the synset *s50724* is in a hypernym relationship with the synset *s50721* (which in turn has a single lexical unit with orthographic form *Bär*). The direction of the semantic relation can be reverted, reading that the synset *s50721* is in a hyponym relationship to the synset *s50724*.

In the same file, we find an example of a lexical relation for our lexical entry *l71792*:

```
<lex_rel name="has_habitat"
         from="l71792"
         to="l69189"
         dir="one" />
```

It shows that it is in an *has_habitat* relationship with "l69189", a lexical unit with the orthographic name *Eis* and class *Substanz*. The relationship is uni-directional.

The lexical entry "l71792" has also been linked with Wiktionary as the following entry from the file *wiktionaryParaphrases-nomen.xml* testifies:

```
<wiktionaryParaphrase
  lexUnitId="l71792"
  wiktionaryId="w19163"
  wiktionarySenseId="0"
  wiktionarySense="Bär mit weißem Fell,
                   lebt in den nörd-
                   lichen Polargebieten"
  edited="no" />
```

And the lexical unit for *Eisbär* is also part of the interlingual index[3] (encoded in the file *interLingualIndex_DE-EN.xml*):

```
<iliRecord
  lexUnitId="l71792"
  ewnRelation="synonym"
  pwnWord="Thalarctos maritimus"
  pwn20Id="ENG20-02049886-n"
  pwn30Id="ENG30-02134084-n"
  pwn20paraphrase="white bear of arctic
                   regions"
  source="initial" >
```

As the examples show, GermaNet provides extensive information about the German language,

[2]Our description lacks some detail. For an in-depth description of the GermaNet data format, see Appendix B of Henrich's dissertation (Henrich, 2015).

[3]GermaNet's interlingual index stems from the EuroWordNet project, for details see (Kunze and Lemnitzer, 2002).

and our resource has grown considerably in the last 25 years. Purpose-built software is used to update GermaNet's database (Henrich and Hinrichs, 2010a), and we publish a new release of GermaNet on a yearly basis.

Users of GermaNet can query the lexical resource via Rover[4], a web-based interface that gives users easy access to all of GermaNet's content, and also allows users to calculate the semantic similarity between synsets.

2.2 Format Evolution of GermaNet

Since its beginning, GermaNet has undergone several format adaptations and conversions. A first version for an XML-based format of GermaNet was proposed by Lemnitzer and Kunze (2002). The current XML format of GermaNet is largely based on the work reported by Henrich and Hinrichs (2010b), with several extensions since then.

In (Henrich and Hinrichs, 2010b), a conversion from GermaNet's XML format to WordNet-LMF (Lexical Markup Framework[5]) is given. The conversion helped identifying some representational shortcomings of WordNet-LMF (*e.g.*, the lack of encoding for lexical relations; the lack of entailment relations for synsets; the omission of syntactic frames for word senses), and hence a number of DTD adaptations were proposed to deal with this issue. Note, however, that the WordNet-LMF format has evolved since then, and that the new version[6] addresses some of these shortcomings.

2.3 Wordnets and their Move to Linked Data

The Princeton WordNet (Fellbaum, 1998) was the first wordnet that was given a representation in RDF.[7] In 2006, two formalisations were created independently from each other. While Graves and Gutierrez (2006) insist on staying within pure RDF, van Assem et al. (2006) give a representation that makes use of RDF-Schema (RDFS)[8] and OWL semantics.[9] In the latter work, classes, sub-classes, and property definitions are explicitly encoded in RDFS, and there are also additional OWL-based restrictions on classes. In this representation it is hence possible to specify that, say, *isAntonym* is a symmetrical relation, or that a fact such as *isAntonym(l60336,l186616)* can be used to automatically derive *isAntonym(l186616, l60336)*.

Recently, the Princeton Wordnet has been forked into the Open English WordNet and given a public repository home on GitHub so that it can be further developed under an open source methodology.[10] There exists a searchable web interface[11] and the wordnet can be downloaded in yet another RDF-based format, one which makes use of the OntoLex[12] conceptualisation. Other download formats include WordNet-LMF, a format advocated by the Global WordNet Association, and Princeton's original format.

There exist linked data wordnets for a number of other languages such as the Danish WordNet[13], the Dutch WordNet[14], and the Polish Wordnet[15], most of which are directly accessible on a central website.[16] The wordnets are available in JSON-LD[17], OntoLex-based RDF (both using the lemon vocabulary), but also in WordNet-LMF.[18]

The benefits of having all wordnets in a common and easily searchable format is demonstrated by a browser-based search interface to the Open Multilingual WordNet[19], where a word can be searched in a selected language, and where the search result can then be used to find semantically equivalent words in the other available languages.

3 GermaNet in RDF

In this section we discuss the design choices of our RDF-based representation of GermaNet. Expressing GermaNet in RDF forces us to express all information in terms of subject-predicate-object triplets.

Clearly, synsets and their lexical entries must be first class citizens of the triple store. It is about these two classes of resources for which GermaNet has an abundance of information. Consequently, they must take the subject position in the triple

[4] https://weblicht.sfs.uni-tuebingen.de/rover/

[5] http://www.lexicalmarkupframework.org

[6] https://github.com/globalwordnet/schemas/blob/master/WN-LMF-1.1.dtd

[7] https://www.w3.org/RDF/

[8] https://www.w3.org/TR/rdf-schema/

[9] https://www.w3.org/TR/owl-ref/

[10] https://github.com/globalwordnet/english-wordnet

[11] https://en-word.net

[12] https://www.w3.org/2016/05/ontolex/

[13] https://github.com/kuhumcst/DanNet

[14] https://github.com/cltl/OpenDutchWordnet

[15] http://plwordnet.pwr.wroc.pl/wordnet/

[16] http://compling.hss.ntu.edu.sg/omw/

[17] http://json-ld.org

[18] https://globalwordnet.github.io/schemas

[19] http://compling.hss.ntu.edu.sg/omw/cgi-bin/wn-gridx.cgi?gridmode=grid

```
PREFIX gn_lex: <https://uni-tuebingen.de/germanet/v16/lexUnit/>
PREFIX gn_syn: <https://uni-tuebingen.de/germanet/v16/synset/>

### https://uni-tuebingen.de/germanet/v16/lexUnit/l71792
gn_lex:l71792 rdf:type owl:NamedIndividual ,
                       <https://www.uni-tuebingen.de/germanet/v16/compound> ,
                       <https://www.uni-tuebingen.de/germanet/v16/lexUnit> ;
              dcterms:identifier "l71792"^^xsd:string ;
              gn:artificial "no"^^xsd:string ;
              gn:compoundHead "Bär"^^xsd:string ;
              gn:compoundModifier "Eis"^^xsd:string ;
              gn:compoundModifierCategory "Nomen"^^xsd:string ;
              gn:hasEWNRelation "synonym"^^xsd:string ;
              gn:hasPWN20Id "ENG20-02049886-n"^^xsd:string ;
              gn:hasPWN20Paraphrase "white bear of arctic regions"^^xsd:string ;
              gn:hasPWN20Synonym "Ursus Maritimus"^^xsd:string ,
                                 "ice bear"^^xsd:string ,
                                 "polar bear"^^xsd:string ;
              gn:hasPWN30Id "ENG30-02134084-n"^^xsd:string ;
              gn:hasPWNWord "Thalarctos maritimus"^^xsd:string ;
              gn:hasSource "initial"^^xsd:string ;
              gn:hasWiktionaryParaphrase "Bär mit weißem Fell, lebt in den nörd-
                                          lichen Polargebieten"^^xsd:string ;
              gn:has_habitat gn_lex:l69189 ;
              gn:isMemberOf gn_syn:s50724 ;
              gn:namedEntity "no"^^xsd:string ;
              gn:orthForm "Eisbär"^^xsd:string ;
              gn:sense "1"^^xsd:string ;
              gn:source "core"^^xsd:string ;
              gn:styleMarking "no"^^xsd:string .

### https://uni-tuebingen.de/germanet/v16/synset/s50724
gn_syn:s50724 rdf:type owl:NamedIndividual ,
                       <https://www.uni-tuebingen.de/germanet/v16/synset> ;
              dcterms:identifier "s50724"^^xsd:string ;
              gn:category "nomen"^^xsd:string ;
              gn:class "Tier"^^xsd:string ;
              gn:hasMember gn_lex:l199681 ,
                           gn_lex:l71792 ;
              gn:has_hypernym gn_syn:s50721 .
```

Figure 2: Lexical unit "Eisbär" and its synset in RDF

representation. Given that GermaNet encodes lexical relations between lexical units and conceptual relations between synsets, it is also clear that the two classes of resources can also take the object position. This also holds for expressing the facts that a lexical unit is part of a synset, or that a synset consists of lexical units.

Reconsider the definition of the synset *s50724* in Fig. 1 with its three attributes *id*, *category*, and *class* and its two children, the lexical units *l71792* and *l199681*. The RDF representation of the synset is given at the bottom of Fig. 2. The synset resource *s50724* is given an identifier with the same name (using Dublin Core terminology), and for the other two attributes (as for all others), we have chosen to keep the attribute name of the XML representation as predicate name in our RDF format. Similarly, the XML names for our lexical and conceptual relations are reused in our RDF representation.

The information that a synset has children, or that a lexical unit node has a synset parent node (in XML, this is encoded through hierarchical embedding) is expressed by introducing two newly defined predicates *hasMember* and *isMemberOf*.

Note that the RDF representation of the lexical unit *l71792* has a corresponding predicate *isMemberOf*, so each lemma has a direct link to the synset it is part of. Clearly, this duplicates information, but we wanted instances of *lexUnit* and *synset* to know about their interrelationship.

The information on compounds is directly encoded using the three relations *compoundHead*, *compoundModifier*, and *compoundModifierCategory*, flattening the tree structure in the XML representation accordingly.[20]

Consider the following lexical relation:

```
<lex_rel name="has_antonym"
         from="l60336"
         to="l186616"
         dir="both"
         inv="has_antonym" />
```

It represents the fact that the lexical unit *l60336* (*Kunstschnee*, engl. *artificial snow*) is an antonym to the lexical unit *l186616* (*Naturschnee*, engl. *natural snow*). In GermaNet, antonymy is a symmetrical sense relation, which is encoded by the attribute value for the relation's direction (*both*). In our conversion to RDF, our algorithm generates two triples for this (only one is shown in Fig. 2).

[20]Here, we could have chosen to introduce a blank node in RDF, and relating it both to the lexical unit it belongs to and the two relations for modifier and head, respectively, but we opted for the simpler, more readable representation.

Similarly, for the example conceptual relation given above two triples are asserted, namely that the synset *s50724* with the lexical units *Eisbär* and *Polarbär* is a hypernym to *S50721* (*Bär*), and that *vice versa*, the latter synset has as hyponym the former synset (only one direction is shown in Fig. 2).

As with the XML representation, all information is *explicitly* encoded. As a consequence, we have refrained from using RDF-Schema or OWL to define an ontology of classes and relations at all. We require no inference mechanism to infer new information as all information is already made explicit. This does not stop Protégé[21], an open-source editor for RDF-based ontologies, to infer a number of RDF class statements or OWL-type statements when it is given our large set of triples (*e.g.*, that *lexUnit*, *synset*, and also *compound* are classes and that, for instance, a lexical unit such as *l71792* is an instance of (*rdf:type*) class *lexUnit* (see Fig. 2).

In our RDF-based representation, the entire information relevant for a lexical unit is directly attached to it. The same holds for synsets. Where multiple database queries would be required to obtain the information (or where multiple XML documents need to be looked up), in SPARQL, a simple query with the subject position instantiated to the lexical unit or synset in question (with the predicate and object position kept variable) is needed.

Our conversion takes GermaNet's XML-based serialisation of its database content as a starting point. The conversion has been implemented in Prolog using SWI-Prolog, its built-in library `sgml` for XML parsing and its semantic web library `semweb/rdf11`. The conversion processes all main input files for nouns, verbs, and adjectives, the XML file that defines conceptual and lexical relations, and the ILI and wiktionary files. While those files are being parsed, RDF triples are being asserted. At the end of the process, the triple store is written into a file resulting in 4015172 RDF triples. We have loaded all triples into Protégé and used the software to export them in turtle format, an excerpt of which is shown in Fig. 2.

A SPARQL end-point for the triple store has been tested and deployed as part of the Text+[22] research infrastructure.

[21]`https://protege.stanford.edu`
[22]`https://www.text-plus.org`

4 Discussion

The Resource Description Framework (RDF) is a representational model that cannot get any more simple. In fact, it almost appears as if the field of knowledge representation with its many high-level representation languages has been given a common, low-level assembly language to which all knowledge can be compiled to. With RDF, each piece of data about some entity can be expressed as a simple statement. This statement consists of a subject (the entity that is talked about), a predicate (the property we would like to attribute to the entity), and an object (the property's value). In RDF, it is important that this information can be combined with information from other sources. For this, the subject must get a unique identifier, preferably a Uniform Resource Identifier that is web-resolvable.

The RDF platform makes it easy to realize the AAA slogan "Anyone can say Anything about Any topic". If two persons say something about the same resource, but they use different identifiers for it, one can combine the varying pieces of information once it is clear that the resource with identifier, say *id-1*, is identical to the resource with, say, identifier *id-2*.[23]

As we have said earlier, we have abstained from defining an RDF schema or even OWL vocabulary that would restrict us to express lexical or semantic information about the German language. As a result, we cannot draw a line between valid and invalid RDF statements, but we do not need to draw that line either.

In the past, we have converted GermaNet also to the Lexical Markup Framework (Henrich and Hinrichs, 2010b). The conversion, however, comes with an information loss as the LMF DTD prevented us to express lexical information in a valid format. Where RDF actively promotes the AAA slogan, the LMF DTD imposes a representational straight-jacket that prevents us from encoding all the information we have.

Moreover, the LMF standard is not open but behind an ISO paywall. This makes it hard to access the currently active standard and update our LMF variant of GermaNet according to the new standard. Open standards such as RDF score much better on this aspect as its W3C specification is readable for anyone.

In contrast to LMF, RDF requires the use of URIs where synsets and lexical units are universally addressable. This makes it much easier to establish links across wordnets and other lexical resources, making it straightforward to incorporate those statements that others made about a particular entity.

5 Conclusion and Future Work

In this paper, we have described our conversion of GermaNet's XML format to a pure RDF representation. This makes it possible for GermaNet to be part of a linked data cloud that combines rich linguistic information from various, high-quality resources.

Future work includes linking GermaNet with other lexical resources. In part, this is already done, but not in an ideal way. Reconsider Fig. 2 where a lexical unit is also described with information stemming from its interlingual index, for instance, the relation *hasPWN20Id* and *hasPWN20Id*. Here, their literal string values *ENG20-02049886-n* and *ENG30-02134084-n* should be replaced by URIs pointing to the respective RDF representation of the Princeton Wordnet, or its new open source equivalent, the Open English WordNet.[24]

At the time of writing, our GermaNet resource identifiers are not yet web-resolvable. In the future, an HTTP request to, say, `https://uni-tuebingen.de/germanet/v16/lexUnit/171792`, will return the top part of Fig. 2.

Rover, a web-based user interface for the exploration and visualization of GermaNet data (Hinrichs et al., 2020) is currently using the XML representation and the Java API in the back-end. In the future, we would like to experiment with using a back-end that executes SPARQL queries on the triple store.

The main reason for having an RDF-based representation of GermaNet, however, is to unleash its potential when properly linked to other high-quality lexical sources. In the context of the Text+ project, it is our aim to link GermaNet with the DWDS dictionary of the German language[25] and also with the Leipzig Corpora Collection[26]. There are plans to convert both resources into RDF, which would allow the creation of a linked data cloud for the

[23] In OWL terms, the relation *owl:sameAs* relation between the two resources can be established: `ns1:id1 owl:sameAs ns2:id2`.

[24] `https://en-word.net/lemma/ice%20bear`

[25] `https://www.dwds.de`

[26] `https://corpora.uni-leipzig.de/`

German language. In addition, linkages to both Babelnet[27] and the lexicographical data of Wikidata[28] will be possible.

In a pilot study, we have started linking GermaNet synsets of type *Ort* (location) to a subset of the *Integrated Authority File* (GND)[29] of the German National Library, namely, the subset holding *Geographika* with approximately 4.5 million triples. In this exercise, for instance, the synset *s43887* with its lexical unit *l63714* and its orthographic form *Potsdam* was automatically linked to the entity `https://d-nb.info/gnd/4046948-7` of the GND dataset. The semantic linkage gives users access to a variety of information such as alternative names or lexicalisations (*e.g.*, Bostanium, Potestampium, Pozdam), the geographical coordinates in terms of latitude and longitude, and other information (*Hauptstadt vom Bundesland Brandenburg, kreisfreie Stadt, 993 als Poztupimi urkundl. erwähnt, 1317 Stadt*), hence demonstrating the potential of linked data. In this initial study, 1764 links between GermaNet entries to entities in the subset of the GND dataset were established.

Mapping location entities of one dataset to the locations of another dataset is relatively straightforward. In general, the main task to properly link together nodes from different RDF graphs is – essentially – a word disambiguation task. Our work will build upon Henrich et al. (2014b), where GermaNet senses were linked to wiktionary senses, and Henrich et al. (2014a), where word senses in GermaNet were linked with those in the DWDS Dictionary of the German Language. The linking task will be supported by the WebCAGe corpus (Henrich et al., 2012).

References

Mark van Assem, Aldo Gangemi, and Guus Schreiber. 2006. Conversion of wordnet to a standard RDF/OWL representation. In *Proceedings of the Fifth International Conference on Language Resources and Evaluation, LREC 2006, Genoa, Italy, May 22-28, 2006*, pages 237–242. European Language Resources Association (ELRA).

Christiane Fellbaum. 1998. *WordNet: An Electronic Lexical Database*. Cambridge, MA: MIT Press.

Alvaro Graves and Claudio Gutierrez. 2006. Data representations for WordNet: A case for RDF. In *3rd International WordNet Conference, GWC 2006*. Masaryk University, Brno. South Jeju Island, Korea.

Birgit Hamp and Helmut Feldweg. 1997. GermaNet - a lexical-semantic net for german. In *Proceedings of the ACL workshop Automatic Information Extraction and Building of Lexical Semantic Resources for NLP Applications*. Madrid, Spain.

Verena Henrich. 2015. *Word Sense Disambiguation with GermaNet*. Ph.D. thesis, Univerisity of Tuebingen. `http://dx.doi.org/10.15496/publikation-4706`.

Verena Henrich and Erhard Hinrichs. 2010a. GernEdiT: A graphical tool for GermaNet development. In *Proceedings of the ACL 2010 System Demonstrations*, pages 19–24, Uppsala, Sweden. Association for Computational Linguistics.

Verena Henrich and Erhard Hinrichs. 2010b. Standardizing wordnets in the ISO standard LMF: Wordnet-LMF for GermaNet. In *Proceedings of the 23rd International Conference on Computational Linguistics (Coling 2010)*, pages 456–464, Beijing, China. Coling 2010 Organizing Committee.

Verena Henrich, Erhard Hinrichs, and Reinhild Barkey. 2014a. Aligning Word Senses in GermaNet and the DWDS Dictionary of the German Language. In *Proceedings of the 7th Global WordNet Conference (GWC 2014)*, pages 63–70. Tartu, Estonia.

Verena Henrich, Erhard Hinrichs, and Tatiana Vodolazova. 2012. WebCAGe – a Web-Harvested Corpus Annotated with GermaNet Senses. In *Proceedings of the 13th Conference of the European Chapter of the Association for Computational Linguistics (EACL 2012)*, pages 387–396. Avignon, France.

Verena Henrich, Erhard Hinrichs, and Tatiana Vodolazova. 2014b. Aligning GermaNet Senses with Wiktionary Sense Definitions. In *Human Language Technology: Challenges for Computer Science and Linguistics*, pages 329–342.

Marie Hinrichs, Richard Lawrence, and Erhard Hinrichs. 2020. Exploring and visualizing wordnet data with germanet rover. In *Proceedings of the CLARIN Annual Conference*, pages 32–36.

Claudia Kunze and Lothar Lemnitzer. 2002. GermaNet - representation, visualization, application. In *Proceedings of the Third International Conference on Language Resources and Evaluation (LREC'02)*, Las Palmas, Canary Islands - Spain. European Language Resources Association (ELRA).

Lothar Lemnitzer and Claudia Kunze. 2002. Adapting GermaNet for the Web. In *Proceedings of the First Global Wordnet Conference*, pages 174–181. Central Institute of Indian Languages, Mysore, India, 21.-25.01.2002.

[27] `https://babelnet.org`

[28] `https://wikidata.org`

[29] `https://gnd.network`

Proceedings of the 18th Conference on Natural Language Processing (KONVENS 2022)

Assessing the Linguistic Complexity of German Abitur Texts from 1963–2013

Noemi Kapusta* and **Marco Müller**† and **Matilda Schauf***
Isabell Siem* and **Stefanie Dipper***
Sprachwissenschaftliches Institut
Fakultät für Philologie
Ruhr-Universität Bochum
* firstname.lastname@rub.de
† Marco.Mueller-z3b@rub.de

Abstract

This paper is about the analysis of the linguistic complexity of texts written by high school graduates as part of the final secondary-school examinations. We measure complexity on different levels (lexical diversity, perplexity of part-of-speech-based language models, and syntactic complexity) and compare the complexity of high school graduation texts from 1963–2013. It turns out that, contrary to our initial assumptions, linguistic complexity increases over time.

1 Introduction[1]

Successful literacy acquisition represents an important building block in the educational process of young people. Literacy is not only about the acquisition of correct spelling and grammar, but also about the ability to understand and produce texts with complex content, and to use appropriate registers in different situations.

Competent handling of texts with complex content is a prerequisite for successful study at university. The teaching of these skills is one of the main goals of the *Gymnasium* (secondary school). The relevant competencies are tested at the *Abitur* (the final secondary-school examinations), where school graduates must produce extensive texts as part of the German exam.

Over the past decades, the Gymnasium in Germany has changed considerably. While nationwide only a small minority of around 7% attended this type of school in the 1960s, today the figure is around 50%. This has been accompanied by a change in the composition of the student body, from a rather homogeneous, male-dominated selection of the educated population to a more diverse composition that includes children from educationally disadvantaged families and children from families with a migration background who may acquire German only as a second language.

In this paper, we investigate whether the changing composition of the school population has a measurable impact on literacy acquisition. For this purpose, we examine texts from the GraphVar corpus (Berg et al., 2021) that were written as part of the final secondary-school examinations for German in the period 1963–2013.

We focus on aspects of linguistic complexity, which we investigate at the lexical and syntactic levels. We pursue two hypotheses:

1. Because of the more homogeneous composition, the results in the 1960s are more homogeneous and have less variance.

2. Because of the more elite composition, the linguistic complexity of the texts is higher in the 1960s than nowadays.

Most work on linguistic complexity concerns data from foreign language (L2) acquisition, typically in the form of longitudinal studies over a few months in instructed settings. Such studies show that lexical and syntactic complexity typically increases over time (cf. Crossley, 2020). Besides complexity, the correctness (error rate) of texts is often investigated.

Written language acquisition in the native language is less frequently studied. A relevant corpus is the KoKo Corpus (Abel et al., 2014, 2016). It contains argumentative essays in German with about 825,000 words, written by students of graduating classes. The corpus is manually annotated for different error types (spelling, grammar). It has also been automatically enriched with part-of-speech (POS) annotations and lemmas. Additionally, it has been annotated on a textual level with

[1] All scripts, result tables and plots related to this work are available at https://github.com/rubcompling/konvens2022.

366 features related to linguistic complexity. However, we are not aware of any studies focusing on the complexity features.

The Falko corpora are a collection of different German-language corpora, mostly of L2 learners.[2] Parallel to the L2 data, there is usually a comparative corpus of L1 students. The data is richly annotated with linguistic information (lemma, POS), and errors are also annotated with corrected forms. In studies using these corpora, the L1 texts usually serve as a reference corpus, but this is not unproblematic, as Shadrova et al. (2021) show.

As a factor influencing complexity, task effects have been examined, and factors such as the task type, topic, and genre have been shown to have a significant impact on complexity (e.g., Alexopoulou et al. (2017); Weiss (2017)).

In contrast to the aforementioned corpora, the GraphVar corpus is a diachronic corpus and our focus is on the change of complexity through time. We investigate linguistic complexity using different methods: word-based measures of lexical complexity, and POS bigram probabilities and a selection of traditional syntactic features for syntactic complexity. For lexical and syntactic features, see, e.g., the overview in Crossley (2020). Further references to related literature can be found in the respective sections.

The paper is structured as follows. In Sec. 2, we present the corpora our investigations are based on. Sec. 3 introduces the different measures that we apply to assess complexity: lexical diversity, POS-based perplexity, and various syntactic features related to complexity. Sec. 4 presents the results and Sec. 5 concludes the paper.

2 Data

For our investigations, we use a subset of the GraphVar corpus (Sec. 2.1).

In addition, we use two reference corpora that we compiled in the context of this work: first, the EXPRESS corpus with a rather simple linguistic style; second, the ZEIT corpus which has a rather complex and sophisticated linguistic style (Sec. 2.2). We exploit the reference corpora in two ways:

First, for measuring POS-based perplexity we train two models on the full reference corpora. Second, for assessing lexical diversity and syntactic complexity, we compare the results from the GraphVar corpus with results from subsets of the reference corpora.

[2] https://hu-berlin.de/falko.

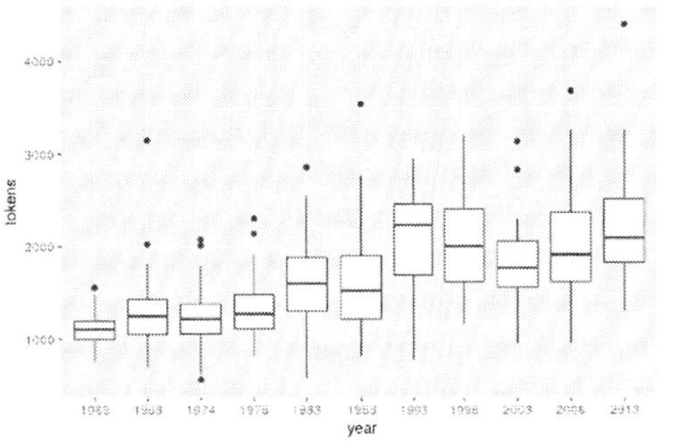

Figure 1: Boxplots of number of tokens per text, grouped by survey year.

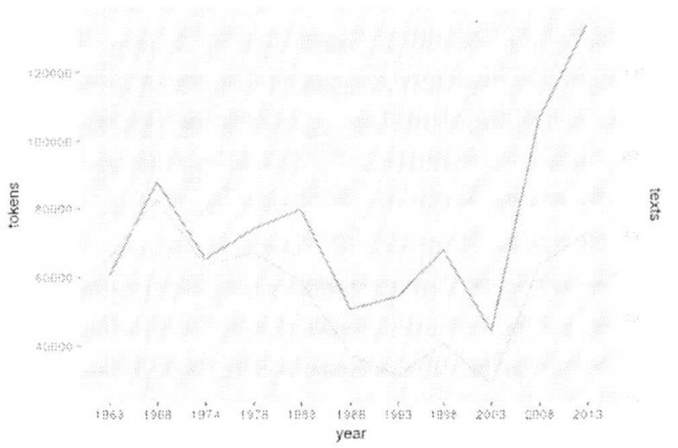

Figure 2: Plot of number of tokens (red) and total number of texts (green) per survey year (rescaled).

Text samples of each corpus can be found in Appendix A.

2.1 The GraphVar Corpus

The current version 1.4.2 of the GraphVar corpus (Berg et al., 2021) contains more than 1600 high school graduation essays from the years 1923–2018 from the subjects German, Biology and History. For our research, we use a subset containing only essays from the subject German from 1963–2013. The texts were collected at intervals of roughly five years.

We preprocessed the texts and excluded all tokens that were annotated as headers. Such tokens were not produced by the students but were part of the task description. Figure 1 displays information on the number of tokens per text. The boxplots show that the average text length has increased continuously since 1963. We decided to consider all data, though, because the subsets (per survey year) are rather small, with an average number of tokens of 75,000 (average per text: 1,600). In studying the development of complexity over time, it is therefore important to use normalized complexity measures or measures that are not sensitive to text length.

Figure 2 shows the total number of tokens and texts per survey year. It can be seen that slightly fewer texts were included in the corpus from the 1980s and 1990s, and the total number of tokens in these years is also slightly lower. In the most recent years, 2008 and 2013, there is a clear increase in the number of texts and tokens.

The GraphVar corpus has been annotated manually and automatically with various linguistic information, including lemma, part of speech (POS) according to the STTS scheme (Schiller et al., 1999), and syntax according to the TüBa/DZ scheme (Telljohann et al., 2012). For calculating lexical diversity and syntactic complexity, we use the lemma forms and syntactic annotations provided by the corpus. Syntactic annotations are represented in GraphVar as spans spanning the dominated tokens. For further processing, we converted the GraphVar data into a column format, translating the syntactic annotation into a path notation that represents the dominating nodes (BIE tags[3]) as a path from the root to the terminal node. For instance, `I-SIMPX|B-MF|NX|PPER` is the syntactic annotation of a personal pronoun (PPER) embedded in a singleton nominal phrase (NX) which is the first node in the middle field (B-MF) inside a clause (I-SIMPX).

We randomly divided the corpus into a dev set (20%, 107 texts) and a test set (80%, 404 texts). The test set is the basis for the evaluations in Sec. 4.

2.2 Reference Corpora

For the EXPRESS corpus, we downloaded articles of the daily German newspaper "EXPRESS" from 2021/01/02 to 2022/07/03. For the ZEIT corpus, we downloaded articles of the German weekly newspaper "DIE ZEIT" from 2021/03/11 to 2022/03/02. Both data sets were downloaded from `wiso-net.de`, an online database that offers eBooks and journals as well as newspaper articles for research purposes.

We filtered out articles from categories that do not consist of plain newspaper text[4] and articles with less than 500 tokens. Both corpora contain roughly the same number of tokens, see Table 1.

Corpus	#Articles	#Tokens	#Types
EXPRESS	4,565	3.4M	180K
ZEIT	2,022	3.4M	190K

Table 1: The two reference corpora.

Subcorpus	#Fragments	#Tokens	#Sentences
EXPRESS	138	70,398	3,758
ZEIT	137	70,134	3,796

Table 2: The subsets of the two reference corpora.

We use the full corpora for training POS-based language models (Sec. 3.2).

In addition, we use randomly selected subsets of the reference corpora for assessing lexical diversity (Sec. 3.1) and syntactic complexity (Sec. 3.3) of the reference texts, see Table 2. These subsets contain about 70,000 tokens, which roughly corresponds to the median size of GraphVar texts of one survey year. The subsets consist of article fragments with at least 500 tokens each.[5]

3 Measures of Complexity

We study linguistic complexity at different levels and with different measures. First, we look at lexical diversity (Sec. 3.1); second, we use perplexity of part-of-speech (POS) based language models to estimate syntactic complexity (Sec. 3.2); third, we apply different measures to syntactic annotations (Sec. 3.3).

3.1 Lexical Diversity

Lexical complexity of learner data is measured in several ways. Lexical sophistication looks at the proportion of "complicated" words in the text. Complicated words are determined, for example, by word lists or by their general frequency: the rarer, the more complicated (Laufer and Nation, 1995).

Another aspect is lexical density, which is measured by measures such as Type-Token Ratio (TTR) or improved variants thereof. TTR is the ratio of word types to the total number of tokens in a text. However, it is well known that TTR depends on

[3] B: begin of a span/node; I: inside a span/node; E: end of a span/node. Singletons are not marked as such.

[4] E.g. "Impressum" (imprint), "Schach" (chess), "Witz der Woche" (joke of the week), "Glückszahlen" (lucky numbers), "Leserbriefe" (letters to the editor).

[5] In calculation the lexical diversity measure MATTR, we use a window of 500 tokens, so this is the minimum length for individual texts (see Sec. 3.1).

the text length, hence, it cannot be used for comparing texts of different length. Other TTR-based measures have been proposed in the past, such as Corrected TTR, Log-TTR, and Root TTR, all of which, however, have been shown to be affected by text length (e.g., Zenker and Kyle, 2021). Measures that turned out stable and are used in the current study are MTLD (McCarthy and Jarvis, 2010), MATTR (Covington and McFall, 2010), and HD-D (McCarthy and Jarvis, 2007), which we describe in the following sections. With all three measures, a higher score indicates a lexically more diverse text.

3.1.1 MTLD

McCarthy (2005) and McCarthy and Jarvis (2010) propose MTLD ("Measure of Textual Lexical Diversity") as a length-independent measure of lexical density. This measure is calculated as the mean length of segments (i.e., sequences of words) with a given TTR. The TTR is calculated for increasing bits of text, with the first round starting at the beginning of the text and going on until the given TTR threshold (default = 0.72) has been reached. At this point, the next round starts with TTR reset to 1. This process is repeated until the end of the text. Usually there are tokens left at the end of a text whose TTR does not reach the threshold. For these tokens, a partial factor is calculated, so that no data is discarded (see McCarthy and Jarvis (2010) for details). The whole process is first run forward and then reverse, hence, bidirectional, which produces consistent and accurate MTLD scores. MTLD is calculated as the total number of words in the text divided by the number of rounds.

MTLD has been proven to be a reliable measure of lexical diversity in studies such as Koizumi and In'nami (2012) and Fergadiotis et al. (2013). Only for short texts (with $<$ 100 words), which do not even reach the given TTR score, the results are unreliable.

3.1.2 MATTR

Covington and McFall (2010) introduce MATTR ("Moving Average Type-Token Ratio"). Similar to MTLD, MATTR is based on TTR. Yet, while MTLD uses segments that can be of different length, MATTR uses a window of a fixed size that moves forward by one token at a time and whose TTR is calculated in each case. Covington and McFall (2010) suggest a large window for lexical diversity. Since the shortest GraphVar texts contain roughly 550 tokens, we chose a window size of 500. The MATTR score of the text is the mean of all these TTR scores.[6]

3.1.3 HD-D

McCarthy and Jarvis (2007) propose HD-D ("Hypergeometric Distribution D"), which is a simplified version of vocd-D (Malvern et al., 2004). vocd-D calculates TTR scores for random samples of different size. In contrast, HD-D is based on probabilities: For every type in a text, the probability of occurring in a sample of n tokens is calculated. As recommended by McCarthy and Jarvis (2007), we use $n = 42$. HD-D is the sum of all probabilities.

3.2 Perplexity of POS-based Language Models

Perplexity is a common measure to evaluate language models, by comparing perplexity of two models on a test set. The model with the lower perplexity score fits the test data better.

We assume that the ZEIT corpus has a more complex language style than the EXPRESS corpus. A language model trained on the ZEIT corpus should therefore have a lower perplexity on a linguistically complex test text than a language model trained on the EXPRESS corpus. However, the perplexity of two models can only be compared if they use identical vocabularies. Therefore, it is not possible to compare language models based on word ngrams here. Instead, we compare POS ngrams (more precisely: POS bigrams), since here the vocabulary of both training corpora is identical. So essentially we compare syntactic properties.

We calculated the perplexity as described in Jurafsky and Martin (2022) with the log probabilities of the bigrams. For the test set, we randomly extracted the same number of bigrams from each text of the same year such that a total of 5000 bigrams per survey year are included in the test set.

3.3 Syntactic Complexity

For measuring syntactic complexity, we use the syntactic annotation provided by the GraphVar corpus, which we converted into path representations (Sec. 2.1). We implemented a range of measures that have been listed in Chen and Meurers (2016) for measuring syntactic complexity, in particular measures that relate to complex constituents (like

[6]MATTR is an improved version of MSTTR ("Mean Segmental Type-Token Ratio"). MSTTR uses non-overlapping segments and has to discard remaining words at the end of the text (for details, see the description in Covington and McFall (2010)).

No	Feature	Definition
1	Mean Sentence Length	#tokens / #sentences
2	Clauses per Sentence	#(SIMPX + R-SIMPX + P-SIMPX) tokens / #sentences
3	Subordinate Clauses per Sentence	#C / #sentences
4	Mean Clause Length	#(SIMPX + R-SIMPX + P-SIMPX) tokens / #(SIMPX + R-SIMPX + P-SIMPX)
5–6	Mean {Simplex | Relative} Clause Length	#{SIMPX | R-SIMPX} tokens / #{SIMPX | R-SIMPX}
7–9	{Simplex | Relative | Paratactic} Clauses Ratio	#{SIMPX | R-SIMPX | P-SIMPX} / #(SIMPX + R-SIMPX + P-SIMPX)
10–12	Mean {Prefield | Middle Field | Postfield} Length	#{VF | MF | NF} tokens / #{VF | MF | NF}
13–14	Mean {NP | PP} Length	#{NX | PX} tokens / #{NX | PX}
15–16	{Verbs | NPs} per Sentence	#{VXFIN + VXINF | NX} tokens / #sentences
17	Verb/Noun Ratio	#VV.* / #NN
18	Mean Token Embedding Depth	#nodes / #tokens
19	Mean Maximum Embedding Depth per Sentence	sum of maximum embedding depth per sentence / #sentences

Table 3: Syntactic complexity features and their definitions.

embedded clauses) within sentences, or length of specific constituents. In addition, we included measures that relate to topological fields, in particular the prefield ("Vorfeld", VF), the middle field ("Mittelfeld", MF), and postfield ("Nachfeld", NF) (cf. Telljohann et al., 2012). Similar features have been used in other studies for automatically evaluating syntactic complexity (Chen and Zechner, 2011; Meyer et al., 2020).

Table 3 shows all of our features along with their definitions.[7] Mean length of constituents is calculated as follows: First, all tokens within the relevant constituents are counted by counting all nodes pertaining to the constituent (i.e., singletons and BIE nodes). Next, this sum is normalized by the total number of relevant constituents, which is calculated by counting the number of nodes marking the beginning of the constituent (singletons and B nodes). For instance, mean length of SIMPX is calculated as shown in (1). In Table 3, we use the simplified notation "#SIMPX tokens / #SIMPX" for the formula in (1).

(1) Mean length of SIMPX

$$= \frac{\#SIMPX + \#B\text{-}SIMPX + \#I\text{-}SIMPX + \#E\text{-}SIMPX}{\#SIMPX + \#B\text{-}SIMPX}$$

Features 1–3 concern the complexity of sentences, measured in number of tokens, clauses, and subordinate clauses.[8]

Features 4–9 concern the complexity of clauses in general and specific clause types. Features 7–9 record the proportions of different clause types. Unfortunately, the annotation scheme only distinguishes between relative clauses, paratactic (i.e., coordinated) clauses, and the rest, called simplex clauses. Simplex clauses cover a huge and heterogeneous class with verb-second main clauses as well as verb-final subordinate clauses.[9]

Features 10–12 and 13–14 measure the length of the topological fields and of NPs and PPs, respectively.

Features 15–17 concerns the number and ratio of verbs and nouns, which can indicate a more verbal (i.e., oral) style vs. a more nominal (i.e., written) style.

Features 18 and 19 concern the depth of embedding in general. Feature 18 calculates an overall mean embedding depth, considering all tokens in the text. The embedding depth is measured by the number of nodes which form the path from the root node to a token's terminal node. Topological field nodes do not contribute to the path length. Feature 19 considers only the maximum embedding depth per sentence, and calculates the mean over all sentences in a text.

Appendix B illustrates the syntactic annotation and the resulting complexity scores with an exam-

[7]"X" as part of a syntactic label stands roughly for "phrase"; e.g., "NX" corresponds to "NP". Syntactic nodes labeled "VXFIN" and "VXINF" dominate a finite or infinite verb (infinitives and participles), respectively (Feature 16). For the exact definitions of the syntactic labels, see Telljohann et al. (2012). "VV.*" and "NN" refer to POS tags (Feature 17).

[8]Virtually all subordinate clauses contain a node labeled "C", which hosts the subordinating conjunction in complementizer and adverbial clauses, the relative pronoun in relative clauses, and the interrogative pronoun in (embedded) interrogative clauses. An exception are embedded verb-second clauses, which do not contain a node C and are therefore not covered here.

[9]We do not include mean length of paratactic clauses because they connect two or more simplex clauses, whose length we include. Moreover paratactic clauses are very rare, as shown by Feature 9.

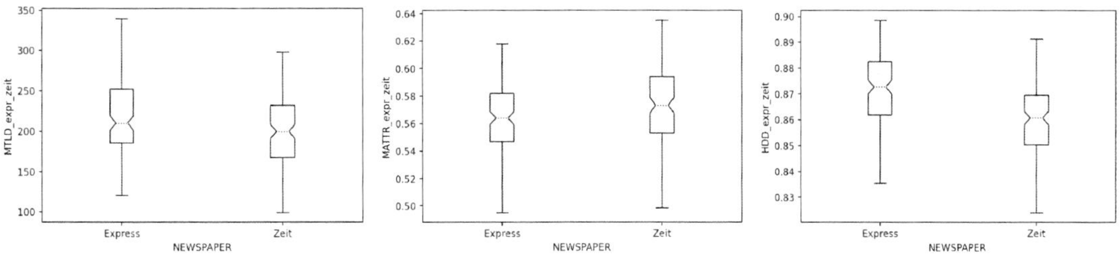

Figure 3: Boxplots of the scores according to *MTLD* (left), *MATTR* (center), and *HD-D* (right) for the EXPRESS and ZEIT corpora (left vs. right box, respectively).

ple sentence from the GraphVar corpus.

Our basic assumption is that a higher number of clauses and a greater length of clauses is an indicator of a higher syntactic complexity.[10] Expectations concerning the topological fields are less straightforward. A complex middle field is often considered a feature of the written register. In contrast, a complex postfield typically results from postponing complex constituents from the middle field and, hence, can possibly be considered a characteristics of the oral register and less complex. Regarding length and embedding depth of constituents, higher scores also imply higher complexity.

4 Results

4.1 Lexical Diversity

4.1.1 Reference Corpora

For the two reference corpora, we assumed that the ZEIT corpus should result in higher scores of lexical diversity than EXPRESS corpus. To validate this assumption, we lemmatized the reference subsets with the TreeTagger (Schmid, 1994) and determined MTLD, MATTR, and HD-D scores for both subsets.

The results vary, as shown in Fig. 3: Contrary to our assumption, the EXPRESS corpus achieves slightly higher MTLD and HD-D scores than the ZEIT corpus, i.e., it is lexically more diverse than the ZEIT corpus according to these scores (the difference is not significant with MTLD, though). Only with MATTR the ZEIT corpus achieves the higher scores (no significant difference, though).

Perhaps this unexpected result can be attributed to the way the subcorpora were sampled, see our considerations in Sec. 5.

[10] However, as mentioned above, a nominal style (i.e., using nominalizations instead of clauses) is also an indication of high complexity (see Features 15–17).

4.1.2 GraphVar Corpus

With regard to the GraphVar corpus, we assumed that due to the changing composition of the students (i) the results from the early years would be more homogeneous and have less variance, and (ii) the lexical diversity of texts written in the 1960s and 1970s would be rather high and would gradually decrease when progressing in time.

However, the results from the lexical diversity study do not confirm our hypothesis. We calculated the measures for each text separately, and computed mean and standard deviation per year.

We start with the second hypothesis. All three measures show an increasing trend over time, see Fig. 4. This is especially clear with MTLD and HD-D, so our hypothesis is clearly refuted. With regard to the first hypothesis, the boxplots in Fig. 4 show that variance is smallest in 2003–2013, again contrary to our expectations.

The texts from 1998 seem to be an interesting outlier: The mean is very clearly below the trend line, and there is also an unusually high variance this year.

Compared to the EXPRESS and ZEIT corpora, the GraphVar texts turn out lexically less diverse than both the EXPRESS and ZEIT texts, with all measures.[11] Presumably, this can be attributed to the different tasks: Essays written as part of the German exam deal with one predefined topic, e.g. a question on a novel that has to be answered and discussed, and therefore tend to use recurring vocabulary rather than newspaper texts, aimed at a broad public.

Regarding the first hypothesis, there seems to

[11] Means per subcorpus:

Measure	EXPRESS	ZEIT	GraphVar
MTLD	215.60	203.11	74.74
MATTR	0.56	0.57	0.41
HD-D	0.87	0.86	0.77

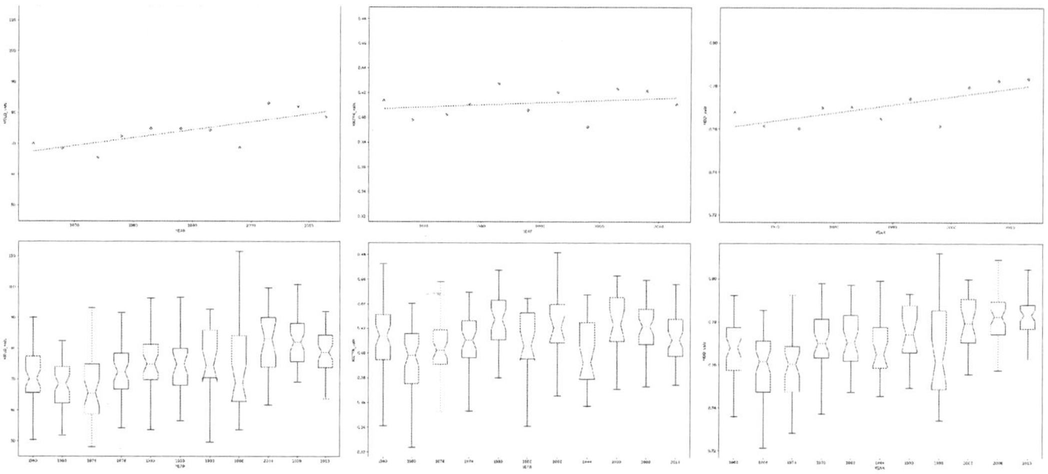

Figure 4: MTLD (left), MATTR (center), and HD-D (right) scores for the GraphVar corpus: means (top) and boxplots (bottom) per year.

be a trend toward less variance, i.e., toward more homogeneous texts, which again contradicts the hypothesis.

4.2 Perplexity of POS-based Language Models

As argued in Sec. 3.2, we assume that a POS-based language model trained on the ZEIT corpus should have a lower perplexity on a linguistically complex text than a POS-based language model trained on the EXPRESS corpus.

We tagged both reference corpora with the SoMeWeTa POS tagger (Proisl, 2018) with the model "german_newspaper_2020-05-28"[12] and trained two models on the POS tags of the ZEIT corpus and the EXPRESS corpus, respectively. We used the same tagger to re-tag the GraphVar corpus such that the annotation can be compared to the reference corpora.[13]

[12]The SoMeWeTa tagger comes with two pre-trained models: "german_newspaper_2020-05-28", which was trained on German newspaper texts, and "german_web_social_media_2020-05-28", which was trained on German web and social media data. In an informal evaluation, we compared these models and evaluated 50 randomly selected tokens from each of the three corpora (EXPRESS, ZEIT, GraphVar) where the models yielded different results. It turned out that the model "german_newspaper_2020-05-28" performed slightly better than the model "german_web_social_media_2020-05-28". In addition, we evaluated the model "german_newspaper_-2020-05-28" on 100 randomly selected tokens from each of the three corpora. The tagger achieved very good accuracies of 97% (ZEIT and GraphVar) and 96% (EXPRESS).

[13]We used the NORMAL forms of the GraphVar texts for tagging. These are normalized word forms with (corrected) modernized spellings.

Fig. 5 displays the result from the POS-based models trained on the ZEIT and EXPRESS corpora when applied to the GraphVar corpus. For each year, first the perplexity of the EXPRESS model is shown, followed by the one of the ZEIT model.

Overall, later years tend to yield higher perplexities, i.e., the syntactic distance between the GraphVar texts and the two newspapers models increases over time. This is remarkable because the newspaper models have been trained on data from 2021 and 2022, but perplexity is very low with the GraphVar data from the 1960s. Interestingly, however, the upward trend breaks off abruptly in 2008 (assuming that 1998 is again an outlier and that the upward trend continues to 2003).

Concerning the reference corpora, it is interesting to note that most of the time, the ZEIT-based perplexity is lower than the EXPRESS-based one, even though the differences are not significant (as indicated by the overlapping regions of the notches).

With regard to our first hypothesis, the boxplots show a relatively high variance for the entire period.

4.3 Syntactic Complexity

4.3.1 Reference Corpora

For the two reference corpora, we assumed that the ZEIT corpus should have a higher syntactic complexity than the EXPRESS corpus. For the comparison, we parsed the subsets of the reference corpora with the Berkeley Parser (Petrov and Klein, 2007), using a model for German that provides

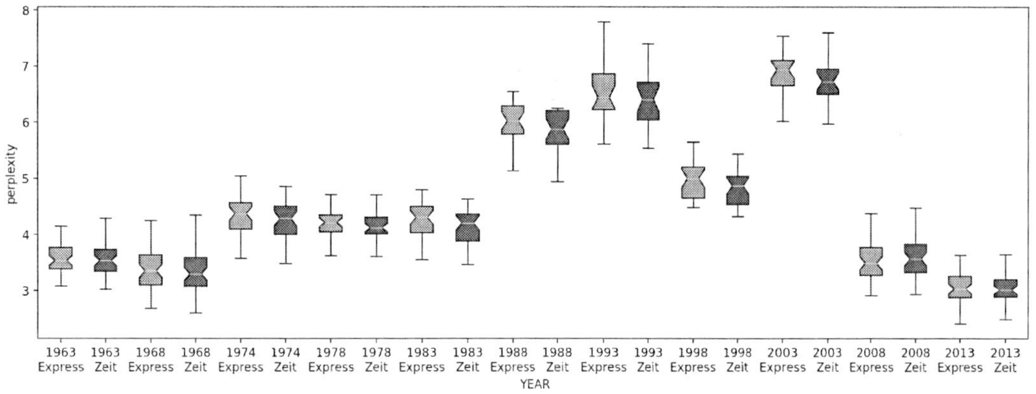

Figure 5: Mean perplexity per year using the EXPRESS and ZEIT models

syntactic as well as topological field annotations (Cheung and Penn, 2009).[14]

Table 4 lists the different measures and scores of the subsets (columns "EXPRESS" and "ZEIT"). As the table shows, ZEIT texts tend to have higher scores (with 12 out of 19 measures, column "E/Z"), although the scores are often close to each other. With Features 3, 6 and 12, the differences are more pronounced. At least for Features 3 and 6, a higher score clearly indicates higher complexity.

We conclude that the ZEIT texts are generally more syntactically complex than the EXPRESS texts, so that our assumption is confirmed here.

4.3.2 GraphVar Corpus

Table 4 shows that the GraphVar corpus achieves higher scores than the reference corpora with most of the measures. In fact, there is often a very clear gap to the scores of the reference corpora, in particular for Features 1–5 and 18–19, which are all clearly related to syntactic complexity.

The final column "Trend" shows that the vast majority of the features tend to have lower scores in early years (1963–1978) and higher scores in late years (1983–2013), clearly contradicting our second hypothesis. These features are marked by "+" in Table 4.[15]

Texts written in 1998 represent a remarkable exception, again, showing low average scores for most of these features, see the plots in Fig. 7 in Appendix C.

Contrary to our initial hypothesis, these results suggest that the syntactic complexity of the GraphVar texts is higher in late years.

With regard to our first hypothesis, the tendencies are less clear and there is a relatively high variance for the entire period, as in the case of perplexity.

5 Conclusion

In this paper, we examined high school graduation texts over five decades (1963–2013). Our initial hypotheses were: (i) variance increases; (ii) complexity decreases. However, these hypotheses were not confirmed by our tests.

Lexical diversity does not distinguish clearly between the two reference corpora EXPRESS and ZEIT. For the GraphVar corpus, diversity increases over time according to all three measures, but variance seems to decrease. The results by perplexity show a growing distance to both reference corpora, with an abrupt break in the year 2008. Variance is rather high for the entire period. There is no real difference in perplexity between the two reference models. According to the syntactic measures, the GraphVar texts are clearly more complex than both of the reference corpora, and the ZEIT texts are slightly more complex than the EXPRESS texts. The GraphVar corpus shows an increase in syntactic complexity over time with most features. Again, variance is rather high for the entire period. In summary, GraphVar texts are becoming more complex over time.

With regard to the reference corpora, we could hypothesize that the unexpected results could be

[14]We downloaded the parser and the model "tuebadz_topf_no_edge.gr" from `https://www.cs.mcgill.ca/~jcheung/topoparsing/topoparsing.html`.

[15]We fit linear models for each of the features, with the year as the predictor and the score as the dependent variable (in R: `lm(formula = score ~ year)`). If the year has a highly significant effect ($p < 0.001$), the feature is marked as "+" in Table 4. A (weak) significant effect ($p < 0.05$) is recorded as "(+)" in the table.

No	Feature	E/Z	EXPRESS	ZEIT	GraphVar	Trend
1	Mean Sentence Length	E	*17.59*	17.57	**21.30**	+
2	Clauses per Sentence	Z	1.90	*1.96*	**2.21**	ns
3	Subordinate Clauses per Sentence	Z	0.40	*0.51*	**0.73**	(+)
4	Mean Clause Length	Z	13.03	*13.30*	**14.63**	+
5	Mean Simplex Clause Length	Z	13.34	*13.61*	**15.19**	+
6	Mean Relative Clause Length	Z	9.04	**10.05**	*9.42*	+
7	Simplex Clauses Ratio	E	**0.92**	*0.90*	0.88	ns
8	Relative Clauses Ratio	Z	0.07	*0.09*	**0.11**	ns
9	Paratactic Clauses Ratio	Z	0.00	0.00	**0.01**	ns
10	Mean Prefield Length	E	**3.64**	3.35	*3.46*	+
11	Mean Middle Field Length	E	*5.14*	5.02	**5.30**	+
12	Mean Postfield Length	Z	9.48	*10.36*	**10.98**	+
13	Mean NP Length	Z	2.46	*2.55*	**2.57**	+
14	Mean PP Length	Z	3.57	*3.72*	**3.82**	+
15	Verbs per Sentence	E	*2.55*	2.53	**2.97**	ns
16	NPs per Sentence	E	*6.96*	6.84	**7.62**	+
17	Verb/Noun Ratio	Z	0.49	*0.51*	**0.52**	ns
18	Mean Token Embedding Depth	E	3.18	*3.27*	**4.13**	+
19	Mean Maximum Embedding Depth per Sentence	Z	*4.62*	4.59	**5.95**	+

Table 4: Results of syntactic complexity measures. Column "E/Z" marks which of the reference corpora achieves the higher score for the respective feature. Columns "EXPRESS", "ZEIT" and "GraphVar" list the average scores of each subcorpus. For each feature, the highest score is in bold, the second highest in italics. The column "Trend" shows the GraphVar trend over the survey years: "+" means that late years show significantly higher scores than early years. The feature marked by "(+)" still shows similar tendencies but the difference is less pronounced. "ns" marks features that do not show clear trends between the scores of the different years of the GraphVar corpus.

Corpus		#Articles	Avg. #Tokens
EXPRESS	complete	30K	295
	filtered	4.6K	740
ZEIT	complete	7.5K	1,094
	filtered	2K	1,670

Table 5: The two reference corpora, complete and filtered.

due to the way the text fragments were sampled. Only articles that were at least 500 tokens long were considered. This excludes a large number of articles, especially in the EXPRESS corpus: out of almost 30,000 articles, only 4,565 remain. The average length of an EXPRESS article before this filtering is 295 tokens, after the filtering 740 (see Table 5). That is, it could be that the filtering sorts out the "typical", linguistically simple EXPRESS articles and the more unusual, more complex articles remain. In contrast, the filter effect with the ZEIT corpus is much smaller.

This could explain why the EXPRESS corpus is lexically more diverse than ZEIT according to MTLD and HD-D, and could also be a reason why the EXPRESS corpus gets quite similar scores as the ZEIT corpus with many syntactic features.

Concerning the GraphVar corpus, we have observed two striking anomalies. First, texts from 1998 stood out as outliers in all studies. Second, perplexity results indicate a major break in 2008. Maybe these anomalies can be explained by some external factor such as an important change in the task.[16]

In general, increasing complexity of GraphVar texts could be traced back to different reasons, all of which require further investigation: Teaching methods could have improved and students are achieving better results in later years. The type of task might have changed more than expected over the years and therefore the results differ. We leave this question open for future research.

Acknowledgments

We would like to thank the reviewers for their constructive and valuable feedback. Many thanks also to Kristian Berg (Bonn), who provided us with the GraphVar corpus and answered numerous questions about it.

[16]The anomalies cannot be due to the spelling reform from 1996: The lexical measures are based on normalized lemma forms, which are not affected by the reform. The perplexity and syntactic measures refer to abstract syntactic categories.

References

Andrea Abel, Aivars Glaznieks, Lionel Nicolas, and Egon Stemle. 2014. KoKo: an L1 learner corpus for German. In *Proceedings of the 9th International Conference on Language Resources and Evaluation (LREC 2014)*, pages 2414–2421, Reykjavik, Iceland.

Andrea Abel, Aivars Glaznieks, Lionel Nicolas, and Egon Stemle. 2016. An extended version of the KoKo German L1 learner corpus. In *Proceedings of the Third Italian Conference on Computational Linguistics (CLIC-it 2016)*, pages 13–18, Naples, Italy.

Theodora Alexopoulou, Marije Michel, Akira Murakami, and Detmar Meurers. 2017. Task effects on linguistic complexity and accuracy: A large-scale learner corpus analysis employing natural language processing techniques. *Language Learning*, 67(S1):180–208.

Kristian Berg, Jonas Romstadt, and Cedrek Neitzert. 2021. GraphVar – Korpusaufbau und Annotation. Version 1.0. Friedrich-Wilhelms-Universität Bonn, https://graphvar.uni-bonn.de/dokumentation.html.

Miao Chen and Klaus Zechner. 2011. Computing and evaluating syntactic complexity features for automated scoring of spontaneous non-native speech. In *Proceedings of the 49th Annual Meeting of the Association for Computational Linguistics: Human Language Technologies*, pages 722–731, Portland, Oregon, USA. Association for Computational Linguistics.

Xiaobin Chen and Detmar Meurers. 2016. CTAP: A web-based tool supporting automatic complexity analysis. In *Proceedings of the Workshop on Computational Linguistics for Linguistic Complexity (CL4LC)*, pages 113–119, Osaka, Japan. The COLING 2016 Organizing Committee.

Jackie Chi Kit Cheung and Gerald Penn. 2009. Topological field parsing of German. In *Proceedings of the Joint Conference of the 47th Annual Meeting of the ACL and the 4th International Joint Conference on Natural Language Processing of the AFNLP*, pages 64–72, Suntec, Singapore. Association for Computational Linguistics.

Michael A. Covington and Joe D. McFall. 2010. Cutting the Gordian knot: The moving-average type–token ratio (MATTR). *Journal of Quantitative Linguistics*, 17(2):94–100.

Scott A. Crossley. 2020. Linguistic features in writing quality and development: An overview. *Journal of Writing Research*, 11(3):415–443.

Gerasimos Fergadiotis, Heather Wright, and Thomas West. 2013. Measuring lexical diversity in narrative discourse of people with aphasia. *American journal of speech-language pathology / American Speech-Language-Hearing Association*, 22:397–408.

Daniel Jurafsky and James H. Martin. 2022. *Speech and Language Processing*. Draft from Jan 12, 2022.

Rie Koizumi and Yo In'nami. 2012. Effects of text length on lexical diversity measures: Using short texts with less than 200 tokens. *System*, 40(4):554–564.

Batia Laufer and Paul Nation. 1995. Vocabulary size and use: Lexical richness in L2 written production. *Applied Linguistics*, 16(3):307–322.

David Malvern, Brian Richards, Ngoni Chipere, and Pilar Duran. 2004. *Lexical diversity and language development: Quantification and assessment. Basingstoke, Hampshire: Palgrave Macmillan*. Cited in McCarthy and Jarvis (2010).

Philip M. McCarthy. 2005. *An Assessment of the Range and Usefulness of Lexical Diversity Measures and the Potential of the Measure of Textual, Lexical Diversity (MTLD)*. Ph.D. thesis, The University of Memphis.

Philip M. McCarthy and Scott Jarvis. 2007. vocd: A theoretical and empirical evaluation. *Language Testing*, 24(4):459–488.

Philip M. McCarthy and Scott Jarvis. 2010. MTLD, vocd-D, and HD-D: A validation study of sophisticated approaches to lexical diversity assessment. *Behaviour Research Methods*, 42(2):381–392.

Jennifer Meyer, Torben Jansen, Johanna Fleckenstein, Stefan Keller, and Olaf Köller. 2020. Machine Learning im Bildungskonstext: Evidenz für die Genauigkeit der automatisierten Beurteilung von Essays im Fach Englisch. *Zeitschrift für Pädagogische Psychologie*, 0:1–12.

Slav Petrov and Dan Klein. 2007. Improved inference for unlexicalized parsing. In *Human Language Technologies 2007: The Conference of the North American Chapter of the Association for Computational Linguistics; Proceedings of the Main Conference*, pages 404–411, Rochester, New York. Association for Computational Linguistics.

Thomas Proisl. 2018. SoMeWeTa: A part-of-speech tagger for German social media and web texts. In *Proceedings of the Eleventh International Conference on Language Resources and Evaluation (LREC 2018)*, pages 665–670, Miyazaki. European Language Resources Association ELRA.

Anne Schiller, Simone Teufel, Christine Stöckert, and Christine Thielen. 1999. Guidelines für das Tagging deutscher Textcorpora mit STTS (Kleines und großes Tagset). Technical report, Universitäten Stuttgart und Tübingen, http://www.ims.uni-stuttgart.de/forschung/ressourcen/lexika/TagSets/stts-1999.pdf.

Helmut Schmid. 1994. Probabilistic part-of-speech tagging using decision trees. In *Proceedings of International Conference on New Methods in Language Processing*.

Anna Shadrova, Pia Linscheid, Julia Lukassek, Anke Lüdeling, and Sarah Schneider. 2021. A challenge for contrastive L1/L2 corpus studies: Large inter- and intra-individual variation across morphological, but not global syntactic categories in task-based corpus data of a homogeneous L1 German group. *Frontiers in Psychology, Section Language Sciences*, 12.

Heike Telljohann, Erhard W. Hinrichs, Sandra Kübler, Heike Zinsmeister, and Katrhin Beck. 2012. *Stylebook for the Tübingen Treebank of Written German (TüBa-D/Z)*. Seminar für Sprachwissenschaft, Universität Tübingen.

Zarah Weiss. 2017. Using measures of linguistic complexity to assess German L2 proficiency in learner corpora under consideration of task-effects. Master's thesis, University of Tübingen, Germany.

Fred Zenker and Kristopher Kyle. 2021. Investigating minimum text lengths for lexical diversity indices. *Assessing Writing*, 47:100505.

A Text Samples

GraphVar corpus (1963)
Franz Werfel setzt über das Gedicht einen lateinischen Spruch, der übersetzt heißt: Komm Schöpfer Geist. So gemahnt dies Gedicht an einen liturgischen Hymnus. In den Versen und mit Endreimen erhält das Gedicht eine andere Form als ein mittelalterlicher Hymnus. Der Dichter hat wohl diese Überschrift gewählt, um den Menschen heute, die auf der Suche nach einem Weltbild sind, die Geschlossenheit des mittelalterlichen Weltbildes zu zeigen, damit sie aus diesem lernen. Rainer Maria Rilke setzt keine Überschrift über das Gedicht. Er gibt keinen Fingerzeig, sondern stellt uns so vor das Gedicht, das kein Versmaß hat, sondern unregelmäßige Langzeilen mit Endreimen. B I Gott kommt zu den Menschen nur durch schöpferische Tätigkeit. Der Mensch muss sich Gott wie ein großes Kunstwerk erst erarbeiten. Er muss um Gott kreisen, "um den alten Turm". Hat der Mensch ihn gefunden, dann kommt er "mit ihm" - mit Gott - "aus der Nacht." Gott führt ihn aus dem Chaos zum Licht.

GraphVar corpus (2013)
In der damaligen Ständegesellschaft waren ständeübergreifende Beziehungen sehr problematisch. Mit einer solchen Beziehung zwischen einer Bürgerlichen und einem Adligen beschäftigt sich auch Theodor Fontane in dem Auszug aus seinem Roman "Irrungen und Wirrungen", erschienen im Jahre 1887. In dem Textauszug aus dem fünften Kapitel findet ein Dialog zwischen der Bürgerlichen Lene und ihrem adeligen Geliebten Botho statt, in welchem die Aussichtslosigkeit der Liebe der beiden aufgrund der Ständegesellschaft thematisiert wird. Das Paar trifft sich bei Nacht in einem Garten zum Spaziergang. Sie unterhalten sich zunächst über die Mutter von Botho, wobei Lene ihre Furcht vor dieser Person äußert. Botho ist der Ansicht, dass sie seine Mutter falsch einschätzt, woraufhin Lene ihre Bedenken bezüglich ihrer Liebe und ihrer Beziehung anspricht.

EXPRESS
Heftiger Regen. Und das fast den ganzen Tag. Zig Straßen sind überflutet, Hunderte Keller sind vollgelaufen, Menschen müssen raus aus ihren Wohnungen, es gibt Vermisste. Tief "Bernd" setzt fast ganz Deutschland mächtig zu. Besonders hart hat der Starkregen Nordrhein-Westfalen getroffen. In Hagen musste ein Altenheim evakuiert werden, weil Wassermassen einströmten. Es ist unbewohnbar geworden. Eltern wurden gebeten, ihre Kinder nicht in die Kita zu schicken. Eine verschüttete Person wurde leicht verletzt gerettet worden. Mehrere Fahrer mussten aus ihren von Wassermassen eingeschlossenen Autos befreit werden. Es gab mindestens 200 Einsatzorte. Einige Ortsteile waren zum Teil nicht mehr zu erreichen. "Die Leute sind verzweifelt", sagte ein Sprecher des Polizeipräsidiums Hagen. Bundeswehrpanzer sollen helfen, die Straßen wieder frei zu machen.

ZEIT
Der zerbrochene Krug, der chaotische Schreibtisch oder die Fahrt nach Rimini mit einem Diesel verbrennenden alten Opel - das alles sind Anwendungsfälle des Zweiten Hauptsatzes der Thermodynamik. Der besagt in aller Kürze, dass jedes System den Zustand höchster Unordnung anstrebt - solange niemand Extraenergie reinsteckt. Dieses »Extraenergiereinstecken« aber ist die vornehmste Aufgabe der Politik. Ein hervorragendes Beispiel dafür ist die Mülltrennung. Früher (bis in die Sechzigerjahre) gab es für den gesamten Müll eine einzige große Tonne : für Zeitungen und faule Äpfel, für leere Flaschen und Konservendosen, für alte Batterien, löchrige Socken und Asche aus dem Kohleofen. Manchmal war die noch heiß, dann fing der Mülleimer an zu qualmen. In dieser (guten) alten Zeit - in Teilen der USA ist das heute noch so - war die einzige ernst zu nehmende Frage: Wer bringt den Müll runter?

B Syntactic Complexity: An Example

We illustrate the Syntactic Complexity measures with an example sentence from the GraphVar corpus, shown in (i).

(i) *Dies ist ein Werk aus der Zeit des Naturalismus.*
'This is a work from the period of naturalism.'

Fig. 6 displays the syntactic analysis produced by the Berkeley parser (Petrov and Klein, 2007), using the model "tuebadz_topf_no_edge.gr" (Cheung and Penn, 2009).[17] It further shows the corresponding BIE path notation and presents the results for the individual syntactic complexity measures.

C Syntactic Complexity: Results

Fig. 7 shows the means and boxplots per survey year for all syntactic features. The numbers refer to the numbered features listed in Table 4 in Sec. 4.3.

[17]The tree view has been produced by the Syntax Tree Generator, `http://mshang.ca/syntree/`.

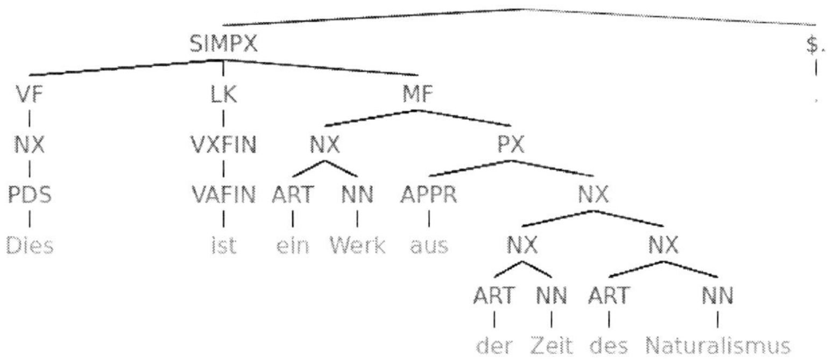

<table>
<tr><th>Word</th><th>Lemma</th><th>POS</th><th>Syntax</th></tr>
<tr><td>Dies</td><td>dies</td><td>PDS</td><td>B-SIMPX | VF | NX | PDS</td></tr>
<tr><td>ist</td><td>sein</td><td>VAFIN</td><td>I-SIMPX | LF | VXFIN | VAFIN</td></tr>
<tr><td>ein</td><td>eine</td><td>ART</td><td>I-SIMPX | B-MF | B-NX | ART</td></tr>
<tr><td>Werk</td><td>Werk</td><td>NN</td><td>I-SIMPX | I-MF | E-NX | NN</td></tr>
<tr><td>aus</td><td>aus</td><td>APPR</td><td>I-SIMPX | I-MF | B-PX | APPR</td></tr>
<tr><td>der</td><td>die</td><td>ART</td><td>I-SIMPX | I-MF | I-PX | B-NX | B-NX | ART</td></tr>
<tr><td>Zeit</td><td>Zeit</td><td>NN</td><td>I-SIMPX | I-MF | I-PX | I-NX | E-NX | NN</td></tr>
<tr><td>des</td><td>die</td><td>ART</td><td>I-SIMPX | I-MF | I-PX | I-NX | B-NX | ART</td></tr>
<tr><td>Naturalismus</td><td>Naturalismus</td><td>NN</td><td>E-SIMPX | E-MF | E-PX | E-NX | E-NX | NN</td></tr>
<tr><td>.</td><td>.</td><td>$.</td><td>$.</td></tr>
</table>

No	Feature	Score
1	Mean Sentence Length	10
2	Clauses per Sentence	1
3	Subordinate Clauses per Sentence	0
4	Mean Clause Length	9.0
5	Mean Simplex Clause Length	9.0
6	Mean Relative Clause Length	–
7	Simplex Clauses Ratio	1
8	Relative Clauses Ratio	0
9	Paratactic Clauses Ratio	0
10	Mean Prefield Length	1.0
11	Mean Middle Field Length	7.0
12	Mean Postfield Length	–
13	Mean NP Length	2.2
14	Mean PP Length	5.0
15	Verbs per Sentence	1
16	NPs per Sentence	5
17	Verb/Noun Ratio	0
18	Mean Token Embedding Depth	3.6
19	Mean Maximum Embedding Depth	5

Figure 6: Syntactic analysis of the example sentence. The tree (top) shows the output of the parser. The first table (center) shows the corresponding path notation using BIE tags in the column "Syntax"; the last node of each path consists of the POS tag. The second table (bottom) lists the scores of the syntactic complexity measures that result for the example sentence; note that Features 18 and 19 do not consider the topological nodes (VF, LK, MF in the example)

Figure 7: Syntactic features: mean and boxplot per survey year.

Proceedings of the 18th Conference on Natural Language Processing (KONVENS 2022)

Measuring Faithfulness of Abstractive Summaries

Tim Fischer **Steffen Remus** **Chris Biemann**

Language Technology Group
Department of Informatics
Universität Hamburg, Germany
{firstname.lastname}@uni-hamburg.de

Abstract

Recent abstractive summarization systems fail to generate factually consistent – faithful – summaries, which heavily limits their practical application. Commonly, these models tend to mix concepts from the source or hallucinate new content, completely ignoring the source. Addressing the faithfulness problem is perhaps the most critical challenge for current abstractive summarization systems. First automatic faithfulness metrics were proposed, but we argue that existing methods do not yet utilize the full potential that this field has to offer and introduce new approaches to assess factual correctness. We evaluate existing and our proposed methods by correlating them with human judgements and find that BERTScore works well. Finally, we conduct a qualitative and quantitative error analysis, which reveals common problems and indicates means to further improve the metrics.

1 Introduction

Abstractive summarization is the task of generating an informative and fluent summary that is faithful to the source document. Recent progress in neural text generation has led to significant improvements and well-performing state-of-the-art abstractive summarization systems (Zhang et al., 2019; Lewis et al., 2020). Despite these advances, recent models fail to meet one of the essential requirements of practical summarization systems: information of a generated summary must match the facts of the source document. We follow Cao et al. (2018) and refer to this aspect as faithfulness in this work. Recent studies have shown that around 30% of automatically generated summaries from neural summarization systems contain unfaithful information (Cao et al., 2018; Falke et al., 2019; Kryscinski et al., 2019), especially when a sentence combines content from multiple source sentences (Lebanoff et al., 2019). Table 1 shows a misleading and unfaithful summary demonstrating this issue.

Source	The restaurant began serving puppy platters after a new law was introduced allowing dogs to eat at restaurants – as long as they were outdoors!
Summary	New rules have come into place that you can eat your dog.

Table 1: A generated, unfaithful summary found in the XSUM hallucination dataset by Maynez et al. (2020).

Researchers identified multiple challenges for developing faithful systems. One challenge is evaluation, as current automatic metrics are inadequate. Typical metrics like ROUGE (Lin, 2004), BLEU (Papineni et al., 2002) or METEOR (Banerjee and Lavie, 2005) are insensitive to semantic errors. These n-gram-based approaches weight all portions of the text equally, even when only a small fraction of the n-grams carry most of the semantic content. Consequently, factual inconsistencies caused by small changes are overshadowed by high n-gram overlaps. Another challenge is the optimization of abstractive models. Generating summaries that highly overlap with human references does not guarantee faithful summaries (Zhang et al., 2020b).

Initial work on metrics to automatically assess faithfulness will be discussed in Section 2 and 3, however, no consensus has been reached to date. We argue that the currently available means to automatically evaluate faithfulness do not use the full potential that current NLP methods offer. In this work, we explore new methods to assess the faithfulness of generated texts and compare them to existing approaches. Finally, we perform a qualitative and quantitative error analysis by investigating the outputs of all methods to analyze their problems and to reveal ways to improve them. We study the following research questions (RQs) in this work:

1. Which faithfulness metric correlates best with human judgements?
2. What are problems of faithfulness metrics and how can we address them?

Together with this work, we release an open-source Python library[1] that allows reproduction of our results and utilization of all discussed metrics by others to evaluate faithfulness.

2 Related Work

The lack of automatic evaluation metrics for faithfulness has motivated researches to develop new metrics that ideally mimic human judgements of factual consistency. Popular approaches are based on question answering (Wang et al., 2020; Durmus et al., 2020), textual entailment (Falke et al., 2019; Maynez et al., 2020) and contextual embeddings (Kryscinski et al., 2020).

Nan et al. (2021) focus on the problem of unfaithful entities where model-generated summaries contain named entities that do not appear in the source document. The authors perform named entity recognition and calculate the percentage of entities in the summary that can be found in the source. A low percentage means entity hallucination is severe. In addition, they propose precision-target and recall-target, which capture the entity-level accuracy of the generated summary with respect to the ground truth summary.

Goodrich et al. (2019) propose to measure the factual correctness with relation extraction methods. Facts are represented as subject-predicate-object triples and faithfulness is defined as the precision between the facts extracted from the generated summary and target summary.

3 Methods

We re-implement and modify popular faithfulness metrics as well as propose new methods (SentSim, NER, SRL) that extract and compare different information from text to assess factual consistency.

3.1 BERTScore

BERTScore (Zhang et al., 2020a) is an automatic evaluation metric for text generation. It utilizes contextual embeddings to compute a similarity score between every token in the candidate sentence and reference sentence. Computing the similarity with contextual embeddings is effective for matching paraphrases as well as capturing distant dependencies and ordering.

Let x be a reference sentence $x = x_1, ..., x_n$ and a y be candidate sentence $y = y_1, ..., y_m$ tokenized into tokens x_i and y_j, respectively. An embedding model maps theses sentences to two sequence of vectors $\mathbf{x_1}, ..., \mathbf{x_n}$ and $\mathbf{y_1}, ..., \mathbf{y_m}$. Every token in x is matched to a token in y to compute recall and each token in y is matched to a token in x to compute precision using maximum matching: each token is aligned to the most similar token in the other sentence. Three variants of BERTScore (precision, recall, F1) are shown below:

$$R_{BERT} = \frac{1}{|x|} \sum_{x_i \in x} \max_{y_j \in y} \mathbf{x_i}^T \mathbf{y_j}$$

$$P_{BERT} = \frac{1}{|y|} \sum_{y_j \in y} \max_{x_i \in x} \mathbf{x_i}^T \mathbf{y_j}$$

$$F1_{BERT} = 2 \frac{P_{BERT} \times R_{BERT}}{P_{BERT} + R_{BERT}}$$

We optimize BERTScore by selecting layer 8 of RoBERTa-large (Liu et al., 2019) fine-tuned on Multi-NLI (Williams et al., 2018) (roberta-large-mnli on Hugging Face) to compute embeddings.

3.2 Textual Entailment (TE)

Textual Entailment (Dagan et al., 2005) is a popular approach to measure factual consistency employed e.g. by Falke et al. (2019), Maynez et al. (2020), Durmus et al. (2020). The basic intuition is that all information in a summary should ideally be entailed by the source document or perhaps be neutral to the source document, but the summary should never contradict it.

Let E be a TE model that predicts the probability $E(a, b)$ that text b is entailed by text a. The faithfulness score f of a summary S consisting of sentences $s_1, ..., s_n$ with respect to the original document D with sentences $d \in D$ can be computed in 3 different ways:

$$f_{s2s}(S) = \frac{1}{n} \sum_{i=1}^{n} max_{d \in D} E(d, s_i)$$

$$f_{d2s}(S) = \frac{1}{n} \sum_{i=1}^{n} E(D, s_i)$$

$$f_{top2s}(S) = \frac{1}{n} \sum_{i=1}^{n} E(P, s_i)$$

The sentence-to-sentence (s2s) scoring method checks if every summary sentence is entailed by any source sentence. The document-to-sentence (d2s) checks if every summary sentence is entailed by the source document. The top-to-sentence (t2s) checks if every summary sentence is entailed by

[1] https://github.com/bigabig/faithfulness

the k (=3) most similar source sentences (calculated by comparing cosine-similarities of sentence embeddings) forming paragraph P.

We use BART-large (Lewis et al., 2020) and RoBERTa-large fine-tuned on Multi-NLI in our experiments to compute entailment and sentence-transformers[2] to compute sentence embeddings (for t2s).

3.3 Question Generation & Question Answering (QGQA)

The QGQA framework was introduced by Durmus et al. (2020) and Wang et al. (2020) and has been used in follow-up work, e.g. Maynez et al. (2020); Dong et al. (2020). The basic intuition of this framework is: if we ask questions about a summary and its source, we expect to receive similar answers if the summary is faithful. Naturally, more matched answers imply a more faithful summary as the information addressed by these questions is consistent between summary and source.

QGQA framework performs the following steps to detect factual inconsistencies:

1. An answer candidate selection (AS) model selects important text spans from the summary.
2. A question generation (QG) model generates a set of question about the summary using the answer candidates.
3. A question answering (QA) model answers these questions using both the source document and the generated text.
4. The faithfulness score is computed based on the similarity of the corresponding answers.

A similarity metric is necessary to compare corresponding answers. We empirically find $F1$ surface (token-level) similarity performs best (Appendix A.1).

We use the transformers library (Wolf et al., 2020) to implement this framework. Named entities and noun phrases are extracted with spaCy[3] as answer candidates. We use T5-base[4] as QG model to generate 5 questions per candidate, but filter out duplicates, bad questions (questions that cannot be answered by QA model given the summary) and low probability questions to have at most 10 questions per summary. RoBERTa-large fine-tuned on SQUAD2 (Rajpurkar et al., 2018) is used as QA model (deepset/roberta-large-squad2 on Hugging Face).

3.4 Sentence Similarity (SentSim)

The intuition of SentSim to measure faithfulness is that the information expressed in the summary should be the same as in the source document but paraphrased. Therefore, a summary sentence should be very similar to one or multiple important source sentences.

Abstractive summaries are written using different wordings and formulations to express the same information. Consequently, SentSim has to successfully deal with highly paraphrased text detecting similar concepts expressed with different words on the one hand. On the other hand, it has to differentiate between similar and contrasting or contradicting information so that it can actually be used to score faithfulness.

We propose the following strategy to asses faithfulness with sentence similarity:

1. Apply sentence splitting to the source document and summary to obtain lists of sentences.
2. Match every summary sentence with the most similar source sentence to compute precision; vice-versa to compute recall.

The precision variant (recall is analog, F1 as usual) of SentSim is defined as follows: let $S = \{s_1, s_2, ..., s_N\}$ be the set of summary sentences and let $D = \{d_1, d_2, ..., d_M\}$ be the set of document sentences, then

$$P_{SentSim} = \frac{1}{|S|} \sum_{s_j \in S} \max_{d_i \in D} sim(d_i, s_j)$$

We utilize spaCy to apply sentence splitting and experiment with various implementations of $sim()$. We empirically find that F1 and BERTScore perform well to score and align sentences (Appendix A.1).

3.5 Named Entity Recognition (NER)

Factual inconsistencies can occur at different levels. The entity hallucination problem occurs when a summary contains named entities that do not appear in the source document. Intuitively, a summary containing many entities that do not appear in the source is less faithful than a summary that contains the same entities as the source.

We propose the following strategy to calculate faithfulness with NER:

[2] all-mpnet-base-v2 from https://www.sbert.net/index.html
[3] en_core_web_lg from https://spacy.io/
[4] https://github.com/fajri91/question_generation

1. Identify entities in summary and source.
2. Group entities by their label (e.g. PER).
3. For each summary entity, calculate the most similar entity of the same group in the source document and its similarity score.
4. The faithfulness score is the average over all similarity scores.

We use spaCy to extract named entities and empirically find that Exact Match and F1 perform well to compare them (Appendix A.1). Please note, this approach does not capture other aspects that influence faithfulness like relations between entities or context surrounding entities.

3.6 Open Information Extraction (Open IE)

At relation level, we compare the relations between entities appearing in the source document and the summary. The relation hallucination problem occurs when a summary contains the same entities as the source document but their relations do not appear in the source document.

Naturally, if a summary contains many relations not present in the source document it is less faithful than a summary that contains the same relations. More matched relations imply a more faithful summary since not only the entities but also their interaction is consistent. In contrast to NER, a perfect match of summary relations with source relations can guarantee a faithful summary.

We propose the following strategy to calculate faithfulness with Open IE:

1. Apply a co-reference resolution system to replace all pronouns in the texts with their respective entity.
2. Apply an Open IE system to extract summary triples ($R(s)$) and source triples ($R(d)$) of the form (subject, relation, object) representing any fact in the given text.
3. Compute a faithfulness score based on the comparison of the extracted relations.

We use the Stanford CoreNLP toolkit for Open IE (Angeli et al., 2015), which includes an option to apply co-reference resolution as pre-processing step. We experiment with different methods to compare triples. The Relation Matching Rate (Zhu et al., 2021) operates on fact triples and basically measures the ratio of correct hits. Additionally, we linearize fact triples by concatenating the subject, relation and object to measure similarity with typical metrics. We empirically find that F1 or BERTScore work best (Appendix A.1).

3.7 Semantic Role Labeling (SRL)

This approach is inspired by the YiSi metric (Lo, 2019). YiSi measures similarity between two sentences by aggregating the semantic similarities of semantic structures. We argue that comparing semantic frames in contrast to comparing tokens as e.g. in BERTScore brings more linguistic structure into the faithfulness assessment. This process can find crucial differences between the argument structure of summary and source, which is a desirable property considering faithfulness. It verifies whether summary phrases are used in a semantically similar way as in the source document and should help to identify cases where the summary differs from the originally intended meaning.

We propose the following strategy to calculate faithfulness with SRL:

1. Apply a SRL model to the summary and source document to obtain labeled phrases.
2. Optionally, filter and merge semantic role labels to increase robustness.
3. Group phrases by their label.
4. Align (a) source and summary phrases with same label using a similarity metric.
5. Aggregate the similarity scores of aligned phrases and average over all labels to compute faithfulness (f).

Formally, this calculation can be denoted as

$$a_{recall}(l) = \frac{1}{|P_{S,l}|} \sum_{p_i \in P_{S,l}} \max_{p_j \in P_{D,l}} sim(p_i, p_j)$$

$$f_{metric} = \frac{1}{|L|} \sum_{l \in L} a_{metric}(l)$$

where $metric \in \{precision, recall, F1\}$. The precision variant of alignment (a) is analog to a_{recall}, F1 is calculated as usual. L is the set of all semantic labels, sim is a similarity metric comparing two texts, $P_{D,l}$ and $P_{S,l}$ are sets of phrases with label $l \in L$ for source D and summary S.

We use SRL BERT (Shi and Lin, 2019) of AllenNLP (Gardner et al., 2018) toolkit trained on the English OntoNotes 5 dataset (Hovy et al., 2006) for semantic role labeling. Following Lo (2019), we merge semantic role labels into more general role types (who, what, whom, when, where, why, how) for more robust performance. We empirically find computing similarity scores of phrases ($sim()$) works best with cosine-similarity (Appendix A.1).

4 RQ1: Best faithfulness metrics

We evaluate all faithfulness metrics described in Section 3 on the XSUM hallucination dataset (Maynez et al., 2020) as well as the SummEval dataset (Fabbri et al., 2021) and compute the correlation with human judgements. XSUM contains human faithfulness judgements (averaged to faithfulness scores) for 2000 document-summary pairs obtained by randomly sampling 500 articles from the XSUM (Narayan et al., 2018) test set and applying four different summarization models. Three annotators per document-summary pair were given the task to identify unfaithful text spans (hallucination spans) in the summary. The faithfulness score is roughly equivalent to the number of faithful words divided by number of total words of a summary. SummEval contains human faithfulness judgements for 1600 document-summary pairs obtained by randomly sampling 100 articles from the CNN/DailyMail (Hermann et al., 2015) test set and applying 16 different neural summarization models. Five crowd-sourced and 3 expert annotators were given the task to rate the factual consistency on a Likert scale from 1 to 5.

We apply a faithfulness metric on all document-summary pairs and calculate Spearman correlation (p) and Pearson correlation (r) coefficients between human judgements and predicted faithfulness scores. Results are reported in Table 2.

On the XSUM dataset, BERTScore achieves the highest correlation with human judgements. Entailment, SentSim and SRL perform similarly. On the SummEval dataset, SentSim and Entailment achieve the best correlation with human judgements. Open IE is last in both rankings.

Comparing XSUM and SummEval, there is a huge performance difference. This reason is twofold: First, we developed and optimized the metrics with the XSUM dataset in mind and checked other available datasets to test the generalizability later. Second, there is a huge methodical difference between the XSUM and SummEval faithfulness annotations. In the XSUM hallucination dataset, annotators worked closely with the text annotating unfaithful passages, whereas in SummEval, annotators used Likert scales, a more distant approach. To exemplify this difference, consider the two sentences "I love you" vs. "I hate you". Using a Likert scale, annotators would most likely rate the summary 1 or 2 (faithfulness score $\leq$ 25%). When using span annotations, the only unfaithful word is "hate", resulting in a faithfulness score of 66%. Both approaches are valid, but for our experiments and quantitative analysis, we stick with the closer, span-annotation-based faithfulness computation.

Method (on XSUM)	Pearson (r)	Spearman (p)
BERTScore	**0.501**	**0.486**
Entailment	0.366	0.422
SentSim	0.392	0.389
SRL	0.393	0.377
NER	0.252	0.259
QGQA	0.228	0.258
Open IE	0.169	0.185
Method (on SummEval)	Pearson (r)	Spearman (p)
SentSim	**0.24**	**0.24**
Entailment	0.22	0.22
BERTScore	0.17	0.17
QGQA	0.13	0.13
SRL	0.13	0.13
NER	0.12	0.12
Open IE	0.10	0.10

Table 2: Pearson (r) and Spearman (p) correlation coefficients for faithfulness measured between human faithfulness judgements and different automatic methods.

Method	Correct	Delta
Random	50.0%	0
NER	29.5%	-20.5
Open IE	49.0%	-1
ESIM (Falke et al., 2019)	67.6%	+17.6
SRL	69.4%	+19.4
SentSim	69.7%	+19.7
FactCC (Kryscinski et al., 2020)	70.0%	+20
QGQA	71.9%	+21.9
BERTScore	77.5%	+27.5
Entailment	**88.5%**	**+38.5**
Human (Falke et al., 2019)	83.9%	+33.9

Table 3: Results on the sentence re-ranking experiment. Human performance was crowd-sourced. Ties are counted as incorrect predictions.

We also evaluate all faithfulness metrics on the sentence re-ranking experiment by Falke et al. (2019). This dataset contains contains 373 triples, each triple consists of a source sentence and two summary sentences. Source sentences are taken from the CNN/DailyMail dataset, summary sentences are generated by the summarization model from Chen and Bansal (2018). One summary sentence is faithful to the source sentence, whereas the other summary sentence is factually inconsistent.

We test how often a metric prefers the correct sentence i.e. gives a higher score to the faithful sentence. Results are shown in Table 3.

Entailment distinguishes best between unfaithful and faithful sentences, achieving 88.5% correct predictions outperforming even human performance. All other faithfulness metrics perform in a comparable range on this task, ranking about 70% example sentences correctly. The only exceptions are Open IE and NER. Both metrics perform worse than Random. We qualitatively find that, in almost every example, the entities mentioned in the summary sentences are also present in the source sentence explaining the poor ranking performance.

Finally, in our search for the best faithfulness metric, we experiment with combining multiple metrics. Since the discussed faithfulness metrics compare fairly different information (tokens, entities, answers to questions etc.), we believe a combination of metrics can lead to a better faithfulness assessment. We correlate all faithfulness metrics with each other using the XSUM hallucination dataset. The results are shown in Figure 1, indicating that a combination of BERTScore, QGQA and either Entailment or NER is promising.

Data to learn a reliable combination of metrics is not available, since manual faithfulness evaluation is time-consuming and expensive. Still, to analyze the effectiveness of combining metrics, we learn a linear combination of multiple metrics with 10-fold cross-validation on the XSUM hallucination dataset. Table 4 shows combining BERTScore, Entailment and QGQA achieves an average Spearman correlation of 0.559, which is a relative improvement of 15% over BERTScore, combining all metrics leads to a relative improvement of 20%.

5 RQ2: Error Analysis of faithfulness metrics

In order to reveal weaknesses and room for improvement, we investigated outputs for 100 randomly selected source-summary pairs of the XSUM hallucination dataset per metric, of which 50 are underprediction cases and 50 are overprediction cases. A detailed breakdown of the most prevalent error categories (E1 - E37) and their relative frequency is shown in Table 5 for all metrics. To set these errors in perspective, Figure 2 visualizes how often, and by how much a metric over- and underpredicts. BERTScore, for example, is much more prone to overpredicting (75%), indicating that these errors are more critical. Next, we discuss ideas to tackle some of the found problems.

The F1 similarity metric is used in many faithfulness metrics (QGQA, SentSim, OpenIE) because it leads to best correlation with human faithfulness.

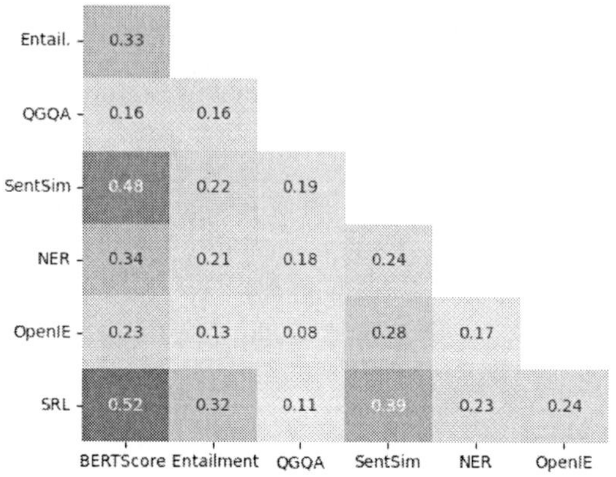

Figure 1: Spearman correlation of faithfulness metrics with each other computed on the XSUM hallucination dataset.

Combination	Correlation
1· BERTScore (BS)	0.485
1.5· BS +0.1· NER	0.493
1.5· BS +0.26· QGQA	0.514
1.3· BS +0.26· Entailment	0.535
1.3· BS +0.24· Entailment +0.24· QGQA	0.559
0.86· BS +0.22· Entailment +0.03· NER +0.21· QGQA + 0.3· SRL +0.34· SS	0.582

Table 4: Averaged Spearman correlations of linear metric combinations with human faithfulness judgements.

This metric performs exact match on a token-level, which comes with many disadvantages: it fails to match synonyms (Error 12 in Table 5), does not comprehend meaning (E14, E29) and stopwords can falsify its results (E24). Further, less frequent errors include inability to correctly compare abbreviations (e.g. "GB" with "Great Britain"), singular and plural (e.g. "men" with "man"), generalizations (e.g. "save 5$" with "save money"),

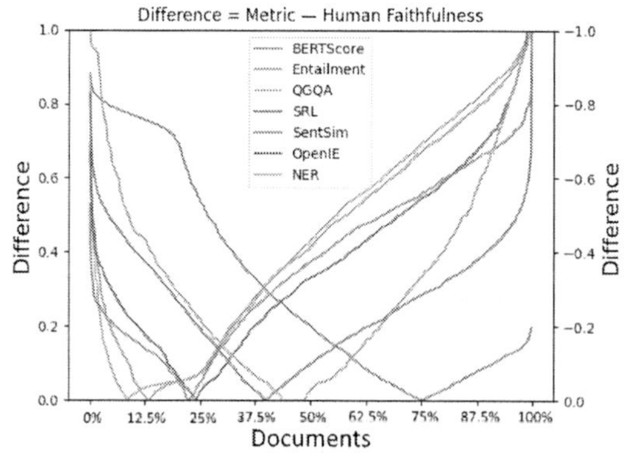

Figure 2: Differences between human and metric faithfulness predictions. Documents and their corresponding difference are sorted in descending order per metric.

locations (e.g. "London" with "England") and e.g. "pharmaceutical firm" with "Accord Healthcare" as it lacks background knowledge. A possible solution is to replace F1 with a metric that has background knowledge and can deal with paraphrases, like BERTScore.

However, the error analysis revealed that BERTScore, which aligns and compares token embeddings, tends to assign too high similarities to phrases that appear in different contexts and to negations, opposites, and contradictions as well as to different numbers. For example, whether someone was jailed for 4 or 7 years makes no difference to BERTScore (similarity of 97%). Currently, BERTScore operates on contextualized embeddings. Paraphrases and synonyms are used in similar context, thus, their embeddings are similar. But, negations, opposites and contradictions typically appear in similar contexts as well, which leads to some of BERTScores problems. Using contrastive embeddings where opposites are distant in the embedding space is a promising direction.

QGQA struggles with questions having not enough variation (E7) or targeting irrelevant information (E9). Questions are generated by providing a model with text and answer candidate, thus, developing an answer candidate selection method that focuses on critical parts of the summary can solve these issues. Further, some generated questions are not answerable, but the QA model finds answers anyway (E8). Here, a QA model that can output "NO ANSWER" is a possible solution.

NER often finds no entities at all (E17) or not enough entities (E20) for the following reason: generated summaries are written in lowercase only. However, one important feature of NER models is capitalization, leading to either not finding entities or incorrect entity labels (E22). Applying a re-capitalization model to generated summaries before extracting entities seems promising.

OpenIE suffers mostly from triples not covering important information (E25). By definition, Open IE triples should cover subject, predicate, object which will always lead to a sentence (or subsentence) representation that misses information. In its current state, we do not think OpenIE is a suitable method to assess faithfulness. Instead, SRL is a solid alternative as these models predict more detailed labels (e.g. who, what, whom, why etc.).

SRL uses cosine similarity of phrase embeddings to align and compare phrases with similar semantics. Similar to BERTScore, cosine similarity of phrases tends to be too high (E30), despite different contexts (E31). We calculate embeddings per phrase and, thus, the remaining sentence has no influence on phrase embeddings. Including more context to the phrase embedding calculations could help issue E31. Other issues attribute to SRL labels. The SRL model predicts wrong labels (E33) or similar summary and source phrases have different labels (E37). We already group SRL labels as described in Section 3.7 to increase robustness and number of matches. Refining this grouping with aid of experts could be beneficial.

The current protocol of SentSim, aligning and comparing one summary with one source sentence, is not a good fit to assess faithfulness (E16). A sophisticated approach that splits sentences into clauses and compares them seems more suitable.

Entailment calculates the entailment probability of a summary sentence given the source document. Analyzing this metric posed quite the challenge as its calculations are in-transparent. We found that verbs have most impact on the predictions: whenever a verb is not entailed, the metric predicts very low scores (E5). Cases where mostly the verbs are unfaithful are problematic as human faithfulness is usually high for summaries that contain few unfaithful words.

6 Conclusion

We re-implemented, modified and proposed new metrics to assess faithfulness of automatically generated summaries. Next, we conducted several experiments and found that BERTscore and Entailment correlate with human judgements and are able to successfully re-rank sentences. In a comprehensive error analysis, we revealed common problems of faithfulness metrics and identified possible solutions to their most prevalent issues. We want to highlight that the discussed metrics do not seem to generalize well to other datasets and cannot replace human faithfulness evaluation yet.

With this work, we laid a solid basis for further development and improvement on faithfulness metrics. We also released an open-source library including all discussed metrics to encourage further experimentation and to facilitate evaluation.

In further work, we experiment with contrastive embeddings and combine multiple metrics to improve performance. Also, we collect new faithfulness datasets to build metrics that generalize well.

#	BERTScore Errors	Over	Under
1	Phrases or entities appearing in different context have too high similarity	45%	-
2	Negations, opposites and contradictions have too high similarity	24%	-
3	Different numbers (amounts, counts, money, age, dates etc.) have too high similarity	13%	-
4	Arbitrarily assembled compound nouns have high faithfulness *e.g. "Macedonia's Prime Minister Justin Riot"*	8%	-
#	**Entailment Errors**	Over	Under
5	Faithful phrases connected by unfaithful verbs drastically reduce the score Summary: *Moscow imposed sanctions on Turkey.* Score: *0%* Src: *Russia suspended all sanctions against Turkey.*	-	52%
6	Robustness: summary contains grammatical errors or word repetitions	-	18%
#	**QGQA Errors**	Over	Under
7	Questions do not have enough variation (target the same information, are similar, too few)	44%	48%
8	Question is not answerable, but an answer matching the unfaithful summary is found anyway *Q: Which county has signed Colin? Src: Worcestershire signed John. A: Worcestershire*	32%	-
9	Questions target irrelevant information (answers do not help to assess the faithfulness of the text)	12%	12%
10	QA component cannot find the correct answer	-	36%
11	Question is unanswerable (since no answer can be found, faithfulness decreases)	-	24%
12	F1 answer similarity fails to match correct answers *e.g. "optometrist"* vs. *"eye specialist"* or *"a number of whales"* vs. *"thirty six whales"*	-	44%
#	**SentSim Errors**	Over	Under
13	Stopwords increase the similarity (faithfulness based on stopwords or incorrect alignment)	52%	-
14	F1 does not comprehend meaning (different terms mean the same, or vice versa) *"police appeal for witnesses"* vs. *"anyone with information can call 101"*	14%	36%
15	Summary sentence paraphrases multiple sentences. Comparing with one sentence is insufficient.	32%	56%
16	Erroneous sentence splitting (information is wrongly split into multiple sentences)	-	12%
#	**NER Errors**	Over	Under
17	No entities in the summary (faithfulness defaults to 100%)	50%	-
18	No source entities with corresponding tag to summary entity (→ not considered in calculation)	16%	-
19	Entities match correctly, but faithfulness is not related to entities	14%	30%
20	Important entities not found in summary and / or source (*e.g. Leukaemia not detected as entity*)	26%	61%
21	Tokenization problems lead to incorrect entities (*e.g. 1.5million = 1[Money].5m[Quantity]*)	-	12%
22	Incorrect entity labels (*e.g. World is labeled as Person*)	-	12%
23	Similarity of different mentions of same entity is low (*e.g. "Myles Anderson"* vs. *"Anderson"*)	-	24%
#	**OpenIE Error**	Over	Under
24	Stopwords increase the similarity of completely different triples	40%	-
25	Summary triples miss important information (dates, locations, etc.) *e.g. a man | has been | found* instead of *a man | has been found guilty | of murdering a soldier* *"More than a third of children in the UK have been sexually abused" → Children | in | UK*	44%	52%
26	Faithful information of source document not part of a triple	-	26%
27	Summary is too abstract (highly paraphrased, aggregate information of multiple sentences)	-	20%
28	Summary has no triples	-	16%
29	F1 does not comprehend meaning (different terms mean the same, or vice versa)	-	8%
#	**SRL Errors**	Over	Under
30	Similarity of (apparently randomly) aligned phrases is incomprehensibly high	44%	-
31	Single word phrases match exactly with other single word phrases, but context is different	28%	-
32	Similarity of detailed, information-rich summary phrases and simple source phrases is too high *e.g. "Double olympic champion Nicola Adams"* is very similar to *"Adams"*	16%	-
33	SRL model errors (incorrect labels, incorrect split of phrases, incorrect grouping of phrases) *e.g. "IS"* (abbreviation of islamic state) or *"united"* of *"Manchester United"* is labeled as verb	12%	-
34	Important information is not part of a phrase and cannot be considered in faithfulness calculation	16%	-
35	Summary phrases are coarse grained. Split into smaller phrases necessary to validate faithfulness	-	40%
36	Summary is too abstract (understanding of whole text necessary to validate faithfulness) *e.g.* summary presents the result of a soccer match, source is soccer live ticker	-	24%
37	Faithful phrases have different tags in summary & source and, thus, are not aligned & compared	-	32%

Table 5: Quantitative error analysis of 100 randomly selected examples of the XSUM hallucination dataset for all faithfulness metrics, of which 50 are underprediction (Under) and 50 are overprediction (Over) cases.

References

Gabor Angeli, Melvin Jose Johnson Premkumar, and Christopher D. Manning. 2015. Leveraging linguistic structure for open domain information extraction. In *Proceedings of the 53rd Annual Meeting of the Association for Computational Linguistics and the 7th International Joint Conference on Natural Language Processing (Volume 1: Long Papers)*, pages 344–354, Beijing, China. Association for Computational Linguistics.

Satanjeev Banerjee and Alon Lavie. 2005. METEOR: An automatic metric for MT evaluation with improved correlation with human judgments. In *Proceedings of the ACL Workshop on Intrinsic and Extrinsic Evaluation Measures for Machine Translation and/or Summarization*, pages 65–72, Ann Arbor, Michigan. Association for Computational Linguistics.

Ziqiang Cao, Furu Wei, Wenjie Li, and Sujian Li. 2018. Faithful to the original: Fact aware neural abstractive summarization. In *Proceedings of the 32th AAAI Conference on Artificial Intelligence*, pages 4784–4791, New Orleans, Louisiana, USA.

Yen-Chun Chen and Mohit Bansal. 2018. Fast abstractive summarization with reinforce-selected sentence rewriting. In *Proceedings of the 56th Annual Meeting of the Association for Computational Linguistics (Volume 1: Long Papers)*, pages 675–686, Melbourne, Australia. Association for Computational Linguistics.

Ido Dagan, Oren Glickman, and Bernardo Magnini. 2005. The pascal recognising textual entailment challenge. In *Proceedings of the First International Conference on Machine Learning Challenges: Evaluating Predictive Uncertainty Visual Object Classification, and Recognizing Textual Entailment*, page 177–190.

Yue Dong, Shuohang Wang, Zhe Gan, Yu Cheng, Jackie Chi Kit Cheung, and Jingjing Liu. 2020. Multi-fact correction in abstractive text summarization. In *Proceedings of the 2020 Conference on Empirical Methods in Natural Language Processing (EMNLP)*, pages 9320–9331, Online. Association for Computational Linguistics.

Esin Durmus, He He, and Mona Diab. 2020. FEQA: A question answering evaluation framework for faithfulness assessment in abstractive summarization. In *Proceedings of the 58th Annual Meeting of the Association for Computational Linguistics*, pages 5055–5070, Online. Association for Computational Linguistics.

Alexander R. Fabbri, Wojciech Kryscinski, Bryan McCann, Caiming Xiong, Richard Socher, and Dragomir R. Radev. 2021. Summeval: Re-evaluating summarization evaluation. *Trans. Assoc. Comput. Linguistics*, 9:391–409.

Tobias Falke, Leonardo F. R. Ribeiro, Prasetya Ajie Utama, Ido Dagan, and Iryna Gurevych. 2019. Ranking generated summaries by correctness: An interesting but challenging application for natural language inference. In *Proceedings of the 57th Annual Meeting of the Association for Computational Linguistics*, pages 2214–2220, Florence, Italy. Association for Computational Linguistics.

Matt Gardner, Joel Grus, Mark Neumann, Oyvind Tafjord, Pradeep Dasigi, Nelson F. Liu, Matthew Peters, Michael Schmitz, and Luke Zettlemoyer. 2018. AllenNLP: A deep semantic natural language processing platform. In *Proceedings of Workshop for NLP Open Source Software (NLP-OSS)*, pages 1–6, Melbourne, Australia. Association for Computational Linguistics.

Ben Goodrich, Vinay Rao, Peter J. Liu, and Mohammad Saleh. 2019. Assessing the factual accuracy of generated text. In *Proceedings of the 25th International Conference on Knowledge Discovery + Data Mining*, page 166–175, New York, New York, USA.

Karl Moritz Hermann, Tomas Kocisky, Edward Grefenstette, Lasse Espeholt, Will Kay, Mustafa Suleyman, and Phil Blunsom. 2015. Teaching machines to read and comprehend. In *Advances in Neural Information Processing Systems*, volume 28, page 1693–1701.

Eduard Hovy, Mitchell Marcus, Martha Palmer, Lance Ramshaw, and Ralph Weischedel. 2006. OntoNotes: The 90% solution. In *Proceedings of the Human Language Technology Conference of the NAACL, Companion Volume: Short Papers*, pages 57–60, New York City, USA. Association for Computational Linguistics.

Wojciech Kryscinski, Nitish Shirish Keskar, Bryan McCann, Caiming Xiong, and Richard Socher. 2019. Neural text summarization: A critical evaluation. In *Proceedings of the 2019 Conference on Empirical Methods in Natural Language Processing and the 9th International Joint Conference on Natural Language Processing (EMNLP-IJCNLP)*, pages 540–551, Hong Kong, China. Association for Computational Linguistics.

Wojciech Kryscinski, Bryan McCann, Caiming Xiong, and Richard Socher. 2020. Evaluating the factual consistency of abstractive text summarization. In *Proceedings of the 2020 Conference on Empirical Methods in Natural Language Processing (EMNLP)*, pages 9332–9346, Online. Association for Computational Linguistics.

Logan Lebanoff, John Muchovej, Franck Dernoncourt, Doo Soon Kim, Seokhwan Kim, Walter Chang, and Fei Liu. 2019. Analyzing sentence fusion in abstractive summarization. In *Proceedings of the 2nd Workshop on New Frontiers in Summarization*, pages 104–110, Hong Kong, China. Association for Computational Linguistics.

Mike Lewis, Yinhan Liu, Naman Goyal, Marjan Ghazvininejad, Abdelrahman Mohamed, Omer Levy,

Veselin Stoyanov, and Luke Zettlemoyer. 2020. BART: Denoising sequence-to-sequence pre-training for natural language generation, translation, and comprehension. In *Proceedings of the 58th Annual Meeting of the Association for Computational Linguistics*, pages 7871–7880, Online. Association for Computational Linguistics.

Chin-Yew Lin. 2004. ROUGE: A package for automatic evaluation of summaries. In *Text Summarization Branches Out*, pages 74–81, Barcelona, Spain. Association for Computational Linguistics.

Yinhan Liu, Myle Ott, Naman Goyal, Jingfei Du, Mandar Joshi, Danqi Chen, Omer Levy, Mike Lewis, Luke Zettlemoyer, and Veselin Stoyanov. 2019. Roberta: A robustly optimized bert pretraining approach. Computation and Language repository, arXiv:1907.11692.

Chi-kiu Lo. 2019. YiSi - a unified semantic MT quality evaluation and estimation metric for languages with different levels of available resources. In *Proceedings of the Fourth Conference on Machine Translation (Volume 2: Shared Task Papers, Day 1)*, pages 507–513, Florence, Italy. Association for Computational Linguistics.

Joshua Maynez, Shashi Narayan, Bernd Bohnet, and Ryan McDonald. 2020. On faithfulness and factuality in abstractive summarization. In *Proceedings of the 58th Annual Meeting of the Association for Computational Linguistics*, pages 1906–1919, Online. Association for Computational Linguistics.

Feng Nan, Ramesh Nallapati, Zhiguo Wang, Cicero Nogueira dos Santos, Henghui Zhu, Dejiao Zhang, Kathleen McKeown, and Bing Xiang. 2021. Entity-level factual consistency of abstractive text summarization. In *Proceedings of the 16th Conference of the European Chapter of the Association for Computational Linguistics: Main Volume*, pages 2727–2733, Online. Association for Computational Linguistics.

Shashi Narayan, Shay B. Cohen, and Mirella Lapata. 2018. Don't give me the details, just the summary! topic-aware convolutional neural networks for extreme summarization. In *Proceedings of the 2018 Conference on Empirical Methods in Natural Language Processing*, pages 1797–1807, Brussels, Belgium. Association for Computational Linguistics.

Kishore Papineni, Salim Roukos, Todd Ward, and Wei-Jing Zhu. 2002. Bleu: a method for automatic evaluation of machine translation. In *Proceedings of the 40th Annual Meeting of the Association for Computational Linguistics*, pages 311–318, Philadelphia, Pennsylvania, USA. Association for Computational Linguistics.

Pranav Rajpurkar, Robin Jia, and Percy Liang. 2018. Know what you don't know: Unanswerable questions for SQuAD. In *Proceedings of the 56th Annual Meeting of the Association for Computational Linguistics (Volume 2: Short Papers)*, pages 784–789, Melbourne, Australia. Association for Computational Linguistics.

Peng Shi and Jimmy Lin. 2019. Simple bert models for relation extraction and semantic role labeling. Computation and Language repository, arXiv:1904.05255.

Alex Wang, Kyunghyun Cho, and Mike Lewis. 2020. Asking and answering questions to evaluate the factual consistency of summaries. In *Proceedings of the 58th Annual Meeting of the Association for Computational Linguistics*, pages 5008–5020, Online. Association for Computational Linguistics.

Adina Williams, Nikita Nangia, and Samuel Bowman. 2018. A broad-coverage challenge corpus for sentence understanding through inference. In *Proceedings of the 2018 Conference of the North American Chapter of the Association for Computational Linguistics: Human Language Technologies, Volume 1 (Long Papers)*, pages 1112–1122, New Orleans, Louisiana. Association for Computational Linguistics.

Thomas Wolf, Lysandre Debut, Victor Sanh, Julien Chaumond, Clement Delangue, Anthony Moi, Pierric Cistac, Tim Rault, Remi Louf, Morgan Funtowicz, Joe Davison, Sam Shleifer, Patrick von Platen, Clara Ma, Yacine Jernite, Julien Plu, Canwen Xu, Teven Le Scao, Sylvain Gugger, Mariama Drame, Quentin Lhoest, and Alexander Rush. 2020. Transformers: State-of-the-art natural language processing. In *Proceedings of the 2020 Conference on Empirical Methods in Natural Language Processing: System Demonstrations*, pages 38–45, Online. Association for Computational Linguistics.

Jingqing Zhang, Yao Zhao, Mohammad Saleh, and Peter J. Liu. 2019. Pegasus: Pre-training with extracted gap-sentences for abstractive summarization. In *Proceedings of the 37th International Conference on Machine Learning*, pages 11328–11339, Vienna, Austria.

Tianyi Zhang, Varsha Kishore, Felix Wu, Kilian Q. Weinberger, and Yoav Artzi. 2020a. Bertscore: Evaluating text generation with bert. In *Proceedings of the 8th International Conference on Learning Representations*, Accepted as poster. Online.

Yuhao Zhang, Derek Merck, Emily Tsai, Christopher D. Manning, and Curtis Langlotz. 2020b. Optimizing the factual correctness of a summary: A study of summarizing radiology reports. In *Proceedings of the 58th Annual Meeting of the Association for Computational Linguistics*, pages 5108–5120, Online. Association for Computational Linguistics.

Chenguang Zhu, William Hinthorn, Ruochen Xu, Qingkai Zeng, Michael Zeng, Xuedong Huang, and Meng Jiang. 2021. Enhancing factual consistency of abstractive summarization. In *Proceedings of the 2021 Conference of the North American Chapter of the Association for Computational Linguistics: Human Language Technologies*, pages 718–733, Online. Association for Computational Linguistics.

A Appendix

A.1 Comparing texts

Most faithfulness metrics introduced in Section 3 compare texts to compute the faithfulness score. We experiment with various similarity metrics to implement the faithfulness metrics and evaluate them on the XSUM hallucination dataset (Table 7 and the sentence re-ranking experiment (Table 8). The cosine-similarity (CS) metric is calculated on sentence embeddings generated by off-the-shelf sentence-transformers[5]. We find using F1 in QGQA is the best trade-off between performance and computation time. SRL performs best with CS. Depending on the task, NER performs best with either F1 or CS. Both, SentSim and Open IE perform best with either F1 or BERTScore.

A.2 Input for textual entailment

We evaluate different input techniques (sentence-to-sentences (s2s), document-to-sentence(d2s), top-to-sentence (top2s) for an entailment model on the XSUM hallucination dataset and find that d2s works best as shown in Table 6.

Method	Pearson (r)	Spearman (p)
s2s	0.152	0.190
d2s	**0.366**	**0.422**
top2s	0.251	0.302

Table 6: Evaluation of different input techniques for entailment models. The table lists correlations with human faithfulness judgements.

Method	Similarity	Pearson (r)	Spearman (p)
QGQA	EM	0.200	0.226
QGQA	F1	0.228	0.258
QGQA	**BERTScore**	**0.252**	**0.258**
QGQA	CS	0.216	0.222
NER	EM	0.251	0.255
NER	**F1**	**0.252**	**0.259**
NER	BERTScore	0.151	0.195
NER	CS	0.200	0.204
SRL	EM	0.234	0.273
SRL	F1	0.359	0.363
SRL	BERTScore	0.270	0.344
SRL	**CS**	**0.393**	**0.377**
SentSim	EM	-0.039	-0.039
SentSim	**F1**	**0.392**	**0.389**
SentSim	BERTScore	0.374	0.372
SentSim	CS	0.387	0.369
Open IE	EM	0.042	0.076
Open IE	**F1**	**0.169**	**0.185**
Open IE	BERTScore	0.013	0.212
Open IE	CS	0.134	0.186

Table 7: Comparison of different similarity metrics used in various faithfulness metrics. The table lists correlations with human faithfulness judgements. We experiment with Exact Match (EM), F1 (on token-level), BERTScore and cosine-similarity of embeddings (CS).

Method	**Similarity**	**Correct**
QGQA	EM	67.29%
QGQA	F1	68.36%
QGQA	BERTScore	69.17%
QGQA	**CS**	**69.71%**
NER	EM	18.50%
NER	F1	18.50%
NER	BERTScore	26.54%
NER	**CS**	**29.49%**
SRL	EM	50.67%
SRL	F1	66.76%
SRL	BERTScore	67.83%
SRL	**CS**	**69.44%**
SentSim	EM	2.95%
SentSim	F1	56.03%
SentSim	**BERTScore**	**69.71%**
SentSim	CS	68.36%
Open IE	EM	26.27%
Open IE	F1	46.11%
Open IE	**BERTScore**	**49.06%**
Open IE	CS	47.99%
Open IE	RMR1	21.98%
Open IE	RMR2	26.27%

Table 8: Comparison of different similarity metrics used in various faithfulness metrics evaluated on the sentence ranking experiment from Falke et al. (2019). We experiment with Exact Match (EM), F1 (on token-level), BERTScore and cosine-similarity of embeddings (CS).

[5]https://www.sbert.net/index.html

Proceedings of the 18th Conference on Natural Language Processing (KONVENS 2022)

Sentiment Analysis on Twitter for the Major German Parties during the 2021 German Federal Election

Thomas Schmidt
Media Informatics Group
University of Regensburg
Regensburg, Germany
thomas.schmidt@ur.de

Jakob Fehle
Media Informatics Group
University of Regensburg
Regensburg, Germany
jakob.fehle@ur.de

Maximilian Weissenbacher
Media Informatics Group
University of Regensburg
Regensburg, Germany
maximilian.weissenbacher@ur.de

Jonathan Richter
Media Informatics Group
University of Regensburg
Regensburg, Germany
jonathan.richter@ur.de

Philipp Gottschalk
Media Informatics Group
University of Regensburg
Regensburg, Germany
philipp.gottschalk@ur.de

Christian Wolff
Media Informatics Group
University of Regensburg
Regensburg, Germany
christian.wolff@ur.de

Abstract

We present the results of a project performing sentiment analysis on tweets from German politicians and party accounts for the 2021 German federal election. We collected over 58,000 tweets from the Twitter accounts of the seven parties represented in the German Bundestag, of which a selection of 2,000 tweets were annotated by three annotators. Based on the annotated data, we implemented multiple sentiment analysis approaches and evaluated the sentiment classification performance. We found that transformer-based models like bidirectional encoder from transformers (BERT) performed better than traditional machine learning models such as Naive Bayes and lexicon-based models like GerVADER. The best performing BERT model achieved an accuracy of 93.3% and macro f1 score of 93.4%. Applying sentiment analysis on the overall corpus via this method showed that overall, negative sentiment was most frequent and that there were multiple major shifts in sentiment a few months before and after the election. Furthermore, we found that tweets from opposition parties had on average more negative sentiment than those from governing parties.

1 Introduction

The 2021 federal election in Germany led to a dramatic change in power of the leading parties. Angela Merkel's chancellorship and the reign of the CDU (Christlich Demokratische Union) came to an end after 16 years and a new coalition now forms the government (see table A.1 in the appendix for election results). Whereas former election campaigns only took place in the real world through posters and election events, ever since the rise of social media, campaigns additionally focus on gaining support on the internet (Freelon, 2017). During elections, politicians of all parties are strategic actors focused on gaining voters' support (Druckman et al., 2010). Besides online advertisements, political discussions via social media have gained more and more importance. This is a worldwide phenomenon but can especially be seen in the United States (Tumasjan et al., 2010) where former president Donald Trump used Twitter almost on a daily basis to share his opinion on a wide variety of topics. Twitter is a micro-blogging platform and one of the most popular social-media channels for online communication. Sharing content takes place in form of a short text, limited to 280 characters, which is called a tweet. Twitter has become an important platform for research in computational social science and a source for research conducting sentiment analysis (Drus and Khalid, 2019). Sentiment analysis is the computational method to predict the sentiment, attitude or opinion of media, predominantly text (Liu, 2015). It is often regarded as a classification task with the categories positive, neutral and negative (Wagh et al., 2018). Sentiment analysis can also be differentiated into three different description levels: document level, sentence level, feature level (Liu, 2015). In this study, we are focusing on complete tweets as level of analysis (i.e. sentiment analysis on document level). There are a variety of methods to perform sentiment analysis ranging from rule-based approaches to the application of transformer-based language models (Drus and Khalid, 2019; Guhr et al., 2020).

In this study, we analyze the social media behaviour of German politicians and parties during the federal election of 2021 by applying sentiment analysis on the tweets of the entire election year for a selection of party accounts (58,864 tweets). The goal of this work is to gain insights about political parties' sentiment during the election year 2021. Our research questions are as follows:

- What is the best performing sentiment analysis technique in this use case of political tweets in regards to common methods and state-of-the-art recommendations?
- How does the sentiment of parties expressed in tweets differ from each other in general and with respect to government/opposition and election winner/loser relations?
- How does the sentiment of parties expressed in tweets change across the election year?

Our main contributions to the research area are as follows:

- The acquisition and preparation of all tweets of 89 Twitter accounts for the year 2021 of the most important German political parties (58,864 tweets)
- The annotation of a subset of 2,000 tweets with sentiment information for evaluation and machine learning (ML) purposes
- The implementation and evaluation of a lexicon-based approach, sentiment analysis based on traditional machine learning and the application of a large German BERT model on our annotated data set and a larger additional corpus
- The investigation of the above research questions applying the best performing sentiment model on our overall corpus

We release our annotated data sets and best performing model as well as additional data and visualizations via GitHub [1] to support further research. We apply the best performing model on our overall corpus to investigate the proposed research questions.

[1] https://github.com/lauchblatt/Twitter_German_Federal_Election_2021

2 Related Work

Ever since the rise of social media, sentiment analysis on social media platforms is a very active research area (Wang et al., 2012; Elbagir and Yang, 2019). Sentiment analysis is used, for example, to explore sentiment in *Reddit* forums (Schmidt et al., 2020c; Moßburger et al., 2020), on Twitter (Elbagir and Yang, 2019) or social media artefacts like memes (Schmidt et al., 2020b). In the following chapters, we summarize important research in the context of political analysis on Twitter and offer an overview of current sentiment analysis methodology.

2.1 Sentiment Analysis on Twitter for Political Research

Research in political sentiment analysis on Twitter differs between the analysis of accounts of political actors and the analysis of public sentiment towards political events or actors. As examples for the latter, Bermingham and Smeaton (2011) investigated whether it is possible to predict the election results for the Irish general election 2011. The results showed that the analysis of sentiment indeed offers predictive qualities. Furthermore, there was a big sentiment-shift two days before the election day which already gave indications on the election results. In similar research for India, Sharma and Moh (2016) showed that parties which were mentioned in tweets with a positive sentiment are more likely to win election votes than parties with a negative sentiment.

Considering the analysis of political actors, Tumasjan et al. (2010) analyzed the sentiment during the German federal election in 2009. For politicians and parties they discovered that the politicians' sentiment profiles reflected different nuances of the election campaign. Furthermore, polarizing politicians from the opposition showed inversed sentiment. Budiharto and Meiliana (2018) focused on the Indonesian presidential candidates and were able to predict popularity with various Twitter metrics including results of sentiment analysis. Recently Costa et al. (2021) analyzed the communication of parties and their sentiments in Portugal in one year. When comparing the results, the authors found a great variability between the parties. They revealed that the party being at the opposition had the most positive sentiment profile and the right wing generally expressed more positive sentiment than the left wing.

Overall, research shows that sentiment analysis of political actors and the public on Twitter can serve as source of analysis and predictor of popularity. Similar to previous research, we will focus on the identification of sentiment shifts and differences among parties.

2.2 Methods for Sentiment Analysis

Large transformer-based language models like BERT and ELECTRA are currently considered state-of-the-art for sentiment analysis tasks (Qiu et al., 2020; Chouikhi et al., 2021; Chan et al., 2020) and outperform traditional ML approaches using Naive Bayes or Support Vector Machines (SVM) (Geetha and Renuka, 2021). The large German language model *gbert* by *deepset* outperforms other models on a variety of tasks including sentiment analysis (Chan et al., 2020).

Nevertheless, another type of regularly used sentiment analysis approaches are lexicon-based methods. Lexicon-based sentiment analysis is a rule-based method using a dictionary, in which words with positive and negative connotations are stored.The basic idea is that the majority of the occurring words (or their values) of a class decides about the classification of a text unit, e.g. if predominantly positive connoted words occur in the text, it will be classified as positive (Jurek et al., 2015; Schmidt et al., 2021a). This branch of rule-based methods, while being outperformed by ML approaches in most settings, is still popular and common for German language research (Fehle et al., 2021). Lexicon-based methods are often applied in settings that lack annotated corpora and ML possibilities in German like literary texts (Schmidt and Burghardt, 2018; Schmidt et al., 2020a) or in human-computer interaction (Ortloff et al., 2019; Schmidt et al., 2020d). Thus we included this method in our evaluation. Indeed, in the context of the U.S. presidential elections 2016, the well-known lexicon-based sentiment analysis module VADER (Hutto and Gilbert, 2014) was used for the analysis of tweets (Elbagir and Yang, 2019). Besides lexicon-based methods, traditional ML approaches have also been used in research of political tweet analysis (Bermingham and Smeaton, 2011; Sharma and Moh, 2016). Traditional ML approaches follow a two-step process, which first extracts manually annotated features from the tweet to subsequently feed them into a classifier, e.g. SVM, which in turn makes predictions on novel (or unseen) data (Minaee et al., 2021). While transformer-based models have shown to outperform the aforementioned methods, we also implemented examples of lexicon-based methods and traditional ML to serve as baselines.

3 Methods

3.1 Data Acquisition

We gathered tweets from the seven parties currently represented in the German Bundestag for an entire year. For each party, we selected the ten most relevant politicians (according to their Twitter follower count) as well as the three largest official party-accounts (as of January 2022), which are mostly the national or regional party accounts (see Fig. 7 and Fig. 8 in the appendix for the full list of accounts). This results to tweets by 89 Twitter accounts (the party-accounts for the parties CDU and CSU were summarized to 4 accounts). In the following we do however report results for 6 parties by combining the tweets by CDU and CSU since both parties are in political proximity and the CSU is basically the Bavarian representative of the party. We used the *Scweet* (Jeddi and Bengadi, 2022) package for the acquisition of tweets, which downloads tweets from specific accounts and stores them in a CSV-File. For the data collection, we set the time frame to January 2021 to December 2021 to cover a large period before the election on September 26th as well as several months after the election. Tweet replies or retweets were not taken into account to obtain only those tweets that were written by the respective user themselves and thus contain the user's own wording and sentiment. The final tweet corpus contains of 58,864 distinct tweets. Table 1 summarizes general corpus statistics and further party information. The corpus consists of over 3 million tokens. A tweet consists on average of 53 tokens and the number of tweets per party differ with the AfD having the most tweets and the FDP the fewest.

3.2 Data Annotation

We selected a subset of 2,000 tweets using stratified (in respect to the proportion of tweets per party) random sampling to create an annotated sub corpus to use for evaluation and machine learning purposes. Each tweet was annotated by three annotators independently from each other. The annotators were three native-speaking students or research assistants respectively. We created an annotation

Partei	political orientation	pre-election	post-election	# tweets	%	# tokens	avg. tweet length
AfD	far right	opposition	opposition	11,625	20	592,828	51.00
CDU/CSU	center right	government	opposition	10,072	17	512,803	50.91
Die Linke	far left	opposition	opposition	9,628	16	522,322	54.25
FDP	liberal	opposition	government	6,610	11	356,789	53.98
Die Grünen	left, ecological	opposition	government	9,576	16	537,408	56.12
SPD	center left	government	government	11,353	19	623,572	54.93
Absolute	-	-	-	58,864	100	3,145,722	53.44

Table 1: General corpus statistics of the overall tweet corpus.

manual with examples and instructions for the annotation of a tweet to ensure consistent annotation. Annotators were instructed to annotate the sentiment the tweet expresses. The annotation-classes were as follow:

1. **Positive.** Tweets with a predominantly positive sentiment
2. **Negative.** Tweets with a predominantly negative sentiment
3. **Neutral.** Tweets expressing no sentiment or neutral
4. **Mixed.** Tweets with a mix of positive and negative sentiment

Table 2 shows annotation examples. We used Fleiss' κ and Krippendorff's α as metrics to measure the inter-rater agreement between annotators. This was implemented with the *Statsmodels* (Seabold and Perktold, 2010) and *Krippendorff*[2] Python packages. The results of Fleiss' κ and Krippendorff's α with a value of 0.53 show moderate agreement according to the interpretation of Landis and Koch (1977). Indeed, agreement metrics for sentiment annotation on tweets do differ between very high and rather low depending on the number of classes and overall setting and our results are slightly below the average in similar settings (cf. Salminen et al., 2018). Studies in the context of German literary texts (Schmidt et al., 2019b,a) or movie subtitles (Schmidt et al., 2020a) do report similar or lower levels of agreement. In our case, the mediocre agreement shows the challenges of the annotation and that the tweets were often open to interpretation.

[2]https://pypi.org/project/krippendorff/

To deal with the mediocre agreement, the final annotation of a tweet was determined according to the majority of individual decisions. If no majority could be determined or the tweets were classified as mixed by the majority, these tweets were not considered in the further process. Table 3 shows the distribution of the annotated tweets. In total, this majority decision leads to an annotated corpus of 1,785 tweets.

3.3 Sentiment Analysis

We regard the sentiment analysis as single-label classification task with the classes positive, neutral and negative. We implemented and evaluated the following approaches:

3.3.1 Lexicon-Based Approaches

We used *GerVADER* (Tymann et al., 2019) which is a German adaption of the English tool *VADER* (Hutto and Gilbert, 2014) and showed positive results in the context of German social media content (Tymann et al., 2019). In *GerVADER* the German sentiment dictionary *SentiWS* (Remus et al., 2010) is used for the sentiment calculation. The lexicon consists of 1,650 positive and 1,818 negative words and their inflections resulting in over 32,000 different word forms. The words' sentiment is scaled between the values -1 and 1.

3.3.2 Traditional Machine Learning Approaches

We compared Multinomial Naive Bayes and Support Vector Machines. To train and test these models, a bag-of-words approach with 5-fold cross-validation was carried out. Since preprocessing of texts is recommended for these approaches (Krouska et al., 2016), we performed the following preprocessing steps: filtering punctuation, stop words and unique words, normalization via lower

Annotation	Tweet	Account
positive	@MikeJosef FFM ist ein engagierter SPD-Kandidat mit viel Einsatz und Ideen für seine Stadt Frankfurt am Main. Am 14.3. könnt Ihr ihn wählen, liebe Frankfurter*innen! Für eine lebenswerte, moderne und soziale Metropole im Herzen von Europa.	@OlafScholz
negative	Die CDU ist die Partei der sozialen Kälte. #Triell	@Ricarda_Lang
neutral	Es ist nicht die Zeit für Einen zu sagen: Ich mache alles. Wir müssen uns jetzt breit aufstellen. #CDUVorsitz #jetztabervoran	@n_roettgen
mixed	Medien berichten über Neuformierung der Parteispitzen von @spdde @Die_Gruenen + @CDU Vergleich hinkt, weil @CDU Weg aus tiefer Orientierungs- +Personalkrise sucht, während @spdde + @Die_Gruenen Personalwechsel eher herausfordernde Begleiterscheinungen politischen Erfolges sind	@Ralf_Stegner
no majority	Wir wollen nicht zurückfallen in ein Spiel der nationalen Mächte, in eine Zeit, in der man im permanenten, destruktiven Wettstreit war - sondern Dinge gemeinsam hinkriegen und an die Entspannungspolitik von Willy Brandt und Helmut Schmidt anknüpfen. #Progressives4Europe	@OlafScholz

Table 2: Annotation examples. First three examples annotators agree upon. Last example is annotated as negative, neutral and mixed.

Sentiment	Count	Percentage
Neutral	**763**	38,15%
Negative	**536**	26,80%
Positive	**486**	24,3%
No Majority	120	6,00%
Mixed	95	4,75%

Table 3: Sentiment class distribution of the annotated subset.

casing and lemmatization. The aforementioned steps were implemented in python using the libraries *NLTK*[3], *sklearn* (Pedregosa et al., 2011) and *spaCy* (Honnibal and Montani, 2017).

3.3.3 Transformer-Based Approaches

We also evaluated the, to our knowledge, one of the largest publicly available German transformer-based language model *gbert-base* by *deepset* (Chan et al., 2020). The model was acquired via the *Hugging Face* platform (Wolf et al., 2020) and was implemented with the library *Simple Transformers* (Rajapakse, 2019), an adaption of *Hugging Face*'s library *Transformers*.

We used gbert-base[4] and fine-tuned it to the downstream task of sentiment classification differing between three different data sets for the training: (1) the 1,785 annotated tweets of our own data set, (2) the freely available *GermEval 2017* data set (Wojatzki et al., 2017), consisting of around 28,000 annotated German posts from various social media sources, representing one of the largest data sets of German sentiment-annotated posts, and (3) the combination of data sets (1) and (2). Each model is trained and evaluated in 5x5 stratified setting containing only the annotated data set. For methods (2) and (3) the *GermEval* data set is added to the training set while the test sets remain the same (consisting only of the annotated data). In the following, we refer to these approaches as BERT-1, BERT-2 and BERT-3 respectively. Each model is fine-tuned according to the default recommendations of BERT (Devlin et al., 2018) and trained for 4 epochs, with a train and evaluation batch size of 32, learning rate of 4e-5 and Adam optimizer for stochastic gradient descent. As GPU, a Tesla K80 was used.

4 Results

4.1 Evaluation of the Different Approaches

To evaluate the different approaches we used well established ML evaluation metrics including accuracy, macro (ignoring class distribution) and weighted (including class distribution in the calculation) f1 score.

Table 4 shows the results of the different approaches. For the traditional ML and transformer-based approaches we report averages over all 5 runs.

[3] https://www.nltk.org/

[4] https://huggingface.co/deepset/gbert-base

	SVM	NB	GerVADER	BERT-1	BERT-2	BERT-3
Accuracy	57.6	65.0	52.0	85.8	81.5	**93.3**
F1 Macro	54.5	65.3	52.0	82.1	73.8	**93.4**
F1 Weighted	55.9	65.1	54.0	85.9	81.5	**93.3**

Table 4: Results of the evaluation of the different sentiment analysis approaches. Best results per metric are marked in bold.

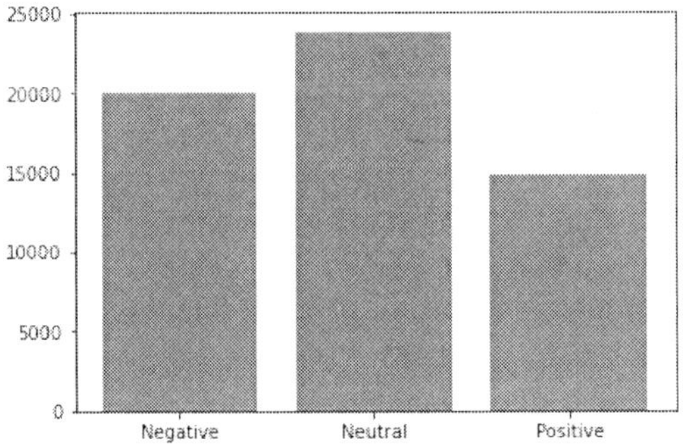

Figure 1: Overall sentiment distribution with 25% positive, 34% negative and 41% neutral tweets.

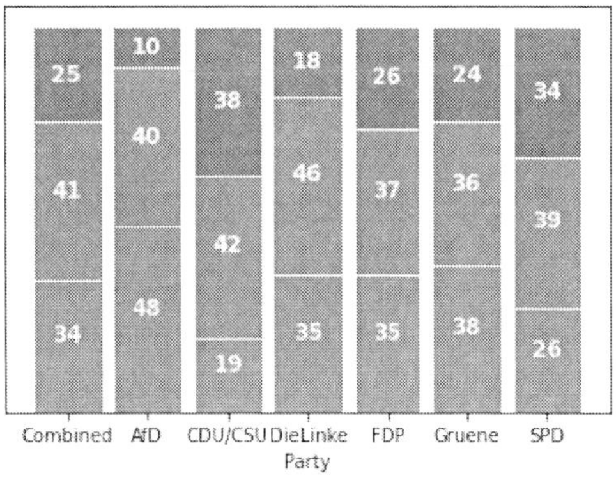

Figure 2: Percentage distribution of sentiment classes for all parties.

The best overall performance was achieved with BERT-3, followed by BERT-1 as the second best approach. The BERT-3 model reached an accuracy of 93.3%, a macro and weighted f1 score of 93.4 % and 93.3%. Thus, the best run of this model was used to predict the sentiment of the whole corpus of 58,864 tweets. In terms of traditional ML approaches, the Naive Bayes classifier performed best with an accuracy of 65.0% and macro and weighted f1 scores of 65.1% and 65.3% respectively. SVM performed considerably worse with an accuracy of 57.6% and macro as well as weighted f1 scores of 54.5% and 55.9%. GerVADER obtained the worst accuracy score with 52.0% and worst macro and weighted f1 scores with 52.0% and 54.0%.

4.2 Data Analysis

We classified each of the tweets of our overall corpus with the best run of BERT-3 and analyze the results in the following chapter. We focus on party-based and diachronic analysis.

Figure 1 shows the distribution of neutral, positive and negative sentiment predictions for all tweets. Figure 2 gives a more detailed view on the sentiment distribution per party. Overall, most of the tweets were predicted as neutral which is in line with the distribution of the annotated data set. Additionally, there are more negative than positive tweets. Regarding specific parties, the AfD (Alternative für Deutschland) is the party with the highest percentage of negative tweets. Die Grünen has the second most percentage of negative tweets. Additionally, AfD got the lowest count of positive tweets. Parties which were part of the opposition before the election such as AfD, FDP (Freie Demokratische Partei), Die Grünen and Die Linke express more negative sentiment than the two government parties SPD (Sozialdemokratische Partei Deutschlands) and CSU/CDU who indeed have the highest percentage of tweets classified as positive.

For semantic analysis, we looked at word clouds for the different sentiment classes after stop words removal. The word clouds for the overall corpus - Figure 3 and Figure 4 - as well as further term frequency analysis that can be found in our github repository, show that topics like "Corona", "lockdown", "Afghanistan" or "Klimawandel" (German for "climate change") are often mentioned in negative tweets. Positive tweets, however, frequently treat acceptance speeches with words like "Danke" (German for "Thanks"). Additionally, they often include mentions of the own party that the specific account represents. In negative tweets, there are regularly mentions of competing parties.

For diachronic analysis, we calculated a mean sentiment value by assigning -1 to negative, +1 to positive and 0 to neutral tweets. We then summed

Figure 3: Word cloud of negative tweets with all parties combined.

Figure 4: Word cloud of positive tweets with all parties combined.

the values for all tweets of a month per party and calculated the average. The lower the number the more negative, the higher the more positive. Figure 5 shows the mean sentiment per month of the different parties in 2021, with the dashed line symbolizing the election month. First, the figure shows that each party has nearly the same tops and valleys. It can be seen that there is a decrease in sentiment from June to August over all parties. This sentiment decrease turns around before the election in September, where all parties increased their mean sentiment. Surprising winners like FDP got a strong increase also after the election, whereas election losers like AfD or Die Linke got a sentiment decrease after the election.

To present more detailed results shortly before and after the election, Figure 6 shows the average sentiment value of each party's tweets over a 6-week period before and after the election on Sept. 26, 2021. For the average sentiment of all parties, there is a noticeable drop for mid to late August. However, the average sentiment of all parties increased significantly one week before the election. For the parties CDU/CSU, SPD, Die Grünen, this trend remains until one week after the election before the average sentiment drops again. For the parties FDP and AfD, sentiment remains roughly the same in the week after the election, while the average sentiment of the party Die Linke drops immediately after the election. A rise in sentiment can be seen again towards the end of October and the beginning of November.

5 Discussion

Considering the performance of the sentiment analysis approaches, results of the current state-of-the-art are confirmed with transformer-based models outperforming other approaches and the best model achieving an accuracy of 93% in a three class setting. However, in regards to the traditional machine learning approaches, please note that we did not include the "GermEval 2017" data set for training as we did in the BERT setting. The lexicon-based approach performs worst which is due to the fact of very bad recall values for the neutral class. Investigating the results of the different BERT approaches, we see that a combination of the "Germeval 2017" data and our data set for training achieves the best results (BERT-3) which proves that more data of the same domain for training is beneficial for overall performance.

Considering the analysis of the tweet classification on the overall corpus, we identified a predominance of neutral sentiment followed by negative sentiment for the overall distributions of the entire year. The higher frequency of negative sentiment compared to positive may be due to the period in which we collected the tweets. In 2021 the Covid pandemic posed major challenges to everyday life and was present all over the media. As the decisions of the government in dealing with the virus were often much disputed by the parties, this may explain the overall negative sentiment. This can be seen by inspecting the word clouds of negative tweets from the different parties. The overall word cloud for the negative tweets (see Fig. 3) indeed contains the word "Corona" in contrast to the positive word cloud for which this word is often missing.

Our results regarding differences between reigning parties and the opposition are contrary to research by Costa et al. (2021). They noticed that parties at the opposition had the most positive sentiment profile. We observed a more negative overall sentiment by the opposition parties AfD, Die Linke, Die Grünen and the FDP in comparison to the reign-

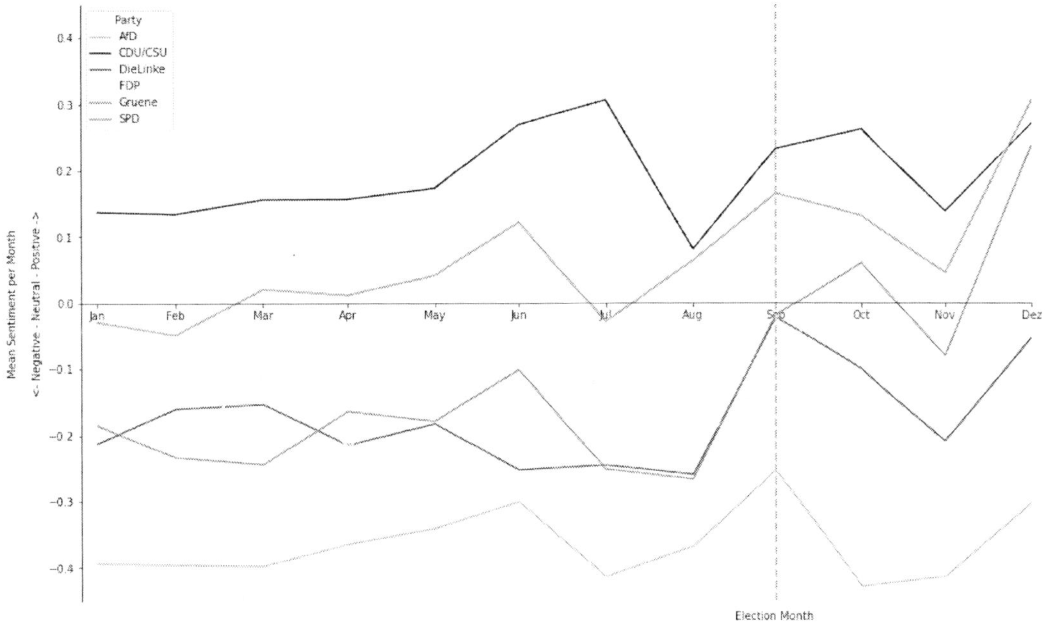

Figure 5: Mean sentiment per month for the political parties over the whole election year.

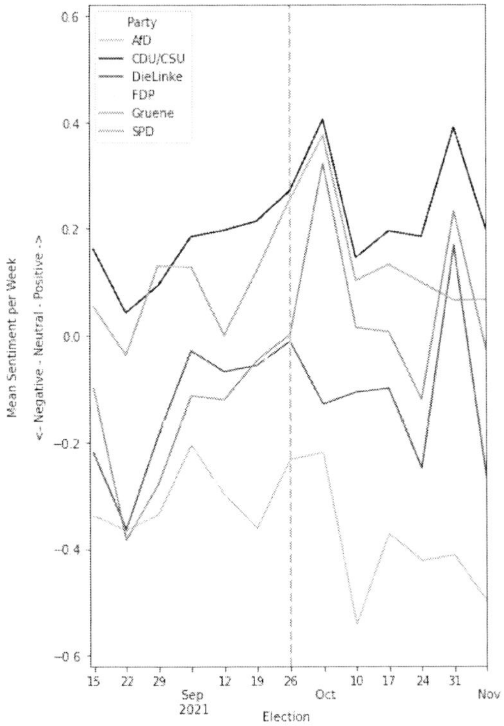

Figure 6: Average sentiment per week for the political parties in the 6-week period before and after the election.

ing parties rather consistently throughout the year with major shifts appearing after the election with the new reigning parties becoming more positive (see fig. 5).

Next to the general distributions, we also investigated sentiment progressions throughout the year. The first shift of sentiment in figure 5, which occurs for almost all parties in July could be explained with the flood disaster in west and middle Europe. It posed tremendous challenges to the country and a lot of people were hurt, lost their homes or died due to the catastrophe. In August, all parties except AfD and SPD had one of their lowest mean sentiment. One reason for this could be the the withdrawal of American troops from Afghanistan which has been heavily debated. One indicator of this is the vocabulary used in negative tweets by all parties in August. Tweets often refer to "Afghanistan," "Kabul," "Taliban" or "Ortskräfte" (German for "local forces"), which leads to the conclusion that topics related to troop withdrawals in Afghanistan were often criticized by the parties.

Looking at the period of a few weeks around the election, several sentiment changes are noticeable (see fig. 6). Towards the election week the sentiment of all parties increased again after the rather low average sentiment of July and August. If we compare the changes in sentiment in detail for the week after the election and in context with the results of the election (see table A.1), we identify that for the clear winners and losers of the election, such as the SPD, Die Grünen (both winners) and Die Linke it is also reflected in their sentiment trend. For those parties for which the proportional change in votes tended to be small, no major changes in sentiment can be observed. Only the CDU/CSU contradicts this pattern: the party records the highest percentage loss of all parties, 8.8 %, but still shows a strong increase in sentiment. This may be due to the optimistic attitude of the CDU/CSU towards the emerging opportunities of once again belonging to the opposition rather than the government-forming parties after a long period of time.

After the average sentiment of the parties went back to previous levels in mid-October, the next burst of positive sentiment towards the end of October and the beginning of November of some parties can be explained by the fact that the formation of a coalition of the governing parties was finalized. It has to be kept in mind that the new government constellation wasn't build directly after the election. The new government constellation with the SPD, FDP and Die Grünen are ruling just since November. In addition, the first session of the Bundestag of the new election period was held and a new president for the Bundestag was chosen. This is reaffirmed with the general vocabulary used between the last week of October and the first week of November. Examples are an increasing use of words and phrases like "Herzlichen Glückwunsch" (German for "congratulations"), "Bundestagspräsidentin" (German for "President of the Bundestag") and "Demokratie" (German for "democracy"). In autumn, it can be seen that the mean sentiment of most parties was on a lower level again, most likely caused by stronger Covid restrictions and more infections in Germany. However, the sentiment of all parties rose to the end of the year with events like Christmas and New year's Eve.

While our work provides in-depth insight on the sentiment of political parties before, during and after the German federal election, there are certain limitations we want to approach in future work. First, we only annotated a small subset of the overall corpus and achieved mediocre agreement among annotators. We currently plan further annotation studies with an extended annotation manual and guided training annotations to improve upon this problem. Furthermore we intend to discuss examples with low agreement to investigate this problem and we will annotate on a more fine-grained level marking words and word sequences to get a better understanding of the sentiment expression in the tweets and explore other prediction approaches. More annotation are beneficial for more precise evaluations and can improve the performance of our models.

On a methodological level, while an accuracy of 93% represents current state-of-the-art results in sentiment analysis in German (Chan et al., 2020), there is room for improvement. We see potential in further pretraining the language model with texts of political Twitter as recommended in the research area of domain adaptation of language models (Gururangan et al., 2020). Furthermore, the exploration of more sophisticated emotion categories instead of basic sentiment could lead to further more fine-grained insights. Indeed, recent experiments in the branch of emotion classification for German texts (Schmidt et al., 2021b,c) show the possibilities of the application of transformer-based models for multi-class emotion classification. We intend to integrate emotion annotation in our annotation process as well.

Please also note that we only investigated a subset of party representatives and that the selection as well as Twitter overall do not represent the entire party and its political dissemination, especially in lights of different parties pursuing different goals on Twitter or even having varying emphasize considering the usage of Twitter. It is also noteworthy that Twitter is not as popular in Germany as in other countries. According to current surveys only 10% of Germans use Twitter regularly[5] compared to 23% of U.S. adults.[6] Thus the implications and the importance of Twitter for political parties are limited. Nevertheless the importance of Twitter grows in Germany as well and we intend to build upon our research as described to further gain insights about the influence and development of sentiment of German political actors.

[5]`https://de.statista.com/statistik/daten/studie/171006/umfrage/in-anspruch-genommene-angebote-aus-dem-internet/`

[6]`https://www.statista.com/statistics/232818/active-us-twitter-user-growth/`

References

Adam Bermingham and Alan Smeaton. 2011. On using twitter to monitor political sentiment and predict election results. In *Proceedings of the Workshop on Sentiment Analysis where AI meets Psychology (SAAIP 2011)*, pages 2–10.

Widodo Budiharto and Meiliana Meiliana. 2018. Prediction and analysis of indonesia presidential election from twitter using sentiment analysis. *Journal of Big data*, 5(1):1–10.

B Chan, S Schweter, and T Möller. 2020. German's next language model. arxiv. *arXiv preprint arXiv:2010.10906*.

Hasna Chouikhi, Hamza Chniter, and Fethi Jarray. 2021. Arabic sentiment analysis using bert model. In *International Conference on Computational Collective Intelligence*, pages 621–632. Springer.

Carlos Costa, Manuela Aparicio, and Joao Aparicio. 2021. Sentiment analysis of portuguese political parties communication. In *The 39th ACM International Conference on Design of Communication*, pages 63–69.

Jacob Devlin, Ming-Wei Chang, Kenton Lee, and Kristina Toutanova. 2018. Bert: Pre-training of deep bidirectional transformers for language understanding. *arXiv preprint arXiv:1810.04805*.

James N Druckman, Cari Lynn Hennessy, Martin J Kifer, and Michael Parkin. 2010. Issue engagement on congressional candidate web sites, 2002—2006. *Social Science Computer Review*, 28(1):3–23.

Zulfadzli Drus and Haliyana Khalid. 2019. Sentiment analysis in social media and its application: Systematic literature review. *Procedia Computer Science*, 161:707–714.

Shihab Elbagir and Jing Yang. 2019. Twitter sentiment analysis using natural language toolkit and vader sentiment. In *Proceedings of the International Multi-Conference of Engineers and Computer Scientists*, volume 122, page 16.

Jakob Fehle, Thomas Schmidt, and Christian Wolff. 2021. Lexicon-based sentiment analysis in German: Systematic evaluation of resources and preprocessing techniques. In *Proceedings of the 17th Conference on Natural Language Processing (KONVENS 2021)*, pages 86–103, Düsseldorf, Germany. KONVENS 2021 Organizers.

Deen Freelon. 2017. Campaigns in control: Analyzing controlled interactivity and message discipline on facebook. *Journal of Information Technology & Politics*, 14(2):168–181.

MP Geetha and D Karthika Renuka. 2021. Improving the performance of aspect based sentiment analysis using fine-tuned bert base uncased model. *International Journal of Intelligent Networks*, 2:64–69.

Oliver Guhr, Anne-Kathrin Schumann, Frank Bahrmann, and Hans Joachim Böhme. 2020. Training a broad-coverage german sentiment classification model for dialog systems. In *Proceedings of The 12th Language Resources and Evaluation Conference*, pages 1627–1632.

Suchin Gururangan, Ana Marasović, Swabha Swayamdipta, Kyle Lo, Iz Beltagy, Doug Downey, and Noah A. Smith. 2020. Don't Stop Pretraining: Adapt Language Models to Domains and Tasks. *arXiv:2004.10964 [cs]*. ArXiv: 2004.10964.

Matthew Honnibal and Ines Montani. 2017. spaCy 2: Natural language understanding with Bloom embeddings, convolutional neural networks and incremental parsing. To appear.

Clayton Hutto and Eric Gilbert. 2014. Vader: A parsimonious rule-based model for sentiment analysis of social media text. In *Proceedings of the international AAAI conference on web and social media*, volume 8, pages 216–225.

Yassine Ait Jeddi and Soufiane Bengadi. 2022. Scweet. a simple and unlimited twitter scraper with python. `https://github.com/Altimis/Scweet`. Accessed on 2022-06-07.

Anna Jurek, Maurice D Mulvenna, and Yaxin Bi. 2015. Improved lexicon-based sentiment analysis for social media analytics. *Security Informatics*, 4(1):1–13.

Akrivi Krouska, Christos Troussas, and Maria Virvou. 2016. The effect of preprocessing techniques on twitter sentiment analysis. In *2016 7th international conference on information, intelligence, systems & applications (IISA)*, pages 1–5. IEEE.

J Richard Landis and Gary G Koch. 1977. The measurement of observer agreement for categorical data. *biometrics*, pages 159–174.

Bing Liu. 2015. Sentiment analysis: mining opinions, sentiments, and emotions.

Shervin Minaee, Nal Kalchbrenner, Erik Cambria, Narjes Nikzad, Meysam Chenaghlu, and Jianfeng Gao. 2021. Deep learning–based text classification: a comprehensive review. *ACM Computing Surveys (CSUR)*, 54(3):1–40.

Luis Moßburger, Felix Wende, Kay Brinkmann, and Thomas Schmidt. 2020. Exploring Online Depression Forums via Text Mining: A Comparison of Reddit and a Curated Online Forum. In *Proceedings of the Fifth Social Media Mining for Health Applications Workshop & Shared Task*, pages 70–81, Barcelona, Spain (Online). Association for Computational Linguistics.

Anna-Marie Ortloff, Lydia Güntner, Maximiliane Windl, Thomas Schmidt, Martin Kocur, and Christian Wolff. 2019. Sentibooks: Enhancing audiobooks via affective computing and smart light bulbs. In *Proceedings of Mensch Und Computer 2019*, MuC'19, page

863–866, New York, NY, USA. Association for Computing Machinery.

F. Pedregosa, G. Varoquaux, A. Gramfort, V. Michel, B. Thirion, O. Grisel, M. Blondel, P. Prettenhofer, R. Weiss, V. Dubourg, J. Vanderplas, A. Passos, D. Cournapeau, M. Brucher, M. Perrot, and E. Duchesnay. 2011. Scikit-learn: Machine learning in Python. *Journal of Machine Learning Research*, 12:2825–2830.

Xipeng Qiu, Tianxiang Sun, Yige Xu, Yunfan Shao, Ning Dai, and Xuanjing Huang. 2020. Pre-trained Models for Natural Language Processing: A Survey. *arXiv:2003.08271 [cs]*. ArXiv: 2003.08271.

T. C. Rajapakse. 2019. Simple transformers. `https://github.com/ThilinaRajapakse/simpletransformers`.

Robert Remus, Uwe Quasthoff, and Gerhard Heyer. 2010. Sentiws-a publicly available german-language resource for sentiment analysis. In *Proceedings of the Seventh International Conference on Language Resources and Evaluation (LREC'10)*.

Joni O Salminen, Hind A Al-Merekhi, Partha Dey, and Bernard J Jansen. 2018. Inter-rater agreement for social computing studies. In *2018 Fifth International Conference on Social Networks Analysis, Management and Security (SNAMS)*, pages 80–87. IEEE.

Thomas Schmidt, Marlene Bauer, Florian Habler, Hannes Heuberger, Florian Pilsl, and Christian Wolff. 2020a. Der einsatz von distant reading auf einem korpus deutschsprachiger songtexte. In Christof Schöch, editor, *DHd 2020: Spielräume; Digital Humanities zwischen Modellierung und Interpretation. Konferenzabstracts; Universität Paderborn, 02. bis 06. März 2020*, pages 296–300. Paderborn, Germany.

Thomas Schmidt and Manuel Burghardt. 2018. An Evaluation of Lexicon-based Sentiment Analysis Techniques for the Plays of Gotthold Ephraim Lessing. In *Proceedings of the Second Joint SIGHUM Workshop on Computational Linguistics for Cultural Heritage, Social Sciences, Humanities and Literature*, pages 139–149, Santa Fe, New Mexico. Association for Computational Linguistics.

Thomas Schmidt, Manuel Burghardt, Katrin Dennerlein, and Christian Wolff. 2019a. Sentiment Annotation for Lessing's Plays: Towards a Language Resource for Sentiment Analysis on German Literary Texts. In Thierry Declerck and John P. McCrae, editors, *2nd Conference on Language, Data and Knowledge (LDK 2019)*, pages 45–50. Leipzig, Germany.

Thomas Schmidt, Johanna Dangel, and Christian Wolff. 2021a. Senttext: A tool for lexicon-based sentiment analysis in digital humanities. In Thomas Schmidt and Christian Wolff, editors, *Information Science and its Neighbors from Data Science to Digital Humanities. Proceedings of the 16th International Symposium of Information Science (ISI 2021)*, volume 74, pages 156–172. Werner Hülsbusch, Glückstadt.

Thomas Schmidt, Katrin Dennerlein, and Christian Wolff. 2021b. Emotion classification in German plays with transformer-based language models pretrained on historical and contemporary language. In *Proceedings of the 5th Joint SIGHUM Workshop on Computational Linguistics for Cultural Heritage, Social Sciences, Humanities and Literature*, pages 67–79, Punta Cana, Dominican Republic (online). Association for Computational Linguistics.

Thomas Schmidt, Katrin Dennerlein, and Christian Wolff. 2021c. Using Deep Learning for Emotion Analysis of 18th and 19th Century German Plays. In Manuel Burghardt, Lisa Dieckmann, Timo Steyer, Peer Trilcke, Niels-Oliver Walkowski, Joëlle Weis, and Ulrike Wuttke, editors, *Fabrikation von Erkenntnis. Experimente in den Digital Humanities*.

Thomas Schmidt, Philipp Hartl, Dominik Ramsauer, Thomas Fischer, Andreas Hilzenthaler, and Christian Wolff. 2020b. Acquisition and analysis of a meme corpus to investigate web culture. In *15th Annual International Conference of the Alliance of Digital Humanities Organizations, DH 2020, Conference Abstracts*, Ottawa, Canada.

Thomas Schmidt, Florian Kaindl, and Christian Wolff. 2020c. Distant reading of religious online communities: A case study for three religious forums on reddit. In *Proceedings of the Digital Humanities in the Nordic Countries 5th Conference (DHN 2020)*, pages 157–172, Riga, Latvia.

Thomas Schmidt, Miriam Schlindwein, Katharina Lichtner, and Christian Wolff. 2020d. Investigating the relationship between emotion recognition software and usability metrics. *i-com*, 19(2):139–151.

Thomas Schmidt, Brigitte Winterl, Milena Maul, Alina Schark, Andrea Vlad, and Christian Wolff. 2019b. Inter-rater agreement and usability: A comparative evaluation of annotation tools for sentiment annotation. In *INFORMATIK 2019: 50 Jahre Gesellschaft für Informatik – Informatik für Gesellschaft (Workshop-Beiträge)*, pages 121–133, Bonn. Gesellschaft für Informatik e.V.

Skipper Seabold and Josef Perktold. 2010. statsmodels: Econometric and statistical modeling with python. In *9th Python in Science Conference*.

Parul Sharma and Teng-Sheng Moh. 2016. Prediction of indian election using sentiment analysis on hindi twitter. In *2016 IEEE international conference on big data (big data)*, pages 1966–1971. IEEE.

Andranik Tumasjan, Timm Sprenger, Philipp Sandner, and Isabell Welpe. 2010. Predicting elections with twitter: What 140 characters reveal about political sentiment. In *Proceedings of the International AAAI Conference on Web and Social Media*, volume 4.

Karsten Tymann, Matthias Lutz, Patrick Palsbröker, and Carsten Gips. 2019. Gervader-a german adaptation of the vader sentiment analysis tool for social media texts. In *LWDA*, pages 178–189.

Bhagyashri Wagh, JV Shinde, and PA Kale. 2018. A twitter sentiment analysis using nltk and machine learning techniques. *International Journal of Emerging Research in Management and Technology*, 6(12):37–44.

Hao Wang, Doğan Can, Abe Kazemzadeh, François Bar, and Shrikanth Narayanan. 2012. A system for real-time twitter sentiment analysis of 2012 us presidential election cycle. In *Proceedings of the ACL 2012 system demonstrations*, pages 115–120.

Michael Wojatzki, Eugen Ruppert, Sarah Holschneider, Torsten Zesch, and Chris Biemann. 2017. Germeval 2017: Shared task on aspect-based sentiment in social media customer feedback. *Proceedings of the GermEval*, pages 1–12.

Thomas Wolf, Lysandre Debut, Victor Sanh, Julien Chaumond, Clement Delangue, Anthony Moi, Pierric Cistac, Tim Rault, Rémi Louf, Morgan Funtowicz, et al. 2020. Transformers: State-of-the-art natural language processing. In *Proceedings of the 2020 conference on empirical methods in natural language processing: system demonstrations*, pages 38–45.

A Appendix

A.1 Results of German Federal Election 2021

Party	Full Name	2021	2017	Change
SPD	Social Democratic Party of Germany	25.7 %	20.5 %	+ 5.2 %
CDU/CSU	Christian Democratic Union/ Christian Social Union (Bavaria)	24.1 %	32.9 %	- 8.8 %
Die Grünen	The Greens	14.8 %	8.9 %	+5.9 %
FDP	Free Democratic Party	11.5 %	10.7 %	+ 0.8 %
AfD	Alternative for Germany	10.3 %	12.6 %	- 2.3 %
Die Linke	The Left	4.9 %	9.2 %	- 4.3 %

Table 5: Election results per party for the election years 2017 and 2021.

A.2 Twitter Accounts from Data Acquisition

AFD	Links	SPD	Grüne	FDP	CDU	CSU
@Alice_Wei del 138k	@SWagenk necht 518k	@Karl_Laut erbach 770k	@cem_oez demir 290k	@c_lindner 552k	@jensspa hn 279k	@Markus_ Soeder 341k
@Joerg_Me uthen 76k	@GregorG ysi 439k	@HeikoMaa s 460k	@GoeringE ckardt 202k	@MaStrackZ i 46k	@ArminLa schet 188k	@DoroBaer 103k
@Beatrix _vStorch 68k	@katjakippi ng 130k	@OlafSchol z 324k	@JTrittin 115k	@MarcoBusc hmann 46k	@Friedrich Merz 179k	@andreass cheuer 63k
@Gofffried Curio 37k	@DietmarB artsch 82k	@KuehniKe v 323k	@Konstanti nNotz 85k	@Konstantin Kuhle 44k	@JuliaKlo eckner 74k	@Manfred Weber 54k
@MalteKau fmann 36k	@anked 43k	@larsklingb eil 116k	@RenateK uenast 77k	@johannesv ogel 38k	@n_roettg en 68k	@DerLenz MdB 10k
@JoanaCot ar 30k	@b_riexing er 41k	@hubertus_ heil 108k	@Ricarda_ Lang 65k	@Wissing 32k	@PaulZie miak 58k	@hahnflo 9k
@Tino_Chr upalla 21k	@jankorte mdb 34k	@EskenSas kia 101k	@KathaSc hulze 37k	@Lambsdorff 27k	@groehe 49k	@smueller mdb 9k
@StBrandn er 23k	@Janine_ Wissler 37k	@Ralf_Steg ner 64,9k	@BriHasse lmann 37k	@ria_schroe der 23k	@HBraun 39k	@DaniLudw igMdB 8k
@GtzFrmmi ng 17k	@SevimDa gdelen 35k	@Karamba Diaby 55,6k	@nouripour 29k	@LindaTeute nberg 23k	@rbrinkha us 30k	@ANiebler 6k
@PetrBystr onAFD 17k	@Susanne Hennig 29k	@MiRo_SP D 39k	@MiKellner 28k	@f_schaeffle r 20k	@tj_tweets 17k	@MarkusFe rber 5k

Figure 7: Ten biggest user user accounts of all parties used for the acquisition of tweets.

AFD	Links	SPD	Grüne	FDP	CDU	CSU
@AfD 173k	@dieLinke 350k	@spdde 417k	@Die_Gruen en 649k	@fdp 414k	@CDU 378k	@CSU 229k
@AfDimBund estag 68k	@Linksfraktio n 108k	@spdbt 217k	@GrueneBun destag 186k	@fdpbt 39k	@cducsubt 166k	
@AfDBerlin 19k	@dielinkeber lin 19k	@jusos 77k	@gruene_jug end 76k	@fdp_nrw 28k	@Junge_Union 79k	

Figure 8: Three biggest main accounts of all parties used for the acquisition of tweets.

Proceedings of the 18th Conference on Natural Language Processing (KONVENS 2022)

Do gender neutral affixes naturally reduce gender bias in static word embeddings?

Jonas Wagner and **Sina Zarrieß**
Bielefeld University
Faculty for Linguistics and Literary Studies
{jonas.wagner,sina.zarriess}@uni-bielefeld.de

Abstract

In German, substituting gendered role nouns with gender neutral versions, known as *gendergerechte Sprache*, has rapidly been gaining ground, with the primary aim being the inclusion of non-male people. Its effectiveness, however, has not been conclusively demonstrated. Previously, word embeddings have been shown to contain gender biases similar to natural language. They thus can be used to measure whether this practice impacts gender association of role nouns. Methods of debiasing pre-trained word embeddings have been devised, but their effectiveness in German, especially compared to *gendergerechte Sprache*, has not been tested. In this paper, we systematically compare two methods of gender neutral affixation to a base corpus to examine the effect on gender bias of role nouns. We also compare the gender biases of analogy resolutions generated with embeddings trained on the base corpus, on the base corpus after undergoing an established post-hoc debiasing method, and the corpus after introduction of gender neutral affixation. Our results show a mixed picture: affixation leads to increased gender bias of role nouns, but decreased gender bias of generated analogy resolutions, even outperforming post-hoc debiasing methods.

1 Introduction

Gender bias in word embeddings and its reduction have received significant attention from computational linguists and NLP researchers over the past years, and a substantial body of research around the topic has accumulated (Bolukbasi et al. 2016; Caliskan et al. 2017; Ethayarajh et al. 2019; Kaneko and Bollegala 2019 among others). Given the wide use of word embeddings and the resulting danger of perpetuating and reinforcing gender stereotypes (Hansen et al., 2015; Musto et al., 2015; Dastin, 2018; Schnitzer et al., 2019), this is a pressing concern. But existing research has failed to address two aspects of the issue: firstly, as is a common problem in NLP, it mostly investigates English (but see Sahlgren and Olsson 2019 and Katsarou et al. 2022 for investigations of Swedish, Chávez Mulsa and Spanakis 2020 for Dutch, and Basta et al. 2020 for Spanish), which, in contrast to German, does not have regular gender marking on nouns.

Secondly, and possibly as a result of this, it ignores societal efforts to mitigate gender bias in natural language. Blodgett et al. (2020, p. 5458) criticise this detachment from such societal processes, instead calling for researchers to "[e]xamine language use in practice by engaging with the lived experiences of members of communities affected by NLP systems". One way in which language users are addressing gender biases in their languages is by changing these gender markings, such as the *-e* suffix in Spanish or the addition of the female suffix *-in* to German role nouns,[1] which is the subject of the present study. Instead, research has focused on post-hoc debiasing of pre-trained word embeddings rather than the impact of these societal processes.

The practice of adding the female role noun affix *-in* to male role nouns in German is known is *gendergerechte Sprache* (henceforth *GGS*). *GGS* has become a controversial topic in Germany (Stöber, 2021), which may (at least partially) be rooted in the fact that a quantitative investigation into its effectiveness has not yet been conducted. While this paper sets out to begin an investigation into quantifiable gender bias reduction through *GGS*, due to the complex nature of the subject and its ideological components, the question whether it measurably reduces gender bias may not be answerable, especially in the short term. Nevertheless, given the tools supplied with word embeddings, an initial

[1] For the purposes of this work, "role noun" refers to nouns that denote someone's activity or occupation, such as *runner*, *teacher*, or *listener*.

investigation is warranted and valuable. We thus investigate two research questions:

RQ1: Does gender neutral language in German lead to a reduction in gender association of role nouns' embeddings?

RQ2: Is altering corpora on which embeddings are trained so as to make their language more gender neutral as effective as post-hoc debiasing of word embeddings?

To answer these questions, we conduct two experiments. First, we train word embeddings on a corpus of German language texts and measure the gender association of role nouns in the text before and after altering them to conform to *GGS* (Section 3.4). Second, we compare the reduction of gender association of this to hard-debias (Bolukbasi et al. 2016; see also Section 2.2) to gauge its effectiveness (Section 3.5). Although it is not its focus, this research will also contribute to the growing body of research of gender bias in word embeddings in non-English languages.

2 Background

2.1 *Gendergerechte Sprache*: gender neutral language in German

German, like many Indo-Eurpean languages, has grammatical gender with a regular derivational pattern for role noun generation. For example, *Programmierer* means "male programmer", while *Programmiererin* means "female programmer"; *-er* serves as a derivational morpheme with which male role nouns can be generated from verbs (*programmieren*, "to program"), and *-in* changes male to female role nouns. Gender neutral alternatives to these gendered suffixes do not exist.

Masculine generics have, therefore, been used to refer to not only male individuals in occupations, but all individuals – *Programmierer* could refer to male as well as female and non-binary programmers, despite being morphologically masculine. Criticism of this practice goes back several decades (see Braun et al., 2005 and Kotthoff, 2020 for an overview), but has been mounting in recent years. This has led to the establishment of more formalised ways of explicitly including none-male people in generic role nouns (Kotthoff, 2020). These largely add the female suffix *-in*, separated by a typographic symbol such as * (see Table 1 for an example).

2.2 Gender bias in word embeddings

Given the wide use of word embeddings in downstream tasks, the mitigation of gender biases present in them has been of interest to researchers. This necessitates a method to measure gender bias in word embeddings first, which Ethayarajh et al. (2019) provide with the *Relational Inner Product Association* (RIPA). This method identifies the vector $\vec{b}$, which captures the subspace of the embedding space that denotes gender. This is done by first creating a set (*S*) of pairs of words that define the gender association. The two words in each pair only differ by gender, but the relationship between the pairs can be arbitrary. An example for *S* would be ($\{woman, man\}$, $\{queen, king\}$, $\{girl, boy\}$). Of these pairs, the difference vectors ($\overrightarrow{woman}$–$\overrightarrow{man}$, $\overrightarrow{queen}$–$\overrightarrow{king}$, etc.) are taken, and the first principal component of all difference vectors is computed. This first principal component is $\vec{b}$, and a word's gender association is simply the dot product of its embedding and $\vec{b}$. RIPA is highly interpretable: if, as in the example, the first word in each pair in the set *S* is the female word, positive RIPA scores show female association and negative scores show male association. The strength of the association is reflected by the absolute value of the score.[2]

Once a gender subspace is captured, debiasing can proceed. Bolukbasi et al. (2016) establish several methods, of which only hard-debias will be discussed here. To hard-debias an embedding, it is re-embedded with the following formula:

$$\vec{w} := \frac{\vec{w} - \vec{w}_B}{||\vec{w} - \vec{w}_B||}$$

Where $\vec{w}$ is the word's embedding and $\vec{w}_B$ is the embedding's projection on the gender subspace - in our case, this subspace is $\vec{b}$ as introduced above. Vectors enclosed in || denote the vectors' norms.

Investigations of gender bias in contextualised embeddings are emerging, but still less well-researched than static embeddings. However, it has been shown that despite their sensitivity to context, gender bias is still present in contextualised embeddings, especially for occupations (Basta et al., 2020), though less pronounced than in static embeddings (Sahlgren and Olsson, 2019). Established debiasing methods may not mitigate gender bias in contextualised embeddings well (Sahlgren and Ols-

[2]For a more in-depth discussion of RIPA and other bias measurements, see Ethayarajh et al., 2019 and Caliskan et al., 2017.

Original sentence (male role noun)	*Der*	*Programmierer*		*schläft*
Original sentence (female role noun)	*Die*	*Programmiererin*		*schläft*
New sentence after affixation	<[ART]>	*Programmierer*in*		*schläft*
New sentence after inserting the **in*-token	<[ART]>	*Programmierx*	<**in*>	*schläft*
Translation	The	*programmer*		sleeps

Table 1: Example of a sentence that was changed with both methods.

son, 2019). Translingual research has also revealed that in Swedish, occupations are less gender biased than in English (Katsarou et al., 2022).

Post-hoc debiasing methods like hard-debias have the advantage of being employable on large pre-trained models, thus circumventing the need to gather large corpora of gender neutral language to train new embeddings. However, they rely on several assumptions. Most importantly, for post-hoc debiasing to be at all effective, it is crucial that the gender subspace with regards to which words are debiased accurately captures gender. But, as Ethayarajh et al. (2019) point out, the selection of words that define the gender subspace is arbitrary and subject to beliefs and biases of those who conduct the debiasing, even with the more robust RIPA. Additionally, they crucially ignore the contextual and societal aspects of language. Language users are already implementing their idea of gender neutral language, but this type of language, which is desired by its users, may not be reflected in the corpora that word embeddings are trained on. Post-hoc debiased word embeddings therefore do not reflect natural gender neutral language, but a computationally altered version of gender biased language. Given that gender bias is, at its core, a societal and cultural phenomenon, this is a serious shortcoming which the present study aims to investigate. For the purposes of this study, we will refer to these natural-language-like debiasing methods as *corpus debiasing*, and to post-hoc debiasing methods like hard-debias as *embedding debiasing*.

3 Experiments

3.1 Data

We use the *Gebrauchsliteratur* subset of the German-language fiction corpus (henceforth *DTA-Gebrauchsliteratur*; available at `https://www.deutschestextarchiv.de/download`) on works from 1750 onwards, totalling some 120 books. Using the CBOW implementation in *Word2Vec* from *gensim* (Řehůřek and Sojka, 2010, version 4.1.2), we train embeddings on this corpus with a vector size of 50 (due to the comparatively small size of the corpus) and a window size of 10.

3.2 Role Nouns

We extract role nouns from the corpus by filtering out capitalised words (as all German nouns are capitalised) that end in *-er* or *-erin* (see Section 2 for information on the morphology of German role nouns). Using *spaCy* (Honnibal and Johnson, 2015), we then filter this list of nouns twice: the first step removes all plural nouns, as *-er* is also a standard plural morpheme for German nouns – not just role nouns – resulting in many false positives. This is filtered again, allowing only entries that were clearly derived from verbs. For this, we remove the role noun suffixes (*-er* and *-erin*) and replace them with *-en*, the default ending for German non-finite verbs. Only if *spaCy* recognises this as a verb is the noun retained in the list. We then manually investigate this final list and remove any false positives. False negatives, however, cannot be added back in. In total, the list includes 764 role nouns: 636 male and 128 female, with 71 of them occurring in both the male and female forms.

3.3 Affixation patterns

Then, we alter the role nouns in the corpus in two ways:

Affixation: Substituting each role noun with a version of itself with the role noun endings removed and *-er*in* appended (both *Programmierer* and *Programmiererin* become *Programmierer*in*

Inserting an **in*-token: Substituting each role noun with a version of itself with the role noun endings removed and *-x* appended (both *Programmierer* and *Programmiererin* become *Programmierx*) and inserting **in* as an additional token **after** every role noun.

In both cases, we replace any determiner preceding the role noun with the token *[ART]* (from German *Artikel*, "determiner"). See Table 1 for an example. We then train embeddings from scratch on both altered versions of the corpus with the same hyperparameters as above.

The reason for inserting **in* as a token after the role nouns is that simple affixation (i.e. exchanging all instances of role nouns with gender neutral versions of themselves) should necessarily lead to a reduction in gender association, provided the male and female versions have different gender associations. If, in a hypothetical corpus, the words *Programmierer* and *Programmiererin* are of equal frequency and the former is male-associated while the latter is female-associated, the new version (which would substitute both in the entire text) would have the mean gender assocation of the two, i.e. it would lie somewhere in between them. This would reduce measurable gender bias, but would likely not work in cases where the two versions' frequencies are unequal or one does not occur at all. Introducing the new token **in* while also changing all role nouns to a gender neutral version allows the gender neutralising effect that *GGS* has on role nouns where both versions occur to carry over to those of which only either the male or the female version occurs – though potentially not as strong – as all role nouns now occur in the vicinity of the **in*-token. The validity of this approach will be tested in this experiment.

Note that if sub-word embeddings had been learned (using e.g. fastText, Bojanowski et al., 2017), this approach may not have been necessary in cases where the role noun would be recognised as consisting of a verb (e.g. *programmier-*) and the derivational affixes (*er* and **in*, respectively). However, gender association and bias are much more well-researched in word embeddings generated with *Word2Vec*, making it the preferred approach here.

3.4 Experiment 1: Impact of *gendergerechte Sprache* on gender association

We calculate the RIPA score (Ethayarajh et al., 2019) of the role nouns we extracted in the base corpus and of the altered role nouns in the corpus-debiased corpora (see Sections 3.2 and 3.3). For the gender defining set *S* we use kinship terms (see Table 2).

Shapiro tests from *scipy.stats* (version 1.6.2, Virtanen et al., 2020) show that RIPA scores are not normally distributed. Thus, we use two-sided Wilcoxon tests (from the same package) for significance testing. We run separate tests for each gender. We use the *median* function from *statistics* to calculate medians, and create boxplots with *pyplot* from *matplotlib* (Hunter, 2007, version 3.3.4). Since multiple tests were run, we Bonferroni adjust *p*-values with *multipletests* from *statsmodels* (Seabold and Perktold, 2010, version 0.12.2).

3.5 Experiment 2: Analogy resolution

We debias the role nouns' embeddings from the base corpus (Sections 3.1 and 3.2) using hard-debias (Bolukbasi et al. 2016; see Section 2.2). It is not possible to evaluate the resulting gender associations with RIPA, since hard-debias reduces gender association w.r.t. RIPA – that is, the RIPA scores of words after undergoing hard-debias are necessarily minimal.

Instead, we alter the methodology used by Bolukbasi et al. (2016), who generate analogy resolutions for each investigated word, e.g. "he is to doctor as she is to X", with the analogy being solved for X. In Bolukbasi et al. (2016), crowd-workers then rate whether the analogy resolution is biased (e.g. *nurse*) or not (e.g. *physician*). This works well for their research, but is expensive and time-consuming. There are also other reasons why it would not work for our experiment:

- **Ambiguity of German nouns and pronouns**. *Sie* is the third person singular female pronoun, but also the gender neutral third person plural pronoun, and, if capitalised, the second person honorific pronoun. *Frau* ("woman") also is a honorific for women ("Mrs"), so they do not differ only by gender. This means that the analogy "er verhält sich zu Arzt wie sie zu X" ("he is to doctor as she is to X") would not necessarily have a gendered resolution, as *sie* does not refer strictly to female individuals. The analogy therefore cannot be constructed using pronouns nor words for *man* and *woman*

- **Loss of natural language gender bias**. The corpus-based gender bias reduction methods introduced in Section 3.3 lead to analogies like "man is to male or female doctor as woman is to male or female nurse". Human raters would rate these as gender neutral, as they employ the gender neutral suffixes that they are used to from natural language

To solve the first issue, we calculate the mean embeddings of the male and female words in *S* (see

German kinship terms	English translation
Frau, Mann	woman, man
Schwester, Bruder	sister, brother
Tante, Onkel	aunt, uncle
Tochter, Sohn	daughter, son
weiblich, männlich	female, male
Cousine, Cousin	female cousin, male cousin
Nichte, Neffe	niece, nephew
Enkelin, Enkel	granddaughter, grandson
Schwägerin, Schwager	sister-in-law, brother-in-law

Table 2: Set S that defines the gender association.

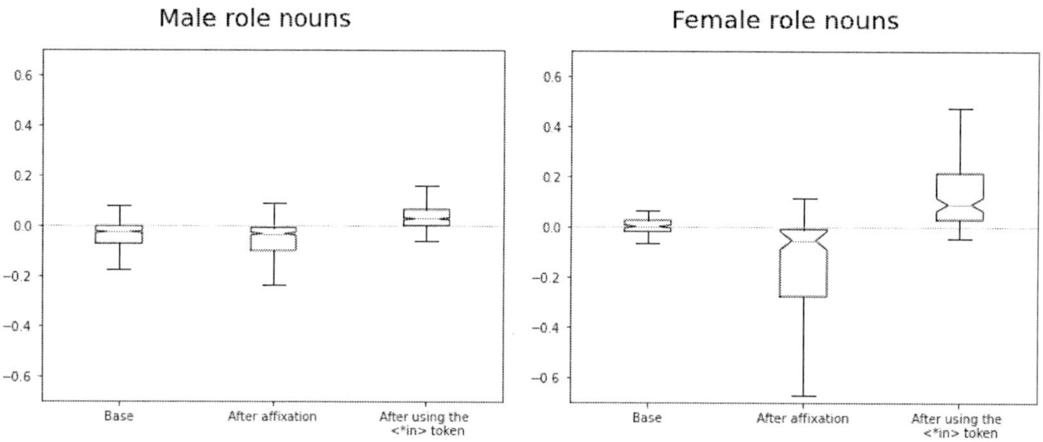

Figure 1: Boxplot of gender associations of role nouns: RIPA scores of unaltered role nouns and after undergoing gender association reduction. Outliers omitted. Whiskers end at 1.5*IQD. Positive scores indicate female, negative scores male association.

Table 2) for each corpus and insert them into their respective embedding spaces, thus getting a better measure of gender than using only a pronoun. Then, we generate ten analogy resolutions per role noun and compute the mean RIPA score for them. The hard-debiased data, however, still poses a problem here. Since, in a good model, role nouns should be generated for the analogy resolutions, we would encounter the same problem as above: the analogy might still be solved as e.g. "man is to doctor as woman is to nurse", only that both *doctor* and *nurse* would have been debiased w.r.t. RIPA. Thus, the model could generate a clearly biased resolution that would still have a low RIPA score.

We generate the analogy resolution in the hard-debiased embedding space and then take the RIPA score of the generated resolutions in the base, non-debiased space. The analogy ($\mu_{male_{HD}}$ *is to male* $doctor_{HD}$ *as* $\mu_{female_{HD}}$ *is to* X_{HD}), where *HD* denotes the hard-debiased embedding space and μ_{male} and μ_{female} are the mean male and female embeddings described above, is solved for X_{HD}. Then, we compute the RIPA scores not of X_{HD}, but of X_{base} in the base corpus. This means that analogy resolutions that would still be perceived as biased by human raters ("he is to doctor as she is to nurse") will be recognised as such. This is not possible for the corpus-debiased embeddings, as role nouns generated in those models have no gender markings on them, meaning it would be impossible to decide whether to calculate the RIPA score of the male or female version in the base corpus. Their RIPA scores are thus computed in their own embedding spaces. We also calculate how many nouns and role nouns are generated for each analogy as an indicator of the quality of the resolutions.

Comparison	1st median	RIPA scores 2nd median	median change (abs.)	p	p_{adj}	signif.
Male role nouns						
base vs affixation	-0.0249	-0.0321	-0.0072	1.24E-16	2.23E-15	···
base vs *in-token	-0.0249	0.0286	-0.0037	2.57E-91	4.63E-90	···
affixation vs *in-token	-0.0321	0.0286	0.0035	1.95E-96	3.51E-95	···
Female role nouns						
base vs affixation	0.0023	-0.0524	-0.0501	2.27E-16	4.08E-15	···
base vs *in-token	0.0023	0.0907	-0.0885	1.34E-17	2.41E-16	···
affixation vs *in-token	-0.0524	0.0907	-0.0384	1.53E-22	2.74E-21	···

Table 3: Gender association of role nouns before and after corpus debiasing, separated by gender. Significance codes: · (p <.05), ·· (p <.01), ··· (p <.001); codes also apply to other tables.

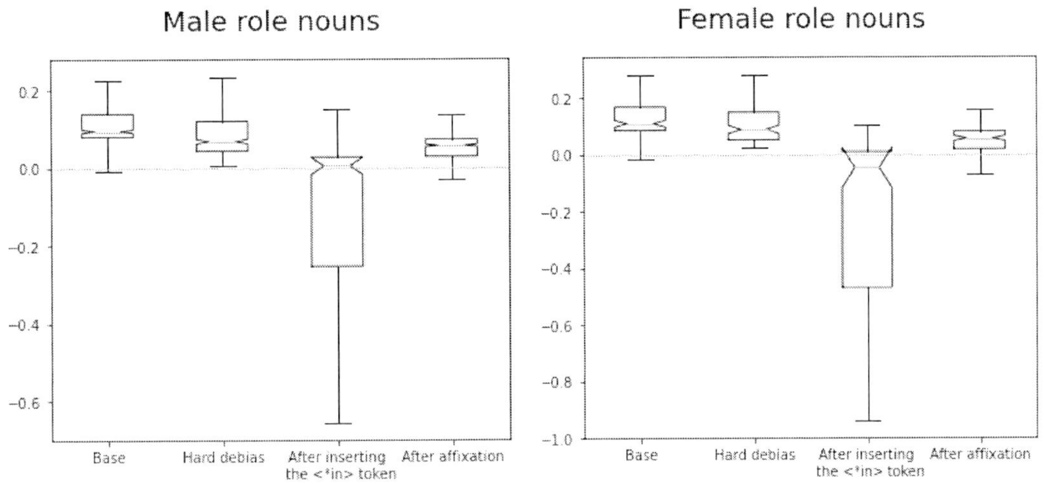

Figure 2: Boxplot of gender associations of role nouns: RIPA scores of unaltered role nouns and after undergoing gender association reduction. Outliers omitted. Whiskers end at 1.5*IQD. Positive scores indicate female, negative scores male association.

4 Results

In Tables 3 and 4, positive RIPA scores show female association and negative RIPA scores show male association. The absolute value of the scores shows the strength of the association. The first median refers to the median RIPA score of the first part of the comparison (e.g. role nouns in the base corpus in the comparison *base vs affixation*), the second median to the second one (e.g. role nouns after undergoing affixation in that same comparison). The higher the absolute value of the RIPA score, the stronger the association. Negative median changes indicate that gender association is stronger in the second part of the comparison, positive ones indicate that it is weaker.

4.1 Experiment 1

The mean absolute RIPA scores for male role nouns in the base corpus (-0.0249, male biased) are lower than after affixation (-0.0321; p_{adj}<0.001) and inserting the **in*-token (0.0286, female biased; p_{adj}<0.001; see Table 3). The difference between both debiasing methods is significant (p_{adj}<0.001).

For female role nouns, mean absolute RIPA scores are lower in the base corpus (0.0023) than after affixation (-0.0524; p_{adj}<0.001) and inserting the **in*-token (0.0907; p_{adj}<0.001 see Table 3). The difference between both debiasing methods is significant (p_{adj}<0.001).

4.2 Experiment 2

For male role nouns, mean absolute RIPA scores of analogy resolutions in the base corpus (0.0935, fe-

Comparison	1st median	RIPA scores 2nd median	median change (abs.)	p	p_{adj}	signif.
Male role nouns						
base vs hard-debias	0.0935	0.0670	0.0264	6.55E-10	1.18E-08	···
base vs affix	0.0935	0.0555	0.0380	5.10E-34	9.19E-33	···
base vs **in*-token	0.0935	0.0037	0.0898	3.86E-65	6.95E-64	···
hard-debias vs affix	0.0670	0.0555	0.0116	3.16E-12	5.69E-11	···
hard-debias vs **in*-token	0.0670	0.0037	0.0633	1.67E-61	3.01E-60	···
**in*-token vs affix	0.0580	0.0572	0.0008	1.14E-13	5.36E-12	···
Female role nouns						
base vs hard-debias	0.1078	0.0866	0.0212	1.63E-06	2.94E-05	···
base vs affix	0.1078	0.0545	0.0533	3.37E-17	6.08E-16	···
base vs **in*-token	0.1078	-0.0486	0.0592	2.95E-20	5.32E-19	···
hard-debias vs affix	0.0866	0.0545	0.0321	2.39E-09	4.30E-08	···
hard-debias vs **in*-token	0.0866	-0.0486	0.0380	1.06E-19	1.90E-18	···
**in*-token vs affix	0.2254	0.0584	0.1670	3.16E-12	1.49E-10	···

Table 4: Gender association of role noun: base, after hard-debias, after affixation, after adding the **in*-token, separated by gender. Significance codes: · (p <.05), ·· (p <.01), ··· (p <.001).

Model	Word	Generated analogy resolutions
Base	Erzieherin	*Erzieherin*, *Lehrerin*, zieherin, *Gesellschafterin*, *Dichterin*
Hard-debiased	Erzieherin	*Erzieherin*, *Dichterin*, Zahl, Cuvier'schen, Aufbewahrung
Affixation	Erzieher*in	*Erzieher*in*, *Lehrer*in*, *Beamter*, *Gesellschafterin*, *Buchhalter*
**in*-token	Erzieherx	*Erziehx*, *Pflegx*, *Leitx*, *Schülx*, *Verwaltx*
Base	Maler	*Maler*, Tieck, verwandt, *Kaufmann*, Nadelbäume
Hard-debiased	Maler	Freundschaft, Censoriade, vollkommnen, Freundin, geneigt
Affixation	Maler*in	*Maler*in*, *Sieger*in*, *Dichter*in*, entschiedener, *Musiker*
**in*-token	Malx	*Malx*, *Beschreibx*, *Kellnx*, *Porträtmalx*, *Nothelfx*

Table 5: Sample analogy resolutions from each model. Role nouns in resolutions in *italics*. First five resolutions per word.

male biased) are significantly higher than after hard-debias (0.0670; p_{adj}<0.001), affixation (0.0555; p_{adj}<0.001), or inserting the **in*-token (0.0037; p_{adj}<0.001). Analogies generated after affixation have significantly (p_{adj}<0.001) weaker gender association than those generated after hard-debias or inserting the **in*-token (see Table 4, Figure 2).

For female role nouns, mean absolute RIPA scores of analogy resolutions in the base corpus (0.1078; female biased) are significantly higher than after hard-debias (0.0866; p_{adj}<0.01), after affixation (0.0545; p_{adj}>0.99), or after inserting the **in*-token (-0.0486, male-biased; p_{adj}>0.99). Affixation leads to significantly (p_{adj}>0.99) lower gender association than hard-debias or inserting the **in*-token (see Table 4, Figure 2).

The base model generates a mean of 0.71 nouns and 0.27 role nouns per analogy resolution, the hard-debiased model 1.20 nouns and 0.85 role nouns, the model that we debiased by inserting the **in*-token 7.54 nouns and role nouns, and the model that we debiased by affixation generates a mean of 2.07 nouns and 1.86 role nouns per analogy resolution (see Table 5 for examples).

5 Interpretation

The experiments conducted in this research have demonstrated that *GGS*, i.e. the practice of substituting role nouns with gender neutral versions (e.g. turning *Programmierer* ("male programmer") and *Programmiererin* ("female programmer") into *Programmierer*in*) does not lead to a significant reduction in gender association of these words' embeddings. As can be seen in Figure 1, the two methods of implementing *GGS* in the corpus (see Section 3.4) lead to different results: affixation leads to an overall shift to male associations, while adding the *in-token shifts gender association to female values. Affixation also leads to a greater spread of gender associations compared to adding the *in-token, especially for female role nouns. While adding the *in-token leads to overall greater absolute gender association for female role nouns, they are shifted towards female association, while they were already almost completely gender neutral in the base corpus. This indicates that *GGS* may simply shift gender associations towards the female end overall.

The second experiment (see Section 3.5) shows that hard-debias (see Bolukbasi et al., 2016) does work on languages with grammatical gender such as German, though it consistently performed worse than corpus debiasing. The results after adding the *in-token also had a far greater spread than any other condition (see also Figure 2), while affixation had the smallest spread.

The corpus-debiased models also generate a far greater proportion of role nouns per analogy resolution, with the model that was debiased by inserting the *in-token performing best in this regard. While this underlines their strong performance, it must be noted that this is not a fair comparison. We compute RIPA scores from the base model for the hard-debiased role nouns, while for the other two we compute them in their respective models. Role nouns, in the two altered corpora, occur in more similar environments, as they (and only they) are often preceded by the token *[ART]*, and in the case of the corpus that we debiased by inserting the *in-token, all role nouns are always followed by the the *in-token (see Table 1). This leads to role nouns' embeddings being more similar compared to other models, impacting the results of the experiment overall. This is a limitation of the methodology that we could not circumvent. However, the fact that all methods, but especially corpus debiasing, outperformed the base model by such a large margin is interesting, as it suggests that debiasing may lead to better analogy resolution performance, at least when it comes to role model analogies.

This may also be the reason for the seemingly contradictory results from both experiments: *GGS* leads to increased gender association in role nouns' embeddings, but reduced bias in analogy resolution. It appears that the analogy resolutions from the base corpus are fewer role nouns, but that those resolutions have stronger gender association than role nouns. The samples in Table 5 also (subjectively) appear qualitatively better to us: for example, *Maler*in* ("painter") is analogous to *Dichter*in* ("poet") and *Musiker*in* ("musician"), and *Malx* ("painter") is analogous to *Porträtmalx* ("portrait painter") after corpus debiasing, but not after other methods. In the base corpus, *Erzieherin* ("governess") is analogous to *Lehrerin* ("female teacher"), but also to *Dichterin* ("female poet") – the latter is not a good analogy, since the only relation appears to be gender.

The poor performance of the base model in analogy resolution, where it only managed to generate a noun in its top ten resolutions in 71% of cases, suggests that there may be issues with the data used, and a larger corpus (or one more tailored to role noun usage) may be necessary.

6 Conclusion and outlook

While *GGS* significantly increases gender association of role nouns, this does not necessarily invalidate the practice. Other than the ideological and philosophical questions that cannot be answered here, initial research on a smaller subset of this corpus yielded different results, where *GGS* significantly reduced gender association for male role nouns, but not female ones. This, once more, points to a weakness of this research: the results seem to depend on the corpus, and the corpus we use is rather small and may be too general, limiting the number of occurrences of role nouns even more. Further research with better suited corpora is necessary. Job postings, as one of the chief domains of *GGS*, would be particularly interesting data, but such corpora were not available. Use of larger or better suited corpora may also address the poor performance of the base model in analogy resolution and yield more informative data. Future research may also investigate if substituting gendered role nouns with gender neutral versions leads to the same results as balancing the occurrences of male and female versions of the role nouns.[3]

The research presented here has also demonstrated an additional weakness of existing debiasing methods, namely that their evaluation is very time consuming and usually involves crowdsourcing (such as in Bolukbasi et al., 2016). For German, no pre-made evaluation methods for hard-debias were available, and the method used here is far from perfect, as it evaluates analogies generated

[3]We would like to thank an anonymous reviewer for this suggestion.

from hard-debiased role nouns in the non-debiased model (to circumvent the problem where effectively, the same metrics to debias the role nouns are used to then measure their remaining bias), but for corpus-debiased embeddings, analogies are generated in their own models. This means that in reality, hard-debias may perform much better than the results in this research indicate. Nevertheless, it must be considered that debiasing methods that alter the data that embeddings are trained on perform comparably to hard-debiasing in this research.

Despite some weaknesses, this research demonstrates that natural language debiasing strategies are fundamentally different from post-hoc debiasing of pre-trained embeddings, and thus, the latter must be viewed with caution. It may still be used for practical purposes, but users must be aware that it is not analogous to societal efforts to reduce gender bias. These results are in line with Blodgett et al. (2020), who encourage researchers to more strongly relate their work to the experiences of real-world members of affected communities. While we do not directly engage with members of such affected communities, our findings that post-hoc debiasing is not equivalent to real-world natural language debiasing strategies lend further weight to their calls.

Lastly, we also partially address the question posed in (Bolukbasi et al., 2016) regarding the use of post-hoc word embeddings debiasing methods for language with grammatical gender. For the limited set of words investigated here, it does indeed lower gender association in analogy resolution. Future research with more sophisticated evaluation methodologies will shed more light on this area.

References

Christine Basta, Marta R. Costa-Jussà, and Noe Casas. 2020. Extensive study on the underlying gender bias in contextualized word embeddings. *Neural Computing and Applications*, 33(8):3371–3384.

Su Lin Blodgett, Solon Barocas, Hal Daumé III, and Hanna Wallach. 2020. Language (technology) is power: A critical survey of "bias" in NLP. In *Proceedings of the 58th Annual Meeting of the Association for Computational Linguistics*, pages 5454–5476, Online. Association for Computational Linguistics.

Piotr Bojanowski, Edouard Grave, Armand Joulin, and Tomas Mikolov. 2017. Enriching word vectors with subword information. *Transactions of the Association for Computational Linguistics*, 5:135–146.

Tolga Bolukbasi, Kai-Wei Chang, James Y Zou, Venkatesh Saligrama, and Adam T Kalai. 2016. Man is to computer programmer as woman is to homemaker? Debiasing word embeddings. In *Advances in Neural Information Processing Systems*, volume 29. Curran Associates, Inc.

Friederike Braun, Sabine Sczesny, and Dagmar Stahlberg. 2005. Cognitive effects of masculine generics in German: An overview of empirical findings. *Communications: The European Journal of Communication Research*, 30(1):1–21.

Aylin Caliskan, Joanna J. Bryson, and Arvind Narayanan. 2017. Semantics derived automatically from language corpora contain human-like biases. *Science*, 356(6334):183–186.

Rodrigo Alejandro Chávez Mulsa and Gerasimos Spanakis. 2020. Evaluating bias in Dutch word embeddings. In *Proceedings of the Second Workshop on Gender Bias in Natural Language Processing*, pages 56–71, Barcelona, Spain (Online). Association for Computational Linguistics.

Jeffrey Dastin. 2018. Amazon scraps secret AI recruiting tool that showed bias against women. *Reuters*.

Kawin Ethayarajh, David Duvenaud, and Graeme Hirst. 2019. Understanding undesirable word embedding associations. In *Proceedings of the 57th Annual Meeting of the Association for Computational Linguistics*, pages 1696–1705, Florence, Italy. Association for Computational Linguistics.

C Hansen, M Tosik, G Goossen, C Li, L Bayeva, F Berbain, and M Rotaru. 2015. How to get the best word vectors for resume parsing. In *SNN Adaptive Intelligence/Symposium: Machine Learning*.

Matthew Honnibal and Mark Johnson. 2015. An improved non-monotonic transition system for dependency parsing. In *Proceedings of the 2015 Conference on Empirical Methods in Natural Language Processing*, pages 1373–1378, Lisbon, Portugal. Association for Computational Linguistics.

J. D. Hunter. 2007. Matplotlib: A 2D graphics environment. *Computing in Science & Engineering*, 9(3):90–95.

Masahrio Kaneko and Danushka Bollegala. 2019. Gender-preserving debiasing for pre-trained word embeddings. In *Proceedings of the 57th Annual Meeting of the Association for Computational Linguistics*, pages 1641–1650, Florence, Italy. Association for Computational Linguistics.

Styliani Katsarou, Borja Rodríguez-Gálvez, and Jesse Shanahan. 2022. Measuring gender bias in contextualized embeddings. *Computer Sciences & Mathematics Forum*, 3(1).

Helga Kotthoff. 2020. Gender-Sternchen, Binnen-I oder generisches Maskulinum: (Akademische) Textstile der Personenreferenz als Registrierungen? *Linguistik Online*, 103(3):105–127.

Cataldo Musto, Giovanni Semeraro, Marco de Gemmis, and Pasquale Lops. 2015. Word embedding techniques for content-based recommender systems: An empirical evaluation. In *RecSys Posters*, volume 1441 of *CEUR Workshop Proceedings*. CEUR-WS.org.

Radim Řehůřek and Petr Sojka. 2010. Software Framework for Topic Modelling with Large Corpora. In *Proceedings of the LREC 2010 Workshop on New Challenges for NLP Frameworks*, pages 45–50, Valletta, Malta. ELRA.

Magnus Sahlgren and Fredrik Olsson. 2019. Gender bias in pretrained Swedish embeddings. In *Proceedings of the 22nd Nordic Conference on Computational Linguistics*, pages 35–43, Turku, Finland. Linköping University Electronic Press.

Steffen Schnitzer, Dominik Reis, Wael Alkhatib, Christoph Rensing, and Ralf Steinmetz. 2019. Preselection of documents for personalized recommendations of job postings based on word embeddings. In *Proceedings of the 34th ACM/SIGAPP Symposium on Applied Computing*, SAC '19, pages 1683–1686, New York, NY, USA. Association for Computing Machinery.

Skipper Seabold and Josef Perktold. 2010. Statsmodels: Econometric and statistical modeling with Python. In *9th Python in Science Conference*.

Robert Stöber. 2021. Genderstern und Binnen-I. *Publizistik*, 66(1):11–20.

Pauli Virtanen, Ralf Gommers, Travis E. Oliphant, Matt Haberland, Tyler Reddy, David Cournapeau, Evgeni Burovski, Pearu Peterson, Warren Weckesser, Jonathan Bright, Stéfan J. van der Walt, Matthew Brett, Joshua Wilson, K. Jarrod Millman, Nikolay Mayorov, Andrew R. J. Nelson, Eric Jones, Robert Kern, Eric Larson, C J Carey, İlhan Polat, Yu Feng, Eric W. Moore, Jake VanderPlas, Denis Laxalde, Josef Perktold, Robert Cimrman, Ian Henriksen, E. A. Quintero, Charles R. Harris, Anne M. Archibald, Antônio H. Ribeiro, Fabian Pedregosa, Paul van Mulbregt, and SciPy 1.0 Contributors. 2020. SciPy 1.0: Fundamental Algorithms for Scientific Computing in Python. *Nature Methods*, 17:261–272.

Proceedings of the 18th Conference on Natural Language Processing (KONVENS 2022)

Improved Open Source Automatic Subtitling for Lecture Videos

Robert Geislinger[1,2] Benjamin Milde[1,2] Chris Biemann[1]

[1]Language Technology Group, Universität Hamburg, Germany
[2]Hamburger Informatik Technologie-Center e.V., Germany
robert.geislinger@uni-hamburg.de
benjamin.milde@uni-hamburg.de
christian.biemann@uni-hamburg.de

Abstract

This paper summarizes the current state of development in improving an open source subtitling tool. This includes improvements to the speech recognition model for German, the replacement for the punctuation reconstruction architecture and the addition of an audio segmentation. The goal of these adjustments is an overall better subtitle quality. The most crucial part of the existing pipeline, the German speech recognition, is replaced by a new Kaldi TDNN-HMM model trained on 70% of additional audio data, resulting in a word error rate of 6.9% on Tuda-De. The punctuation reconstruction model for German texts is replaced by a Transformer-based approach that is also trained on new data. English is added as a fully supported second language, including speech recognition and punctuation reconstruction models. Furthermore, to improve speech recognition in long videos, audio segmentation was also added into the pipeline to support long videos flawlessly without quality issues.

1 Introduction

Remote learning with lecture videos has become the norm in the Covid-19 pandemic. Subtitling videos make them accessible for persons with hearing limitations. Since subtitling videos by hand is a time-consuming and cost-intensive task, this work offers a solution for automatic subtitling. Automatic speech recognition (ASR) is the most important step in the creation of subtitles, but for sufficient results, the text must also be supplemented with punctuation marks and be separated at appropriate places to achieve a good reading flow.

This paper presents the results of a revised pipeline to create German and English subtitles with open source algorithms and models. It also introduces the addition of audio segmentation as well as improvements to automatic speech recognition and punctuation reconstruction models. The entire pipeline is shown in Figure 1. The model for German ASR was revised and a model for English language was added. Also, the existing punctuation reconstruction model is replaced by a new Transformer-based architecture and trained on new data. It is now also possible to get live status information about the current processing step via a Redis database.

The tool is already in operation at the Universität Hamburg lecture video portal Lecture2Go[1] and the generated subtitles serve as a starting point for further manual annotation. Users of the platform can also correct the subtitles with a web-based subtitle editor.

2 Related Work

Generating subtitles with ASR can be performed both semi-automatically and automatically. In semi-automatic generation systems, texts are respoken in a controlled environment by a trained speaker (Sperber et al., 2013; Romero-Fresco, 2020; Vashistha et al., 2017). However, automatic systems are already being used to subtitle videos and conferences (Milde et al., 2021; Geislinger et al., 2021).

There are several models for German speech recognition available. A model based on Kaldi TDNN-HMM with ARPA rescoring and RNNLM achieved a word error rate (WER) of 7.4% on Tuda-De (Milde, 2022). The currently lowest WER on Tuda-De is a Conformer Transducer model with 5.8%, which is trained on about 4,600 hours of training data (Wirth and Peinl, 2022). The model presented in this paper with Kaldi TDNN-HMM architecture is trained on about 1,720 hours with a WER of 6.9%. A model for English speech recog-

[1]https://lecture2go.uni-hamburg.de

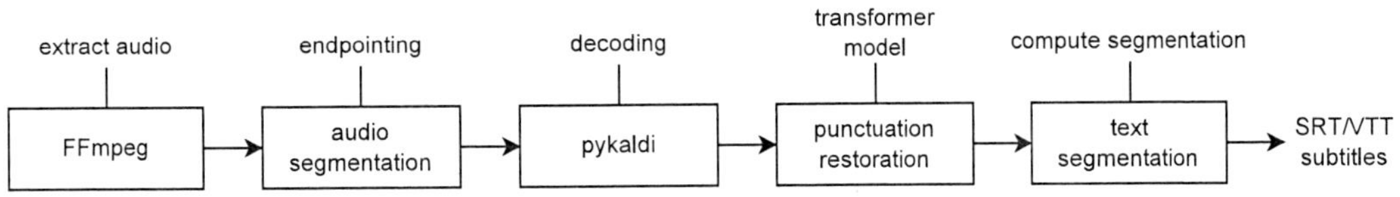

Figure 1: Full processing pipeline of the tool

nition achieved a WER of 5.9% on Switchboard (Tüske et al., 2021).

For punctuation reconstruction, there are also several available models. Multilingual models for German, English, French as well as Transformer based models for Polish (Chordia, 2021; Guhr et al., 2021; Wróbel and Zhylko, 2021). Recurrent Neural Networks are used by Hládek et al. (2019) to supplement a Slovak speech recognition system.

3 Speech Recognition Models

The most important feature that is needed in order to create suitable and understandable subtitles is a well-trained ASR model. This work is divided into the improvement of an existing, freely available German model speech recognition model and the creation of a new English speech recognition model under the Apache License 2.0 . Kaldi was used as a speech recognition framework to train our ASR models, as it is under the Apache License 2.0 and provides multiple training scripts for German and English, which were used as a starting point for this work (Povey et al., 2011). For decoding, we use Kaldi's nnet3 lattice decoder with PyKaldi (Can et al., 2018).

3.1 German Model

For automatic speech recognition in German, the freely available Kaldi-Tuda-De model was used as a basis for improvement. The training script uses 1,000 hours of audio data to train the acoustic model and about 100 million German sentences from several free available sources to train the language model (Milde and Köhn, 2018).

The training data for the acoustic model was increased from 1,000 hours by 720 hours to a total of 1,720 hours. This was achieved by replacing the Common Voice version 3 data set with the updated Common Voice version 8 data set (Ardila et al., 2020). This resulted in an expansion of the number of speakers about all data used from 5,546 to a total of 16,929. One of the model training data sets is Tuda-De which was also revised in this work to remove errors (Radeck-Arneth et al., 2015). Several broken audio files in the test and training data were removed and corrections were made to the transcript. In total, these corrections removed less than one minute of data, which is far less than one percent of the total data.

The training data for the language model were also part of the revision with the aim to achieve a lower WER and also to incorporate current words and terms into the language model. The data was crawled for this purpose from several freely available sources with the german-asr-lm-tools[2] project. The data consist mainly of articles from the news program Tagesschau, German Wikipedia, subtitles of German TV stations such as ARD and proceedings of the EU Parliament (Koehn, 2005).

The script to train the model itself was also improved to remove pitfalls in the training and make it easier to train and extend it with additional data for individual purposes (e.g. adding university lectures as training data). This should also give persons with limited language processing knowledge the possibility to train a model for their requirements.

The modifications in the Tuda-De data set and the additional data for the language and acoustic model lead to lower WER. The previous WER of the model was 14.4% with a lexicon of more than 350,000 words and without LM rescoring (Milde and Köhn, 2018). The newly trained model lowered the WER to 10.2% which is 29% relatively lower. This may be due to the increased lexicon of more than 900,000 words as well as the 70% more data.

When also using ARPA and RNNLM rescoring the model performs at 6.9% WER which is a relative reduction of 52% compared with the previous model. The results in comparison with other models are shown in Table 1. The training script and pretrained models are available[3] under the Apache License 2.0.

[2] https://github.com/bmilde/german-asr-lm-tools/

[3] https://github.com/uhh-lt/kaldi-tuda-de

System	Model	Data	test WER
Radeck-Arneth et al., 2015	TDNN-HMM hybrid, FST	108h	20.5
Milde and Köhn, 2018	"	375h	14.4
Milde, 2022	"	1720h	7.4
Wirth and Peinl, 2022	E2E / Conformer CTC	4520h	7.8
"	E2E / Conformer T	"	5.8
This model	TDNN-HMM hybrid, FST	1720h	6.9

Table 1: The WER results of the German models on the Tuda-De test set

3.2 English Model

To support speech recognition for English videos as well, an own expandable training script for English was created. The script is based on the TEDLIUM TDNN-HMM script for Kaldi. The TEDLIUM corpus consists of recordings of TED Talks. In total, the data set contains 118 hours of audio data (Hernandez et al., 2018).

To expand the training data, the Librispeech corpus was added. Librispeech contains recordings of audiobooks of the LibriVox and Gutenberg Project (Panayotov et al., 2015). This dataset is read speech, i.e. books read aloud in a quiet environment. A total of 100 hours of audio data are added to the script. This makes a total training data for the acoustic model of 218 hours.

Language model training material was expanded by YouTube subtitles from the pile data set. These additional texts add current topics and words to the training data (Gao et al., 2020). To prepare the texts, punctuation as well as languages other than English are removed. The toolkit to clean up English texts for language modelling in an ASR contest is available as a separate project[4]. Unknown words in the lexicon were added by using a Sequitur G2P model (Bisani and Ney, 2008), which was trained on already existing words in the combined lexicon of the TEDLIUM and Librispeech data set.

After Arpa and RNNLM rescoring the WER of the new model is 13.1% on Librispeech test set "test-other" and 4.8% on "test-clean" which is 12% lower compared to the model by Panayotov et al., 2015. On the TEDLIUM test data the WER is 10.3% which is 53% higher than the model by Hernandez et al., 2018. In their current state, the results on the TEDLIUM test set are still clearly in need of improvement. This can be achieved by adding further data sets like Gigaspeech, increasing the training data for the language model or train on further adapted training scripts (Chen et al., 2021). The results are shown in Table 2. The training script and pretrained English ASR models are available[5] under the Apache License 2.0.

System	Data	WER LS	WER TED
Panayotov et al., 2015	100h	5.5	
Hernandez et al., 2018	118h		**6.7**
This model	218h	**4.8**	10.3

Table 2: The WER results of Kaldi TDNN-HMM models on librispeech and TEDLIUM test set

4 Punctuation reconstruction

Text transcriptions generated by ASR often lack punctuation and capitalization. To make the text more human-readable in post-processing, punctuation is reconstructed. For German punctuation reconstruction, Milde et al. (2021) used Punctuator2 which was trained on 5 million lines of German text. This architecture is based on a recurrent neural network (Tilk and Alumäe, 2016). The goal of this work is to outperform the error rate of the German model and also train an English model. For both languages, pretrained BERT-based models are used. As a starting point to fine-tune the models, the trainings scripts of Daulet Nurmanbetov[6] are used. The pretrained German model used for later fine-tuning is GBERT (Chan et al., 2020). The German punctuation reconstruction model is fine-tuned on 94 million lines of German subtitles and Wikipedia articles. For evaluation, the NoSta-D corpus was used (Benikova et al., 2014). The model by Milde et al., 2021 achieved an error rate

[4] https://github.com/uhh-lt/english-asr-lm-tools

[5] https://github.com/uhh-lt/kaldi-asr-english

[6] https://github.com/Felflare/rpunct

Model	System	error rate
Milde et al., 2021	BRNN	9.1%
This model	BERT-based	6.2%

Table 3: Comparison German Punctuation reconstruction error rates on NoSta-D for period, comma and questionmark

of 9.1% for reconstruction of period, comma and question mark in German texts. The new model achieved an error rate of 6.2% which is relative reduction of 31%. The results are also shown in Table 3.

5 Changes in the Tool Pipeline

Further changes to the pipeline involve an added language selection, audio segmentation and process feedback. The pipeline with all parts is shown in Figure 1. The language can now be changed before each video and the languages are managed via a configuration file. To support a wider range of Kaldi models, support for CMVN and RNNLM rescoring was added to the decoder.

5.1 Audio segmentation

Processing longer videos as a whole can lead to unpredictable behavior in Kaldi. This can result in segments being skipped and gaps in the transcript. One reason for this behavior is the rising memory demand with every minute of decoding. To work around this problem and process videos of several hours running time flawlessly, the file must be split into smaller chunks. The easiest approach could be a hard cut after a fixed amount of time but that would also cut in the middle of words and thus increase the error rate. To avoid the problem of splitting during a word, an beam search based endpointing algorithm was implemented (Reddy, 1976).

The algorithm finds the best segmentation that breaks on pauses in the signal. It also seeks to fulfill an average segment length criteria (default 1 minute). For this, the energy of the signal is analyzed and splitting costs are assigned to all positions in the audio. The energy function is smoothed with a Gaussian filter, so that longer periods of low energy (longer pauses) have the lowest splitting cost. The search algorithm combines this with a segment length criteria and finds a solution that compromises between both criteria. These resulting segments can be passed to Kaldi as input. This also makes it possible for later enhancements to use multithreading to maximize the performance of the pipeline by decoding the segments simultaneously.

5.2 Process feedback

The new version of the tool adds also additional functionality to receive update messages about the progress of the pipeline when using the tool in a backend (e.g. a video platform). The tool sends information to registered services via a Redis pub/sub channel. These messages contain information about the current processing step. The status messages can be used to visualize the progress to a frontend while creating the subtitles. The additional feedback helps the user to understand the current progress of the processing job and there is also more information should a processing step fail.

6 Conclusion

Creating automatic subtitles for videos needs a lot of well-tuned models to attain good results. Even if an ASR system is the most important part of the pipeline, good models for punctuation reconstruction are also a necessity for well readable subtitles. Previously, our tool was only able to subtitle German videos. We were able to improve the German ASR model and significantly improved WER results. We also expanded language support and added models for English. Further additions presented in this paper added more possibilities in the existing tool, especially when used in a backend of a video platform.

The subtitling software is published[7] under the Apache License 2.0, with instructions and download scripts for all necessary models.

7 Outlook

Since the project is still in development at this point, we hope that the results will continue to improve. This concerns in particular the punctuation model as well as the English ASR model.

When Kaldi's successor K2 (Żelasko et al., 2021) is more stable, a new German and English model based on the presented training scripts can be developed and trained. With this new architecture and additional data sets, this could also lead to better results due to new acoustic modelling techniques.

The reconstruction of punctuation could be further optimized with usage of Transformer-based

[7] https://github.com/uhh-lt/subtitle2go

models. This could be done with more training data and also with new models and architectures. Platforms with Transformer models bring a wide range of pre-trained models and training scripts (Wolf et al., 2019). Research on the post-processing pipeline could also lead to a new end-to-end model to summarize the different steps into one specially adapted model for the purpose of subtitle creation. Besides the added English models, other languages could bring the project to a wider audience outside of German and English videos.

For longer videos, multithreading could be used on the segmented audio, to transcribe different parts of one video in parallel.

References

Rosana Ardila, Megan Branson, Kelly Davis, Michael Kohler, Josh Meyer, Michael Henretty, Reuben Morais, Lindsay Saunders, Francis Tyers, and Gregor Weber. 2020. Common voice: A massively-multilingual speech corpus. In *Proceedings of the 12th Language Resources and Evaluation Conference*, pages 4218–4222, Marseille, France.

Darina Benikova, Chris Biemann, and Marc Reznicek. 2014. Nosta-d named entity annotation for german: Guidelines and dataset. In *Proceedings of the Ninth International Conference on Language Resources and Evaluation (LREC'14)*, pages 2524–2531, Reykjavik, Iceland.

Maximilian Bisani and Hermann Ney. 2008. Joint-sequence models for grapheme-to-phoneme conversion. *Speech communication*, 50(5):434–451.

Dogan Can, Victor Martinez, Pavlos Papadopoulos, and Shrikanth Narayanan. 2018. PyKaldi: A python wrapper for Kaldi. In *Proc. Acoustics, Speech and Signal Processing (ICASSP)*, pages 5889–5893, Calgary, Canada.

Branden Chan, Stefan Schweter, and Timo Möller. 2020. German's next language model. In *Proceedings of the 28th International Conference on Computational Linguistics*, pages 6788–6796, Barcelona, Spain (Online).

Guoguo Chen, Shuzhou Chai, Guanbo Wang, Jiayu Du, Wei-Qiang Zhang, Chao Weng, Dan Su, Daniel Povey, Jan Trmal, Junbo Zhang, Mingjie Jin, Sanjeev Khudanpur, Shinji Watanabe, Shuaijiang Zhao, Wei Zou, Xiangang Li, Xuchen Yao, Yongqing Wang, Yujun Wang, Zhao You, and Zhiyong Yan. 2021. Gigaspeech: An evolving, multi-domain asr corpus with 10,000 hours of transcribed audio. In *Proc. Interspeech 2021*, pages 3670–3674, Brno, Czech Republic.

Varnith Chordia. 2021. PunKtuator: A multilingual punctuation restoration system for spoken and written text. In *Proceedings of the 16th Conference of the European Chapter of the Association for Computational Linguistics: System Demonstrations*, pages 312–320, Online. Association for Computational Linguistics.

Leo Gao, Stella Biderman, Sid Black, Laurence Golding, Travis Hoppe, Charles Foster, Jason Phang, Horace He, Anish Thite, Noa Nabeshima, Shawn Presser, and Connor Leahy. 2020. The Pile: An 800gb dataset of diverse text for language modeling. *arXiv preprint arXiv:2101.00027*.

Robert Geislinger, Benjamin Milde, Timo Baumann, and Chris Biemann. 2021. Live Subtitling for BigBlueButton with Open-Source Software. In *Proc. Interspeech 2021*, pages 3319–3320, Brno, Czech Republic.

Oliver Guhr, Anne-Kathrin Schumann, Frank Bahrmann, and Hans Joachim Böhme. 2021. Fullstop: Multilingual deep models for punctuation prediction. In *Proceedings of the Swiss Text Analytics Conference 2021*, Winterthur, Switzerland.

François Hernandez, Vincent Nguyen, Sahar Ghannay, Natalia Tomashenko, and Yannick Esteve. 2018. Tedlium 3: twice as much data and corpus repartition for experiments on speaker adaptation. In *International conference on speech and computer*, pages 198–208.

Daniel Hládek, Ján Staš, and Stanislav Ondáš. 2019. Comparison of recurrent neural networks for slovak punctuation restoration. In *2019 10th IEEE International Conference on Cognitive Infocommunications (CogInfoCom)*, pages 95–100, Naples, Italy.

Philipp Koehn. 2005. Europarl: A parallel corpus for statistical machine translation. In *Proceedings of Machine Translation Summit X: Papers*, pages 79–86, Phuket, Thailand.

Benjamin Milde. 2022. *On Representation Learning in Speech Processing and Automatic Speech Recognition.* Ph.D. thesis, Universität Hamburg, Germany.

Benjamin Milde, Robert Geislinger, Irina Lindt, and Timo Baumann. 2021. Open source automatic lecture subtitling. In *Proceedings of ESSV 2021*, pages 128–134, Virtual Berlin, Germany.

Benjamin Milde and Arne Köhn. 2018. Open source automatic speech recognition for German. In *Proceedings of ITG 2018*, pages 251–255, Oldenburg, Germany.

Vassil Panayotov, Guoguo Chen, Daniel Povey, and Sanjeev Khudanpur. 2015. Librispeech: An asr corpus based on public domain audio books. In *2015 IEEE International Conference on Acoustics, Speech and Signal Processing (ICASSP)*, pages 5206–5210, Brisbane, Australia.

Daniel Povey, Arnab Ghoshal, Gilles Boulianne, Lukas Burget, Ondrej Glembek, Nagendra Goel, Mirko Hannemann, Petr Motlicek, Yanmin Qian, Petr Schwarz, Jan Silovsky, Georg Stemmer, and Karel

Vesely. 2011. The kaldi speech recognition toolkit. In *IEEE 2011 Workshop on Automatic Speech Recognition and Understanding*, Hilton Waikoloa Village, Hawaii, USA.

Stephan Radeck-Arneth, Benjamin Milde, Arvid Lange, Evandro Gouvea, Stefan Radomski, Max Mühlhäuser, and Chris Biemann. 2015. Open Source German Distant Speech Recognition: Corpus and Acoustic Model. In *Proceedings Text, Speech and Dialogue (TSD)*, pages 480–488, Pilsen, Czech Republic.

Raj Reddy. 1976. *Summary of Results of the Five-Year Research Effort at Carnegie-Mellon University*. Carnegie-Mellon University, Department of Computer Science.

Pablo Romero-Fresco. 2020. *Subtitling through speech recognition: Respeaking*. Routledge.

Matthias Sperber, Graham Neubig, Christian Fügen, Satoshi Nakamura, and Alex Waibel. 2013. Efficient speech transcription through respeaking. In *Proceedings of Interspeech 2013*, pages 1087–1091, Lyon, France.

Ottokar Tilk and Tanel Alumäe. 2016. Bidirectional recurrent neural network with attention mechanism for punctuation restoration. In *Proceedings of Interspeech 2016*, pages 3047–3051, San Francisco, California, USA.

Zoltán Tüske, George Saon, and Brian Kingsbury. 2021. On the limit of english conversational speech recognition. *arXiv preprint arXiv:2105.00982*.

Aditya Vashistha, Pooja Sethi, and Richard Anderson. 2017. Respeak: A voice-based, crowd-powered speech transcription system. In *Proceedings of the 2017 CHI conference on human factors in computing systems*, pages 1855–1866, Denver, Colorado, USA.

Johannes Wirth and Rene Peinl. 2022. Asr in german: A detailed error analysis. *arXiv preprint arXiv:2204.05617*.

Thomas Wolf, Lysandre Debut, Victor Sanh, Julien Chaumond, Clement Delangue, Anthony Moi, Pierric Cistac, Tim Rault, Rémi Louf, Morgan Funtowicz, et al. 2019. Huggingface's transformers: State-of-the-art natural language processing. *arXiv e-prints*, pages arXiv–1910.

Krzysztof Wróbel and Dmytro Zhylko. 2021. Punctuation restoration with transformers. In *Proceedings of the PolEval 2021 Workshop*, pages 33–37, Warsaw, Poland.

Piotr Żelasko, Daniel Povey, and Sanjeev Khudanpur. 2021. Speech recognition with next-generation kaldi (k2, lhotse, icefall). In *Proc. Interspeech 2021*, Brno, Czech Republic.

Proceedings of the 18th Conference on Natural Language Processing (KONVENS 2022)

Constructing a Derivational Morphology Resource with Transformer Morpheme Segmentation

Łukasz Knigawka
Warsaw University of Technology
Faculty of Electrical Engineering ul. Koszykowa 75
00-662 Warszawa, Poland
lukasz.knigawka.stud@pw.edu.pl

Abstract

This paper describes a framework for the creation of new derivational morphology databases for a selected set of productive affixes in English. The sample resource obtained comprises almost 120k English words with morpheme segmentations generated by Transformer. The model and the database have been compared against other existing solutions. Moreover, this study offers an overview of potentially problematic cases encountered during the process of automatic word segmentation.

1 Introduction

Derivational morphology studies the formation of new words (lexemes) "rather than forms of a single word (cf. inflection)" (Bauer, 2004). The most common way of deriving new English words is affixation, which involves combining potential bases with affixes so that a new, morphologically complex word can be built. In the present study, two kinds of affixation are considered: suffixation (suffixes are the affixes placed after a base) and prefixation (prefixes precede a base). Affixes, as well as the bases, can be subsumed under morphemes, which are the smallest meaningful morphological units of a language (Hockett, 1958). Morphological segmentation divides words into morphemes, hence automatic morpheme segmentation employs computational methods of morpheme boundary identification. The main focus of this paper is canonical segmentation, first introduced in Cotterell et al. (2016b). It analyses a word as a sequence of canonical morphemes representing the underlying forms of morphemes, which may differ from their orthographic representations. For example, the canonical segmentation of the word *funniest* is *fun-y-est*. In principle, canonical morphological segmentation constitutes a useful, though insufficient, tool for the analysis of morphologically complex words. In this work, methods of automatic morpheme segmentation are reviewed with the aim to create new morphological resources. Initially, a machine learning model is trained to perform canonical morphological segmentation. Subsequently, English words consisting of more than one morpheme are selected for further analysis. All the model input words are potentially affixed, i.e. they contain one of the affixes (prefixes and suffixes) under review. This study also investigates how the trained segmentation model would deal with problematic morphological cases.

2 Related Work

Several recent studies have focused on automatic morphological segmentation. The log-linear model proposed in Cotterell et al. (2016b) is to learn to segment and restore orthographic changes jointly. In Kann et al. (2016), a character-level model consisting of five encoder-decoders is introduced and has become the new state-of-the-art. Convolutional neural networks have been applied in the process of morphological segmentation of Russian words in Sorokin and Kravtsova (2018). A discriminative joint model for canonical segmentation, with a context-free grammar backbone, has been introduced in Cotterell et al. (2016a). After applying it to a subset of the English portion of the CELEX data (Baayen et al., 1996), an annotated treebank consisting of over 7k English words was released. Importantly, Mager et al. (2020) propose two new approaches to obtaining canonical segmentations of words whilst working with limited training data: an LSTM pointer-generator and a neural transducer trained with imitation learning. The two recommended methods outperformed baselines in the low-resource setting while achieving scores close to the best models in the high-resource cases. Another attempt at generating canonical segmentations of lexical items from low-resource languages is described in Moeng et al. (2022), where Transformer obtained not only the highest performance score but also the supervised models outperformed the unsupervised ones. On the other hand, a novel, semi-automatic method of the construction of word-formation networks, focusing mainly on derivation, is proposed in Lango et al. (2021), where sequential pattern mining is used in an unsupervised manner to construct morphological features.

The application of neural networks in different computational morphology tasks, such as morphological segmentation, is delineated in Liu (2021). A model capable of building better word representations for morphologically complex words is proposed in Luong et al. (2013), where RNNs are combined with neural language models to learn morphologically-aware word representations. Other studies, such as Jurdzinski (2017) and El-Kishky et al. (2019), show that performing morpheme segmentation may facilitate the capturing of word properties more efficiently when creating word embeddings. Song et al. (2020) demonstrate that adopting Transformer (Vaswani et al., 2017) to process morpheme information on the input layer may improve performance in the semantic textual similarity task. Hofmann et al. (2021) examine how the input segmentation of BERT (Devlin et al., 2018) affects its interpretations of derivationally complex words and suggests afterwards that the generalisation capabilities of pretrained language models could be improved if a morphologically-informed vocabulary of input tokens has been applied. Hofmann et al. (2020) focus on productive derivational morphology and indicate that pre-trained language models, BERT specifically, could generate correct derivatives in a sentence cloze task.

Although many modifications to the standard Transformer architecture have been proposed since the original paper was published, many of them failed to do well across different applications, as demonstrated in Narang et al. (2021). Some Transformer implementations aim explicitly at improving model efficiency. For instance, Primer (So et al., 2021) achieved a smaller training cost thanks to squaring ReLU activations and adding depthwise convolution layers in self-attention. As per Wu et al. (2021), the batch size was crucial in the performance of Transformers on character-level tasks, and with a large enough batch size, recurrent networks are outperformed.

This paragraph presents several recent studies that have attempted to create morphological resources. For instance, Universal Derivations constitutes a collection of harmonised (converted into a common file format and partially converted to a shared schema) word-formation resources (Kyjánek et al., 2020), while DErivBase is a rule-based framework for inducing derivational families for German (Zeller et al., 2013). That approach is further developed for Russian in DErivBase.Ru (Vodolazsky, 2020), whereas almost 70k English words were gathered in the derivational database named MorphoLexEN and presented in Sánchez Gutiérrez et al. (2017). Similar procedures for word segmentation as those used in MorphoLexEN are utilised in MorphoLexFR (Mailhot et al., 2019) which includes almost 39k French words. A derivational and inflectional morphology database (extracted from Wiktionary and consisting of about 519k derivatives in 15 languages) called Morphynet is proposed in Batsuren et al. (2021).

3 Experiments

A transformer model[1] consisting of encoding and decoding blocks was used to obtain word morpheme segmentations. The encoder block comprised positional embedding, multi-head attention, feed-forward and dropout, while the decoder blocks were constructed with the same layers, but the positional embedding layer was masked. The Transformer implementation used for experiments differed slightly from the one proposed in Vaswani et al. (2017). Learned positional encoding was applied instead of a static one, the optimiser's learning rate was static instead of one with warm-up and cool-down, and no label smoothing was utilised. The implementation of the model was inspired by that explored in Moeng et al. (2022). The hidden dimension was set to 256, and the learning rate worked best at 0.0005. A relatively small dropout of 0.1 was applied. Various optimizers available in PyTorch were tested, e.g., Adam (Kingma and Ba, 2014), RAdam (Liu et al., 2019), NAdam (Dozat, 2016), AdamW (Loshchilov and Hutter, 2017), Adadelta (Zeiler, 2012) and Adagrad (Duchi et al., 2011). Adam was chosen in Vaswani et al. (2017) and Moeng et al. (2022), but AdamW led to slightly better results in BERT. NAdam performed best in this research. Different activation functions were tested to replace ReLU (which was used in Moeng et al., 2022), and even though the differences

[1]The code is accessible at `https://anonymous.4open.science/r/CanonicalSegmentationTransformers-81ED/`

Type	List
Prefix	after, anti, back, circum, contra, counter, de, dis, ex, extra, fore, hyper, im, in, inter, intra, macro, mal, mega, mis, non, out, over, post, pre, pro, pseudo, re, retro, sub, super, supra, trans, ultra, un, under
Suffix	able, age, al, an, ance, ancy, ant, ary, ate, dom, ee, eer, en, er, ess, esque, ette, ful, hood, ian, ic, free, ify, ion, ise, ize, ite, ish, ism, ist, ity, ive, less, let, like, ment, ness, or, ous, ship, some, ster, th, wise, y

Table 1: Lists of considered productive affixes.

in the model scores obtained were not significant, consistently, the best results were obtained with GeLU (Hendrycks and Gimpel, 2016). Squaring ReLU activations, as proposed in Primer slightly decreased performance which decreased even more after trying out Swish units (Ramachandran et al., 2017).

The new derivational morphology resource was built with Transformer word morpheme segmentation. The model was trained on the data from MorphoLexEN. The words used to develop this resource were obtained from the English Lexicon Project (Balota et al., 2007) and were already segmented into morphemes. Inflectional suffixes such as *-s*, *-ing* or *-ed* and contractions such as *'ll* or *'s* were removed manually. Out of 68,624 words in the database, 80% formed the training set, and 10% were assigned to validation and test sets.

A relatively extensive list of English words was compiled out of lexical items from various sources: NLTK corpus (Bird and Loper, 2004), Brown corpus (Francis and Kucera, 1979) and built-in English word lists of macOS and Ubuntu. Each word was case-insensitive. Many words overlapped, so all the duplicates had to be removed. Then, all the individual lists were merged into one list containing 315,404 words. Finally, each word from the list was automatically segmented and entered in the morphological resource, provided that the relevant number of automatically segmented morphemes was greater than one and the lexical item under study started or ended with one of the selected affixes. A set of recognisable productive affixes considered in this study is presented in Table 1.

Model	Accuracy	F1
Semi-CRF	0.54 (.018)	0.75 (.014)
Joint	0.77 (.013)	0.87 (.007)
Joint+Vec	0.82 (.020)	0.90 (.008)
Transformer	0.77 (.015)	0.79 (.015)

Table 2: Results of the canonical segmentation task on a subset of the English part of the CELEX database. Standard deviation is given in parentheses.

4 Results

In this section, model performance is compared to other solutions, the new derivational morphological resource is evaluated, and puzzling morphological cases are analysed.

4.1 Model performance

The model used to create the morphological resource was trained on the subset (Cotterell, 2016) of the English portion of the CELEX lexical database with the view to compare model performance with other modern solutions. The reported results were obtained with 10-fold cross-validation. The training, validation and test sets consisted of 8k, 1k and 1k samples, respectively. Encoder and decoder dropouts were increased to 0.3 to account for limited data issue. Adam optimization and ReLU activations seemed to work best in this low-resource setting. Two metrics were used for comparison: accuracy and morpheme F1 (Van den Bosch and Daelemans, 1999). Segmentation accuracy measured whether every canonical morpheme was identified correctly. This implies that this metric is very harsh, and very close answers are penalized equally as the wrong ones. Morpheme F1 would give credit only if some canonical morphemes were identified correctly. Results are exhibited in Table 2, where the developed model was compared with Semi-CRF (Sarawagi and Cohen, 2004), Joint (Cotterell et al., 2016b) and Joint+Vec (Cotterell and Schütze, 2018).

The Transformer accuracy and F1 measure are close to the scores of other models. More data would probably significantly increase the performance of the tested model. The model used to create the new resource was trained on a several times larger dataset (a subset of MorphoLexEN) and achieved over 94% morpheme F1 and almost 93% segmentation accuracy on the test dataset.

	Morphynet	MorphoLexEN	Morfem (non-strict matching)	Morfem (strict matching)	Combined
Size	67,412	68,624	163,036	118,900	235,579
Precision	0.628	0.592	0.594	0.700	0.561
Recall	0.814	0.848	0.879	0.754	0.929
F1	0.709	0.697	0.709	0.723	0.700

Table 3: Word count, precision, recall and F1 comparison of two chosen linguistic resources, two variants of the proposed one and a combination of Morphynet, MorphoLexEN and Morfem without strict matching.

4.2 The new resource

The obtained morphological resource, named Morfem, consists of 118,900 words supplied with their segmentations[2]. In what follows, the evaluation of the database is discussed.

One thousand random words from the database were manually checked to determine whether their morphological status was correctly recognised. It turned out that over 90% of the randomly selected words constituted complex words derived with one of the selected affixes. The words which were manually marked as simplex yet segmented by the model could be subsumed under different categories. The general list included some proper names, e.g., *Demontez* was segmented as *De-montez*, along with lexical items that were not listed in English dictionaries, e.g., *unie*, or, misspelled words, e.g., *tecnology*. Some morphological cases appeared to be problematic. Certain primarily lexicalized words with potentially divisible internal structures may pose some obstacles, e.g., the words *delay* and *discard* may be treated either as delay and *discard* or *de-lay* and *dis-card*. In MorphoLexEN, *delay* was treated as a single morpheme, while *discard* was divided. The model managed to learn that, and thus only *discard* was included in the resulting database (was divided into *dis* and *card*).

To automatically validate the resource, 901 derivatives containing one of the affixes under study were retrieved manually from Joseph Conrad's Heart of Darkness (Conrad, 1899/2006). Precision and recall measures were calculated for the new database, MorphyNet and MorphoLexEN, to compare the coverage of the created resource with other morphological databases. Words that were present in both, a database and in the manually selected set of derivatives from the book, were marked as true positives. Words that were present in the book and a database, but not in the manually selected set were counted as false positives. Finally, the words that were manually selected, but not found in a resource were designated as false negatives. The test results are presented in Table 3. Two versions were compared with the other databases. One with strict matching, where a word was noted in the resource only if one of the identified morphemes overlapped with an affix from the list. The other, without strict-matching, included all the words which contained more than one morpheme, and started or ended with at least one of the selected affixes. Morfem with strict matching achieved the highest precision while lacking in recall. Morfem with non-strict matching achieved the highest coverage of the derivatives, which is indicated by the highest recall score among the compared databases. Combining the non-strict Morfem with other resources (excluding the strict-matching Morfem) to form a unified vocabulary resulted in even higher recall alongside a significant precision decrease. Deciding which metric is the most relevant depends on the specific application.

5 Conclusion

The proposed framework allows for creating morphological resources larger than those currently available. The automatic morpheme segmentation task results are promising, but there is still some room for improvement. Therefore, a more reliable linguistic resource could be compiled when built upon a more reliable segmentation algorithm. Current state-of-the-art methods of canonical morphological segmentation do not consider the word's context. Knowing that words can be divided differently depending on their context (e.g., *recover* or *re-cover*), methods consulting the context should be developed.

[2]The resource is available at https://anonymous.4open.science/r/CanonicalSegmentationTransformers-81ED/src/CanonicalSegmentationTransformers/experiments/db.txt

References

R Harald Baayen, Richard Piepenbrock, and Leon Gulikers. 1996. The CELEX lexical database (cd-rom).

David A Balota, Melvin J Yap, Keith A Hutchison, Michael J Cortese, Brett Kessler, Bjorn Loftis, James H Neely, Douglas L Nelson, Greg B Simpson, and Rebecca Treiman. 2007. The English Lexicon Project. *Behavior Research Methods*, 39(3):445–459.

Khuyagbaatar Batsuren, Gábor Bella, and Fausto Giunchiglia. 2021. Morphynet: a Large Multilingual Database of Derivational and Inflectional Morphology. In *Proceedings of the 18th SIGMORPHON Workshop on Computational Research in Phonetics, Phonology, and Morphology*, pages 39–48.

Laurie Bauer. 2004. *A Glossary of Morphology*. Washington, D.C.: Georgetown University Press.

Steven Bird and Edward Loper. 2004. NLTK: The Natural Language Toolkit. In *Proceedings of the ACL Interactive Poster and Demonstration Sessions*, pages 214–217, Barcelona, Spain. Association for Computational Linguistics.

Joseph Conrad. 1899/2006. *Heart of Darkness*. Project Gutenberg, https://www.gutenberg.org/ebooks/219.

Ryan Cotterell. 2016. Canonical segmentation data. `https://github.com/ryancotterell/canonical-segmentation/tree/master/english`. [Online; accessed 14-November-2021].

Ryan Cotterell, Arun Kumar, and Hinrich Schütze. 2016a. Morphological Segmentation Inside-Out. In *Proceedings of the 2016 Conference on Empirical Methods in Natural Language Processing*, pages 2325–2330.

Ryan Cotterell and Hinrich Schütze. 2018. Joint Semantic Synthesis and Morphological Analysis of the Derived Word. *Transactions of the Association for Computational Linguistics*, 6:33–48.

Ryan Cotterell, Tim Vieira, and Hinrich Schütze. 2016b. A Joint Model of Orthography and Morphological Segmentation. In *Proceedings of the 2016 Conference of the North American Chapter of the Association for Computational Linguistics: Human Language Technologies*, pages 664–669, San Diego, California. Association for Computational Linguistics.

Jacob Devlin, Ming-Wei Chang, Kenton Lee, and Kristina Toutanova. 2018. BERT: Pre-training of Deep Bidirectional Transformers for Language Understanding. *arXiv preprint arXiv:1810.04805*.

Timothy Dozat. 2016. Incorporating Nesterov Momentum into Adam. *ICLR Workshop*.

John Duchi, Elad Hazan, and Yoram Singer. 2011. Adaptive Subgradient Methods for Online Learning and Stochastic Optimization. *Journal of Machine Learning Research*, 12(Jul):2121–2159.

Ahmed El-Kishky, Frank F. Xu, Aston Zhang, and Jiawei Han. 2019. Parsimonious Morpheme Segmentation with an Application to Enriching Word Embeddings. *2019 IEEE International Conference on Big Data (Big Data)*, pages 64–73.

W Nelson Francis and Henry Kucera. 1979. Brown corpus manual. *Letters to the Editor*, 5(2):7.

Dan Hendrycks and Kevin Gimpel. 2016. Gaussian Error Linear Units (GELUs). *arXiv preprint arXiv:1606.08415*.

Charles F. Hockett. 1958. *A course in Modern Linguistics*. New York: The Macmillan Company.

Valentin Hofmann, Janet Pierrehumbert, and Hinrich Schütze. 2021. Superbizarre Is Not Superb: Derivational Morphology Improves BERT's Interpretation of Complex Words. In *Proceedings of the 59th Annual Meeting of the Association for Computational Linguistics and the 11th International Joint Conference on Natural Language Processing (Volume 1: Long Papers)*, pages 3594–3608.

Valentin Hofmann, Janet B Pierrehumbert, and Hinrich Schütze. 2020. DagoBERT: Generating Derivational Morphology with a Pretrained Language Model. *arXiv preprint arXiv:2005.00672*.

Grzegorz Jurdzinski. 2017. Word Embeddings for Morphologically Complex Languages. *Schedae Informaticae*, 25.

Katharina Kann, Ryan Cotterell, and Hinrich Schütze. 2016. Neural Morphological Analysis: Encoding-Decoding Canonical Segments. In *Proceedings of the 2016 Conference on Empirical Methods in Natural Language Processing*, pages 961–967.

Diederik P Kingma and Jimmy Ba. 2014. Adam: A Method for Stochastic Optimization. *arXiv preprint arXiv:1412.6980*.

Lukáš Kyjánek, Zdenek Zabokrtsky, Magda Sevcikova, and Jonáš Vidra. 2020. Universal Derivations 1.0, A Growing Collection of Harmonised Word-Formation Resources. *The Prague Bulletin of Mathematical Linguistics*, 115:5–30.

Mateusz Lango, Zdenek Zabokrtsky, and Magda Sevcikova. 2021. Semi-automatic construction of word-formation networks. *Language Resources and Evaluation*, 55.

Ling Liu. 2021. Computational Morphology with Neural Network Approaches. *arXiv e-prints*, pages arXiv–2105.

Liyuan Liu, Haoming Jiang, Pengcheng He, Weizhu Chen, Xiaodong Liu, Jianfeng Gao, and Jiawei Han. 2019. On the Variance of the Adaptive Learning Rate and Beyond. *arXiv preprint arXiv:1908.03265*.

Ilya Loshchilov and Frank Hutter. 2017. Decoupled Weight Decay Regularization. *arXiv preprint arXiv:1711.05101*.

Minh-Thang Luong, Richard Socher, and Christopher D Manning. 2013. Better Word Representations with Recursive Neural Networks for Morphology. In *Proceedings of the Seventeenth Conference on Computational Natural Language Learning*, pages 104–113.

Manuel Mager, Özlem Çetinoğlu, and Katharina Kann. 2020. Tackling the Low-resource Challenge for Canonical Segmentation. In *Proceedings of the 2020 Conference on Empirical Methods in Natural Language Processing (EMNLP)*, pages 5237–5250.

Hugo Mailhot, Maximiliano Wilson, Joël Macoir, Hélène Deacon, and Claudia Sánchez Gutiérrez. 2019. Morpholex-FR: A derivational morphological database for 38,840 French words. *Behavior Research Methods*, 52.

Tumi Moeng, Sheldon Reay, Aaron Daniels, and Jan Buys. 2022. Canonical and Surface Morphological Segmentation for Nguni Languages. In *Artificial Intelligence Research*, pages 125–139, Cham. Springer International Publishing.

Sharan Narang, Hyung Won Chung, Yi Tay, William Fedus, Thibault Fevry, Michael Matena, Karishma Malkan, Noah Fiedel, Noam Shazeer, Zhenzhong Lan, et al. 2021. Do Transformer Modifications Transfer Across Implementations and Applications? *arXiv preprint arXiv:2102.11972*.

Prajit Ramachandran, Barret Zoph, and Quoc V Le. 2017. Searching for Activation Functions. *arXiv preprint arXiv:1710.05941*.

Sunita Sarawagi and William W Cohen. 2004. Semi-Markov Conditional Random Fields for Information Extraction. *Advances in Neural Information Processing Systems*, 17.

David So, Wojciech Mańke, Hanxiao Liu, Zihang Dai, Noam Shazeer, and Quoc V Le. 2021. Searching for Efficient Transformers for Language Modeling. *Advances in Neural Information Processing Systems*, 34:6010–6022.

Yuncheng Song, Shuaifei Song, Juncheng Ge, Menghan Zhang, and Wei Yang. 2020. Incorporating Morphological Compostions with Transformer to Improve BERT. *Journal of Physics: Conference Series*, 1486:072071.

Alexey Sorokin and Anastasia Kravtsova. 2018. *Deep Convolutional Networks for Supervised Morpheme Segmentation of Russian Language: 7th International Conference, AINL 2018, St. Petersburg, Russia, October 17–19, 2018, Proceedings*, pages 3–10.

Claudia Sánchez Gutiérrez, Hugo Mailhot, Hélène Deacon, and Maximiliano Wilson. 2017. MorphoLex: A derivational morphological database for 70,000 English words. *Behavior Research Methods*, http://link.springer.com/article/10.3758/s13428-017-0981-8:1–13.

Antal Van den Bosch and Walter Daelemans. 1999. Memory-Based Morphological Analysis. In *Proceedings of the 37th Annual Meeting of the Association for Computational Linguistics*, pages 285–292.

Ashish Vaswani, Noam Shazeer, Niki Parmar, Jakob Uszkoreit, Llion Jones, Aidan N Gomez, Łukasz Kaiser, and Illia Polosukhin. 2017. Attention Is All You Need. *Advances in Neural Information Processing Systems*, 30.

Daniil Vodolazsky. 2020. DerivBase.Ru: a Derivational Morphology Resource for Russian. In *Proceedings of the 12th Language Resources and Evaluation Conference*, pages 3937–3943, Marseille, France. European Language Resources Association.

Shijie Wu, Ryan Cotterell, and Mans Hulden. 2021. Applying the Transformer to Character-level Transduction. In *EACL*.

Matthew D Zeiler. 2012. ADADELTA: An Adaptive Learning Rate Method. *arXiv preprint arXiv:1212.5701*.

Britta Zeller, Jan Šnajder, and Sebastian Padó. 2013. DErivBase: Inducing and Evaluating a Derivational Morphology Resource for German. In *Proceedings of the 51st Annual Meeting of the Association for Computational Linguistics (Volume 1: Long Papers)*, pages 1201–1211.

Proceedings of the 18th Conference on Natural Language Processing (KONVENS 2022)

Improved Opinion Role Labelling in Parliamentary Debates

Laura Bamberg University of Mannheim
Ines Rehbein University of Mannheim
Simone Paolo Ponzetto University of Mannheim
{rehbein,ponzetto}@uni-mannheim.de

Abstract

This paper presents a model for German Opinion Role Labelling (ORL), using the data from the IGGSA-STEPS 2014 and 2016 shared tasks. We frame the problem as a token classification task and employ a simple transformer-based model that achieves new state-of-the-art results on the data. Then we investigate whether we can further improve our model by transferring knowledge from a related task, i.e., Semantic Role Labelling. Our results show that, despite the small size of our data, this transfer learning step yields further improvements for ORL, mostly regarding recall for target prediction. Finally, we present an error analysis, showing where knowledge transfer from SRL can help and what is still difficult for German ORL.

1 Introduction

The extraction of subjective expressions together with their opinion holders and targets is not only an important processing step for the analysis of argumentation mining but is also relevant for political text analysis. For English, the seminal work of Stoyanov et al. (2004) and Wiebe et al. (2005) has provided resources for training and evaluation of opinion mining models for newswire. However, resources for other languages, domains and text types are still scarce.

Previous work on German has focussed on the political domain where Ruppenhofer et al. (2014, 2016) have presented a corpus of Swiss-German parliamentary debates annotated with subjective expressions, their opinion holders (or sources) and targets (Figure 1). The data set has been used in two shared tasks.[1] However, compared to the MPQA 2.0 corpus (Wiebe et al., 2005; Wilson, 2008) which includes more than 8,500 sentences,

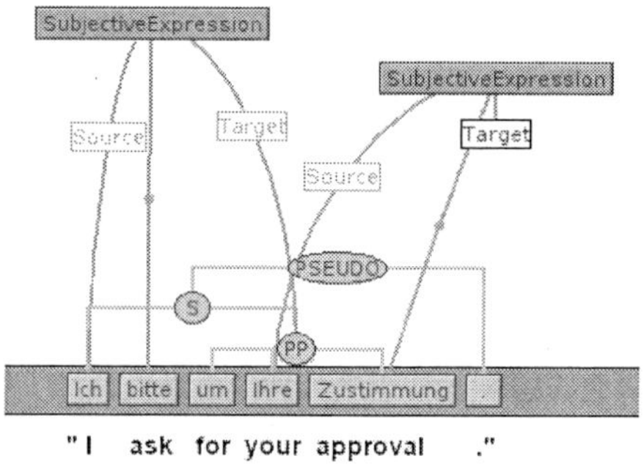

Figure 1: Screenshot of example annotations from the IGGSA-STEPS shared task data for the verb "bitten" (*ask*) and the noun "Zustimmung" (*approval*), visualised in Salto (Burchardt et al., 2006a).

the data is rather small with less than 1,200 sentences. This is reflected in the low results for opinon holder and target extraction, where scores for the best systems from the 2016 shared task were in the range of 46% F1 (micro) for holders and 40% F1 for targets. Follow-up work by Wiegand et al. (2019a) has improved the extraction of opinion holders by around 4 percentage points but failed to increase results for target extraction. The low results imply that, at this stage, the models are not yet good enough to be used in downstream applications.

Since then, transformer-based models (Vaswani et al., 2017; Devlin et al., 2019) and transfer learning approaches have brought huge improvements to the field of Natural Language Understanding (NLU) and are particularly well suited for task settings where only small data are available. Therefore, in our work we exploit the expressive power of transformers and transfer learning and present a simple transformer-based system for German opinion holder and target extraction.

As expected, our baseline system already beats previous work by far, yielding improvements in the range of 10-15 percentage points. We then explore

[1] See the IGGSA-STEPS 2014 shared task: https://sites.google.com/site/iggsasharedtask/task-1 and for 2016: https://iggsasharedtask2016.github.io.

whether we can further improve results by transferring knowledge from a related task, i.e., Semantic Role Labelling (SRL). Transfer from SRL to ORL has been successful for improving results for English Opinion Role Labelling (ORL) (Marasovic and Frank, 2018). However, it is unclear whether a similar approach will work for German where the size of the training data is only a fraction of the English ORL data. To answer this question, we exploit a German newspaper corpus with frame-semantic annotations (Burchardt et al., 2006b) and introduce an intermediate training step where we fine-tune our model on the SRL data, showing that this intermediate training step can further improve results, mostly in terms of recall.

The contributions of this work are as follows. We present a neural system for German opinion holder and target extraction, based on transformer-based transfer learning, and report new state-of-the-art results. We replicate previous results obtained for English, using SRL data for transfer learning, and show that this approach also works when substantially less data is available. Our final system outperforms previous best results by more than 15 percentage points.[2]

2 Related Work

Opinion mining, the "computational study of opinions, sentiments, and emotions expressed in text" (Liu, 2010), has become a vivid field of research in the last 20 years. Among the main goals of opinion mining is the extraction of the source or opinion holder (the one who has the opinion) and its topic or target (what the opinion is about).

Opinion Role Labelling (ORL) for English Most work on ORL has been conducted for English. Initially, the task has been modelled in a pipeline approach where the models first identify the opinion (or subjective expression) and then, given the opinion, in a second step predict the roles of *opinion holder* and *target*. There is, of course, a close link to semantic role labelling, and many works have exploited that link.

Kim and Hovy (2006), for example, have augmented the frame-semantic annotations in FrameNet (Baker et al., 1998) with opinion holder and target roles and used clustering techniques to predict semantic frames for subjective expressions not known by FrameNet. They then decompose the task into three phases where they first identify all opinion-bearing predicates in a sentence, then use SRL to label the semantic roles for the predicate and, finally, identify the holder and topic of the opinion-bearing expression among the labeled semantic roles.

Other work has tried to jointly learn the opinion-bearing expressions and their roles (Choi et al., 2006; Yang and Cardie, 2013; Katiyar and Cardie, 2016). The most recent one of those works, Katiyar and Cardie (2016), use deep bidirectional LSTMs to jointly extract opinion expressions and their holders and targets. The neural model does not outperform previous work that uses CRFs in combination with Integer Linear Programming (ILP) (Yang and Cardie, 2013). However, one advantage of the neural approach is that, unlike other work (Kim and Hovy, 2006; Johansson and Moschitti, 2013; Yang and Cardie, 2013; Wiegand and Ruppenhofer, 2015), it does not depend on external resources such as opinion lexicons, dependency parsers or SRL systems.

Marasovic and Frank (2018) present a neural approach, based on BiLSTMs and CRFs, that exploits external knowledge from SRL in a multi-task learning (MTL) setup. They focus on holder and target prediction and show that the MTL approach results in substantial improvements over a single-task baseline.

Quan et al. (2019) are the first to apply a transformer-based architecture (Vaswani et al., 2017; Devlin et al., 2019) for ORL. Their approach is similar to the one of Katiyar and Cardie (2016) and jointly learns the opinion expressions, their holders and targets. Their end-to-end model integrates BERT with a BiLSTM and CRF component and improves over a simple BiLSTM baseline. However, it fails to outperform the previous state-of-the-art of Katiyar and Cardie (2016) by far. The authors ascribe this to the limited size of the training data and the resource hunger of neural approaches. If that is true, then we cannot expect improvements for German where the size of the training data is even smaller than for English ORL and SRL. We thus want to explore whether is is possible to transfer knowledge from SRL to ORL for German in a low(er)-resource setting.

Our work is similar to Marasovic and Frank (2018) in that we also use Semantic Role Labelling data to address the problem of data sparsity for Opinion Role Labelling, which is much more se-

[2]Our models are available for download from https://github.com/umanlp/ORLde.

DE	Die Kantone	können,	wenn sie wollen,	also	eine Regelung treffen.	dummy-token
EN	The cantons	can,	if they wish,	therefore	make a regulation.	
TRANS	"The cantons can therefore, if they wish, make a regulation."					
instance 1	*Die Kantone*	können,	wenn sie wollen,	*also eine Regelung treffen .*		**inferred**
instance 2	Die Kantone	können,	wenn **sie** wollen	*also eine Regelung treffen .*		–
instance 3	**Die Kantone**	können,	wenn sie wollen	also eine Regelung treffen .		–

Table 1: Three example subjective expressions (underlined) within the same sentence, with their opinion holders (red) and targets (blue); example taken from the IGGSA-STEPS 2016 shared task test set.

vere for German than for English. We do not use a multi-task learning setup, as the size of the SRL data is around 8 times as large as the ORL data and we expect this imbalance to be a challenge for the MTL approach. Instead, we apply transfer learning through intermediate training where we first fine-tune a pretrained BERT model on the SRL data and then use the learned model to initialise the weights for our final ORL model that we fine-tune on the downstream task, i.e., Opinion Role Labelling.

ORL for German Most work on Opinion Role Labelling for German has been conducted in the context of two shared tasks, the IGGSA-STEPS 2014 and 2016 Shared Task on Source and Target Extraction from Political Speeches (Ruppenhofer et al., 2014, 2016). The data for the shared task includes debates from the Swiss parliament, annotated with subjective expressions, their opinon holders and targets. The data set is fairly small with 605 sentences for training and 581 sentences for testing. The number of annotated instances in the data, however, is substantially higher and amounts to 1,115 subjective expressions, 997 opinion holders (excluding *inferred opinion holders*, see §3.1 below) and 1,608 targets for training (see Table 2).

As reported in Wiegand et al. (2019b), 845 (850) subjective expression frames in the training (test) data include both, holder *and* target, while 152 (214) subjective expressions include only the holder. More frequent are subjective frames that include only the target, with a count of 763 (920). Subjective frames with neither holder nor target amount to 468 (433) in the training (test) set.

This is a typical low-resource scenario, and we thus want to investigate whether (and by how much) we are able to improve results over previous work that employs linguistic features, information from external knowedge bases and linguistic modelling. Our work addresses the following research questions:

RQ1: Can transformer-based transfer learning improve results for German ORL over previous best work, despite the small size of the training data?

RQ2: Can we replicate previous work on English and further improve results by harvesting information from German SRL?

We address RQ1 by fine-tuning a pretrained transformer-based language model on the ORL task and compare results to previous work on the same data. To answer our second RQ, we use the German SRL data from the CoNLL 2009 shared task "Syntactic and Semantic Dependencies in Multiple Languages" (Hajič et al., 2009) for transfer learning and investigate whether we will find similar improvements as have been reported for English.

3 A BERT model for German ORL

3.1 Task description and data

The task of opinion role labelling consists in identifying all opinion holders and targets for a given subjective expression. For illustration, see the example in Table 1 where three subjective expressions are given (können (*can*), wollen (*want*), Regelung treffen (*make regulation*)). The task then is to predict the opinion holder and target for each of these expressions.

In the first instance extracted from the example, only the target is expressed overtly while the opinion holder of können (*can*) has to be inferred as the speaker of the utterance. Those *inferred holders* are quite frequent and amount to 26% of all holders in the data (Wiegand et al., 2019b). In the

	#sent	SE (toks)	SE (types)	Holder	Target
train	605	2,105	1,115	997	1,608
test	581	2,166	1,110	1,064	1,770
Total	1,186	4,271		2,061	3,378

Table 2: Some statistics on the IGGSA shared task data.

second instance where the subjective expression is wollen (*want*), both holder and target are realised as arguments of the subjective predicate. Finally, the subjective expression Regelung treffen (*make regulation*) in the third instance is a support verb construction with an explicitly stated holder but the target role remains unfilled.

As in Marasovic and Frank (2018), we assume that the subjective expressions are given and focus on the ORL task. Given an input sentence, the task then consists in detecting the respective token spans for holder and target and assigning the correct label to each role.

Preprocessing We preprocess the data so that we extract one training (or test) instance for each subjective expression and its opinon roles, i.e., its opinion holder and target (including *inferred holders*). Please note that not each sentence includes a subjective expression (SE), and not every SE has an opinion holder and target.

Experimental setup In our first set of experiments, we train an ORL classifier for German, using the data from the IGGSA-STEPS 2014 and 2016 shared tasks (Ruppenhofer et al., 2014, 2016). To make our results comparable, we follow the setup of the 2016 shared task setup, using the data from the 2014 shared task for training and development (605 sentences) and evaluate our models on the same test portion used in the 2016 shared task, including 581 sentences. Table 2 shows some statistics for the data.

We model the task as a token classification task and use the BIO schema to distinguish the first token of each span from the tokens inside a span. We use the "O" label for all tokens that are not part of either holder or target. In the shared task data, the inferred holders are annotated by means of a flag and have to be predicted. We follow Wiegand et al. (2019a) and add a dummy token at the end of each instance which is assigned the label "Inferred" for all instances with implicit opinion holders. For instances with explicitly expressed holders and those without a holder, the dummy token is assigned the label "O" instead.

3.2 Baseline model

Our baseline model for ORL uses a simple token classification setup, similar to the argument detection and labelling step in the BERT-based SRL model of Shi and Lin (2019). There are, however, two differences between their model and ours. The first one concerns the model architecture, the second the representation of the input. The model of Shi and Lin (2019) integrates a BiLSTM layer on top of the BERT encoder, followed by a Multi-Layer Perceptron (MLP). To encode the information about the predicate (for SRL) or subjective expression (for ORL), they concatenate the classification [CLS] token, the input sentence, a separator token [SEP] and the predicate and input the whole sequence into the BERT encoder.

Instead of concatenating the input sentence and the predicate (or subjective expression), we use BERT's token-type-ids to encode this information. Specifically, we set the token type ids of all tokens that are part of the subjective expression to 1 and all other token ids to 0. Our model does not use an additional BiLSTM on top of BERT but, following the NER model presented in Devlin et al. (2019), inputs the encoded sequence directly into the MLP layer.

	ORL	SRL
optimizer	AdamW	AdamW
learning rate	2.693154582157772e-05	0.00003808
batch size	16	8
weight decay	0.019840937077311938	0.055
epsilon	5.45374378277376e-07	0.000001194

Table 3: Hyperparameters used for the ORL/SRL tasks.

Training details We implement our models with the huggingface transformers library (Wolf et al., 2020) and pytorch (Paszke et al., 2017) and do hyperparameter tuning with Weights & Biases (Biewald, 2020). We limit the input sequence length to 120 subword tokens and train in batches of 16 instances, using the AdamW optimizer with random search to determinine the optimal learning rate α, weight decay and epsilon ϵ (sampled from a uniform distribution with $min = 0.02$ and $max = 0.00001$ for α, $min = 0$ and $max = 0.1$ for weight decay and $min = 5e - 9$ and $max = 0.000002$ for ϵ), with the objective to minimize the training loss.

Then we use the same tuned (hyper)parameters to train three independent versions of our model with different initialisations, each for 25 epochs. We select the best performing model on the development set and report results for each indiviual run and averaged results and standard deviation over all three runs.[3] Table 3 shows the (hyper)parameter

[3]Given that standard deviation between the different initialisations was quite low (see Table 4), we decided to report

System		*Holder* Prec	Rec	F1	*Target* Prec	Rec	F1
UDS-supervised		59.4	38.3	46.6	42.6	31.7	36.3
UDS-rulebased		59.9	28.6	38.7	**69.2**	28.9	40.8
WCR19		58.0	44.0	50.3	48.1	35.0	40.5
ORL-ST	avg.	**67.8**$\pm$ 0.6	**63.5**$\pm$ 0.3	**65.6**$\pm$ 0.2	54.2$\pm$ 0.7	**53.2**$\pm$ 0.3	**53.9**$\pm$ 0.2

Table 4: Results for ORL on the STEPS-2016 test set (UDS-sup: supervised UDS system, UDS-rule: rule-based UDS system; WCR19: Wiegand et al. (2019a); ORL-ST: BERT-based single-task ORL system; results averaged over 3 runs; stdev reports standard deviation over 3 runs.).

settings for our experiments.

3.3 Baseline results

We now report results for our BERT single-task model, ORL-ST, and compare them to previous work (Table 4). For evaluation, we use the scorer from the IGGSA-STEPS shared tasks, kindly provided by the organisers, to ensure the comparability of the results.[4] We report the strict measure for (micro) precision, recall and F1 for opinion holders and targets that only considers a predicted holder or target as correct if *all tokens that belong to this entity have been predicted correctly*. Please note that the results for opinion holders also include predictions for inferred holders (see Table 1, instance 1).

We compare against the University of Saarland (UDS) contributions from the IGGSA-STEPS 2016 shared task (UDS-supervised and UDS-rulebased) (Wiegand et al., 2016) and the supervised feature-based approach of Wiegand et al. (2019a). The authors refer to the moderate results reported for deep learning approaches for ORL (Katiyar and Cardie, 2016) as motivation for not using deep learning in their work, and highlight the importance of linguistic information and, in particular, syntactic dependency relations for resolving opinion holders and targets. Finally, the small size of the German data questions the benefits to be expected from neural approaches, which is why Wiegand et al. (2019a) decided to employ SVMs in their work.

Table 4 shows that the baseline BERT model outperforms previous work by a large margin, with improvements in the range of 15-22% for opinion holders and 13-17% for the identification of targets. The rule-based approach (UDS-rulebased), however, beats the BERT system wrt. precision, but at the cost of a very low recall. For all other models, results increase for both, precision and recall.

This answers our first research question, **RQ1**: Transfer learning approaches are well suited to increase results for German ORL over previous feature-based approaches even in low-resource scenarios.

4 SRL for German ORL

We now turn to our second research question and investigate whether it is possible to further improve results for German ORL by means of an additional knowledge transfer from the semantic role labelling (SRL) task. As training data for SRL, we use the German part of the CoNLL 2009 shared task data (Hajič et al., 2009) and train a BERT-based classifier, using the same model architecture and setup as for the ORL task. The data comes originally from the SALSA corpus (Burchardt et al., 2006b), a corpus of newspaper text from a German daily newspaper (*Frankfurter Rundschau*). SALSA includes verbal predicates and their frame elements, with annotations in the flavor of Berkeley FrameNet (Baker et al., 1998). The semantic frames and roles have been automatically converted from FrameNet-style annotations to PropBank (Palmer et al., 2005) style for the shared task.

The data we use for training includes over 36,000 sentences, out of which 14,282 sentences include at least one annotated predicate. The number of training instances (where sentences with more than one annotated predicate result in multiple instances, as described for the ORL preprocessing step) thus amounts to 17,400 instances. The development set includes 2,000 sentences and the test data 400 sentences.

Please note that our goal is not to optimize results for the SRL task but to use SRL as an auxiliary task to transfer knowledge about predicate argument structure to ORL. For this, we compare

results for 3 individual runs only.

[4] We would like to thank the shared task organisers for providing us with the scorer and system outputs from the IGGSA-STEPS shared task.

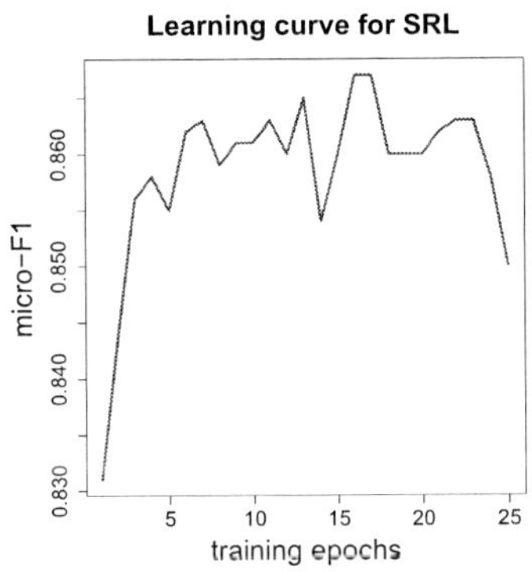

Figure 2: Learning curves for SRL over 25 epochs of training (micro-F1 on the SRL development set).

two different settings. In the first setting, we select the best performing model for SRL, based on the F1 scores on the development set, and use this model to initialise the BERT parameters for subsequent ORL fine-tuning. In the second setting, we do not fully train the model on the SRL data until convergence but stop the training process when the learning curve starts to flatten, which happens after the third training epoch (see Figure 2). Table 5 reports results on the SRL development set for both models (Exp. 1 and 2).

Training details We use this model to initialise the parameters of the ORL model that we then fine-tune on the downstream task (ORL). Model architecture and parameter settings are the same as described in Section 3.2 and Table 3. As before, we train 3 individual models with different initialisations for 25 epochs and select the best performing model for each run on the development set. We report results for each individual run and averaged results and standard deviation over all runs.

4.1 Results for transfer learning from SRL

Table 6 shows results for transfer learning from SRL to ORL. We notice that the intermediate training has a noticable effect on the downstream task. The SRL model that has been trained for 16 epochs and achieved best results on the SRL dev set (Figure 2) fails to further improve results for ORL. Using the parameters from the ORL-3 model that has been trained for 3 epochs only to initialise the BERT ORL model, however, results in another increase in results. This increase is rather small for target prediction with 0.7% but more pronounced for the prediction of opinion holders with 1.6%.

A possible explanation for the better performance of the undertrained SRL model as source of knowledge transfer is that the size of the ORL training data is only a fraction of the SRL data (605 sentences versus 14,282 sentences). Thus, the model has been fitted for a different task (SRL) and has not seen enough data to adapt to the new task (ORL). This suggests that other architectures might be more promising for a low-resource setting like this, such as adapter-based fine-tuning (Rebuffi et al., 2018; Houlsby et al., 2019; Bapna and Firat, 2019; Pfeiffer et al., 2020). We plan to explore this in future work.

Exp.	Model	Prec	Rec	F1
SRL-1	best-on-dev	86.7	86.7	86.7
SRL-2	3-epochs	86.2	85.1	85.6

Table 5: Results for SRL with BERT (dev set).

As mentioned above, the results in Table 6 come from a strict evaluation where we only count roles as correct if *all* tokens that belong to that role have been identified correctly. This explains why results for targets are substantially lower than the ones for holders, given their average lengths (2.1 tokens for opinion holders vs. 5.5 tokens for targets). To add another perspective, we augment the results reported above by a token-based evaluation (Table 7) where we remove the prefixes from the BIO scheme and compute precision, recall and F1 on the token level. Table 8 illustrates the difference between the two evaluation measures, using a constructed example sentence.

For the *strict* evaluation in Table 8, we count one correctly identified role, i.e., the target. We also count one false positive, as we have predicted a span that does not exist in the gold standard. Additionally, we count one false negative because we failed to identify the correct holder (or source) span. For the *token-based* evaluation, on the other hand, we count 7 true positives (2 for the holder and 5 for the target) and one false negative for the missed token "auch" (*also*).

As expected, results for target prediction are much higher in the token-based evaluation setting in Table 8. While the general trends are the same as for the strict evaluation, with best results being obtained by the ORL-3 system (transfer from SRL to ORL), we note that the single-task model, ORL-1, outperforms the transfer model in terms of precision for all three roles (holder, target, inferred holder) while the transfer step mostly helps to increase recall (Table 7).

Exp.	Model	Run	Prec	Rec *Holder*	F1	Prec	Rec *Target*	F1
ORL-1	single-task best-on-dev	1	67.1	63.8	65.4	53.4	52.8	53.6
		2	68.2	63.3	65.7	54.5	53.2	53.9
		3	68.2	63.3	65.7	54.8	53.5	54.1
		avg	67.8	63.5	65.6	54.2	53.2	53.9
ORL-2	SRL-to-ORL best-on-dev	1	66.9	63.3	65.0	52.0	51.2	51.6
		2	66.4	65.3	65.8	52.9	52.4	52.6
		3	64.2	64.5	64.3	53.2	52.9	53.1
		avg	65.8	**64.4**	65.0	52.7	52.2	52.4
ORL-3	SRL-to-ORL 3 epochs	1	70.7	64.7	67.5	54.3	55.0	54.6
		2	71.6	63.8	67.5	54.0	53.7	53.8
		3	68.7	64.7	66.6	55.2	55.4	55.3
		avg	**70.3**	**64.4**	**67.2**	**54.5**	**54.7**	**54.6**

Table 6: Results for the single-task ORL baseline (ORL-1) and for the transfer learning experiments (ORL-2, ORL-3) with intermediate training on SRL (best-on-dev: model that gave best results on the development set; 3 epochs: model has been trained for 3 epochs only).

Exp.	Model	Run	Holder Prec	Holder Rec	Holder F1	Target Prec	Target Rec	Target F1	Speaker (inferred) Prec	Speaker (inferred) Rec	Speaker (inferred) F1
ORL-1	single-task best-on-dev	1	76.1	50.7	60.9	73.5	74.5	74.0	71.2	79.3	75.0
		2	78.8	49.8	61.1	67.6	81.4	73.9	68.6	75.3	71.8
		3	71.0	56.2	62.7	70.9	80.6	75.4	70.5	73.0	71.8
		avg	**75.3**	52.2	61.6	**70.7**	78.8	74.4	**70.1**	75.9	72.9
ORL-2	SRL-to-ORL best-on-dev	1	72.0*	52.1	60.5*	67.3	82.5***	74.1	67.4	78.1	72.4
		2	68.2**	56.0*	61.5***	69.1	80.6	74.4	67.4	76.6	71.7
		3	70.3	54.7	61.5	67.2	81.7	73.7	61.1***	83.1***	70.4***
		avg	70.2	54.3	61.2	67.9	81.6	74.1	65.3	**79.3**	71.5
ORL-3	SRL-to-ORL 3 epochs	1	74.1***	55.3***	63.3***	68.4	85.0***	75.8***	70.7	77.6	74.0
		2	76.0	52.4	62.0	65.2	86.4**	74.3	71.8	76.9	74.3
		3	72.7	55.7	63.1	69.1	83.8*	75.8	67.8**	77.6**	72.4**
		avg	74.3	**54.5**	**62.8**	67.6	**85.1**	**75.3**	**70.1**	77.4	**73.6**

Table 7: Token-based evaluation: precision, recall and F1 (micro) for holders, targets and inferred speakers (asterisks indicate statistical significance for ORL-1 vs. ORL-2 and ORL-1 vs. ORL-3 according to an approximate randomisation test where * $p \leq 0.01$; ** $p \leq 0.001$; *** $p \leq 0.0001$).

	Example sentence					*measure*	**TP**	**FP**	**FN**
DE	Diese Auffassung	wird	auch	in einem Großteil der Lehre	vertreten.				
EN	This view	will	also	in a large part of the doctrine	be held.				
TRANS	"This view is also held by a large part of the doctrine."								
gold	Target		Holder	Holder					
auto	Target			Holder		*strict*	1	1	1
						tok-based	7	0	1

Table 8: Example sentence (constructed) illustrating the difference between the *strict* and the *token-based* evaluation (gold: gold annotation; auto: predicted labels; TP: true positives, FP: false positives, FN: false negatives).

Exp.	Frames		Holder			Target			Speaker (inferred)		
		#	Prec	Rec	F1	Prec	Rec	F1	Prec	Rec	F1
ORL-1	*holder-only*	214	94.6	38.5	54.7	0	0	0	0	0	0
	target-only	247	0	0	0	86.0	79.4	82.6	0	0	0
	target+inferred	923	0	0	0	67.0	81.1	73.4	91.9	77.7	84.2
	holder+target	847	90.6	52.7	66.6	72.6	81.7	76.9	0	0	0
ORL-3	*holder-only*	214	92.0	45.3	60.7	0	0	0	0	0	0
	target-only	247	0	0	0	82.4	86.6	84.4	0	0	0
	target+inferred	923	0	0	0	64.3	86.1	73.6	94.4	79.7	86.4
	holder+target	847	90.4	54.2	67.8	70.5	86.7	77.8	0	0	0

Table 9: Token-based evaluation for different subsets of the test set.

Exp.	subjective expr.		Holder			Target			Speaker (inferred)		
	POS	#	Prec	Rec	F1	Prec	Rec	F1	Prec	Rec	F1
ORL-1	V	823	84.0	62.6	71.7	69.2	88.8	77.8	64.9	70.2	67.4
	N	849	76.1	27.2	40.1	72.8	56.4	63.5	47.9	59.6	53.1
	A	404	66.2	36.2	46.8	67.7	78.8	72.8	78.9	95.1	86.3
ORL-3	V	823	82.1	65.0	72.6	67.7	91.7	77.9	68.3	73.6	70.8
	N	849	71.0	31.6	43.7	68.4	67.8	68.1	58.9	55.9	57.4
	A	404	59.2	30.5	40.2	64.6	84.0	73.0	76.5	93.3	84.0

Table 10: Token-based evaluation for verbal, nominal and adjectival subjective expressions (test set), excluding multi-word expressions.

We run an approximate randomisation test with 10,000 iterations on the output of the different models (ORL-1 vs. ORL-2 and ORL-1 vs. ORL-3) (Table 7). We can see that not all improvements are statistically significant. Only recall for target prediction (ORL-3) yields significant improvements for each individual run over the single-task system (ORL-1).

Table 7 also shows that, according to the token-based evaluation, the inferred holders are easier to identify than the explicit opinion holders, with around 10% higher F1. This is in contrast to the findings of Wiegand et al. (2019b, p.26) who state that inferred sources are "more difficult to detect than normal sources".

We can now answer our second research question, **RQ2**, and conclude that despite the small size of the German data set, it is possible to transfer knowledge from SRL to ORL. Improvements, however, are far more modest than the ones reported for English (Marasovic and Frank, 2018) and mostly improve recall.

4.2 Error analysis

We now take a closer look at the results, to find out where transfer learning helps and what is still difficult for our models. For our error analysis, we look at the predictions of the ORL-1 single task model and the ORL-3 (SRL-to-ORL transfer) model.[5] We first compare the output of the two models, focussing on the performance on different subsets of the data, i.e., subjective frames that include only a holder (but no target), a target (but no holder), targets with inferred sources and frames with both, holder and target.

Table 9 shows that the largest improvements for the transfer model (Exp.3) are due to a higher recall for the subjective frames that include holders only. Here we observe an increase in F1 of 6% (from 54.7% to 60.7%) over the single-task model. The results also suggest that holder-only frames are the most difficult category for opinion role prediction, while F1 for holder prediction for frames that include both, holder *and* target, are substantially higher for both, the single-task and the transfer model.

Next, we investigate how our models perform on subjective expressions with different parts of speech (Table 10). Interesting but by no means unexpected is the decrease in results for the SRL-to-ORL model on adjectival triggers for opinion holders and inferred sources (for explicit holders from 46.8% to 40.2% and for inferred holders from 86.3% to 84%). The largest improvements can be observed for nominal subjective expressions. Here the additional knowledge about predicate argument structure helps the most which, on first glance, is a bit surprising, given that the German SRL data includes semantic roles for verbal predicates only. However, keeping in mind that the subjective expressions are already given, what we need to know in order to predict the opinion roles is which token spans are probable arguments. Our transfer model seems to have learned useful information for this task from SRL, as shown by the increase in F1 for nominal subjective expressions in the range of 3.6% (for holders) to 4.6% (for targets).

5 Conclusions

In the paper, we have presented a transformer-based system for German ORL on parliamentary debates, with new state-of-the-art results for the IGGSA-STEPS shared task. We have further shown that we can improve our baseline system through transfer learning, based on knowledge about predicate argument structure learned from SRL. We include this information via intermediate training and show that we mostly obtain improvements for recall and, in particular, for nominal subjective expressions and subjective frames where only the holder is expressed.

One challenge for transfer learning is the imbalance between the SRL and ORL training data. In future work, we would thus like to explore whether adapters might help us to make more efficient use of the data by injecting knowledge about predicate argument structure in our model without outweighing the information learned from the ORL data.

Acknowledgements

This work was supported in part by a Research Seed Capital (RiSC) grant, funded by the "Ministerium für Wissenschaft, Forschung und Kunst Baden-Württemberg" (MWK BW). We would like to thank the reviewers for their thorough and constructive feedback.

[5] We use the models for Exp. ORL-1 and ORL-3 from the 2nd run in our analysis.

References

Collin F. Baker, Charles J. Fillmore, and John B. Lowe. 1998. The Berkeley FrameNet Project. In *Proceedings of the 36th Annual Meeting of the Association for Computational Linguistics and 17th International Conference on Computational Linguistics - Volume 1*, ACL '98/COLING '98, page 86–90, USA. Association for Computational Linguistics.

Ankur Bapna and Orhan Firat. 2019. Simple, scalable adaptation for neural machine translation. In *Proceedings of the 2019 Conference on Empirical Methods in Natural Language Processing and the 9th International Joint Conference on Natural Language Processing (EMNLP-IJCNLP)*, pages 1538–1548, Hong Kong, China. Association for Computational Linguistics.

Lukas Biewald. 2020. Experiment tracking with weights and biases. Software available from wandb.com.

Aljoscha Burchardt, Katrin Erk, Anette Frank, Andrea Kowalski, and Sebastian Pado. 2006a. SALTO: A versatile multi-level annotation tool. In *Proceedings of the Fifth International Conference on Language Resources and Evaluation, LREC 2006, Genoa, Italy, May 22-28, 2006*, pages 517–520, Genoa, Italy.

Aljoscha Burchardt, Katrin Erk, Anette Frank, Andrea Kowalski, and Sebastian Padó. 2006b. The SALSA Corpus: a German Corpus Resource for Lexical Semantics. In *Proceedings of the Fifth International Conference on Language Resources and Evaluation, LREC 2006, Genoa, Italy, May 22-28, 2006*, pages 969–974. European Language Resources Association (ELRA).

Yejin Choi, Eric Breck, and Claire Cardie. 2006. Joint extraction of entities and relations for opinion recognition. In *EMNLP 2006, Proceedings of the 2006 Conference on Empirical Methods in Natural Language Processing, 22-23 July 2006, Sydney, Australia*, pages 431–439. ACL.

Jacob Devlin, Ming-Wei Chang, Kenton Lee, and Kristina Toutanova. 2019. BERT: pre training of deep bidirectional transformers for language understanding. In *Proceedings of the 2019 Conference of the North American Chapter of the Association for Computational Linguistics: Human Language Technologies, NAACL-HLT 2019, Minneapolis, MN, USA, June 2-7, 2019, Volume 1 (Long and Short Papers)*, pages 4171–4186. Association for Computational Linguistics.

Jan Hajič, Massimiliano Ciaramita, Richard Johansson, Daisuke Kawahara, Maria Antònia Martí, Lluís Màrquez, Adam Meyers, Joakim Nivre, Sebastian Padó, Jan Štěpánek, Pavel Straňák, Mihai Surdeanu, Nianwen Xue, and Yi Zhang. 2009. The CoNLL-2009 shared task: Syntactic and semantic dependencies in multiple languages. In *Proceedings of the Thirteenth Conference on Computational Natural Language Learning (CoNLL 2009): Shared Task*, pages 1–18, Boulder, Colorado. Association for Computational Linguistics.

Neil Houlsby, Andrei Giurgiu, Stanislaw Jastrzebski, Bruna Morrone, Quentin De Laroussilhe, Andrea Gesmundo, Mona Attariyan, and Sylvain Gelly. 2019. Parameter-efficient transfer learning for NLP. In *Proceedings of the 36th International Conference on Machine Learning*, volume 97 of *Proceedings of Machine Learning Research*, pages 2790–2799. PMLR.

Richard Johansson and Alessandro Moschitti. 2013. Relational features in fine-grained opinion analysis. *Computational Linguistics*, 39(3):473–509.

Arzoo Katiyar and Claire Cardie. 2016. Investigating LSTMs for joint extraction of opinion entities and relations. In *Proceedings of the 54th Annual Meeting of the Association for Computational Linguistics (Volume 1: Long Papers)*, pages 919–929, Berlin, Germany. Association for Computational Linguistics.

Soo-Min Kim and Eduard Hovy. 2006. Extracting opinions, opinion holders, and topics expressed in online news media text. In *Proceedings of the Workshop on Sentiment and Subjectivity in Text*, pages 1–8, Sydney, Australia. Association for Computational Linguistics.

Bing Liu. 2010. *Sentiment analysis and subjectivity*, volume 2, pages 627–666. Taylor and Francis Group.

Ana Marasovic and Anette Frank. 2018. SRL4ORL: Improving Opinion Role Labeling Using Multi-Task Learning with Semantic Role Labeling. In *Proceedings of the 2018 Conference of the North American Chapter of the Association for Computational Linguistics: Human Language Technologies, NAACL-HLT 2018, New Orleans, Louisiana, USA, June 1-6, 2018, Volume 1 (Long Papers)*, pages 583–594. Association for Computational Linguistics.

Martha Palmer, Daniel Gildea, and Paul Kingsbury. 2005. The Proposition Bank: An Annotated Corpus of Semantic Roles. *Computational Linguistics*, 31(1):71–106.

Adam Paszke, Sam Gross, Soumith Chintala, Gregory Chanan, Edward Yang, Zachary DeVito, Zeming Lin, Alban Desmaison, Luca Antiga, and Adam Lerer. 2017. Automatic differentiation in PyTorch. In *NIPS Autodiff Workshop*.

Jonas Pfeiffer, Andreas Rücklé, Clifton Poth, Aishwarya Kamath, Ivan Vulić, Sebastian Ruder, Kyunghyun Cho, and Iryna Gurevych. 2020. AdapterHub: A framework for adapting transformers. In *Proceedings of the 2020 Conference on Empirical Methods in Natural Language Processing: System Demonstrations*, pages 46–54, Online. Association for Computational Linguistics.

Wei Quan, Jinli Zhang, and Xiaohua Tony Hu. 2019. End-to-End Joint Opinion Role Labeling with BERT. In *2019 IEEE International Conference on Big Data (Big Data)*, pages 2438–2446, Los Alamitos, CA, USA. IEEE Computer Society.

Sylvestre-Alvise Rebuffi, Hakan Bilen, and Andrea Vedaldi. 2018. Efficient parametrization of multi-domain deep neural networks. In *2018 IEEE/CVF Conference on Computer Vision and Pattern Recognition*, pages 8119–8127.

Josef Ruppenhofer, Julia Maria Struß, Jonathan Sonntag, and Stefan Gindl. 2014. IGGSA-STEPS: Shared Task on Source and Target Extraction from Political Speeches. *Journal for Language Technology and Computational Linguistics*, 29(1):33 – 46.

Josef Ruppenhofer, Julia Maria Struß, and Michael Wiegand. 2016. Overview of the IGGSA 2016 Shared Task on Source and Target Extraction from Political Speeches. In *Proceedings of the IGGSA Shared Task 2016 Workshop*, pages 1–9.

Peng Shi and Jimmy J. Lin. 2019. Simple BERT Models for Relation Extraction and Semantic Role Labeling. *CoRR*, abs/1904.05255.

Veselin Stoyanov, Claire Cardie, Diane Litman, and Janyce Wiebe. 2004. Evaluating an opinion annotation scheme using a new multi-perspective question and answer corpus. In *Proceedings of the AAAI Spring Symposium on Exploring Attitude and Affect in Text: Theories and Applications*.

Ashish Vaswani, Noam Shazeer, Niki Parmar, Jakob Uszkoreit, Llion Jones, Aidan N. Gomez, Lukasz Kaiser, and Illia Polosukhin. 2017. Attention is all you need. In *Advances in Neural Information Processing Systems 30: Annual Conference on Neural Information Processing Systems 2017, December 4-9, 2017, Long Beach, CA, USA*, pages 5998–6008.

Janyce Wiebe, Theresa Wilson, and Claire Cardie. 2005. Annotating expressions of opinions and emotions in language. *Language Resources & Evaluation*, 39(2-3):165–210.

Michael Wiegand, Nadisha-Marie Aliman, Tatjana Anikina, Patrick Carroll, Margarita Chikobava, Erik Hahn, Marina Haid, Katja König, Leonie Lapp, Artuur Leeuwenberg, Martin Wolf, and Maximilian Wolf. 2016. Saarland University's Participation in the Second Shared Task on Source, Subjective Expression and Target Extraction from Political Speeches. In *Proceedings of the IGGSA Shared Task 2016 Workshop*, pages 14–23.

Michael Wiegand, Margarita Chikobava, and Josef Ruppenhofer. 2019a. A Supervised Learning Approach for the Extraction of Sources and Targets from German Text. In *Proceedings of the 15th Conference on Natural Language Processing, KONVENS 2019, Erlangen, Germany, October 9-11, 2019*.

Michael Wiegand, Leonie Lapp, and Josef Ruppenhofer. 2019b. A descriptive analysis of a German corpus annotated with opinion sources and targets. In *Proceedings of the 15th Conference on Natural Language Processing (KONVENS 2019)*, pages 20 – 29, München [u.a.]. German Society for Computational Linguistics & Language Technology und Friedrich-Alexander-Universität Erlangen-Nürnberg.

Michael Wiegand and Josef Ruppenhofer. 2015. Opinion holder and target extraction based on the induction of verbal categories. In *Proceedings of the Nineteenth Conference on Computational Natural Language Learning*, pages 215–225, Beijing, China. Association for Computational Linguistics.

Theresa Ann Wilson. 2008. *Fine-Grained Subjectivity And Sentiment Analysis: Recognizing The Intensity, Polarity, And Attitudes Of Private States*. Ph.D. thesis, University of Pittsburgh.

Thomas Wolf, Lysandre Debut, Victor Sanh, Julien Chaumond, Clement Delangue, Anthony Moi, Pierric Cistac, Tim Rault, Rémi Louf, Morgan Funtowicz, Joe Davison, Sam Shleifer, Patrick von Platen, Clara Ma, Yacine Jernite, Julien Plu, Canwen Xu, Teven Le Scao, Sylvain Gugger, Mariama Drame, Quentin Lhoest, and Alexander M. Rush. 2020. Transformers: State-of-the-art natural language processing. In *Proceedings of the 2020 Conference on Empirical Methods in Natural Language Processing: System Demonstrations, EMNLP 2020 - Demos, Online, November 16-20, 2020*, pages 38–45. Association for Computational Linguistics.

Bishan Yang and Claire Cardie. 2013. Joint inference for fine-grained opinion extraction. In *Proceedings of the 51st Annual Meeting of the Association for Computational Linguistics (Volume 1: Long Papers)*, pages 1640–1649, Sofia, Bulgaria. Association for Computational Linguistics.

Proceedings of the 18th Conference on Natural Language Processing (KONVENS 2022)

ABSINTH: A small world approach to word sense induction

Victor Zimmermann[1], Maja Hoffmann[2]
Leipzig University[1], Leipzig University of Applied Sciences (HTWK)[2]
victor.zimmermann@uni-leipzig.de
maja_katharina.hoffmann@stud.htwk-leipzig.de

Abstract

ABSINTH[1] provides a novel unsupervised graph-based approach to word sense induction. This work combines small world coöccurrence networks with a graph propagation algorithm to induce per-word sense assignment vectors over a lexicon that can be aggregated for classification of whole snippets.

1 Introduction

As late as twelve years after publication, the graph-based approach to word sense induction proposed in Véronis (2004) was still cited as 'state-of-the-art' (Tripodi and Pelillo 2017, Ustalov et al. 2017) and only recently surpassed by neural substitution-based approaches (Amrami and Goldberg 2018, Amrami and Goldberg 2019). Our goal with this work is to evaluate an approach native to small-world graphs for the word sense induction task. We build on the principles laid out in Hyperlex (Véronis, 2004) with a more dynamic feature set and a graph propagation algorithm previously used for sentiment analysis (Hamilton et al., 2016).
Our system, ABSINTH[1], provides a simple two-step approach to SemEval-2013 Task 11 (Navigli and Vannella, 2013). To achieve this, we utilise the properties of small world graphs for language (Cancho and Solé, 2001) in general and semantic relations (Newman, 2003) in particular. We extract senses using the root hub algorithm proposed in Véronis (2004).
For word sense disambiguation we use the sense inventory created in previous steps and a graph propagation algorithm to assign each node a sense distribution vector. Lastly, the vectors of each word in a given context are summed up and the context is assigned the sense of the best cumulative weight.

[1]Association Based Semantic Induction Tools for root Hub propagation

Parameter	ABSINTH	Hyperlex	Baseline
Min. context	4	4	4
Min. #nodes	Avg. #nodes	10	9
Min. #edges	Avg. #edges	5	3
Max. weight	0.9	0.9	0.9

Table 1: Minimum context size, minimum number of nodes, minimum number of edges and maximum edge weight for our system, Hyperlex and our Baseline.

In addition to the SemEval scoring methods to evaluate our results we use characteristic path length and global clustering coëfficient to evaluate the properties of our coöccurrence graphs.
Our system achieves better results in three out of four metrics than a classifier similar to Hyperlex without label propagation.

2 Related Work

Graph-based approaches to word sense induction have been successfully used since the early 2000s (Véronis 2004, Di Marco and Navigli 2013, Amplayo et al. 2019). Véronis proposes the use of root hub detection and minimum spanning trees (Kruskal, 1956) to induce senses and disambiguate search results.
The usefulness of small world graph properties for sense disambiguation has previously been shown in Newman (2003). The term 'small world' was introduced by Travers and Milgram, using it to describe the connectedness of acquaintance networks (Travers and Milgram, 1969). According to their findings, the average path length between two people living in the United States lies around five or six, even though they are selected from a relatively large number of people. The properties of these small world graphs have been formally described in Watts and Strogatz (1998). We show that Hyperlex graphs are indeed small world graphs with the words connected in a similar way to real world

relations between people.
Because of this property, nodes with a high degree (number of outgoing edges) can be selected as so called 'root hubs'. It is assumed that words belonging to a sense are clustered around these root hubs and meaning can be induced by mapping a vocabulary to them.

2.1 Coöccurrence graphs & root hub detection

Véronis uses paragraphs including the target string (the word or multi-word expression for which senses are to be induced) from a web corpus as contexts for building coöccurrence graphs. Words in the vocabulary constitute nodes and have an undirected edge when they appear in the same context window. Paragraphs with fewer than 4 words are discarded, further limits on nodes, edges and their weights are introduced (see table 1). The target string is not included in the graph.
Edges with a high association frequency are assigned lower weights using a weighting system described in (Véronis, 2004). Why this weighting algorithm is chosen over a more traditional measure like Dice weights is not further explained, but we expect an algorithm using Dice weights would artificially limit the number of possible neighbours for each node and therefore reduce the number of possible root hubs substantially.
Root hubs are chosen iteratively from the set of graph nodes, limited by the following criteria:

1. the number of neighbours, excluding root hubs and neighbours of root hubs,
2. the mean weight of the candidate's most frequent neighbours, excluding root hubs and neighbours of root hubs.

Additionally, the candidate may not be neighbour to a previously chosen root hub.
Before building the minimum spanning tree, the target string is inserted back into the graph with a distance of 0 to each root hub. This results in the root hubs being selected as the direct children of the target string, allowing the easy mapping of components to a hub.
For disambiguation, Véronis iterates over each node v in the minimum spanning tree and assigns each a weight vector ω:

$$\omega_i = \begin{cases} \frac{1}{1+d(h_i,v)}, & \text{if } v \text{ belongs to component i,} \\ 0 & \text{else.} \end{cases}$$

with $d(h_i, v)$ being the distance between a root hub h_i and a node v.
For a given context, the weight vectors of each token are added up and the sense with the highest cumulative weight is chosen.
We use Véronis' root hub algorithm broadly with more flexible parameters for our corpus. Our disambiguation system still uses Hyperlex' minimum spanning tree as a backup, but fundamentally builds on labelled graph propagation (Hamilton et al., 2016).

3 Task Set-up

We evaluate our algorithm on Task 11 of the SemEval-2013 Workshop (Navigli and Vannella, 2013). The aim of the task is to develop a word sense induction (WSI) tool that can be used in web search result clustering. The data is structured as follows:
Each topic is given by a target string. For every topic there is a list of the first hundred internet search results, containing information for the result, namely the URL, title and a text snippet (see table 2).

3.1 Corpus

We use an unordered plain-text Wikipedia dump from 2014 as context data to construct the word sense graphs which was not supplied with the shared task. As the sense set used in the task is sourced from Wikipedia as well, using Wikipedia for this purpose satisfies domain and style consistency. Because of soft limits on how many nodes and edges ABSINTH considers, an ordered corpus may favour one sense over another based on if its article randomly fell into our sample.
Additionally we add the titles and snippets of each query to our corpus, since it offers us a guaranteed baseline of around 500 nodes per sense.

4 Small World Graphs

Our graphs are so called 'small world graphs'. The connection topography of a small world graph, as described in Watts and Strogatz (1998), lies between a completely random and a completely ordered graph. Therefore small world graphs can be highly clustered, but still have relatively short path lengths between the nodes.
The structural properties of these graphs are defined by characteristic path length L(p) which measures the average separation between nodes of a graph

ID	47.6
url	`http://us.imdb.com/title/tt0120169/`
title	Soul Food (1997)
snippet	Directed by George Tillman Jr.. With Vanessa Williams, Vivica A. Fox, Nia Long. ...

Table 2: Example dataset entry for 'soul food'.

Target	L_{sys}	C_{sys}	L_{rand}	C_{rand}
cool_water	3.675	0.528	6.025	0.030
soul_food	4.664	0.604	4.992	0.022
stephen_king	3.649	0.552	3.791	0.014
the_block	3.905	0.329	3.721	0.006
Average	3.973	0.503	4.632	0.018

Table 3: Characteristic path length (L) and global clustering coëfficient (C) for our system and a random graph.

and global clustering coëfficient C(p) which measures the cliquishness of a typical neighbourhood. The global clustering coëfficient ranges between 0 (for a completely disconnected graph) and 1 (for a highly connected graph). Characteristic path length and global clustering coëfficient are calculated as follows:

$$L = \frac{1}{N}\sum_{i=1}^{N} d_{min}(i,j)$$

$$C = \frac{1}{N}\sum_{i=1}^{N} \frac{|E(\Gamma(i))|}{\binom{|\Gamma(i)|}{2}},$$

with node count (N), the shortest distance between two nodes i, j ($d_{min}(i,j)$), degree of a node i ($\Gamma(i)$) and proportion of connection between neighbours $\Gamma(i)$ of a node i ($E(\Gamma(i))$). To determine whether a graph is indeed a small world graph, L(p) and C(p) have to be evaluated against a random connection topography of a graph of the same size.

The random measures are calculated as follows:

$$L_{rand} \sim log(N)/log(k)$$
$$C_{rand} \sim 2k/N.$$

A small world graph is defined as follows (Véronis, 2004):

$$L \sim L_{rand}$$
$$C >> C_{rand}.$$

As can be seen in table 3, our graphs resemble small world graphs, as they feature short average path lengths, but substantially higher clustering coëfficients, compared to what would be expected of random graphs.

Véronis uses these properties mostly for root hub detection. We included a graph propagation system for disambiguation that utilises these graph properties as well.

Because our corpus is much less balanced than Véronis (2004) and our task is more varied[2], we use a more flexible set of parameters and methods. The task set-up does not support the use of heuristic variables, as some terms are simply too infrequently represented in our corpus to build meaningful graph representations. While setting the euclidean mean of node/edge frequency as a minimum offers a solution to the problem of sparse graphs for less represented terms, more frequent terms seem to over-generate root hubs.

Graph propagation offers a simple method in reducing the total number of senses by essentially merging related root hubs, while retaining the characteristic distribution of senses shown in (Véronis, 2004).

5 System

The sense induction works with the properties of small world graphs in mind. The degree of certain nodes makes them ideal root hubs from which a sense distribution can be propagated somewhat organically. The work flow of our system can be roughly translated into induction and disambiguation. The goal of the first task is to produce sensible root hubs. These can be more varied and numerous than in Véronis (2004), as ABSINTH merges and shifts the overlying concepts after initial induction. The root hubs do not themselves carry lexicon definitions of meaning, but provide a structure onto definitions can (hopefully) easily map through propagation.

5.1 Word Sense Induction

Induction consists of two steps:

[2] Véronis mostly disambiguates highly polysemous terms and no proper names.

Parameter	ABSINTH	Hyperlex
Min. degree	5	6
Max. mean weight	0.8	0.8

Table 4: Minimum degree and maximum mean weight for root hub detection.

1. Construction and weighting of a coöccurrence graph.

2. Inducing root hubs from this graph.

Our graph is constructed in a straightforward approach, only considering paragraphs including our target string. All nouns and verbs of this sub-corpus are counted, with each coöccurrence within a paragraph being an edge. Stop words are filtered, as is the target string itself, after which every paragraph containing less than four relevant tokens is discarded.
Every node or edge whose frequency falls under a certain threshold (see table 1.) is also discarded. ABSINTH uses the average number of occurrences instead of a heuristic measure, as it is robust enough to deal with over-generation of root hubs and our sub-corpora vary in size too considerably to allow heuristic senses without under-generating root hubs for less frequent targets.
The graph is weighted using the following method from (Véronis, 2004):

$$\omega_{a,b} = 1 - \max[p(A|B), p(B|A)], \quad \text{with}$$
$$p(A|B) = f_{A,B}/f_B \quad \text{and}$$
$$p(B|A) = f_{A,B}/f_A.$$

This weighting method is preferred to a measure like Sørensen-Dice-Weight, as it allows root hubs to have many outgoing edges, while their neighbours can each have a meaningful relation to the root hub without the edge being discarded. We use the algorithm shown in Véronis (2004) to detect root hubs, iteratively choosing hubs by their degree and average weight with their most frequent neighbours (see table 4). We then delete the root hub and its neighbours from the graph before selecting the next hub. After no viable candidates are left, the list of root hubs is returned.

5.2 Word Sense Disambiguation

For allocating contexts to senses, our system uses the graph and list of root hubs built in previous steps. Again, disambiguation is a two step process, mirroring the induction process.

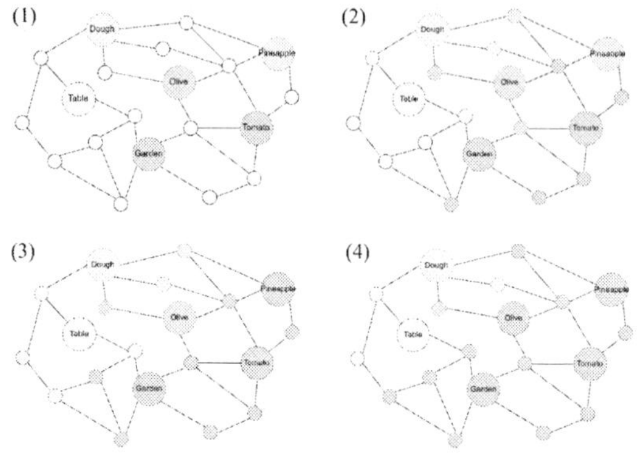

Figure 1: Example of Propagation for the target 'Pizza'.

First, nodes are labelled according to their 'sense preference' using a propagation algorithm similar to ones used to model voting behaviour (Fowler, 2005) or for sentiment analysis (Newman, 2003). The result is a labelled graph with a sense distribution vector for each node. The best sense of the cumulative vector for a given context is chosen for clustering.
Véronis' algorithm using minimum spanning trees[3] is used as a backup for contexts that could not be matched using the propagation algorithm.

5.2.1 Sense Propagation

The goal of our propagation algorithm is to provide an approximation of how indicative a node is for a sense from the root hub inventory. As the sense of a word here is defined by its neighbours, it would follow that whether or not a node is indicative of a sense is also defined by its neighbours. Véronis (2004) offers an algorithm that maps senses to nodes in a binary fashion, but in our understanding a probabilistic distribution would be a more fitting annotation of each node, as this leaves the possibility of a node supporting multiple senses while excluding others, without dividing sense groups.
Our system does not necessarily retain all original root hubs, as they too can be assigned a different sense during iteration (see figure 1). This allows us to over-generate root hubs in earlier steps without much repercussion.

[3] A minimum spanning tree is defined as a sub-graph containing all nodes of the original graph and whose cumulative edge weights are a minimum (Kruskal, 1956).

Algorithm 1 Graph labelling

```
procedure LABEL_GRAPH
    G ← coöccurrence graph
    H ← list of root hubs
    stable ← False
    for node ∈ G do
        node.ω ← (ω_1...ω_n)
        ω_1^0...ω_n^0 ← 0
        if node = h ∈ H then
            ω_h^0 ← 1
    i ← 1
    while stable = False do
        stable = True
        for node ∈ G, h ∈ H do
            for nbr ∈ neighbours do
                if h = argmax(nbr.ω) then
                    ω_h^i ← ω_h^i + (1 − d(node, nbr))
        node.ω ← 1/(i+1) Σ_{j=0}^{i} ω^j
        if argmax(ω) ≠ argmax(1/i Σ_{j=0}^{i−1} ω^j) then
            stable = False
        i ← i + 1
    return G
```

Algorithm 1 shows the process in which each node is assigned a sense distribution vector. Notably only the best sense of each neighbour and the weight of their edge[4] (d) is considered, not the entire distribution. As our graph is undirected, two conflicting nodes would, should a node's distribution be based on a neighbours own vector, tend to balance each other out, with the graph only reaching a stable state when every connected node features the same distribution, including the same 'best sense'. This is of course not a desirable outcome.

Algorithm 2 Disambiguation w/ labelled graph

```
procedure DISAMBIGUATE
    S ← context string
    G ← labelled graph
    H ← list of root hubs
    v ← score vector with length H
    for token ∈ S do
        if token ∈ G then
            for h ∈ H do
                v_h ← v_h + token.ω_h · 1/(1 + d(token, h))
    return argmax(v)
```

Our disambiguation algorithm (see algorithm 2) uses a score vector with weights for each root hub. For each token in a given context, the sense distribution vector is added to the score vector, with each sense weight adjusted by the distance of the token to the root hub.

[4]We defined the weight of an edge earlier as the inverted coöccurrence probability. As we aim to match the node to the highest score, we chose to invert the measure back for this step. An $argmin$ function would work in much the same way as our method.

ABSINTH retains some binding of a sense to a root hub, using the adjustment to counteract a sense straying too far from its root during the propagation step.

5.2.2 Minimum Spanning Tree

Contexts that could not be disambiguated using the propagation algorithm are then processed by the algorithm proposed in Véronis (2004). Target string and root hubs are added to the graph with edge weights of 0. A minimum spanning tree is constructed (Kruskal, 1956) and each node assigned a score in a similar way as above:

$$score_{node} = \frac{1}{1 + d(node, roothub)}$$

Again, the scores for each token in a context are accumulated and the best sense is chosen for clustering.

ABSINTH returns this cumulative mapping of our propagation algorithm, supported by Véronis' components algorithm.

5.3 Baseline

We will be comparing our results to different baselines. Firstly we will use singleton and all-in-one clustering. These are not linguistically or even mathematically motivated clustering methods, our Baseline, which is a more naïve approach to graph based word sense induction, features a basic version of Véronis' algorithm, but using conceptually simple methods and measures. Instead of the root hub selection algorithm detailed above, the baseline simply selects the ten most frequent nodes as root hubs.

The propagation and minimum spanning tree algorithms are replaced by a distance-based scoring measure. Nodes v are assigned one-hot-vectors based on distance d to each root hub $h \in H$.

$$\omega_i = \begin{cases} 1, & \text{if } h_i = argmax_{h \in H}(d(h_i, v)), \\ 0 & \text{else.} \end{cases}$$

The final cumulative score vector for a given context of length n is essentially comprised of the counts of tokens w corresponding to each sense. The sense with the highest score is selected:

$$sense = argmax_{h \in H}(\sum_{h \in H} \omega_{w_1}, ..., \omega_{w_n}).$$

6 Evaluation

We evaluate on the MORESQUE development training set (Navigli and Crisafulli, 2010), consisting of 114 topics and their according search results.
To evaluate the properties of our coöccurrence graph, we use the characteristic path length and the clustering coëfficient (see table 3).

6.1 Clustering Quality

SemEval-2013 Task 11 evaluates clustering quality on the basis of the following four metrics:

- F_1-score,
- Rand index
- adjusted Rand index
- Jaccard index.

Additionally, S-recall at K and S-precision at r are measured, as well as the average number of clusters and average cluster size.

7 Results

System	F_1	JI	RI	ARI
ABSINTH	**55.21**	31.73	54.73	6.98
w/o MST	53.57	33.00	**56.21**	**9.08**
w/o labelling	50.13	**46.20**	53.63	5.51
Baseline	49.87	42.52	51.76	3.26
Singletons	**68.66**	0.00	49.00	-0.07
All-in-one	47.42	**51.00**	51.00	0.00

Table 5: Results for F_1-score, Jaccard index (JI), Rand index (RI) and adjusted Rand index (ARI).

We will compare the results of our system to the results of two different versions of itself. The first variant does not use minimum spanning tree for disambiguation. The second is based on the algorithm proposed in Véronis (2004) and uses the same parameters (w/o labelling). It however is not a one-to-one recreation of the original system, as the corpus used is not extracted from the target URLs. We use these two versions for ablation studies.

System	50	60	70	80
ABSINTH	33.99	22.51	**17.78**	**14.51**
w/o MST	**36.82**	**22.98**	17.18	13.94
w/o labelling	31.73	20.68	15.83	12.57
Baseline	32.75	22.47	15.21	13.96

Table 6: Subtopic precision at recall r (S-precision@r).

ABSINTH outperforms every baseline on the development data, as expected. The three versions of our system vary heavily in F_1-score and adjusted Rand index. Our system with propagation algorithm and minimum spanning tree as backup performs well on F_1-score, but lacks in Jaccard index (see table 5). Our recreation of Hyperlex has the best Jaccard index, but is behind every other system in all other measures. Jaccard index may be biased towards fewer larger clusters, as both our system without labelling and all-in-one clustering perform best in this category. Removing the minimum spanning tree as backup boosts adjusted Rand index significantly, with a smaller bump in Rand index.

System	# cl	ACS
Gold standard	3.98	19.83
ABSINTH	5.39	22.99
w/o MST	4.82	20.61
w/o labelling	1.46	74.81
Baseline	4.54	33.69

Table 7: Average number of clusters (# cl.) and average cluster size (ACS).

The gold standard features a smaller number of clusters with a high average cluster size, which would indicate that the development data may not be an entirely accurate representation of most sense distributions, as other sets have shown to have different distributions (Navigli and Vannella, 2013). We expect better efficacy for Rand index and adjusted Rand index on a different dataset.
We are hesitant to remove Véronis' components algorithm as backup, as the influence of the minimum spanning tree is only minimal, but it supports our system with a tried and tested approach which may outweigh the efficacy gain indicated on the development set.
The low average cluster count may also have affected the remarkably high efficacy of all-in-one clustering, outperforming every other system in Jaccard index and Rand index by a large margin. We expect this measure to drop significantly when testing on datasets with higher cluster counts.
In terms of precision (see table 6) and recall (see table 8), our full system and our system without minimum spanning tree perform about the same, which is expected due to the small influence the minimum spanning tree has on the results. In both metrics, ABSINTH without label propagation and

dynamic limits trails behind every other version of our system, as well as the baseline.

Across the board, adjusted Rand index has been the most stable measure of the system's efficacy, with the other measures being more susceptible to changes in cluster size and count. While accurate prediction of number of senses is certainly an important part of the task, we felt overall clustering quality had to be optimised before any reasonable approach in this direction could be taken.

System	5	10	20	40
ABSINTH	51.58	**70.32**	**78.21**	**88.44**
w/o MST	53.46	69.52	77.83	88.21
w/o labelling	**55.99**	65.77	73.75	84.69
Baseline	55.14	66.25	76.18	87.41

Table 8: Subtopic recall at rank K (S-recall@K)

8 Conclusion

The similarity of coöccurrence networks and human relations in small world graphs lead to a broad spectrum of possible approaches to optimising a system that had been tried and tested for over a decade. Our system produced solid results on the development data despite the age of the basic components.

Hyperlex has proved to be a very robust baseline on which to build on. Using graph-based algorithms on top of the networks built by Hyperlex could open up interesting avenues for further research and improvement in (non-neural) word sense induction.

Small world graphs, not really a native field of computational linguistic research, have proven themselves quite apt in modelling semantic relations. Even though the graphs built were useful and stable, better results could be obtained by using various sources instead of the Wikipedia corpus. Especially proper names of obscure bands and other pop culture references have posed a challenge to our system which could have been solved with a less information- and more entertainment-based corpus.

As graphs tend to explode with a larger prominence of the target string in the context corpus (see figure 2), parameters such as minimum number of neighbours should be tied to a dependent variable in future work. $log(\Gamma(i)) \cdot \Gamma(i)$ was tested, but still performed worse than the heuristic measure[5].

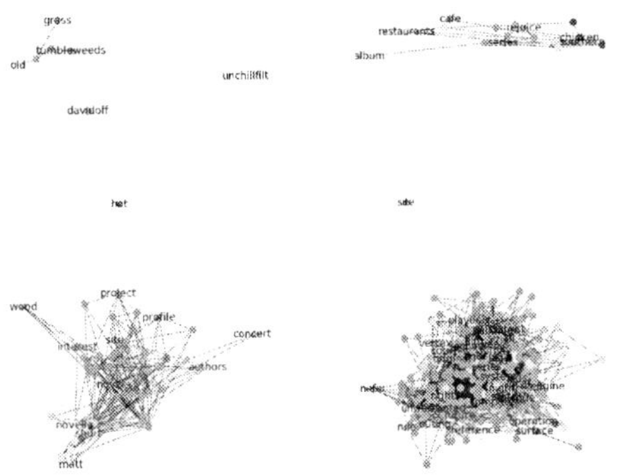

Figure 2: Graphs of different sizes.[6]

This small study hints towards the small world property of semantic graph networks opening up a larger world of established tools and methods from intersecting fields of research that can be appropriated and employed for semantic modelling tasks.

References

Reinald Kim Amplayo, Seung-won Hwang, and Min Song. 2019. Autosense model for word sense induction. In *Proceedings of the AAAI Conference on Artificial Intelligence*, volume 33, pages 6212–6219.

Asaf Amrami and Yoav Goldberg. 2018. Word sense induction with neural biLM and symmetric patterns. In *Proceedings of the 2018 Conference on Empirical Methods in Natural Language Processing*, pages 4860–4867.

Asaf Amrami and Yoav Goldberg. 2019. Towards better substitution-based word sense induction. *arXiv preprint arXiv:1905.12598*.

Ramon Ferrer i Cancho and Richard V. Solé. 2001. The small world of human language. *Proceedings of the Royal Society of London B: Biological Sciences*, 268(1482):2261–2265.

Antonio Di Marco and Roberto Navigli. 2013. Clustering and diversifying web search results with graph-based word sense induction. *Computational Linguistics*, 39(3):709–754.

James H Fowler. 2005. Turnout in a small world. *The social logic of politics: Personal networks as contexts for political behavior*, 269.

[5] We lowered the heuristic minimum number of neighbours from 6 to 5 for our system based on limited tests on a subset of the development data, to some minimal improvements.

[6] From top left to bottom right: cool_water, soul_food, stephen_king, the_block

William L. Hamilton, Kevin Clark, Jure Leskovec, and Dan Jurafsky. 2016. Inducing domain-specific sentiment lexicons from unlabeled corpora. In *Proceedings of the 2016 Conference on Empirical Methods in Natural Language Processing, EMNLP 2016, Austin, Texas, USA, November 1-4, 2016*, pages 595–605.

Joseph B. Kruskal. 1956. On the shortest spanning subtree of a graph and the traveling salesman problem. *Proceedings of the American Mathematical Society*, 7(1):48–50.

Roberto Navigli and Giuseppe Crisafulli. 2010. Inducing word senses to improve web search result clustering. In *Proceedings of the 2010 conference on empirical methods in natural language processing*, pages 116–126.

Roberto Navigli and Daniele Vannella. 2013. SemEval-2013 Task 11: Word sense induction and disambiguation within an end-user application. In *Proceedings of the 7th International Workshop on Semantic Evaluation, SemEval@NAACL-HLT 2013, Atlanta, Georgia, USA, June 14-15, 2013*, pages 193–201. The Association for Computer Linguistics.

M. E. J. Newman. 2003. The structure and function of complex networks. *SIAM REVIEW*, 45:167–256.

Jeffrey Travers and Stanley Milgram. 1969. An experimental study of the small world problem. *SOCIOMETRY*, 32(4):425–443.

Rocco Tripodi and Marcello Pelillo. 2017. A game-theoretic approach to word sense disambiguation. *Computational Linguistics*, 43(1):31–70.

Dmitry Ustalov, Alexander Panchenko, and Chris Biemann. 2017. Watset: Automatic induction of synsets from a graph of synonyms. In *Proceedings of the 55th Annual Meeting of the Association for Computational Linguistics (Volume 1: Long Papers)*, pages 1579–1590, Vancouver, Canada. Association for Computational Linguistics.

Jean Véronis. 2004. Hyperlex: lexical cartography for information retrieval. *Computer Speech & Language*, 18(3):223–252.

Duncan J. Watts and Steven H. Strogatz. 1998. Collective dynamics of 'small-world' networks. *Nature*, 393(6684):440–442.

Proceedings of the 18th Conference on Natural Language Processing (KONVENS 2022)

This isn't the bias you're looking for: Implicit causality, names and gender in German language models

Sina Zarrieß and **Hannes Gröner** and **Torgrim Solstad** and **Oliver Bott**
Bielefeld University
Linguistics Department
{sina.zarriess,hannes.groener,torgrim.solstad,oliver.bott}@uni-bielefeld.de

Abstract

To assess whether neural language models capture discourse-level linguistic knowledge, previous work has tested whether they exhibit the well-known implicit causality (IC) bias found in various interpersonal verbs in different languages. Stimuli for analyzing IC in computational and psycholinguistic experiments typically exhibit verb arguments with different genders. In this paper, we revisit IC in German neural language models, analyzing gender and naming bias as a potential source of confusion. Indeed, our results suggest that IC biases in two existing models for German are weak, unstable, and behave in unexpected and unsystematic ways, when varying names or gender of verb arguments.

1 Introduction

In recent years, large-scale pretrained neural language models (PLMs) have not only become an important component in modeling many NLP tasks (Devlin et al., 2019; Liu et al., 2019; Sanh et al., 2019; Lewis et al., 2020; Brown et al., 2020), but the models themselves have turned more and more into the subject of linguistic analysis and probing: One prominent line of work has investigated undesired social biases, e.g. gender or racial biases, that PLMs inherit from the large and often unmoderated resources for training (Bordia and Bowman, 2019; Blodgett et al., 2020; Meade et al., 2022). Another line of work has examined the linguistic knowledge and desirable biases captured in PLMs, ranging from morphological, syntactic and semantic to discourse-related probing tasks (Belinkov and Glass, 2019; Ettinger, 2020).

In this work, we built upon a series of recent papers that investigated a desirable linguistic bias in PLMs: the implicit causality bias (Upadhye et al., 2020; Davis and van Schijndel, 2020; Kementchedjhieva et al., 2021). Implicit Causality (IC) is a property of a wide range of interpersonal verbs like *annoy*, which display a preference for establishing coreference to one of the verb's argument over the other in explanations:

(1) Peter annoyed Mary because ... ...

When asked to continue a sentence like (1), human subjects have a strong preference towards referring to *Peter*, as in *because he sang loudly*, attributing the implicit cause to the stimulus argument (the subject of *annoy*, in this case). In order to be able to experimentally assess such next-mention biases, studies in (computational) psycholinguistics commonly use stimuli where the verb's arguments mismatch in their gender, so that continuations with a female or male pronoun unambiguously refer to the subject or object of the main clause.

Previous studies on testing IC in PLMs designed stimuli with two NPs in different genders, generating language model prompts with varying names and orders, carefully balanced for gender (Upadhye et al., 2020; Kementchedjhieva et al., 2021). However, they did not explicitly examine the potential interactions with underlying gender bias in PLMs, despite the fact that this a well-known and widely discussed phenomenon in recent work in NLP.

In this paper, we revisit the IC bias for two German language models, BERT and GPT-2, based on Solstad and Bott (2022)'s experimental data. We analyze PLMs' predicted continuations of prompts with an interpersonal verb and two gender-mismatched arguments followed by a connective, as shown in example (1). As in previous studies, we vary and balance prompts for the names and gender of verb arguments and introduce a further condition that manipulates the form of names: next to first names like *Anna, Paul*, we test surnames like *Herr Müller (Mr. Müller), Frau Fischer (Ms. Fischer)*, which in German carry accusative case marking (*Herrn Müller*). Our analysis shows that the manipulation of names' form and gender uncovers various inconsistencies in the continuations predicted by German PLMs for IC prompts.

2 Background

2.1 IC: Implicit Causality and Consequentiality

As discussed by Solstad and Bott (2022), psychological verbs like the stimulus-experiencer (SE) verb *annoy* and the experiencer-stimulus (ES) verb *fear* display biases for establishing coreference to one of the verbs arguments in the context of explanation and consequence. In explanation contexts (introduced by the connective *because*), continuations have a strong referential bias to re-mention the stimulus argument. In consequence contexts (introduced by the connective *and so*), however, an equally strong re-mention bias towards the mention of the experiencer argument is observed. As shown in Examples (2)-(3), this leads to a mirror subject bias pattern: the ES-verb in Example (2) has a bias towards the subject in explanation and towards the object in consequence contexts (the preferred continuation is shown in brackets), whereas the SE-verb in Example (3) shows the complementary bias pattern:

(2) a. Mary fears Peter because... [he] is always so aggressive.
   b. Mary fears Peter and so ... [she] tries to avoid him.

(3) a. Mary annoys Peter because... [she] is so ignorant.
   b. Mary annoys Peter and so... [he] acted rather impolite.

In psycholinguistic sentence completion studies, participants generally receive a prompt including the connective. In their continuations they typically provide reference to the biased argument (in square brackets).

In the following, we will subdivide IC into Implicit Causality (I-Caus) and Implicit Consequentiality (I-Cons). For I-Caus, Solstad and Bott (2022) found a subject-bias for SE verbs and an object-bias for ES verbs with 87.4% and 4.0% subject coreference in continuations, respectively. I-Cons continuations displayed the exact opposite biases with 4.8% subject continuations for SE and 77.9% subject continuations for ES verbs. The opposite I-Caus and I-Cons biases were reflected by an almost perfect negative correlation between I-Caus and I-Cons biases ($r = -0.94, p < .001$) making I-Caus and I-Cons biases of the two psych-verb classes a very interesting testing ground for language models.

Upadhye et al. (2020) used a similar set-up to ours, distinguishing between IC1 and IC2 verbs as well as explanations and consequences. These correspond to SE and ES verbs as well as the I-Caus and I-Cons condition in our setting. Kementchedjhieva et al. (2021) investigate IC in PLMs, but do not discuss mirror biases in their set-up. In general, these previous studies obtained mixed but overall rather promising results in favour of predictions congruent with human-like next-mention biases. Upadhye et al. (2020) find that two English PLMs (Transformer-XL, GPT-2) are not sensitive to manipulations of connectives in IC contexts, but that GPT-2 assigns higher probability to subject-referring pronouns when the respective interpersonal verb exhibits a strong subject bias in human completions, and vice versa for object-referring pronouns. Kementchedjhieva et al. (2021) test a wider range of English PLMs and find that bidirectional models in particular show a moderate to strong correlation with human completions in IC contexts. They also report results on German and Spanish, with German BERT achieving moderate correlations with human IC bias data.

2.2 Gender Bias and Implicit Causality

Bias studies often employ two different-gender names to ease the assessment of coreference with subject or object arguments, i.e. there is a subject bias when the prnoun is male and the first argument of the main verb is a male first name. Typically, the order of male and female referents is included as a counterbalancing factor (e.g., *Peter/Mary annoyed Mary/Peter*) to exclude that gender biases interfere with coreference biases. For instance, a gender bias would be observed if the subject bias for SE verbs in I-CAUS context is less strong when the stimulus is female as compared to male.

Mostly, as in Solstad and Bott's (2022) study, no gender effects have been found. However, Ferstl et al. (2011) did find the proportions of coreference for IC ('because') to be skewed towards male referents. Importantly, Ferstl et al. observed an interaction with participant gender to the extent that male participants were more likely to attribute the cause to the male referent, irrespective of subject or object position. In light of the well-known and widely attested gender bias in neural language models and word embeddings (Blodgett et al., 2020), we argue that the lack of analysis of gender bias in the context of implicit causality constitutes an interesting research gap, that the current study is aiming to fill.

3 Experiments

3.1 Materials

We based our study on I-Caus and I-Cons in German on Experiment 1 in Solstad and Bott (2022). The experiment employed a 2×2(×2) within-participants and within-items design manipulating the factors VERB CLASS (German stimulus-experiencer vs. experiencer-stimulus verbs) and CONNECTIVE (*weil* 'because' vs. *sodass* 'and so'). They chose these two connectives because of their optimal syntactic parallelism. Differently from *daher* or *deswegen* ('therefore') the chosen connectives both select for subordinate sentences with pronouns typically immediately following the connective (similar to the English examples in (2)/(3)). This is a very important prerequisite for probing pronoun production. The form *sodass* is nowadays the most frequent variant of this connective (as suggested by the google books ngram viewer), while forms such as *so dass*, *sodaß* and *so daß* are more infrequent in use.

In addition, GENDER ORDER (male>female vs. female>male) was included as a counterbalancing factor. Solstad and Bott (2022) included 20 stimulus-experiencer and 20 experiencer-stimulus verbs, which were chosen for their stable and pronounced biases. Items were constructed according to a *name*$_1$ *verb-ed name*$_2$ *connective* scheme in line with the above design. Verbs were paired in items matching them semantically as closely as possible. The resulting 20 items in eight conditions were distributed to four list using a Latin Square design, with proper names chosen from publicly available lists of the most frequent first names in Germany.[1] Sentence completions were elicited from 52 participants (39 female; 13 male).

3.2 Language Model Prompts

We use Solstad and Bott (2022)'s experimental items to generate German prompts to be completed by the language models. As in the above examples, prompts consist of a simple sentence introducing the verb, the verb's arguments and the connective:

(4) a. Peter langweilte Marie, sodass ...
Peter bored Mary and so ...

b. Frau Müller sorgte sich um Herrn Schmidt, weil ...
Mrs. Müller was worried about Mr. Schmidt because ...

In contrast to the English Examples (2)-(3), the German Example (4-a) allows for both subject-before-object (SVO) as well as object-before-subject (OVS) interpretations, i.e. *Peter* could be the stimulus or experiencer of the event. The ambiguity does not arise when the arguments are realized as surnames, as in Example (4-b), due to the accusative marking on the word *Herr*. Solstad and Bott (2022) explicitly annotated whether their human participants had assigned an OVS interpretation to the prompts and observed that against this potential concern overwhelmingly SVO interpretations were chosen in more than 95% of the cases. In our study, we assume that the first argument always refers to the subject. In future work, it may be of interest to estimate the amount of OVS interpretations assigned by PLMs, too.

We balanced the prompts according to the following properties:

ES vs. SE Our set of verbs divides into 20 experiencer-stimuli verbs (ES, see Example (4-b)) and 20 stimuli-experiencer verbs (SE, see Example (4-a)).

I-CAUS vs. I-CONS For each verb, we created templates with the connective *weil* 'because' for implicit causality (I-Caus, see Example (4-b)) and *sodass* 'and so' for implicit consequentiality (I-Cons, see Example (4-a)).

First names vs. surnames For each template, we created prompts using five surnames and five first names, e.g., *Herr Schmidt, Paul, Anna.* In each case, both verb arguments were instantiated witht the same type of name.

[np1] We balanced the prompt set for each verb such that the gender of the first argument (i.e. the subject) in the sentence is male/female in 50% of the cases. In Example (4-a), [np1] is male (m), in Example (4-b) it is female (f).

Taken together, we obtain a set of 100 prompts for each of the 40 verbs.

[1] Full materials at https://osf.io/5ewbd/

Bias type	NP-type	BERT	GPT-2
overall	all	0.581	0.560
	firstn	0.556	0.568
I-CAUS	all	0.576	0.548
	firstn	0.503	0.577
I-CONS	all	0.585	0.571
	firstn	0.609	0.559

Table 1: Completion sensitivity for BERT and GPT-2 in I-CAUS and I-CONS contexts, with all types of names and first names (firstn) only

3.3 Models and Metrics

We used two German language models to generate continuations of the set of prompts: (i) the pre-trained DBMZ German **GPT-2** model[2], and (ii) the cased DBMZ German **BERT** model [3], a fully bidirectional model.

From these models, we obtain the likelihood assigned to the continuations *er* (*he*) and *sie* (*she*). We calculate the subject bias for human and model continuations and use the metrics of Prediction Accuracy and Completion Sensitivity from Ettinger (2020).

Completion Sensitivity For each prompt, there is a presumed bias on either the first or the second noun phrase. A pronoun is said to be congruent with the bias if it refers to the noun phrase specified by the bias. Completion Sensitivity scores are calculated as the percentage of prompts where the predicted pronoun is congruent with the bias.

Prediction Accuracy (Acc@2) Prediction Accuracy scores are calculated as the percentage of prompts, where *he* or *she* are among the top 2 continuations.

Subject Bias Subject bias scores are calculated as the percentage of prompts where the pronoun referring to the subject ([np1]) has a higher probability than the pronoun referring to the object ([np2]).

[2]https://huggingface.co/dbmdz/german-gpt2

[3]https://huggingface.co/dbmdz/bert-base-german-cased

4 Results

Table 1 shows completion sensitivity results aggregated for all types of verbs and names. To ease comparison with previous studies, we also report aggregated results on prompts with first names only. In general, these scores suggest that both language models have a weak but seemingly consistent tendency to generate continuations congruent with human biases, i.e. more than 50% of the predictions are congruent in I-Caus and I-Cons conditions. However, results shown in Table 2 suggest that generated continuations are much less consistent than scores in Table 1 may lead us to expect.

As shown in the more detailed breakdown in Table 2, continuations predicted by GPT-2 generally exhibit a strong object bias (low subject bias scores in all conditions), a finding that aligns well with Kementchedjhieva et al. (2021)'s results on German PLMs. This object bias is less strong, however, in some conditions where the subject is female, but only when it is additionally realized as a first name (I-Caus/SE and I-Cons/SE+ES). Moreover, we note that GPT-2 prediction accuracy (Acc@2) drops substantially for all I-Cons/SE verbs, as well as for some I-Caus/ES verbs with female subjects or surname subjects. For the I-Cons/ES condition with female surname subjects, the prediction accuracy is close to 0. This indicates that GPT-2 does not only fail in capturing next-mention biases for interpersonal verbs in our data, but rather fails to compute reliable representations of complex entity names and clauses embedded with *sodass* (*and so*).

Continuations predicted by BERT do not exhibit any systematic object or subject bias across conditions, nor do they exhibit biases that align well with human continuations. For instance, in I-Caus contexts with ES verbs, BERTs predictions display an object bias (in line with humans), except when the subject is female and realized as a surname. In I-Caus contexts with SE verbs, BERTs predictions display an object bias for first name (not in line with humans), but a subject bias for surnames (which would be in line with humans). Similar patterns arise in I-Cons contexts: for ES verbs, predictions tend towards an object bias, except when the subject is a female surname (94% subject bias). Additionally, prediction accuracies in I-Cons contexts drop systematically and dramatically across different verb and name types. Again, this indicates that the model fails to compute reliable representations of prompts ending in *sodass* (*and so*), which,

Bias type	V-type	NP-type	[np1]	BERT Acc@2	BERT Subject Bias	GPT-2 Acc@2	GPT-2 Subject Bias	Human Subject Bias
I-CAUS	ES	firstn	m	0.814	0.118	0.926	0.004	0.06
			f	0.922	0.148	0.826	0.092	0.02
		surn	m	0.898	0.264	0.872	0.000	
			f	0.954	0.520	0.462	0.000	
	SE	firstn	m	1.000	0.200	1.000	0.008	0.885
			f	1.000	0.080	1.000	0.396	0.862
		surn	m	0.998	0.564	1.000	0.074	
			f	0.928	0.818	1.000	0.002	
I-CONS	ES	firstn	m	0.578	0.398	1.000	0.134	0.81
			f	0.568	0.436	0.992	0.368	0.748
		surn	m	0.528	0.462	0.958	0.330	
			f	0.156	0.944	1.000	0.004	
	SE	firstn	m	0.522	0.344	0.736	0.000	0.05
			f	0.336	0.054	0.820	0.266	0.045
		surn	m	0.698	0.518	0.778	0.000	
			f	0.744	0.640	0.072	0.000	

Table 2: Top-2 prediction Accuracy (Acc@2), and Subject Bias for BERT and GPT-2 predictions, and human continuations for different contexts (I-Caus/I-Cons, Experiencer-Stimuli (ES) Stimuli-Experiencer (SE) verbs, NPs with first names (firstn) and surnames (surn). Human scores for prompts using surnames are not available.)

in German, is less frequent than *weil* (*because*).

Discussion Generally, our results indicate that the large-scale German PLMs we tested in this study are not able to compute reliable discourse-level representations of our prompts that are abstract enough to capture next mention bias for interpersonal verbs, regardless of the realization of the names in verbs' arguments. This mirrors Abdou et al. (2020)'s findings on Winograd schema perturbations, showing that language models are sensitive to minimal changes in prompts that do not affect human understanding. Our results also support proposals to improve the modeling of names and entities in neural language models (Ji et al., 2017; Févry et al., 2020; Holgate and Erk, 2021). Concerning gender bias, BERT's continuations show tendencies towards a female bias when NPs are realized as surnames, which may be related to the fact that German *sie* is ambiguous and can refer to female singular and plural entities.

5 Conclusion

We have investigated implicit causality and consequentiality biases in two German PLMs. We find that GPT-2 shows a strong object bias, which is weaker for prompts where the verb arguments are realized as surnames and the subject's gender is female. BERT does not exhibit any systematic next-mention bias for I-Caus and I-Cons conditions when gender and name type are varied. Thus, none of the models show evidence for human-like next-mention biases in explanation or consequence contexts. In line with Abdou et al. (2020), we conclude that perturbation and variation of experimental stimuli is an important tool when testing PLMs on data collected in psycholinguistic studies with humans.

References

Mostafa Abdou, Vinit Ravishankar, Maria Barrett, Yonatan Belinkov, Desmond Elliott, and Anders Søgaard. 2020. The sensitivity of language models and humans to Winograd schema perturbations. In *Proceedings of the 58th Annual Meeting of the Association for Computational Linguistics*, pages 7590–7604, Online. Association for Computational Linguistics.

Yonatan Belinkov and James Glass. 2019. Analysis methods in neural language processing: A survey. *Transactions of the Association for Computational Linguistics*, 7:49–72.

Su Lin Blodgett, Solon Barocas, Hal Daumé III, and Hanna Wallach. 2020. Language (technology) is power: A critical survey of "bias" in NLP. In *Proceedings of the 58th Annual Meeting of the Association for Computational Linguistics*, pages 5454–5476, Online. Association for Computational Linguistics.

Shikha Bordia and Samuel R. Bowman. 2019. Identifying and reducing gender bias in word-level language models. In *Proceedings of the 2019 Conference of the North American Chapter of the Association for Computational Linguistics: Student Research Workshop*, pages 7–15, Minneapolis, Minnesota. Association for Computational Linguistics.

Tom Brown, Benjamin Mann, Nick Ryder, Melanie Subbiah, Jared D Kaplan, Prafulla Dhariwal, Arvind Neelakantan, Pranav Shyam, Girish Sastry, Amanda Askell, et al. 2020. Language models are few-shot learners. *Advances in neural information processing systems*, 33:1877–1901.

Forrest Davis and Marten van Schijndel. 2020. Discourse structure interacts with reference but not syntax in neural language models. In *Proceedings of the 24th Conference on Computational Natural Language Learning*, pages 396–407, Online. Association for Computational Linguistics.

Jacob Devlin, Ming-Wei Chang, Kenton Lee, and Kristina Toutanova. 2019. BERT: Pre-training of deep bidirectional transformers for language understanding. In *Proceedings of the 2019 Conference of the North American Chapter of the Association for Computational Linguistics: Human Language Technologies, Volume 1 (Long and Short Papers)*, pages 4171–4186, Minneapolis, Minnesota. Association for Computational Linguistics.

Allyson Ettinger. 2020. What BERT is not: Lessons from a new suite of psycholinguistic diagnostics for language models. *Transactions of the Association for Computational Linguistics*, 8:34–48.

Evelyn C. Ferstl, Alan Garnham, and Christina Manouilidou. 2011. Implicit causality bias in English: a corpus of 300 verbs. *Behavior Research Methods*, 43(1):124–135.

Thibault Févry, Livio Baldini Soares, Nicholas FitzGerald, Eunsol Choi, and Tom Kwiatkowski. 2020. Entities as experts: Sparse memory access with entity supervision. In *Proceedings of the 2020 Conference on Empirical Methods in Natural Language Processing (EMNLP)*, pages 4937–4951, Online. Association for Computational Linguistics.

Eric Holgate and Katrin Erk. 2021. "politeness, you simpleton!" retorted [MASK]: Masked prediction of literary characters. In *Proceedings of the 14th International Conference on Computational Semantics (IWCS)*, pages 202–211, Groningen, The Netherlands (online). Association for Computational Linguistics.

Yangfeng Ji, Chenhao Tan, Sebastian Martschat, Yejin Choi, and Noah A. Smith. 2017. Dynamic entity representations in neural language models. In *Proceedings of the 2017 Conference on Empirical Methods in Natural Language Processing*, pages 1830–1839, Copenhagen, Denmark. Association for Computational Linguistics.

Yova Kementchedjhieva, Mark Anderson, and Anders Søgaard. 2021. John praised Mary because _he_? implicit causality bias and its interaction with explicit cues in LMs. In *Findings of the Association for Computational Linguistics: ACL-IJCNLP 2021*, pages 4859–4871, Online. Association for Computational Linguistics.

Mike Lewis, Yinhan Liu, Naman Goyal, Marjan Ghazvininejad, Abdelrahman Mohamed, Omer Levy, Veselin Stoyanov, and Luke Zettlemoyer. 2020. BART: Denoising sequence-to-sequence pre-training for natural language generation, translation, and comprehension. In *Proceedings of the 58th Annual Meeting of the Association for Computational Linguistics*, pages 7871–7880, Online. Association for Computational Linguistics.

Yinhan Liu, Myle Ott, Naman Goyal, Jingfei Du, Mandar Joshi, Danqi Chen, Omer Levy, Mike Lewis, Luke Zettlemoyer, and Veselin Stoyanov. 2019. Roberta: A robustly optimized bert pretraining approach. *arXiv preprint arXiv:1907.11692*.

Nicholas Meade, Elinor Poole-Dayan, and Siva Reddy. 2022. An empirical survey of the effectiveness of debiasing techniques for pre-trained language models. In *Proceedings of the 60th Annual Meeting of the Association for Computational Linguistics (Volume 1: Long Papers)*, pages 1878–1898, Dublin, Ireland. Association for Computational Linguistics.

Victor Sanh, Lysandre Debut, Julien Chaumond, and Thomas Wolf. 2019. Distilbert, a distilled version of bert: smaller, faster, cheaper and lighter. *arXiv preprint arXiv:1910.01108*.

Torgrim Solstad and Oliver Bott. 2022. On the nature of implicit causality and consequentiality: the case of psychological verbs. *Language, Cognition and Neuroscience*, 37:1–30. Ahead-of-print version.

Shiva Upadhye, Leon Bergen, and Andrew Kehler. 2020. Predicting reference: What do language models learn about discourse models? In *Proceedings of the 2020 Conference on Empirical Methods in Natural Language Processing (EMNLP)*, pages 977–982, Online. Association for Computational Linguistics.

Proceedings of the 18th Conference on Natural Language Processing (KONVENS 2022)

Evaluation of Automatic Speech Recognition for Conversational Speech in Dutch, English, and German: What Goes Missing?

Alianda Lopez, Andreas Liesenfeld, Mark Dingemanse
Centre for Language Studies
Radboud University, Nijmegen, The Netherlands
{ada.lopez,andreas.liesenfeld,mark.dingemanse}@ru.nl

Abstract

As voice user interfaces and conversational agents grow in importance, automatic speech recognition (ASR) encounters increasingly free-form and informal input data. Conversational speech is at once the most challenging and the most ecologically relevant type of data for speech recognition in this context. Here we evaluate the performance of several ASR engines on conversational speech in three languages, focusing on the fate of backchannels and other interactionally relevant elements of talk. We propose forms of error analysis based on ngram salience scoring that can complement default measures like word error rates (WER) and are more informative of ASR's ability to live up to the task of accurately representing real-world interaction.

1 Introduction

Conversational agents and voice-driven virtual assistants are becoming more and more integrated into our daily lives. However, users are still dissatisfied with their conversational abilities, describing them as frustrating, stilted, and unnatural (Clark et al., 2019; Moore, 2017; Kopp and Krämer, 2021). One likely reason is that most automatic speech recognition (ASR) systems are trained on carefully read monological speech (Panayotov et al., 2015; Ardila et al., 2020) rather than on free-flowing informal conversational interaction.

One of the key ways conversational speech differs from read speech is the nature of its production: planned and produced in real-time by people together. Conversation bears the traces of its dialogical origins in the form of elements like backchannels (Yngve, 1970; Fujimoto, 2007), disfluencies (Ginzburg et al., 2014; Hough and Schlangen, 2017), and other forms of speech management (Allwood et al., 1990), collateral signals (Clark, 1996) and non-lexical conversational sounds (Ward, 2006). The variety of terms in this area highlights the disparate strands of research concerned with such phenomena, and also encodes an implicit evaluation of these elements as somehow missable, marginal, or straying from the norm. Quite some work has focused on "disfluency detection", often with the goal of 'cleaning up' transcripts for use in downstream natural language understanding pipelines or for public consumption (Hough and Schlangen, 2017; Shalyminov et al., 2018; Zayats et al., 2019). However, a recent upsurge in research shows the importance of these elements as metacommunicative tools for streamlining conversation (Buschmeier and Kopp, 2018; Kosmala and Morgenstern, 2018; Dingemanse and Liesenfeld, 2022), and this is where their relevance for some ASR applications lies. For instance, interjections like *mhmm* and *uh-huh* in English serve as a cue for the speaker to continue talking, while others like *huh?* instead indicate a need for repetition or clarification — quite an important distinction to get for voice user interfaces. Likewise, items like *uh* and *um* are easily seen as irregularities to be cleaned up, but they can also do interactional work, such as signalling upcoming complexities or interactionally delicate moments (Clark and Fox Tree, 2002; Kosmala, 2020). While there are use cases for ignoring them, there are also contexts where natural language processing pipelines can benefit from keeping them available in some form (Dinkar, 2022).

The most common methods for benchmarking ASR systems are hardly relevant to conversations. The popular metric of word error rate (WER) compares ASR output against reference transcripts in terms of insertions, deletions, and substitutions. While useful, it has its limitations (Aksënova et al., 2021; Errattahi et al., 2018). For one, it gives more weight to insertions than deletions. It also does not take into account that there are different types of words, even when work on ASR transcription errors in English showed that errors are more likely to occur for conversational interjections (Zayats et al., 2019). Indeed, some applications of WER exclude interjections because they are not well-represented in the training data in the first place (Papadopoulos Korfiatis et al., 2022). Because WER is computed at utterance level, it fails when whole utterances go missing – which is proportionally more likely for shorter utterances, one study on Swedish found (Cumbal et al., 2021). A recent error analysis of ASR performance across types of English speech shows that it fares worst for informal conversation. Furthermore, among function words, content words, and conversational words, it is the latter that cause the biggest drop in performance (Mansfield et al., 2021).

As ASR systems are stress-tested and the limitations of WER become more apparent, the need for complementary evaluation methods arises. Here, we build on the work reviewed above and provide two novel contributions. First, where most prior work has focused on English, we add two other languages. This baby step towards taking more of the world's linguistic diversity into account allows us to see to what extent prior findings generalize (Besacier et al., 2014). Second, we focus on error analysis not at the level of word classes but at the level of interactionally relevant phenomena: conversational words, self-repairs, and phonetic reductions. Both contributions are in line with our larger aim to improve human language technology through looking at linguistically diverse and ecologically valid conversational data (Bird, 2020; Birhane and Guest, 2021).

2 Data and Methods

To investigate how an ASR system processes conversational speech, we use data from English, Dutch, and German – three languages for which there are available corpora along with ASR solutions.

Human Transcripts. Human transcripts were obtained from three different conversational corpora, all of which capture natural conversations. For English, we use CallHome American English (Canavan et al., 1997), a corpus of informal telephone conversations between native speakers of American English from various places in the United States. A total of 140 recordings were used that ranged from 5 to 10 minutes in length. For Dutch, we use the IFA Dialog Video Corpus (van Son et al., 2008) of informal conversations between native Dutch speakers from different parts of the Netherlands. Transcripts follow the the Spoken Dutch Corpus format (Oostdijk, 2000). We used a total of 20 sound files with an average length of 15 minutes. For German, we use the Forschungs- und Lehrkorpus Gesprochenes (FOLK) Deutsch (Reineke and Schmidt, 2022), including 7 files of 10 to 30 minutes long. One sound file was excluded due to poor audio quality. Transcripts in all three corpora mark interjections, phonetically reduced forms, word fragments due to self-repairs and nonverbal conduct like coughs and lip smacks. We unified transcription formats to time-aligned utterance-level annotations, with nonverbal conduct and untranscribed stretches marked in "[]" and not included in our comparisons.

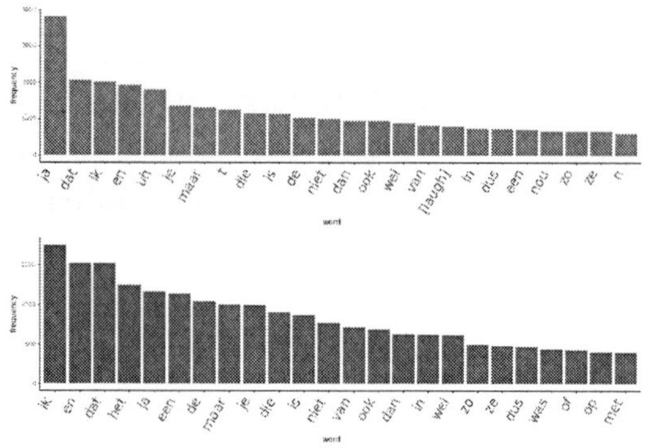

Figure 1: Most frequent words in Dutch human and ASR transcripts of conversational speech. See Appendix B for more details as well as English and German data.

ASR Transcripts. To generate ASR transcripts, we used three general purpose speech recognition engines made available through the Bavarian Archive for Speech Signals' CLARIN Transcription Portal (Draxler et al., 2020).[1] We picked these engines as examples of a class of widely available ASR solutions that are trained on large amounts of written language and that are designed to behave in a roughly comparable way: (i) emphasising textual representations over speech, and (ii) habitually removing some elements of language labeled as disfluencies. While specialist ASR solutions do exist, these general purpose engines are used in many applications and products that deal with conversational speech, such as voice assistants and social robots like Furhat (Al Moubayed et al., 2012) and Pepper (Pandey and Gelin, 2018).[2]

[1]https://clarin.phonetik.uni-muenchen.de/apps/TranscriptionPortal/

[2]*Cobalt Speech* is an example of specialist ASR engine for

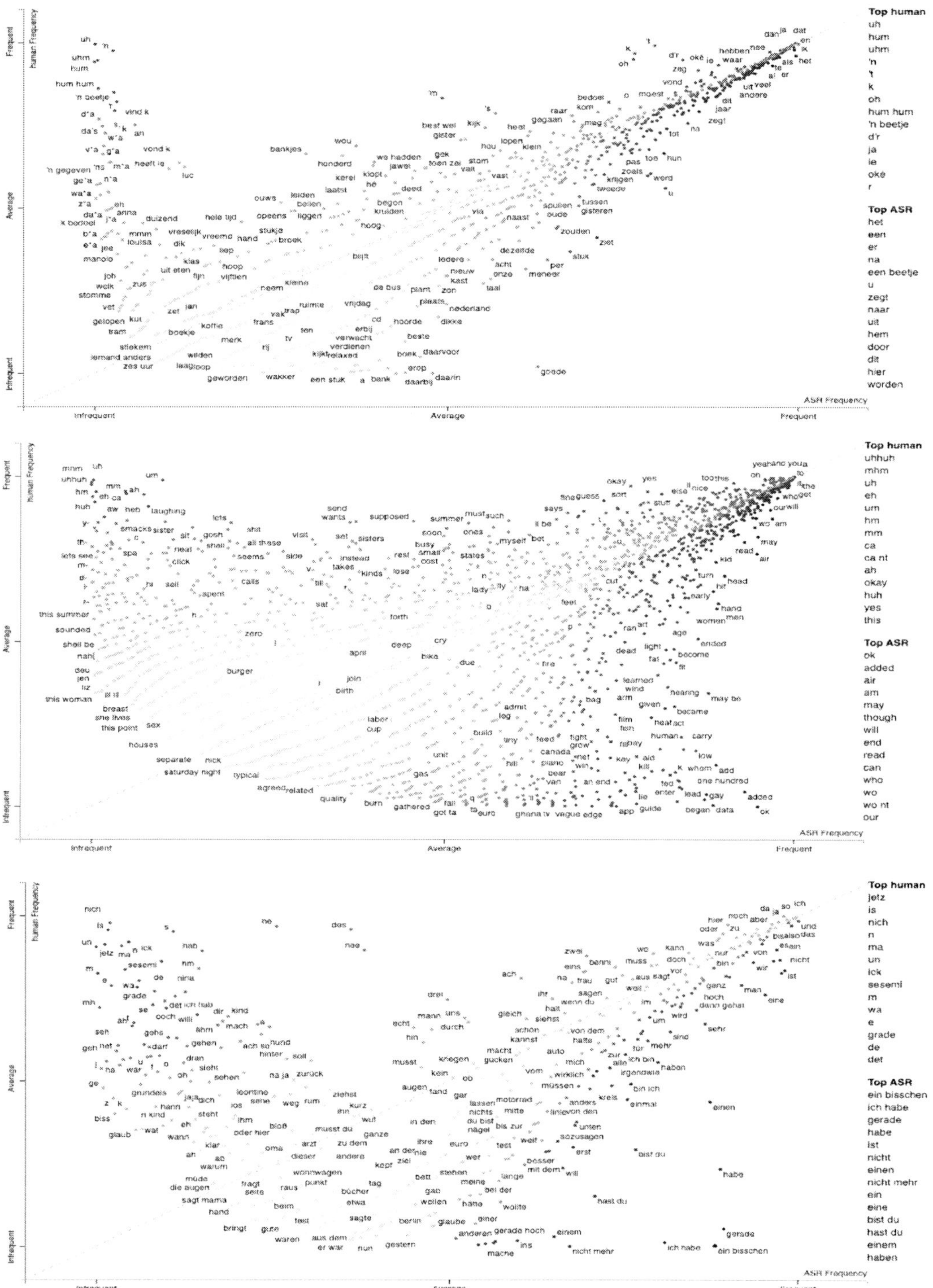

Figure 2: Most characteristic elements in human-transcribed (orange) and ASR transcribed (purple) conversational speech in Dutch, English and German, with right panels showing the top 10 most distinctive items for each type. Plotted using `scaled F score` metric using `scattertext` (Kessler, 2017).

	Dutch	English	German
Conversational Words	*uh, hum, uhm, hum hum, oh, ja*	*uhhuh, mhm, uh, eh, um, hm, mm, ah, huh, okay*	*hm, mh*
Reductions	*d'r (haar), , 'n (een), 'n beetje (een beetje), 't (het), ie (hij)*		*'n (ein), wa (wir), grade (gerade), det (das)*
Self-repairs	*k-, r-*	*m-, e-*	*se-*

Table 1: Top elements that are underrepresented (or missing) in the ASR versus human-produced transcripts. Three interactional phenomena make up most of the top 20 salient tokens by Scaled F score: short *conversational words* (this includes backchannels, response tokens, continuers, non-lexical utterances), phonetic *reductions* (including contractions), and *self-repairs* (also known as word fragments or truncated words).

2.1 Pre-Processing

Transcripts were processed to bring them to a more comparable format. This entailed removing punctuation, correcting the spelling for proper names, and removing capitalization. For the English ASR transcript, the inconsistent formats for contractions were changed to match the human transcript (i.e *can' t* to *cant*). Word fragments and shortened forms were left untouched. To further enhance comparability, tags and other special characters from the human transcripts were removed. All transcripts were then tokenized using `spaCy`'s "Core web" language models.[3]

2.2 Error Analysis

We investigate systematic differences between human-produced and ASR transcripts in the three languages. Which elements are underrepresented in ASR transcripts, and which elements go missing completely? We adopt the `scaled F-Score` introduced by Kessler (2017) as a metric of n-gram salience scoring to compare the two types of transcripts (see appendix A for details). We make the processing and error analysis pipeline available via an OSF repository as part of this paper.[4]

3 Results and Analysis

Across all languages, we find three systematic differences between human and ASR transcripts. This shows that there are indeed certain elements in conversational speech that are incongruously represented.

Shorter output text: In all cases, the ASR transcripts contained fewer words than their human counterparts with a 33% difference for Dutch, 37% for English, and 57% for German. This indicates a significant gap between how humans and ASR engines transcribe conversational speech (Scharenborg, 2007; Mansfield et al., 2021).

Skewed frequency distributions: Furthermore, the frequency distributions of the human transcripts are skewed differently from the ASR transcripts (see Figure 1).

Missing elements: The ngram salience score-based error analysis, visualized in Figure 2, revealed that the words missed by the ASR are notably similar in all the languages studied. First, the lack of conversational words in the ASR transcript indicate that current systems have difficulties picking up these short but important utterances regardless of the language. For reductions, only those in English were well detected by the ASR. This may be because Dutch and German reductions are more exclusive to conversational speech; thus occurring less frequently in written language than their English counterpart. On instances when these reductions are actually detected, the ASR then tends to transcribe them in their expanded form instead of how they were actually said. Lastly, self-repairs are completely missed too. Aside from these self-repairs also being short, they are often omitted from speech datasets as well due to their "incompleteness". However, these word fragments were nonetheless uttered and consequently still carry meaning in conversations.

These findings indicate that current general-purpose ASR engines tend to struggle with three interactional phenomena: short conversational words, reductions, and self-repair (see Table 1).

4 Limitations

We are aware of several limitations. First, the examined corpora are too small to provide a com-

conversational speech. Such products are not only few and far between, but also proprietary and expensive.

[3] https://spacy.io

[4] https://osf.io/7ts3y

prehensive overview of the missing interactional elements. It is likely that a larger dataset will help to discover even more elements that this study has missed. Next, while our analysis revealed the disparity in the representation of certain elements between human and ASR transcripts, an analysis at the utterance level will provide more insight on how and why this disparity exists (Cumbal et al., 2021). An accurate representations of conversational speech has to not only take into account what is being say, but also how it is said, which makes the task a lot harder. This may require a whole new ASR processing pipeline design (Faruqui and Hakkani-Tür, 2022; Merz and Scrivner, 2022; Wepner et al., 2022). Finally, we have not computed WER and similar measures – making it harder to relate such measures to our results (cf. Georgila et al. 2020).

5 Conclusion

Conversation is the primary ecology of natural language use (Schegloff, 2006). ASR systems are an integral part of conversational agents and any technology that deals with speech input, and they are increasingly exposed to conversational settings (Baumann et al., 2017). However, they are far from able to handle free-flowing conversations (Addlesee et al., 2020), a major cause of interactional turbulence and user dissatisfaction (Hoegen et al., 2019; Clark et al., 2019). Here we have shown that across three languages, off-the-shelf ASR solutions have trouble with quintessentially interactional phenomena like conversational words (backchannels, delay markers, and other interjections) and word fragments resulting from self-repair. Yet, it is precisely these items that people use to streamline interaction. Dealing with these items as interactional tools, rather than indiscriminately erasing them, represents the next frontier in the development of voice-driven human language technologies.

Acknowledgments

This work was supported by NWO Vidi 016.vidi.185.205.

References

Angus Addlesee, Yanchao Yu, and Arash Eshghi. 2020. A Comprehensive Evaluation of Incremental Speech Recognition and Diarization for Conversational AI. In *Proceedings of the 28th International Conference on Computational Linguistics*, pages 3492–3503, Barcelona, Spain (Online). International Committee on Computational Linguistics.

Alëna Aksënova, Daan van Esch, James Flynn, and Pavel Golik. 2021. How Might We Create Better Benchmarks for Speech Recognition? In *Proceedings of the 1st Workshop on Benchmarking: Past, Present and Future*, pages 22–34, Online. Association for Computational Linguistics.

Samer Al Moubayed, Jonas Beskow, Gabriel Skantze, and Björn Granström. 2012. Furhat: A Back-Projected Human-Like Robot Head for Multiparty Human-Machine Interaction. In *Cognitive Behavioural Systems*, Lecture Notes in Computer Science, pages 114–130, Berlin, Heidelberg. Springer.

Jens Allwood, Joakim Nivre, and Elisabeth Ahlsén. 1990. Speech Management—on the Non-written Life of Speech. *Nordic Journal of Linguistics*, 13(01):3–48.

Rosana Ardila, Megan Branson, Kelly Davis, Michael Kohler, Josh Meyer, Michael Henretty, Reuben Morais, Lindsay Saunders, Francis Tyers, and Gregor Weber. 2020. Common voice: A massively-multilingual speech corpus. In *Proceedings of the 12th language resources and evaluation conference*, pages 4218–4222.

Timo Baumann, Casey Kennington, Julian Hough, and David Schlangen. 2017. Recognising Conversational Speech: What an Incremental ASR Should Do for a Dialogue System and How to Get There. In Kristiina Jokinen and Graham Wilcock, editors, *Dialogues with Social Robots: Enablements, Analyses, and Evaluation*, Lecture Notes in Electrical Engineering, pages 421–432. Springer, Singapore.

Laurent Besacier, Etienne Barnard, Alexey Karpov, and Tanja Schultz. 2014. Automatic speech recognition for under-resourced languages: A survey. *Speech Communication*, 56:85–100.

Steven Bird. 2020. Decolonising Speech and Language Technology. In *Proceedings of the 28th International Conference on Computational Linguistics*, pages 3504–3519, Barcelona, Spain (Online). International Committee on Computational Linguistics.

Abeba Birhane and Olivia Guest. 2021. Towards Decolonising Computational Sciences. *Kvinder, Køn & Forskning*, (2):60–73.

Hendrik Buschmeier and Stefan Kopp. 2018. Communicative listener feedback in human–agent interaction: Artificial speakers need to be attentive and adaptive. In *Proceedings of the 17th International Conference on Autonomous Agents and Multiagent Systems*.

Alexandra Canavan, David Graff, and George Zipperlen. 1997. CALLHOME American English Speech. Artwork Size: 1830160 KB Pages: 1830160 KB Type: dataset.

Herbert H. Clark. 1996. *Using Language*. Cambridge University Press, Cambridge.

Herbert H. Clark and Jean E. Fox Tree. 2002. Using uh and um in spontaneous speaking. *Cognition*, 84:73–111.

Leigh Clark, Nadia Pantidi, Orla Cooney, Philip Doyle, Diego Garaialde, Justin Edwards, Brendan Spillane, Emer Gilmartin, Christine Murad, Cosmin Munteanu, Vincent Wade, and Benjamin R. Cowan. 2019. What Makes a Good Conversation? Challenges in Designing Truly Conversational Agents. In *Proceedings of the 2019 CHI Conference on Human Factors in Computing Systems*, CHI '19, pages 1–12, New York, NY, USA. Association for Computing Machinery.

Ronald Cumbal, Birger Moell, José Lopes, and Olov Engwall. 2021. "You don't understand me!": Comparing ASR results for L1 and L2 speakers of Swedish. In *Proceeding of Interspeech 2021*, pages 4463–4467.

Mark Dingemanse and Andreas Liesenfeld. 2022. From text to talk: Harnessing conversational corpora for humane and diversity-aware language technology. In *Proceedings of the 60th Annual Meeting of the Association for Computational Linguistics (Volume 1: Long Papers)*, pages 5614–5633, Dublin. Association for Computational Linguistics.

Tanvi Dinkar. 2022. *Computational models of disfluencies : fillers and discourse markers in spoken language understanding*. These de doctorat, Institut polytechnique de Paris.

Christoph Draxler, Henk van den Heuvel, Arjan van Hessen, Silvia Calamai, and Louise Corti. 2020. A CLARIN Transcription Portal for Interview Data. In *Proceedings of the 12th Language Resources and Evaluation Conference*, pages 3353–3359, Marseille, France. European Language Resources Association.

Rahhal Errattahi, Asmaa El Hannani, and Hassan Ouahmane. 2018. Automatic Speech Recognition Errors Detection and Correction: A Review. *Procedia Computer Science*, 128:32–37.

Manaal Faruqui and Dilek Hakkani-Tür. 2022. Revisiting the Boundary between ASR and NLU in the Age of Conversational Dialog Systems. *Computational Linguistics*, 48(1):221–232.

Donna T. Fujimoto. 2007. Listener responses in interaction: A case for abandoning the term, backchannel. *Bulletin paper of Osaka Jogakuin College*, 9(28):35–54.

Kallirroi Georgila, Anton Leuski, Volodymyr Yanov, and David Traum. 2020. Evaluation of Off-the-shelf Speech Recognizers Across Diverse Dialogue Domains. In *Proceedings of the 12th Language Resources and Evaluation Conference*, pages 6469–6476, Marseille, France. European Language Resources Association.

Jonathan Ginzburg, Raquel Fernández, and David Schlangen. 2014. Disfluencies as intra-utterance dialogue moves. *Semantics and Pragmatics*, 7.

Rens Hoegen, Deepali Aneja, Daniel McDuff, and Mary Czerwinski. 2019. An End-to-End Conversational Style Matching Agent. In *Proceedings of the 19th ACM International Conference on Intelligent Virtual Agents*, IVA '19, pages 111–118, New York, NY, USA. Association for Computing Machinery.

Julian Hough and David Schlangen. 2017. Joint, Incremental Disfluency Detection and Utterance Segmentation from Speech. In *Proceedings of the 15th Conference of the European Chapter of the Association for Computational Linguistics: Volume 1, Long Papers*, pages 326–336. Association for Computational Linguistics.

Jason Kessler. 2017. Scattertext: a Browser-Based Tool for Visualizing how Corpora Differ. In *Proceedings of the 55th Annual Meeting of the Association for Computational Linguistics (System Demonstrations)*, pages 85–90.

Stefan Kopp and Nicole Krämer. 2021. Revisiting Human-Agent Communication: The Importance of Joint Co-construction and Understanding Mental States. *Frontiers in Psychology*, 12. Publisher: Frontiers.

Loulou Kosmala. 2020. Euh le saviez-vous ? le rôle des (dis)fluences en contexte interactionnel : étude exploratoire et qualitative. *SHS Web of Conferences*, 78:01018. Publisher: EDP Sciences.

Loulou Kosmala and Aliyah Morgenstern. 2018. Should 'uh' and 'um' be categorized as markers of disfluency? The use of fillers in a challenging conversational context. In *Fluency and Disfluency across Languages and Language Varieties*.

Courtney Mansfield, Sara Ng, Gina-Anne Levow, Richard A. Wright, and Mari Ostendorf. 2021. Revisiting Parity of Human vs. Machine Conversational Speech Transcription. In *Interspeech 2021*, pages 1997–2001. ISCA.

Megan Merz and Olga Scrivner. 2022. Discourse on ASR Measurement: Introducing the ARPOCA Assessment Tool. In *Proceedings of the 60th Annual Meeting of the Association for Computational Linguistics: Student Research Workshop*, pages 366–372, Dublin, Ireland. Association for Computational Linguistics.

Roger K. Moore. 2017. Is Spoken Language All-or-Nothing? Implications for Future Speech-Based Human-Machine Interaction. In Kristiina Jokinen and Graham Wilcock, editors, *Dialogues with Social Robots: Enablements, Analyses, and Evaluation*, Lecture Notes in Electrical Engineering, pages 281–291. Springer, Singapore.

Nelleke Oostdijk. 2000. The Spoken Dutch Corpus: Overview and first evaluation. In *Proceedings of the second international conference on language resources and evaluation (LREC'00)*.

Vassil Panayotov, Guoguo Chen, Daniel Povey, and Sanjeev Khudanpur. 2015. Librispeech: an ASR corpus based on public domain audio books. In *2015 IEEE international conference on acoustics, speech and signal processing (ICASSP)*, pages 5206–5210. IEEE.

Amit Kumar Pandey and Rodolphe Gelin. 2018. A Mass-Produced Sociable Humanoid Robot: Pepper: The First Machine of Its Kind. *IEEE Robotics & Automation Magazine*, 25(3):40–48. Conference Name: IEEE Robotics & Automation Magazine.

Alex Papadopoulos Korfiatis, Francesco Moramarco, Radmila Sarac, and Aleksandar Savkov. 2022. PriMock57: A Dataset Of Primary Care Mock Consultations. In *Proceedings of the 60th Annual Meeting of the Association for Computational Linguistics (Volume 2: Short Papers)*, pages 588–598, Dublin, Ireland. Association for Computational Linguistics.

Silke Reineke and Thomas Schmidt. 2022. Das Archiv für Gesprochenes Deutsch und das Forschungs-und Lehrkorpus für Gesprochenes Deutsch. In *Sprache in Politik und Gesellschaft*, pages 323–330. de Gruyter.

Odette Scharenborg. 2007. Reaching over the gap: A review of efforts to link human and automatic speech recognition research. *Speech Communication*, 49(5):336–347.

Emanuel A. Schegloff. 2006. Interaction: The Infrastructure for Social Institutions, the Natural Ecological Niche for Language, and the Arena in which Culture is Enacted. In Nick J. Enfield and Stephen C. Levinson, editors, *Roots of human sociality: Culture, cognition, and human interaction*, pages 70–96. Berg, Oxford.

Igor Shalyminov, Arash Eshghi, and Oliver Lemon. 2018. Multi-Task Learning for Domain-General Spoken Disfluency Detection in Dialogue Systems.

Rob van Son, Wieneke Wesseling, Eric Sanders, and Henk van den Heuvel. 2008. The IFADV corpus: A free dialog video corpus. In *Proceedings of the Sixth International Conference on Language Resources and Evaluation (LREC'08)*.

Nigel Ward. 2006. Non-lexical conversational sounds in American English. *Pragmatics & Cognition*, 14:129–182.

Saskia Wepner, Barbara Schuppler, and Gernot Kubin. 2022. How prosody affects ASR performance in conversational Austrian German. pages 195–199.

Victor Yngve. 1970. On getting a word in edgewise. In *Papers from the Sixth Regional Meeting, Chicago Linguistic Society*, pages 567–578.

Vicky Zayats, Trang Tran, Richard Wright, Courtney Mansfield, and Mari Ostendorf. 2019. Disfluencies and Human Speech Transcription Errors. In *Proceedings of Interspeech 2019*, pages 3088–3092. ISCA.

6 Appendix

A `Scaled F-score`: measuring ngram salience by class

`Scaled F-score` is a modified version of the vanilla F-score calculated by taking the harmonic means of precision and frequency. Given a word $w_i \in W$ and a category $c_j \in C$, the precision of word w_i with respect to a category c_j is defined as the following:

$$\text{prec}(i,j) = \frac{\#(w_i, c_j)}{\sum_{c \in C} \#(w_i, c)}$$

The function $\#(w_i, c_j)$ represents either the number of times w_i occurs in an utterance labeled with the category c_j or the number of utterances labeled c_j which contain w_i. The frequency of a word within a category is defined as:

$$\text{freq}(i,j) = \frac{\#(w_i, c_j)}{\sum_{w \in W} \#(w, c_j)}$$

Then, the harmonic mean of these two values is defined as:

$$\mathcal{H}_\beta(i,j) = (1+\beta^2)\frac{\text{prec}(i,j) \cdot \text{freq}(i,j)}{\beta^2 \cdot \text{prec}(i,j) + \text{freq}(i,j)}$$

$\beta \in \mathcal{R}^+$ is a scaling factor where frequency is favored if $\beta < 1$, precision if $\beta > 1$, and both are equally weighted if $\beta = 1$. F-score is equivalent to the harmonic mean where $\beta = 1$.

This score is then modified in two ways to address two issues, namely that (1) harmonic means are dominated by precision, and that (2) low scores are "low-frequency brittle terms". In short, the Scaled F-Score aims to better take into account tokens of extremely high and low token frequencies and balances the score to this end. On a scale from -1 to 1, the score indicates whether an n-gram exhibits an association with a class (positive score) or not (negative score). For a more detailed explanation of these modification, see: https://github.com/JasonKessler/scattertext#understanding-scaled-f-score

B Word Frequency distributions in human versus ASR transcripts

Dutch

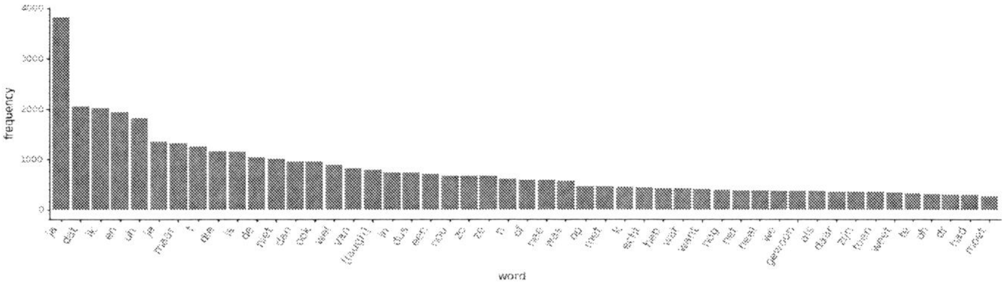

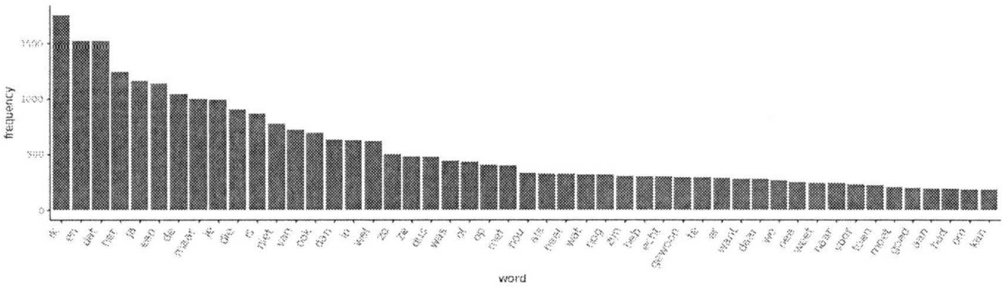

English

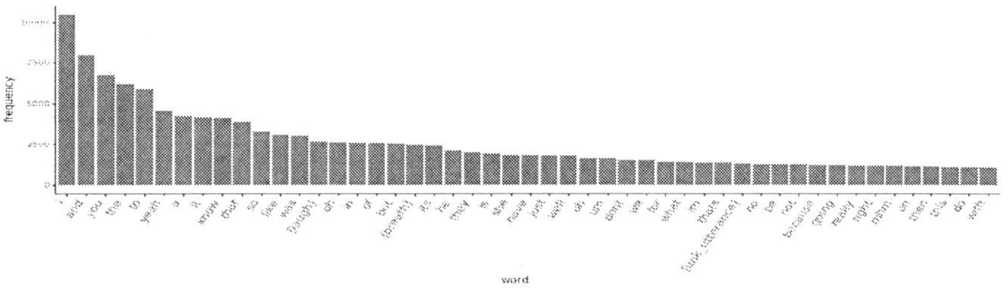

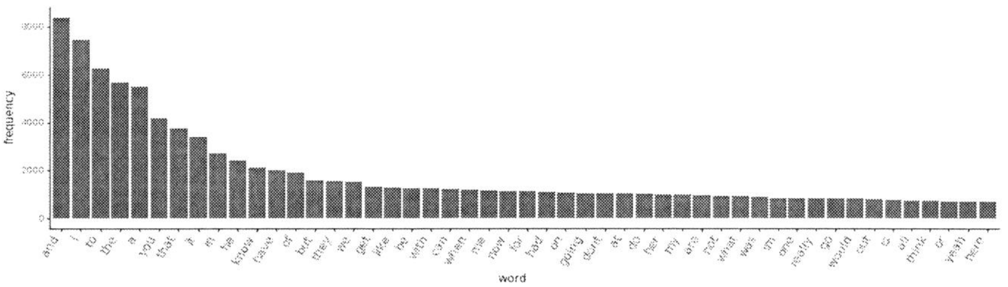

German

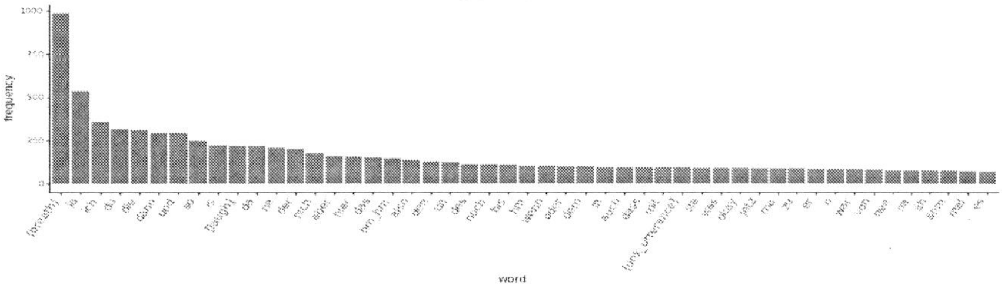

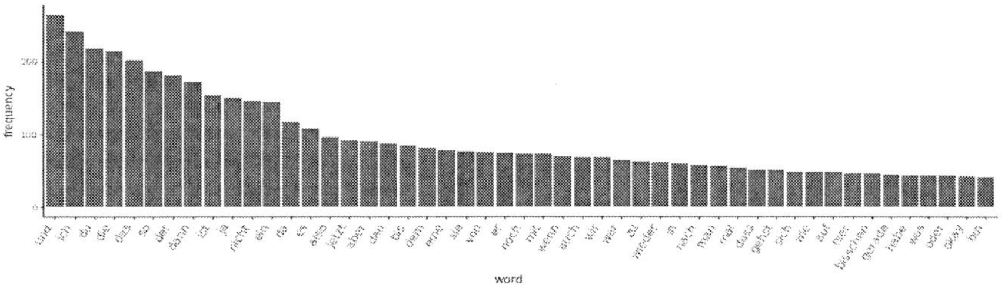

Figure 3: Most frequent words in Dutch, English, and German human (orange) and ASR (purple) transcripts of conversational speech.

Proceedings of the 18th Conference on Natural Language Processing (KONVENS 2022)

Semantic Role Labeling for Sentiment Inference: A Case Study

Manfred Klenner, Anne Göhring
Department of Computational Linguistics
University of Zurich
{klenner,goehring}@cl.uzh.ch

Abstract

In this paper, we evaluate in a case study whether semantic role labelling (SRL) can be reliably used for verb-based sentiment inference (SI). SI strives to identify polar relations (against, in-favour-of) between discourse entities. We took 300 sentences with 10 different verbs that show verb alternations or are ambiguous in order to find out if current SRL systems actually can assign the correct semantic roles and find the correct underlying predicates. Since in SI each verb reading comes with a particular polar profile, SRL is useful only if its analyses are consistent and reliable. We found that this is not (yet) given for German.

1 Introduction

Sentiment Inference (SI) is the task of predicting opponents and proponents given a text. SI reveals how the writer conceptualises the world and how she perceives the discourse entities she refers to. Take for instance the sentence *This government cheats the world.* The writer tries to convey that the government is against the world and that it is - in the perspective of the writer - a negative actor and the world is the victim, which means that there is a negative effect on the world. We, thus, can talk about positive and negative actors, positive and negative effects, about negative (opponents) and positive (proponents) relations. We call these specifications the polar profile of a verb.

In (Klenner et al., 2017), we introduced a verb-based SI system that uses dependency labels in order to express such polar profiles. For instance, the subject of the verb *cheat* - if used in a factual sentence - is identified as indicating a negative actor, the filler of the direct object receives a negative effect, and a negative relation (against) between the two is casted. Even after normalization of dependency trees, e.g. by resolving passive voice, some problems remain, namely verb alternations and verb ambiguity. It certainly will lead to false analyses. Verb alternation, among others, is given if a semantic role changes its syntactic host. As an example of an instrument-subject verb alternation, compare *The police man killed the aggressor with a knife* versus *The knife killed the aggressor.* For a dependency-based approach the police man and the knife are both the subjects although the police man is the agent and the knife is the instrument. There should be a negative polar relation between police man and aggressor, but not between knife and aggressor (a knife cannot be against somebody). If SRL was used instead of dependency parsing, the agent role would indicate the against relation while the instrument role would block such an inference[1] and thus might be a means to provide a general solution to this problem.

SRL could also be useful for verb sense disambiguation. Part of SRL is a step called predicate identification (Conia et al., 2021b), where a verb is mapped to a predicate frame covering the semantic roles of the underlying verb reading. Take as an example German *bedauern* which has a subject and a direct object. It could mean either *feel sorry for* as in *Ich bedauere diese Menschen* (I feel sorry for these people), or *regret* as illustrated by *Ich bedauere den Vorfall* (I regret the incident). In the first case, there is a in-favour-of relation while in the second one the relation is against. In this example, it is not the semantic role that makes the difference in the first place, but the predicate identification (*feel sorry for* versus *regret*).

In this paper, we describe a case study applying SRL to cases of verb alternations and verb ambiguity. For SRL to be applicable, it must hold that the identification of semantic roles is consistent given some verb and that predicate identification is reliable. We found both requirements are currently

[1]The SRL approach InVeRo using VerbAtlas actually produces this result, see https://verbatlas.org

not given for German.

2 Verb Alternations and Verb Ambiguity

As a first step, we identified 10 German verbs[2] from our verb lexicon (Klenner and Amsler, 2016) that have verb alternations or are ambiguous. We focused on challenging cases where a verb has at least two semantic frames given a **single** dependency frame. Take the transitive (i.e. subject,object) and ambiguous verb *verbessern* which might mean *improve* or *correct*. In a dependency setting we just have the subjects and objects of the particular verb *verbessern*. In our current system we cannot distinguish the readings and, thus, only have one polar profile. But in fact we'd need two: for both readings. So either verb disambiguation (which is not available for German) or SRL might do the trick.

As an example of verb alternation take *drohen* (threaten), which has an instrument alternation:

(1) Er droht ihm mit Vergeltung
subject verb object oblique
He threatens him with retaliation

(2) Ihm droht Vergeltung
object verb **subject**
He is threatened with retribution

Only in (1) there is a polar relation (against) between the agent (He) and the recipient (him). In our case study we looked at the transitive versions of such cases: *Er droht ihm* versus *Vergeltung droht ihm* (a bit unusal word order, but correct). Again, in the dependency setting we have a single transitive verb with two unaccesible readings (*threaten* versus *face*).

We semi-automatically extracted 300 sentences from a newspaper corpus where for each verb at least two different semantic frames were given. For instance for the verb *drohen,* we found 5 sentences with an actor as subject (one reading) and 8 with a theme as subject (the second reading).

We applied InVeRo in the PropBank and the VerbAtlas mode and manually analysed the results. We will now introduce these tools.

3 Semantic Role Labeling for German

We have tried to find SRL systems for German, but only InVeRo (Conia et al., 2021b) using VerbAtlas (Di Fabio et al., 2019) was available. It was not possible to install SRL-S2S[3] (Daza and Frank, 2019), and the DameSRL[4] system described in (Do et al., 2018a,b) has no predicate identification model for German which is needed for a proper SRL. Another option was to train our own model. However after we have analysed the available resources, the CoNLL shared task description and data (Hajič et al., 2009), and the Universal Proposition Bank (Akbik et al., 2015), we skipped this idea. The German data from CoNLL is derived from Salsa (Erk et al., 2003), the German version of FrameNet. It came into existence by mapping FrameNet roles, which are very fine-grained, to more coarse-grained PropBank semantic roles (Palmer et al., 2005). However, the mapping procedure is hardly described and no quality control is reported. We do not know how much noise was introduced by this mapping. In a footnote, Daza and Frank (2020) reflect on the difficulty of using heterogeneous SRL styles, above all for a cross-lingual comparison, and comment that "annotations for German use a role inventory with roles A0-A9, and a one-to-one mapping to all English labels is not available". Also, after we analysed a few entries in the German Universal Propositions Bank[5], we had to recognise that this semi-automatically generated resource is too noisy. Training our own SRL model no longer was an option. We, thus, carried out our experiments with InVeRo (Conia et al., 2021a).

InVeRo is a multi-lingual SRL model that was trained on various languages including German. Given a (German) sentence, predicate identification yields an English (predicate) frame and the corresponding semantic roles. The frames are from VerbAtlas, a hand-crafted lexical-semantic resource that uses the verb synsets of BabelNet (Navigli and Ponzetto, 2010), a multilingual encyclopedic dictionary that covers 500 languages (actually the synsets of WordNet are used via BabelNet which integrates Wordnet). VerbAtlas frames specify a prototypical argument structure including implicit and so-called shadowed arguments (Conia et al., 2021a). Such a frame clusters verb meanings having similar semantics. Also selectional preferences (not restrictions) are formulated on the basis of WordNet synsets.

[2]See the appendix for the full verb list.

[3]https://github.com/Heidelberg-NLP/SRL-S2S

[4]https://liir.cs.kuleuven.be/software_pages/damesrl.php

[5]http://alanakbik.github.io/UniversalPropositions_German

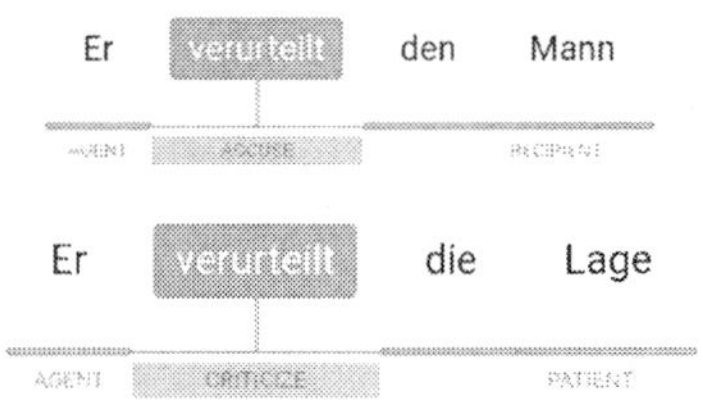

Figure 1: InVero's predicate identification for two German sentences with the verb *verurteilen*, and their corresponding semantic role frames ('He accuses the man' versus 'He criticizes the situation').

Semantic roles are either in PropBank style or following VerbNet nomenclature (25 roles like agent, patient, etc.) (Kipper Schuler et al., 2009).

In Figure 1 predicate identification maps the verb *verurteilen* to *accuse* and *criticize*. As a consequence, two different roles for the direct object become available, namely *recipient* and *patient*. The selectional preferences for the patient role of *criticize* are *individual* and *social group*. Although *situation* is not subsumed under neither restriction, we get a result. The system is robust, thus. However sometimes restrictions seem to be taken seriously and no result appears. The sentence *Sie kämpft für mehr Geld* (She fights for more money) is correctly analysed. If we substitute *Gerechtigkeit* (justice) for *Geld* (money), no result is given, presumably since *Gerechtigkeit* is not subsumed under the restriction which is *entity*.

4 Empirical Evaluation

We manually analysed the output of InVeRo for the 300 sentences. Three types of errors or problems can be distinguished:

- predicate identification (disambiguation) fails
- assigning different semantic roles given a single predicate
- assigning a particular semantic role to syntactically different phrases for the same verb (under a particular reading)

Why are these three points problematic in SI? As we have discussed on various examples, each verb reading has its own polar profile, thus it is crucial to find the right reading (problem 1). A polar profile assigns a directed polar relation (against, in-favour-of) to a verb as well as a holder role (e.g. the agent) and a target role (e.g. theme). That is, in order to specify these relations, the semantic roles of the holder and target roles must be known and they must be stable (not assigned to different roles), otherwise no lexical entry is possible (problem 2). If SRL assigns for a verb reading different roles and role pairings, it is unclear how to anchor the relation correctly. Finally, SRL is syntax-agnostic (problem 3): the same semantic role of a verb might be assigned to different syntactic phrases thereby possibly collapsing verb readings. In the examples (3) and (4) both sentences (according to VerbAtlas[6] have a theme role. In sentence (3) it is realized as a to-infinitive, in sentence (4) as a prepositional phrase (PP).

(3) Er droht zu scheitern
agent verb to-infinitive-**theme**
He is in danger to fail

(4) Er droht mit Konsequenzen
agent verb PP-**theme**
He threatens consequences

As a consequence, these two verb readings would have the same semantic role frame. However, their polar profiles differ. Sentence (3) casts a negative effect on the experiencer (He), while in (4) there is a negative actor, but no negative effect. SRL is not helpful in these cases, it also collapses readings (*danger, threatens*).

Predicate identification failure is most problematic. In the examples above, both (3) and (4) get the same predicate assigned: *guarantee/ensure/promise*[7]. However, only sentence (4) is an instance of this predicate.

This problem becomes clearer, in our case study, if we quantify the number of predicates and predicate frames[8] that were chosen by InVeRo per verb (see the last line of Table 2 in the appendix). For PropBank a verb is, in the mean, mapped to 1.55 predicates, and 3.7 different frames, i.e. pairing of semantic roles, per predicate are used. For VerbAtlas it is 2.75 and 4.5, respectively. Ideally, only one mapping would be given: a verb maps to one or more predicates, each predicate has a stable subcategorization frame (expressed with semantic roles). If this was the case, we could assign a single polar profile to a particular verb reading.

Table 1 shows the mappings for *bedauern*. In the first column the *feel-sorry-for* reading is given.

[6] `https://verbatlas.org`, accessed 2022-06-03.

[7] Predicates in VerbAtlas are sometimes specified with reference to more than one label.

[8] *frame* here refers to role pairings.

	feel-sorry-for	regret
DE	bedauern.2 (A0,A1) [1]	bedauern.1 (A0,A1) [4] (A0,A3) [11] bedauern.2 (A0,A1) [15] (A0,A3) [8]
VA	DISLIKE (Agent,Theme) [1]	DISLIKE (Agent,Theme) [2] (Exp.,Stimulus) [4] REGRET_SORRY (Agent,Theme) [25] (Exp.,Stimulus) [1] (Agent,Attribute) [1] CRITICIZE (Agent,Theme) [5]

Table 1: Different predicates and roles for the verb 'bedauern' according to two readings: *feel-sorry-for* and *regret*. In square brackets are the numbers of sentences labeled with the given semantic roles.

Here we have a single mapping, both with respect to PropBank (DE) and VerbAtlas style (VA). However in the second column, the *regret* reading, PropBank mode shows a variation in the assignment of semantic roles (A0,A1 versus A0, A3). The VerbAtlas analysis is even more confusing. Here three predicates are identified and within the same predicate (e.g. REGRET_SORRY), different roles and role pairings are present. We carried out an error analysis in order to find out how many of the 38 sentences with *bedauern* are wrongly analysed either by choosing the wrong predicate or the wrong semantic role pairing (the subcategorization frame): 7 cases (18.5%) are clearly wrong, 8 cases are hard to decide. Not in every case does the usage of *bedauern* actually involve a (real) regret. Sometimes it is used in more formal way in order to express dislike (as suggested by InVeRo): without context this cannot be resolved reliably (some of the 8 cases are of that type). But nevertheless, even if InVeRo sometimes is right to map a verb to more than one predicate, the diversity of suggested solutions makes it impossible to carry out SI in a lexicon-based way: the necessary mapping from a single polar profile of a verb to some VerbAtlas representation in a one-to-many fashion is bound to produce errors, as our little error analysis with *bedauern* reveals.

Also, although in principle assigning semantic roles depending on the filler object is a desirable solution, if it comes in such an unpredictable diverse way, a lexicon-based approach cannot make use of it. The problem is not neglectable, since the distribution of semantic role pairings for different VerbAtlas predicates is high. The numbers at the end of the roles pairings (in square brackets) in Table 1 indicate the frequency of a pairing. For instance, DISLIKE (Agent,Theme) was assigned 2 times, DISLIKE (Experiencer,Stimulus) 4 times.

The statistics we have gathered on the diversity of predicate and frame mappings coming with InVeRo makes it superfluous to have a full-fledged error analysis for all 300 sentences (like we did for *bedauern*). The InVeRo results are just too diverse to be useful (see Table 2 in the appendix).

In the course of our case study, we have noticed that there is a correlation between the (non)animacy of role fillers and different verb readings. Actually, all examples in this paper could be analysed correctly by taking (non)animacy into account: compare e.g. *er bedauert sie* (he feels sorry for her) with *er bedauert den Vorfall* (he regrets the incident). We have trained an animacy classifier (Klenner and Göhring, 2022) and are about to apply it to the small data set of 300 sentences. To sketch the idea: depending on the animacy of the filler of a dependency label of a verb, different polar profiles become available.

5 Related Work

Sentiment inference is sometimes called sentiment propagation (Deng and Wiebe, 2014) and opinion implicature. It also shares similarities with fine-grained opinion analysis (Marasović and Frank, 2018a). Our positive/negative effects are comparable to the GoodFor/BadFor distinction of (Choi and Wiebe, 2014). However, we also distinguish positive/negative actors. In (Wiebe and Deng, 2014) a sophisticated rule-based system was introduced that specifies general inference rules on the basis of GoodFor/BadFor effects.

Approaches exist that claim that the combination of SRL and Opinion Role Labeling, i.e. the identification of opinion holder and target, is beneficial, e.g. in (Marasović and Frank, 2018b) a multi-task learning-based joint model is introduced.

6 Conclusion

German Semantic Role Labeling does not provide a suitable solution for our task: German sentiment inference based on polar profiles of verb readings.

With InVeRo, lexicon design is difficult since (too) many verb-predicate mappings and role pairings occur. InVeRo is only partially able to deal with the - admittedly - difficult cases of verb alternations and verb ambiguity. Instead of SRL, a combination of dependency parsing and animacy detection might be useful for the task at hand. We are currently evaluating such a disambiguation strategy for sentiment inference.

References

Alan Akbik, Laura Chiticariu, Marina Danilevsky, Yunyao Li, Shivakumar Vaithyanathan, and Huaiyu Zhu. 2015. Generating high quality proposition Banks for multilingual semantic role labeling. In *Proceedings of the 53rd Annual Meeting of the Association for Computational Linguistics and the 7th International Joint Conference on Natural Language Processing*, pages 397–407, Beijing, China. ACL.

Yoonjung Choi and Janyce Wiebe. 2014. +/- effectwordnet: Sense-level lexicon acquisition for opinion inference. In *Proceedings of the 2014 Conference on Empirical Methods in Natural Language Processing, EMNLP, SIGDAT*, pages 1181–1191.

Simone Conia, Andrea Bacciu, and Roberto Navigli. 2021a. Unifying cross-lingual semantic role labeling with heterogeneous linguistic resources. In *Proceedings of the 2021 Conference of the North American Chapter of the ACL: Human Language Technologies*, pages 338–351.

Simone Conia, Riccardo Orlando, Fabrizio Brignone, Francesco Cecconi, and Roberto Navigli. 2021b. InVeRo-XL: Making cross-lingual Semantic Role Labeling accessible with intelligible verbs and roles. In *Proceedings of the 2021 Conference on Empirical Methods in Natural Language Processing: System Demonstrations*, pages 319–328, Online and Punta Cana, Dominican Republic. ACL.

Angel Daza and Anette Frank. 2019. Translate and label! an encoder-decoder approach for cross-lingual semantic role labeling. In *Proceedings of the 2019 Conference on Empirical Methods in Natural Language Processing and the 9th International Joint Conference on Natural Language Processing*, pages 603–615, Hong Kong, China.

Angel Daza and Anette Frank. 2020. X-SRL: A parallel cross-lingual semantic role labeling dataset. In *Proceedings of the 2020 Conference on Empirical Methods in Natural Language Processing (EMNLP)*, pages 3904–3914, Online. ACL.

Lingjia Deng and Janyce Wiebe. 2014. Sentiment propagation via implicature constraints. *Meeting of the European Chapter of the Association for Computational Linguistics (EACL-2014)*.

Andrea Di Fabio, Simone Conia, and Roberto Navigli. 2019. VerbAtlas: a novel large-scale verbal semantic resource and its application to semantic role labeling. In *Proceedings of the 2019 Conference on Empirical Methods in Natural Language Processing and the 9th International Joint Conference on Natural Language Processing*, pages 627–637, Hong Kong, China. ACL.

Quynh Ngoc Thi Do, Artuur Leeuwenberg, Geert Heyman, and Marie-Francine Moens. 2018a. A flexible and easy-to-use semantic role labeling framework for different languages. In *Proceedings of the 27th International Conference on Computational Linguistics: System Demonstrations*, pages 161–165, Santa Fe, New Mexico. ACL.

Quynh Ngoc Thi Do, Artuur Leeuwenberg, Geert Heyman, and Marie-Francine Moens. 2018b. How to use damesrl: A framework for deep multilingual semantic role labeling. In *Proceedings of the CLARIN Annual Conference*, pages 159–162, Pisa, Italy.

Katrin Erk, Andrea Kowalski, Sebastian Padó, and Manfred Pinkal. 2003. Towards a resource for lexical semantics: A large German corpus with extensive semantic annotation. In *Proceedings of the 41st Annual Meeting of the Association for Computational Linguistics*, pages 537–544, Sapporo, Japan. ACL.

Jan Hajič, Massimiliano Ciaramita, Richard Johansson, Daisuke Kawahara, Maria Antònia Martí, Lluís Màrquez, Adam Meyers, Joakim Nivre, Sebastian Padó, Jan Štěpánek, Pavel Straňák, Mihai Surdeanu, Nianwen Xue, and Yi Zhang. 2009. The CoNLL-2009 shared task: Syntactic and semantic dependencies in multiple languages. In *Proceedings of the 13th. Conference on Computational Natural Language Learning (CoNLL 2009)*, pages 1–18, Boulder, Colorado. ACL.

Karin Kipper Schuler, Anna Korhonen, and Susan Brown. 2009. VerbNet overview, extensions, mappings and applications. In *Proceedings of Human Language Technologies: The 2009 Annual Conference of the North American Chapter of the Association for Computational Linguistics, Companion Volume: Tutorial Abstracts*, pages 13–14, Boulder, Colorado. ACL.

Manfred Klenner and Michael Amsler. 2016. Sentiframes: A resource for verb-centered German sentiment inference. In *Proceedings of the Tenth International Conference on Language Resources and Evaluation (LREC 2016)*, Paris, France. European Language Resources Association (ELRA).

Manfred Klenner, Simon Clematide, and Don Tuggener. 2017. Verb-mediated composition of attitude relations comprising reader and writer perspective. In *18th International Conference on Computational Linguistics and Intelligent Text Processing*. ResearchBib.

Manfred Klenner and Anne Göhring. 2022. Animacy denoting german nouns: Annotation and classification. In *Proceedings of the Language Resources and*

Evaluation Conference, pages 1360–1364, Marseille, France. European Language Resources Association (ELRA).

Ana Marasović and Anette Frank. 2018a. SRL4ORL: Improving opinion role labeling using multi-task learning with semantic role labeling. In *Proceedings of the 2018 Conference of the North American Chapter of the Association for Computational Linguistics: Human Language Technologies, Volume 1 (Long Papers)*, pages 583–594, New Orleans, Louisiana. ACL.

Ana Marasović and Anette Frank. 2018b. SRL4ORL: Improving opinion role labeling using multi-task learning with semantic role labeling. In *Proceedings of the 2018 Conference of the North American Chapter of the Association for Computational Linguistics, Volume 1*, pages 583–594, New Orleans, Louisiana. ACL.

Roberto Navigli and Simone Paolo Ponzetto. 2010. BabelNet: Building a very large multilingual semantic network. In *Proceedings of the 48th Annual Meeting of the ACL*, pages 216–225, Uppsala, Sweden.

Martha Palmer, Daniel Gildea, and Paul Kingsbury. 2005. The Proposition Bank: An annotated corpus of semantic roles. *Computational Linguistics*, 31(1):71–106.

Janyce Wiebe and Lingjia Deng. 2014. An account of opinion implicatures.

Appendix

	DE			VA		
verb	pr	fr	fr/pr	pr	fr	fr/pr
akzeptieren	1	1	1.00	4	4	1.00
	1	2	2.00	9	11	1.22
bedauern	1	1	1.00	1	1	1.00
	2	8	4.00	3	7	2.33
bedrohen	2	5	2.50	7	11	1.57
	3	8	2.67	7	13	1.86
belastern	2	2	1.00	1	2	2.00
	2	3	1.50	4	9	2.25
blockieren	3	6	2.00	1	2	2.00
	3	6	2.00	1	3	3.00
schaden	1	3	3.00	2	3	1.50
	1	2	2.00	2	2	1.00
töten	1	5	5.00	1	5	5.00
	1	5	5.00	1	3	3.00
unterstützen	1	1	1.00	1	1	1.00
	2	6	3.00	2	5	2.50
verbessern	1	1	1.00	1	1	1.00
	1	3	3.00	3	3	1.00
vergewaltigen	1	5	5.00	3	3	1.00
	1	1	1.00	1	1	1.00
avg	1.55	3.70	**2.43**	**2.75**	4.50	1.81

Table 2: Number of predicates (pr), frames (fr) and frames per predicate (fr/pr) the SRL assigned to example sentences of the listed 10 pairs of verb profiles (each verb has 2 profiles). Average (avg) over all profiles (macro = micro). The German PropBank scheme (DE) seems to assign less different predicates per verb profile than the VerbAtlas (VA) scheme (1.55 compared to 2.75), though with proportionally more frames (fr/pr= 2.43).

Proceedings of the 18th Conference on Natural Language Processing (KONVENS 2022)

Building an Extremely Low Resource Language to High Resource Language Machine Translation System from Scratch

Flammie A Pirinen
UiT Norgga árktalaš universitehta
Tromsø, Norway
`firstname.lastname@uit.no`

Linda Wiechetek
UiT Norgga árktalaš universitehta
Tromsø, Norway
`firstname.lastname@uit.no`

Abstract

Building a machine translation system for an extremely low-resource language is a problem in contemporary computational linguistics. In this article, we show how to use existing morpho-syntactic analysers and a modern rule-based machine translation system to rapidly build a baseline system for a language pair where a neural model approach is not feasible due to the total lack of high-quality parallel corpora. Our experiment produces a freely available open-source North Sámi to German machine translator, which provides us useful insights into rule-based machine translation of unrelated languages with varying levels of morphological complexity. As German is a language taught in Scandinavian schools this MT system would be of immediate relevance for Sámi school children learning German. In addition, there is a strong Finno-Ugric tradition in the German linguistics space that has in the past produced important publications on the Sámi language, so the system is immediately useful for researchers and enthusiasts as well as language users.

1 Introduction

1.1 Motivation

Machine translation is an important tool for language users. The most common contemporary method for implementing machine translation is to curate professionally translated texts and use machine learning methodology to learn the translations. This presupposes the availability of perhaps several millions of professionally translated sentences, which is unfeasible for under-resourced marginalised languages, where very little parallel corpora or even monolingual corpora are available. To put the low-resourcedness of North Sámi in context, the largest available monolingual corpus (SIKOR, 2018) is only 38 million tokens, and for the bilingual corpora at most 10,000s of aligned phrases, most of which are from Linux program GUI translations[1]. Given the circumstances, we do not find it reasonable to try to train a neural network for this task. The sensible solution is to use linguistic knowledge to build a rule-based machine translation system. What we are presenting in this article is a machine translation from North Sámi to German, a language pair that to our knowledge has not brought forth any system before, and that does not have enough resources for a neural machine translation system. Furthermore, our contribution consists in exploring a newly created module in a rule-based machine translation system, and we are looking at workflows for the rapid development of a baseline machine translator.

The rule-based system took us only some 100 hours to write and is the work of one programmer/linguist/advanced learner of German and native speaker of Finnish, an expert on Apertium - and one computational linguist, native speaker of German with high proficiency in North Sámi (but not a native speaker of it). The system described here is a work-in-progress, yet it is a proof-of-concept that rapid building of a machine translation system is plausible without big data corpus resources. Our motivation to build this system is two-fold: we are building a tool for users, as well as surveying the use of newly introduced techniques in a language pair that is not within the same language family and not English. This is also the *novel research* in our experiment: we provide further insights on the usage of the *new additions* to methodologies in a recently updated machine translation system in a typologically varied setting, that has not been tried before to our knowledge.

In the context of machine translation as a tool for supporting under-resourced language use, one must practice a certain level of carefulness in order

[1] `https://opus.nlpl.eu/KDE4.php`

to not cause more damage than good. For example, creating a system for generating large amounts of translations from the majority language to minority languages, for example, might sound like a lucrative offering to generate big data, but may result in creating larger bodies of automatically translated texts that overtake what there exists of naturally written texts which in the long run can be rather problematic. On the other hand, creating a system that translates well enough for *language understanding* (gisting) for majority language users will enable the minority language communities to wider use of their language in digital contexts. We stick to the ethics of not flooding the web with low-quality North Sámi text by building the system the other way around (German - North Sámi). Clean data is still of great value, and we do not want to put that in danger.

The machine translation system we created is freely available and open source in Apertium's GitHub repository[2]. The dependent North Sámi language model we developed earlier is also available at our github[3] and German model from Apertium's collection[4].[5]

1.2 Languages

North Sámi is a Finno-Ugric language belonging to the Uralic languages spoken in Norway, Sweden, and Finland by approximately 25,700 speakers (Eberhard et al., 2018). It is a synthetic language, where the open *parts-of-speech* (PoS) – e.g. nouns, adjectives – inflect for case, person, number, and more. The grammatical categories are expressed by a combination of suffixes and stem-internal processes affecting root vowels and consonants alike, making it perhaps the most fusional of all Uralic languages. In addition to compounding, inflection and derivation are common morphological processes in North Sámi. German, on the other hand, is an Indo-European language. In contrast to all previous work, there is neither language family similarity, nor geographical proximity or political relation. The latter would be the case for Sámi - Norwegian where despite language typological unrelatedness there are (even syntactic) loans due to coexistence and interaction of the languages.

As German was the previous century's language of science, a lot of scientific literature on the Sámi language was published in German. Newer publications include the North Sámi - German, German - North Sámi dictionary (Sammallahti and Nickel, 2006) of high quality (containing valencies, idiomatic phrases, examples of use). German has also been one of the languages that school children get to pick as a foreign language at school. For both these reasons, it makes sense to have MT systems between these two languages.

Morphologically, the languages have similar features: both are morphologically richer and suffixing, and mark case for nominals and some tense, aspect, and mood as well as person for verbs, however, North Sámi also marks other grammatical features such as possession and aktionsart in morphology. Both languages also have the productive compounding of nominals. The syntactic differences are notable, while the neutral word order for both is SVO, there are a number of mismatching features in the syntax: pro-drop for 1. and 2. person in Sámi, separable verbs in German, adverbial positioning, word order in sub-clauses, question clauses or after adverbial extensions, etc.

2 Background

Previous MT systems involving North Sámi are North Sámi - Lule Sámi (Tyers et al., 2009) (Wiechetek et al., 2010), North Sámi - Norwegian (Trosterud and Unhammer, 2012), North Sámi - South Sámi (Antonsen et al., 2016), North Sámi - Finnish (Pirinen et al., 2017). The systems were all based on previous versions of Apertium, the state-of-the-art in rule-based machine translation.

There is an Apertium-based system for translating North Sámi to Norwegian,[6] that has been in end-user use. As German and Norwegian (Bokmål) are related languages, we expect to be able to use them as a reference when implementing our system.

We chose to use Apertium (Khanna et al., 2021) as it is popular in the context of under-resourced languages. The system is based, roughly speaking, on doing a morpho-syntactic analysis of the source text, transferring the analysis to the target language morpho-syntactic description, and generating it into the target text. There is a diagrammatic presentation of the system pipeline in Figure 1. This means that the system consists of

[2] `https://github.com/apertium/apertium-sme-deu`

[3] `https://github.com/giellalt/lang-sme`

[4] `https://github.com/apertium/apertium-deu`

[5] For reproducibility purposes, the tag `konvens2022` is available in the mentioned repos

[6] `https://gtweb.uit.no/jorgal`

morphological analyser-generators of target and source languages, based on finite-state morphology (Beesley and Karttunen, 2003), and a constraint grammar (Karlsson, 1990; Didriksen, 2010) for syntactic and semantic analysis suitable for transferring the source language structures to target language structures.

See examples (1) and (2) for a concrete example. In our experiment, we had pre-existing morphological analysers for North Sámi[7]and German[8], and we have written a bilingual translation dictionary as well as the grammatical rules.

(1) Boadát go dál?
come.V.2SG QST now.ADV?
'Are you coming now'

(2) Kommst du jetzt?
come.V.2SG you.PRN.2SG now.ADV?
'Are you coming now?'

From the example we see that there is some level of syntactic mapping to be done between the languages: North Sámi is generally pro-drop i.e. missing the subject pronoun morphologically encoded in the verb where German requires this. Furthermore, North Sámi indicates question with a question particle that is not easily glossed in English or German—perhaps an approximate gloss could be 'is it such that'—in German, the word order change indicates the question-format of the sentence.

We base our system on the tools developed within the *GiellaLT* infrastructure for North Sámi and tools developed within Apertium community for German, these include state-of-the-art FST-based morphological analyzers, with Constraint Grammar syntactic analysis and disambiguation. We have done a few slight adjustments to both monolingual systems, but our main work is in the bilingual part. In Figure 1, the part we work on concerns the part under *transfer*, specifically we have used the *recursive structural transfer* path in this experiment, which is a newly built part of Apertium in 2021 (Khanna et al., 2021).

To give an impression of concrete resources and rules, we show in Figure 2[9] what the dictionaries and the rules look like:

[7]https://github.com/giellalt/lang-sme

[8]https://github.com/apertium/apertium-deu

[9]anonymised

3 Development

We predominantly used pre-existing morphological analysers and morpho-syntactic disambiguation for the North Sámi morphological analysis and disambiguation and German morphological generation (and vice versa, but this direction was not the main objective of this article). Our contribution in terms of developed resources is a bilingual lexicon i.e. North Sámi to German translation dictionary, and the development of bilingual grammatical rules that determine for example word order changes and introduction of words that don't exist in the source language, such as articles.

The bilingual lexicon development was done by hand by a linguist, in the following three steps:

1. Translating words of initial reference bilingual corpus[10]
2. Translating high-frequency words (from SIKOR)[11]
3. Translating words from a random sample of large monolingual corpus (from SIKOR)

The final result has been verified by a linguist with near-native language skills. The first two steps ensure high coverage in general, whereas the third step is necessary to have high enough coverage in the genres of evaluation corpus for the human evaluation to even be possible.

The grammatical transfer was developed based on the reference bilingual corpus first. We ran the translation system through our reference corpus and located easy-to-fix syntactic differences, such as missing articles and pronouns, and local word order changes, and wrote the rules for those. We also needed to write transfer rules to account for purely morphological mismatches: for example, German only has grammatical cases: nominative, genitive, accusative, and dative, whereas North Sámi also has local cases and other cases that translate into prepositional phrases in German. The prepositions for each case do not translate one-to-one. Typically, one case will translate into several prepositions depending on the semantic/valency context.

The resulting lexicon and rules are summarised in Table 1.

[10]https://github.com/apertium/apertium-sme-deu/blob/master/sme-deu-corpus.txt

[11]https://gtsvn.uit.no/langtech/trunk/words/lists/sme/sme_lemma.freq

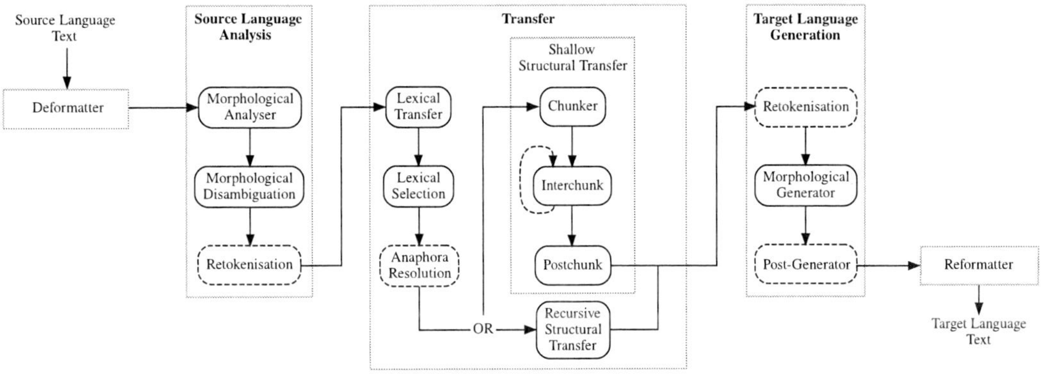

Figure 1: Apertium pipeline structure from (Khanna et al., 2021)

Bilingual dictionary

```
<e><p><l>áddet</l><r>verstehen</r></p><par n="vblex"/></e>
<e><p><l>addit</l><r>geben</r></p><par n="vblex"/></e>
<e><p><l>addit</l><r>liefern</r></p><par n="vblex"/></e>
<e><p><l>álbmut</l><r>schaufeln</r></p><par n="vblex"/></e>
<e><p><l>álggahit</l><r>anfangen</r></p><par n="vblex"/></e>
```

Syntactic rules

```
S -> VP NP { 1 _
    *(maybe_adp)[case=2.case]
    *(maybe_art)[number=2.number, case=2.case, gender=2.gender, def=ind]
    2 } ;
V -> %vblex {1[person = (if (1.tense = imp) "" else 1.person),
               number = (if (1.number = du) pl else 1.number)] } ;
```

Figure 2: Bilingual dictionary format and syntactic rule format

4 Evaluation

As a corpus for evaluation of the translation quality, we randomly picked 300 paragraphs from *SIKOR*. This corpus is summarised in Table 1. We measured the naïve coverage of the monolingual analyser as well as our bilingual dictionary of the whole corpus to get an idea of how far we are in the process of building a translation dictionary suitable for any running texts.

4.1 Word Error Rate on Post-Edited text

We did a *Word Error Rate* (WER) test on our randomly selected corpus that was post-edited by a native speaker of German. Word error rate is a simple measure that calculates the proportion of the wrongly translated words, in this case when comparing the machine translation output to the translation that a human translator has post-edited. For example, if one word in a 10-word sentence is mistranslated, the word-error rate is 10 % and an exact match is 0 %. Notably, if the translation contains too many words, the word error rate can exceed 100 %. It is noteworthy that WER is also a rather naïve metric, for example, a wrong article or case is given the same weight as a completely wrong word. However, for understandability the latter is a much bigger obstacle than the wrong article. For the WER test, we used the `apertium-eval` tool available on their github[12]. The results of this evaluation are shown in Table 2.

5 Discussion and error analysis

One of the prevailing problems at this point of development is dictionary coverage. Creating the dictionary is one of the most time-consuming parts of the rule-based machine translation work. However, the resulting human-curated translation dictionary is a very valuable resource and therefore worth the effort. Once created, a translation dictionary can be included in any other future tool. Many of the errors we saw in the evaluation were due to low frequency, rather domain-specific words, such as *attorney general* or *vice candidate*, which had not been added to the bilingual dictionary yet.

[12] `https://github.com/apertium/apertium-eval-translator`

Data set	Data size	Note
Translation dictionary	4,340 LU pairs	newly built
Translation grammar	17 rules	newly built
German dictionary	100,390 LUs	extended
North Sámi dictionary	154,557 LUs	extended
Development corpus	1469 sentences	manually translated
SIKOR	38,94 Mtokens	monolingual corpus
Test set	7083 tokens	random sample

Table 1: *LU* is a lexical unit e.g. an entry in the dictionaries, *token* is a token in a running text e.g. word-form or punctuation, *Mtokens* is millions of tokens, and *sentences* in the text are based on our sentence boundary finding algorithm.

Corpus	Naïve coverage
Development corpus	99.8 %
Test set	88.2 %
SIKOR	84.6 %

Metric	Test Corpus
Post-Edit WER	77 %

Table 2: Evaluation of our North Sámi - German MT system

Some of the machine-translated sentences are intelligible despite grammatical errors. The translation of ex. (4) in ex. (3) requires lexical edits: *saamisch*→*Saamischsprachige*, *des Saamen*→*saamische*, *um*→*über*, *Lebensunterhalte*→*Gewerbe*, most of which are at least semantically related as can be seen in the correct translation of the sentence in ex. (4). In addition to the lexical edits, there are a number of word order issues, e.g. *treffen andere ...* →*andere ... treffen*. And also, e.g.*aufhören* → *hören ... auf*.

(3) So können die Schüler treffen andere *saamisch, und lernen bißchen traditioneller *um *Lebensunterhalte *des Saamen.

(4) Nu besset oahppit deaivvadit eará
so können.3PL Schüler.PL treffen andere
sámegielagiiguin, ja oahppat
Saamischsprachig.KOM.PL, und lernen
veaháš árbevirolaš sámi
etwas traditionell saamisch
ealáhusaid birra.
Gewerbe.AKK.PL über;um
'So können die Schüler andere Saamischsprachige treffen, und ein bißchen über die traditionellen saamischen Gewerbe lernen.'

One of the interesting findings in this experiment is that, since the source and target languages are not related to each other[13] and the syntactic differences are notable, one focus of our work has been the tasks of word reordering and generation, which have typically been ignored in rule-based approaches to machine translation earlier. We found that the new recursive syntax-based approach in Apertium together with the high-quality Constraint Grammar-based syntactic analysis in the source language allows us to resolve reordering in an efficient way.

Looking at the edits we made in the post-edit, some errors are not as critical as the raw WER might suggest, for example, problems with the grammatical forms of the articles or compound splitting as well as separable verb processing may falsely increase the error rate more than it affects the readability. In the future, we will continue adding words as well as improve the description.

In a qualitative evaluation we found a lot of noise in the source text that affected the quality of our output. Noise in source texts is a much bigger problem in extremely low-resource languages like North Sámi and is due to newer or lacking language norms, lesser literacy and lesser use of the language in writing. (Wiechetek et al., 2022) We found the following types of noise: formatting errors and syllable splitting (potentially caused by corpus collection methods), spelling errors like accent errors and compound misspellings, grammatically doubtful sentences (potentially due to translations) and other grammatical errors like case errors.

6 Conclusion

We have developed the first North Sámi - German machine translation system in a short amount of

[13]Within Europe, the Finno-Ugric and Indo-European are as far apart as they can get.

time (100h) without any bilingual big data, based on the well-known Apertium system and the rule-based morpho-syntactic tools for North Sámi that are available in the *GiellaLT* infrastructure. The system is able to handle a number of syntactic transfer issues such as the generation of articles and longer distance reordering, such as the verb placement in a subordinate clause. We have evaluated our system and managed to develop a state-of-the-art system that is useful in terms of gisting, but still needs further development to serve as a post-editing tool. Our research contribution is not only an MT tool for a new language pair of completely unrelated languages but also, because of the unrelatedness, practical solutions to structural transfer problems that have been either ignored or marginalised in the past.

Acknowledgments

We thank Daniel Swanson from Apertium for his help and answers about the new system and Lene Antonsen for her help with the North Sámi Apertium usage.

References

Lene Antonsen, Trond Trosterud, and Francis M. Tyers. 2016. A North Saami to South Saami machine translation prototype. *Northern European Journal of Language Technology*, 4:11–27.

Kenneth R. Beesley and Lauri Karttunen. 2003. *Finite State Morphology*. CSLI Studies in Computational Linguistics. CSLI Publications, Stanford.

Tino Didriksen. 2010. *Constraint Grammar Manual: 3rd version of the CG formalism variant*. GrammarSoft ApS, Denmark.

David M. Eberhard, Gary F. Simons, and Charles D. Fennig, editors. 2018. *Ethnologue: Languages of the World*, twenty-fifth edition. SIL International, Dallas, Texas.

Fred Karlsson. 1990. Constraint grammar as a framework for parsing unrestricted text. In *Proceedings of the 13th International Conference of Computational Linguistics*, volume 3, pages 168–173, Helsinki.

Tanmai Khanna, Jonathan North Washington, Francis Morton Tyers, Sevilay Bayatlı, Daniel Swanson, Flammie Pirinen, Irene Tang, and Héctor Alos i Font. 2021. Recent advances in Apertium, a free/open-source rule-based machine translation platform for low-resource languages. *Machine Translation*.

Tommi Pirinen, Francis M. Tyers, Trond Trosterud, Ryan Johnson, Kevin Unhammer, and Tiina Puolakainen. 2017. North-sámi to Finnish rule-based machine translation system. In *Proceedings of the 21st Nordic Conference on Computational Linguistics*, pages 115–122, Gothenburg, Sweden. Association for Computational Linguistics.

Pekka Sammallahti and Klaus Peter Nickel. 2006. *Sámi-duiskka sátnegirji=Saamisch-deutsches Wörterbuch*. Davvi Girji, Kárášjohka.

SIKOR. 2018. SIKOR uit norgga árktalaš universitehta ja norgga sámedikki sámi teakstačoakkáldat, veršuvdna 06.11.2018. `http://gtweb.uit.no/korp`. Accessed: 2018-11-06.

Trond Trosterud and Kevin Brubeck Unhammer. 2012. Evaluating North Sámi to Norwegian assimilation RBMT. In *Proceedings of the Third International Workshop on Free/Open-Source Rule-Based Machine Translation (FreeRBMT 2012)*, 2013:03, pages 13–26, Gothenburg, Sweden. Chalmers University of Technology.

Francis M. Tyers, Linda Wiechetek, and Trond Trosterud. 2009. Developing Prototypes for Machine Translation between Two Sámi Languages. In *EAMT-2009*, pages 120–127, Barcelona, Spain. Universitat Politècnica de Catalunya.

Linda Wiechetek, Katri Hiovain-Asikainen, Inga Lill Sigga Mikkelsen, Sjur Moshagen, Flammie Pirinen, Trond Trosterud, and Børre Gaup. 2022. Unmasking the myth of effortless big data - making an open source multi-lingual infrastructure and building language resources from scratch. In *Proceedings of the Language Resources and Evaluation Conference*, pages 1167–1177, Marseille, France. European Language Resources Association.

Linda Wiechetek, Francis M. Tyers, and Thomas Omma. 2010. Shooting at flies in the dark: Rule-based lexical selection for a minority language pair. In *Proceedings of the 7th International Conference on NLP (IceTAL 2010)*, volume 6233 of *Lecture Notes in Computer Science*, pages 418–429, Berlin, Heidelberg. Springer.

Proceedings of the 18th Conference on Natural Language Processing (KONVENS 2022)

More Like This: Semantic Retrieval with Linguistic Information

Steffen Remus[*] **Gregor Wiedemann**[*†]

Saba Anwar **Fynn Petersen-Frey** **Seid Muhie Yimam** **Chris Biemann**

Universität Hamburg
first.last@uni-hamburg.de

[†]Leibniz-Institute for Media Research |
Hans-Bredow-Institute
g.wiedemann@leibniz-hbi.de

Abstract

We investigate the semantic retrieval potential of pre-trained contextualized word embeddings (CWEs) such as BERT, in combination with explicit linguistic information, for various NLP tasks in an information retrieval setup. In this paper, we compare different strategies to aggregate contextualized word embeddings along lexical, syntactic, or grammatical dimensions to perform semantic retrieval for various natural language tasks. We apply this for fine-grained named entities, word senses, short texts, verb frames, and semantic relations, and show that incorporating certain linguistic knowledge improves the retrieval performance over various baselines. In a simulation study, we demonstrate the practical applicability of our findings to speed up the linguistic annotation of datasets. We also show that nearest neighbor classification, which implicitly uses the retrieval setup, works well with only small amounts of training data.[1]

1 Introduction

Neural language models (NLMs) producing contextualized word embeddings (CWEs) such as ELMo (Embeddings from Language Models; Peters et al., 2018), FLAIR (Akbik et al., 2018), or BERT (Bidirectional Encoder Representations from Transformers; Devlin et al., 2019), or one of its many successors have been a leap forward for multiple NLP tasks. One major reason for this is the fact that current NLMs can generate compositional vector space representations of a word based on the sequential context in which it appears, thus sufficiently representing its compositional meaning. CWEs allow the disambiguation of a word's meaning up to a certain degree, such that, for example, sequence tagging models can distinguish two identical surface forms when used in different contexts. For example, both instances of each of the two words 'can' and 'open' in the following two sentences *"Alice opens the can"* and *"Alice can open the box"* will be represented with quite distinct embeddings. Whereas vectors are expected to be very similar for the word 'open', both representations for 'can' are expected to be inherently different, indicating a syntactic and semantic shift.

Still, although certain dependency relations are implicitly encoded in BERT, no equivalent to holistic parsing of syntactical or grammatical structures can be assumed from BERT's attention mechanism (Htut et al., 2019). We thus hypothesize that downstream NLP tasks benefit from exploiting explicit syntactical and grammatical cues derived from linguistic knowledge in addition to the contextual embeddings. To investigate this hypothesis, we define a set of aggregation strategies for word embeddings along linguistically informed dimensions. Such representations are used to address several downstream tasks: *a*) labeling on the sentence level, where we experiment with *sentiment detection*, *relation identification*, and *semantic frame induction*, and *b*) word-level- and sequence labeling, where we experiment with *named entity recognition* and *word sense disambiguation*.

The explicit use of syntactic information to aggregate CWEs can be regarded as feature extraction or feature transformation. Such features may not only be useful in classification scenarios but also for retrieval tasks. Particularly, they can be useful in the context of a retrieval scenario in which the ultimate goal is to enable users to rapidly find semantically similar word patterns or sentences in their datasets.

In this regard, there are three main contributions of this paper: *a*) We introduce several different strategies to incorporate explicit linguistic informa-

[*]Equal contribution

[1]Our code, experiments and results are published as open source software under a permissive Apache v2 license: https://github.com/uhh-lt/cwe-ling

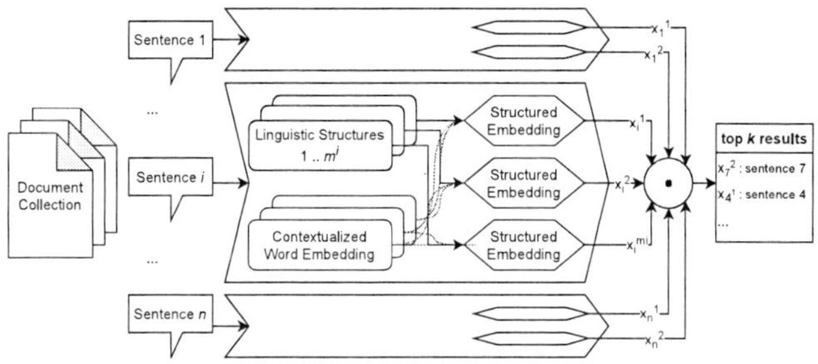

Figure 1: Overview of the retrieval process.

tion for embedding-based feature representations. *b*) We evaluate these strategies in an information retrieval setup to find semantically related items for various downstream NLP tasks. *c*) We demonstrate two potential applications of our findings 1) for speeding up manual annotation of text data, and 2) for fast nearest neighbor classification with little training data. Depending on the task, our retrieval evaluation shows the retrieval precision and nearest neighbor classification indeed profit from the incorporation of additional explicit linguistic knowledge. Depending on the complexity of the task, and correlating it with a simulated cognitive shift between dissimilar texts and distinct categories, our simulation shows that the use of linguistic structures in a retrieval scenario can speed up the manual annotation of text data, e.g. to create training data more rapidly.

2 Related Work

The LISA (linguistically-informed self-attention) approach by Strubell et al. (2018) showed the benefit of injecting syntactic information into a neural network using self-attention for multi-task learning. LISA was applied for dependency parsing, part-of-speech tagging, predicate detection, and semantic role labeling, where the results for all tasks showed significant improvements over the previous state-of-the-art, particularly when using ELMo embeddings (Peters et al., 2018).

Wiedemann et al. (2019) showed that contextual embeddings, particularly BERT (Devlin et al., 2019) inherit a certain degree of sense representation, i.e. polysemous words appear in different areas of the embedding space depending on their context. Wang et al. (2019) implement Elman (1990)'s theory, which states that neural language models are sensitive to word order regularities in simple sentences, by specifically exploiting the inner-sentence structure (word-level ordering) and inter-sentence structure (sentence-level ordering) as training objectives. They argue that their StructBERT model successfully captures the structure of sentences during pre-training.

Htut et al. (2019) and Clark et al. (2019) analyze to which extent attention heads in BERT can track linguistic dependencies. Both works conclude that some attention heads specialize in syntactic structure. Wu et al. (2020) measure the impact one word has on another in a sentence by using a so-called perturbed masking technique. They can derive a syntax tree from a word-word matrix. Soares et al. (2019) used a so-called masking technique to specifically force the model to learn entity locations in a sentence. By doing so, specific representations for particular relations within text can be learned.

SBERT (SentenceBERT; Reimers and Gurevych, 2019) is an extension to pre-trained transformer architectures such as BERT or RoBERTa, which is specifically targeted for sentence similarity search, i.e. finding similar sentences by using cosine similarity. SBERT outperforms most other embedding strategies for multiple sentence similarity tasks. However, it requires labeled data in form of similar/dissimilar sentences.

3 Retrieval of Linguistic Patterns

We approach the problem of semantic retrieval with linguistic structures as follows: Let S $:= [s_1, \ldots, s_n]$ be a dataset with n instances, where s_i represents a sentence. For our retrieval experiments, we use datasets with corresponding class labels $\mathbf{y} = [y_1, \ldots, y_n]$, where y_i is a list of labels in case of word-level tasks. Instances are decomposed into a set of finer-grained, lexical structures such as tokens, multi-word units, chunks, dependency relations, etc. (see Section 3.1 for reference), which we use as the basic unit of retrieval. For each instance s_i, a unique set of m^i linguistic structures $s_i \mapsto \{\mathbf{x}_i^1, \ldots, \mathbf{x}_i^{m^i}\}$, with replicated y_i labels $\{y_i^1, \ldots, y_i^{m^i}\}$, is extracted by using a particular linguistic pattern. Further, $\mathbf{x}_i^j$ represents a single feature vector extracted by a particular lexical template, for example, it could be the actual sentence embedding or word embedding of s_i. We call $\mathbf{x}_i^j$ a *structured embedding*.

The goal is to retrieve the k most relevant instances for a given query instance q and its extracted *structured embeddings* $q \mapsto \{\hat{\mathbf{x}}^1, \ldots, \hat{\mathbf{x}}^{m^q}\}$ of a target class c:

$$[r_1, \ldots, r_k] := \underset{i\in\{1\ldots n\}}{\text{top}_k} \; \{ \underset{\substack{h\in\{1\ldots m^q\} \\ j\in\{1\ldots m^i\}}}{\arg\max} \; \text{sim}(\hat{\mathbf{x}}^h, \mathbf{x}_i^j) \; \} \, ,$$

where top_k is defined as a function that selects the top k indices as an ordered list from the entire set of labeled instances regarding their maximum similarity score. The sim function is defined to be a similarity function for two vectors; we use *cosine similarity* in our experiments. Figure 1 illustrates the indexing and retrieval process.

3.1 Lexical Structures

For the linguistic pre-processing, i.e. tokenization, part-of-speech tagging (PoS), and dependency parsing we use *spaCy*[2] (unless stated otherwise) and for chunking we use *FLAIR*[3]. For CWEs based on RoBERTa (Liu et al., 2019), we sum the output of the last four layers of the model, and if a token comprises several word piece tokens, the corresponding embeddings are averaged to obtain a single vector for a lexical token. We describe our linguistically informed structures in the following.

3.2 Word-level structures

We use the following two word-level structures to find similar entity spans:

token: Each token of the dataset is considered a single item. Consequently, the unit of retrieval is always a single token.

SPS (same-PoS-span)**:** In order to capture nouns and noun phrases, each sequence of tokens having the same PoS tag within a sentence is considered as one structure. Thus, the unit of retrieval is a variable-length span of one or more tokens.

3.3 Sentence-level structures

We use the following sentence-level structures to find similar sentences.

[2] `https://spacy.io/`

[3] `https://github.com/flairNLP/flair`

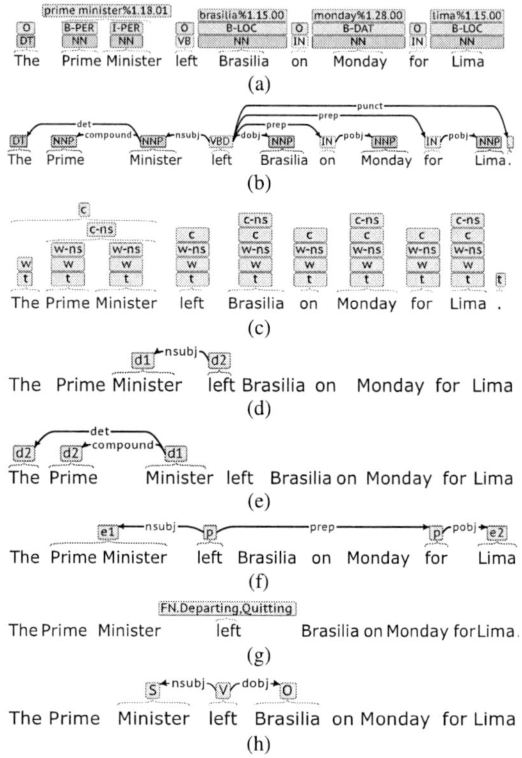

Figure 2: (a) Word-level structures with BIO-labels for NER and WordNet sense information. (b) shows the automatically extracted dependency graph and syntax features. (c-h) Sentence-level structures: (c) shows the aggregation strategy for `token` (t), `word` (w), `word-NS` (w-ns), `chunk` (c), and `chunk-NS` (c-ns). (d) shows the aggregation strategy for `dep-{concat,avg}` for a single dependency edge, i.e. $d1$ and its governor (dependency head) $d2$. (e) illustrates the `dep-depavg` strategy for the word 'Minister', where $d1$ is the actual word and all $d2$ are dependents of $d1$. (f) shows the task dependent `dependency-path` structure for relation identification. (g) and (h) show the task dependent `lexical-unit` and `subj-v-obj` structures for frame identification.

token: each token of a sentence is considered a structure.

word: same as `token`, w/o punctuation.

word-NS: same as `word`, w/o stop-words.

chunk: each extracted chunk of a sentence is a structure. For this, token embeddings of a single chunk's constituents are averaged. For the short text retrieval task, these chunk representations again are averaged to obtain a single vector representation for the sentence.

chunk-NS: same as `chunk`, w/o stop-words.

dep: dependency relations are encoded as a combined vector of its head and tail word. Three strategies are tested to encode dependency relations as vectors *a*) both vectors are concatenated (`-concat`) *b*) both vectors are averaged (`-avg`) *c*) for each word, we concatenate the word vector itself with the averaged vectors of its dependents (`-depavg`).

Figures 2 (c-e) show the structures for an example sentence. The following two baseline approaches produce a single vector representation for the entire sentence:

CLS: the artificial `[CLS]` token of BERT-based models, which is added to every sentence as a meta-token and which is frequently used as a vector representation for the entire sequence in downstream tasks;

BoW: all embeddings are averaged (bag-of-words).

4 Experiments

Several word-level- and sentence-level retrieval tasks of different granularity are tested. We also compare with static word embeddings provided by Mikolov et al. (2013, word2Vec)[4] since our linguistic structures enable the composition of meaning due to the use of multiple tokens for a single structured representation. We investigate the retrieval performance using precision at k (P@k, $k = 1$ and $k = 5$) and mean average precision (mAP) and refer to the static word2Vec embedding as w2v and to the contextualized RoBERTa embedding as RB. To perform the retrieval evaluation based on gold standard data, we use labeled datasets, which means each word or sentence is labeled with one specific target class. We use the standard train and test splits for indexing and querying as indicated by each task-specific dataset.

We additionally run a simple classification benchmark test using the same datasets. As a classification approach, we opted to use a k-nearest neighbor (kNN) approach, which heavily relies on the retrieval performance and, thus, implicitly evaluates the retrieval performance. The kNN approach groups and counts the class labels of the top k retrieved training samples and uses the most prominent class label as a classification result. In case of ties, a random label of the most prominent class labels is chosen. Here, we report F_1 scores on the test sets and determine the hyper-parameter k by using the validation set of the respective task benchmarks.[5]

4.1 Word-level tasks

Named Entity Recognition (NER) We use NER as a coarse-grained task. We evaluate the retrieval performance on the two common English benchmark datasets *CoNLL-2003* (Tjong Kim Sang and De Meulder, 2003) and *OntoNotes Release 5.0* (Weischedel et al., 2013).[6]

For retrieval, we only use structures consisting of entity-labeled tokens, i.e. excluding the 'other' class — with the goal to find more structures having the same label as the query. For NER, searching for non-entities, and including their scores, would only increase the reported performance, because the majority of labels are actually 'other'.

Both word-level structures explained in Section 3.2 are tested. An issue arises when retrieving token spans instead of whole sentences because the unit of retrieval is some linguistic structure that does not necessarily map perfectly to an entity span. Since there is no proper solution to this issue, we validate the appropriateness of our linguistic structures used for retrieval via named-entity classification. The classification scores allow interpretation and connection to SOTA results, but we note that those results are only for anecdotal purposes and cannot be properly compared to SOTA systems because of the simplicity and different objective of our approach.

Word Sense Disambiguation (WSD) can be considered as a fine-grained multi-class problem with thousands of classes where each word sense is a class. We evaluate retrieval and classification performance on a wide range of WSD datasets. In particular, we use the following datasets provided by UFSAC (Vial et al., 2018)[7]: *SemCor* (Miller et al., 1993), *WordNet Gloss Tag*[8] (WNGT) consisting of all WordNet (Miller, 1995) definitions, SensEval 2 (Edmonds and Cotton, 2001) & 3 (Litkowski, 2004) as well as SemEval 2007 Task 7 (Navigli et al., 2007) & 17 (Pradhan et al., 2007). The *SemCor* and WNGT datasets are used as training corpora with SemEval 2007 Task 7 and 17 as query

[4] `https://code.google.com/archive/p/word2vec/`

[5] If an explicit validation set is not supplied, we split the original training set (80/20) and use a random subset for validation and the remainder for training.

[6] We apply the split proposed by Pradhan et al. (2013) for OntoNotes as there is no official dataset split.

[7] `https://github.com/getalp/UFSAC`

[8] `https://wordnetcode.princeton.edu/glosstag.shtml`

datasets. For SensEval 2 and 3, we use their respective training and test sets.

In analogy to NER, we only use words that need disambiguation as queries for the retrieval evaluation. Since WSD is mostly the task of disambiguating a single word, we only use the `token` structure.

4.2 Sentence Level Tasks

Short-text retrieval evaluates the performance of retrieving semantically similar sentences ideally labeled with the same class. This task can be seen as a binary text classification problem. First, we try to find more tweets containing offensive language given an offensive tweet from the OLID dataset (Zampieri et al., 2019)[9] provided by the OffensEval 2019 Shared Task. Second, we want to obtain more negative or positive tweets from the Twitter Airline sentiment dataset[10]. Our intuition is that some very specific parts of a sentence (comparable to a particular linguistic structure) are responsible for triggering a particular class, e.g. making a tweet sound either offensive or negative.

Relation Identification is a multi-class classification problem, where the label space contains between 10 and 19 classes. We use three standard benchmarks from the SemEval[11] challenges for relation classification: SE'07 (SemEval 2007; Girju et al., 2007), SE'10 (SemEval 2010; Hendrickx et al., 2010), and SE'18 (SemEval 2018; Gábor et al., 2018). SE'07 and SE'10 focus on the classification of semantic relations between pairs of nominals. E.g. 'tea' and 'ginseng' are in an ENTITY-ORIGIN(e_1, e_2) relationship in the sentence 'The cup contained tea from dried ginseng'. SE'18 focuses on domain-specific semantic relations from scientific articles and provides entire paragraphs instead of single sentences.

We apply the sentence-level templates mentioned in Section 3.1 and additionally apply a specifically designed template structure, which involves the path between two given entities in a dependency path. The dependency path as a feature has been proven to be beneficial for relation extraction in multiple previous works.We define the feature vector $\mathbf{x}$ to be the concatenation of vectors for each entity $\mathbf{e}_{\{1,2\}}$ and the path $\mathbf{p}$, where each individual vector is the average vector of the words included: $\mathbf{x} := \mathbf{e}_1 \oplus \mathbf{e}_2 \oplus \mathbf{p}$ (cf. Fig. 2f).

Frame Identification or classification is considered to be a fine-grained multi-class classification problem since every frame is its own class. We evaluate the performance on FrameNet (Baker et al., 1998). The latest release of the dataset is FrameNet-1.7, but FrameNet-1.5 is by far the most commonly used one in the literature. We report results for both versions. For this work, we only use the dataset of fulltext annotations which provides 78 documents for FrameNet-1.5 and 108 documents for FrameNet-1.7. To generate data splits for both versions, we use 23 documents to extract the test set following the previous work (Das et al., 2014; Peng et al., 2018) and 16 documents are used as development set (Hermann et al., 2014), whereas the remaining documents are used as training set. Each frame is associated with one or more frame evoking elements commonly referred to as `lexical-units`. For example, the frame 'Abandonment' can be evoked by the `lexical-units` 'abandon', 'depart' or 'leave'. To find sentences that represent the same frame, we use the following task-dependent structures in addition to the default structures:

`lexical-unit`: This structure is based on the target words and phrases corresponding to the `lexical-unit` of the respective frame. Unlike PropBank (Palmer et al., 2005), where the target predicate is always a verb, FrameNet contains ten different types of lexical units such as nouns, adjectives, and prepositions. Embeddings of multi-token lexical units are averaged.

`subj-v-obj`: This structure is based on the concatenation of `subject-verb-object` triples, which have demonstrated competitive performance for unsupervised semantic frame induction tasks (Ustalov et al., 2018). For non-verb lexical units with no subject and object, we just consider the lexical unit.

5 Results

For discussion, we focus on P@1 scores because we believe this is the most important metric for practical applicability. As expected, we observe significantly better performance using contextual word embeddings as compared to static word embeddings across all tasks. However, our goal is not to compare these two types of embeddings,

[9] https://competitions.codalab.org/competitions/20011
[10] https://www.kaggle.com/crowdflower/twitter-airline-sentiment
[11] https://semeval.github.io/

Data	Aggregation token	SPS	
CoNLL-2003 (w2v)	37.1	*38.9*	mAP1K
	71.3	*79.8*	P@1
	64.5	*70.3*	P@5
CoNLL-2003 (RB)	***48.0***	***48.0***	mAP1K
	87.3	87.2	P@1
	78.1	***79.3***	P@5
OntoNotes-v5 (w2v)	26.6	*29.6*	mAP1K
	49.7	*50.5*	P@1
	38.7	*44.9*	P@5
OntoNotes-v5 (RB)	***38.4***	36.0	mAP1K
	75.7	75.3	P@1
	64.4	***64.5***	P@5

Table 1: NER retrieval results. We use the mean average precision (mAP) estimate of the top 1K nearest neighbors.

Data	Embedding w2v	RB	
SensEval 2	45.9	***65.9***	mAP1K
	38.8	***75.1***	P@1
	40.4	***69.7***	P@5
SensEval 3	45.7	***64.2***	mAP1K
	40.5	***72.3***	P@1
	45.1	***68.7***	P@5
SemEval '07 T7 (SemCor)	35.6	***41.4***	mAP1K
	22.3	*27.8*	P@1
	22.5	*26.5*	P@5
SemEval '07 T7 (WNGT)	31.8	*38.6*	mAP1K
	25.0	***32.7***	P@1
	24.7	***29.9***	P@5
SemEval '07 T17 (SemCor)	50.0	***63.3***	mAP1K
	41.7	***62.6***	P@1
	42.7	***57.5***	P@5
SemEval '07 T17 (WNGT)	37.1	*53.0*	mAP1K
	32.4	*54.7*	P@1
	29.6	*44.5*	P@5

Table 2: WSD Retrieval results for the `token` structure.

but to evaluate if aggregation of embeddings along linguistically informed lexical structures provides benefits for retrieval compared to the baselines regardless of the type of embedding.

Named-entity recognition: Table 1 shows the retrieval results for the CoNLL-2003 and OntoNotes v5 datasets. The retrieval performances of the two structures differ depending on the type of word embedding, we can see a rough increase of 10-15% for each dataset and aggregation strategy. With static word embeddings, the SPS structure shows improved performance compared to the token structure. A likely explanation is that averaging vectors of neighboring words inherently creates a kind of composite embedding that is unique for the combination of words. This is supported by the observation that for CWEs, there is only a minor difference between both linguistic structures. For small k, `SPS` is marginally better while `token` outperforms `SPS` on the mAP1K metric on the OntoNotes dataset.

The classification results for CoNLL-2003 and OntoNotes-v5 are shown in Table 6[12]. Overall, the picture is very similar to retrieval. There is only a minor difference between both structures when using contextual embeddings. While the classification with the k-NN approach does not reach SOTA performance, the scores show that both linguistic structures are generally useful to retrieve named entities of the same type.

Data	CLS	BoW	token	word	word-NS	chunk	chunk-NS	dep-cat	dep-avg	dep-depavg	
	Aggregation										
Twitter-	-	*75.9*	63.0	64.3	64.3	66.2	65.6	65.4	66.0	65.6	mAP
Airline	-	*85.6*	71.9	27.4	71.9	56.4	70.6	62.4	59.1	65.2	P@1
(w2v)	-	*86.2*	58.6	51.9	59.5	62.0	57.9	62.6	59.2	62.3	P@5
Twitter-	73.7	***79.0***	63.8	64.7	65.7	78.8	77.9	63.4	65.1	64.3	mAP
Airline	23.5	88.9	74.4	77.5	81.2	***90.0***	89.0	67.8	71.3	68.4	P@1
(RB)	35.3	88.3	72.7	75.8	79.3	***89.7***	88.2	67.1	68.5	67.2	P@5
Offens-	-	39.3	47.5	48.4	***51.5***	47.9	49.2	45.4	45.7	46.0	mAP
Eval'19	-	52.5	60.4	66.2	*69.2*	60.8	62.5	57.5	56.2	60.0	P@1
(w2v)	-	46.8	61.2	64.5	*66.4*	62.4	63.5	58.7	56.8	60.8	P@5
Offens-	29.6	39.4	43.1	43.2	*44.7*	40.2	40.2	41.8	39.9	43.8	mAP
Eval'19	62.5	49.2	67.5	66.2	***70.4***	48.8	48.3	59.2	63.3	63.3	P@1
(RB)	56.7	47.6	66.8	66.3	***68.8***	52.3	50.9	62.3	56.8	63.5	P@5

Table 3: Short text retrieval results.

Word sense disambiguation: Table 2 shows the WSD retrieval results for the various pairs of query and background datasets. For SemEval '07 scores for task 17 are considerably higher as it is not as fine-grained as task 7. Furthermore, the use of SemCor as a background corpus is superior to WNGT. These dataset characteristics are independent of the choice of word embedding type.

The performance of k-NN classification with static word embeddings is always close to the most frequent sense (MFS) baseline (cf. Tab. 7 in the appendix). With CWEs, however, this baseline is beaten by a large margin (cf. Tab. 6).

Short-text retrieval: Table 3 shows the retrieval results for tweet labels. Aggregating embeddings with the `chunk` structure improves the retrieval performs best for sentiment analysis (90% for TwitterAirline and RB). For offensive language, the `word-NS` strategy performs best (70.4% for OffensEval'19 and RB). The reason for this could be that longer phrases are required to express a sentiment but a single word is enough to express offensive content. It is thus highly category-dependent which strategy to use for semantic retrieval.

Relation identification: A common pattern for all datasets is that simple linguistic structures perform worse in terms of P@1 than the baseline BoW approach (cf. Tab. 4). Among the simple linguis-

[12]Complete results can be found in Tables 7 and 8 in the appendix.

Data	CLS	BoW	token	word	word-NS	chunk	chunk-NS	dep-cat	dep-avg	dep-depavg	dep-path	
	Aggregation											
SE'18 (w2v)	-	32.9	31.1	30.4	31.2	31.0	30.9	30.6	30.8	31.2	***36.8***	mAP
	-	39.1	33.1	29.7	30.3	30.6	31.4	25.7	27.7	31.7	*46.0*	P@1
	-	34.6	30.9	31.7	33.4	31.4	31.3	27.1	30.2	31.1	*43.3*	P@5
SE'18 (RB)	31.9	34.5	32.1	31.4	32.0	32.1	32.2	31.8	32.2	32.4	*35.3*	mAP
	35.4	40.3	29.7	32.0	34.9	37.7	32.9	33.7	32.9	34.9	***52.9***	P@1
	34.6	37.8	33.5	32.2	35.0	33.4	34.9	35.0	33.4	34.1	***46.9***	P@5
SE'10 (w2v)	-	12.7	9.0	9.5	9.8	10.8	10.6	11.1	11.3	11.4	*22.2*	mAP
	-	35.5	9.9	14.4	15.6	21.9	21.8	22.7	22.5	23.0	*58.6*	P@1
	-	30.3	10.0	11.3	14.6	19.3	19.2	19.7	19.9	20.4	*50.0*	P@5
SE'10 (RB)	10.3	14.1	11.5	12.6	12.3	12.8	13.2	15.1	13.5	15.5	***26.5***	mAP
	31.6	40.6	26.0	26.8	27.3	32.0	32.4	38.3	27.5	37.6	***73.0***	P@1
	27.0	35.9	22.0	23.3	23.5	28.6	29.0	34.0	26.3	33.4	***66.5***	P@5
SE'07 (w2v)	-	32.2	29.2	29.6	29.8	30.5	30.4	30.5	30.6	30.8	***37.9***	mAP
	-	39.2	17.9	15.1	32.8	31.9	33.2	37.0	35.2	34.8	*53.6*	P@1
	-	36.5	20.2	22.9	30.2	32.2	32.4	31.8	32.6	33.3	*49.3*	P@5
SE'07 (RB)	30.8	31.6	30.6	31.2	31.5	31.1	31.3	32.2	31.3	32.5	*37.0*	mAP
	36.8	39.9	36.2	37.7	40.4	40.8	39.5	43.2	34.8	43.7	***61.9***	P@1
	33.7	37.3	32.9	34.9	35.6	37.2	35.3	39.9	34.3	38.6	***53.8***	P@5

Table 4: Relation identification retrieval results.

tic structures, the dependency-depavg still performs consistently better than other structures, probably because it covers more words than others. BoW also consistently produces better results than the CLS approach, which questions the practical usability of the [CLS] meta-token for downstream tasks. The specialized dependency-path structure, however, improves the results by a large margin, almost doubling the BoW results and even tripling the token-based results (cf. e.g. 73% P@1 for SE'10 and RB). We believe that BoW and dependency-path work so well because relations require even more content than sentiments and dependency-path focuses the content on the important part of the sentence.

Frame identification: Table 5 shows the retrieval results for frame identification. The lexical-unit structure has shown the best performance (~84% P@1 for RB), followed by subj-v-obj (~77% P@1 for RB). All other simple sentence-level structures perform significantly worse. In FrameNet, one sentence can have multiple lexical units which invoke different frames. Simple structures do not capture this and treat each structure as a representative for the whole sentence. The performance is further negatively affected by the very large number of classes in FrameNet (1,000+) in comparison to other tasks discussed in this work. Thus, high precision, i.e. one representative embedding laying out only the frame evoking lexical unit suppresses the noise that other structures introduce.

6 Application

Based on our findings, we investigate two downstream applications. First, similarity-based re-

Data	CLS	BoW	token	word	word-NS	chunk	chunk-NS	dep-cat	dep-avg	dep-depavg	lexical-unit	subj-v-obj	
	Aggregation												
FN1.5 (w2v)	-	1.8	0.9	1.0	1.2	1.6	1.5	1.5	1.5	1.4	***45.1***	41.7	mAP
	-	3.2	0.6	0.8	1.4	2.1	1.8	1.2	1.7	1.9	*80.3*	70.2	P@1
	-	3.3	0.7	0.9	1.3	2.0	1.5	1.5	1.7	1.8	*73.4*	66.8	P@5
FN1.5 (RB)	1.2	1.6	1.3	1.3	1.4	1.6	1.6	1.7	1.4	1.5	*38.0*	31.1	mAP
	1.6	2.2	1.8	2.2	1.8	2.4	2.5	2.7	2.0	2.3	***83.4***	77.0	P@1
	1.8	2.5	1.7	2.1	2.2	2.6	2.5	2.7	2.3	2.5	***74.2***	67.1	P@5
FN1.7 (w2v)	-	1.7	0.8	0.9	1.1	1.4	1.4	1.5	1.4	1.3	***44.6***	41.4	mAP
	-	3.5	0.9	0.8	1.4	2.3	1.6	1.2	1.4	1.5	*79.3*	70.6	P@1
	-	3.4	0.8	0.7	1.2	1.8	1.6	1.5	1.5	1.5	*74.7*	67.5	P@5
FN1.7 (RB)	1.1	1.5	1.2	1.3	1.4	1.5	1.5	1.6	1.3	1.5	*37.8*	30.8	mAP
	1.7	2.7	1.7	2.0	2.4	2.6	2.8	2.8	2.1	2.5	***84.0***	77.1	P@1
	1.8	2.4	1.8	1.9	2.2	2.5	2.4	2.7	2.2	2.6	***75.5***	68.2	P@5

Table 5: Frame identification retrieval results.

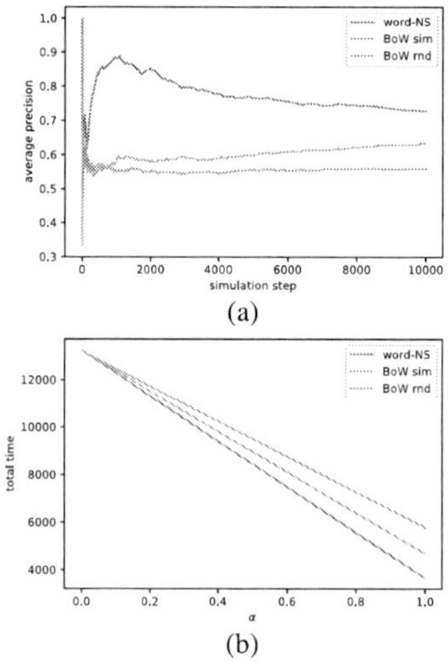

Figure 3: Simulation of similarity-based data labeling for offensive tweets: average agreement of subsequent sample labels (a), simulated label cost reduction depending on relative time saving due to reduced cognitive shifting (b).

trieval improved with linguistic information can be used to speed up manual labeling of text data. Second, aggregated CWEs can be used for rapid nearest neighbor classification with small training data.

Data labeling: Utilizing similarity information during annotation tasks can reduce annotation time and costs. In neuroscience, task switching is a well-studied phenomenon describing prolonged cognitive processing times due to altered tasks and task parameters (Rogers and Monsell, 1995). Vice versa, tasks can be solved faster in a series if parameters stay similar. This circumstance can be used to improve data labeling processes by presenting more similar instead of random samples to human annotators. We simulate the potential gains of such a process for selected aggregation strategies.

For this, we assume that labeling a single random example s_i takes the maximum amount of one time unit t. Labeling of the next most similar sample reduces cognitive processing time to $t - \alpha \times t \times sim(s_i, s_{i+1}) \times \beta$ with regard to the similarity of the two samples and a task-dependent parameter α representing its complexity, i.e. the upper bound of potential speed-up relative to t. Speed-up is expected if the labels of s_i and s_{i+1} agree, in this case setting $\beta = 1$, and $\beta = 0$ otherwise. Figure 3 shows the result of such a simulation on the OLID dataset. Similarity-based retrieval of samples for labeling achieves higher agreement between consecutive labels than random sample selection (cf. Fig. 3a). The best performing strategy `word-NS` outperforms `BoW`, especially in the early steps of the simulation. Figure 3b shows that significant time savings can be expected. For $\alpha = .4$, an assumed upper bound of 40% reduction of cognitive processing time per sample, for instance, the simulation shows a total time saving of ca. 10 %.

Rapid nearest neighbor classification: Table 6 shows a summary of kNN classification experiments with the best performing setup for each task and dataset, which was identified using a held-out validation set and evaluated on the held-out test set. Interestingly, the best classification setups do not correlate with the precision at k scores in the retrieval setup, but rather the mAP scores. While the classification results do not reach SOTA, they still achieve considerable results over a standard baseline. Much shorter training and prediction times of kNN-classification compared to fine-tuning transformers make it an appealing approach in some scenarios despite the lower performance.

Furthermore, kNN can be used in few-shot classification scenarios. We test the performance of the classifier with increasing dataset size, where we randomly select training sentences for indexing. Results are plotted in Figure 4. For the word-level task of NER (Fig. 4a), we can see that as few as 3,000 sentences are sufficient to reach a decent performance that only slightly increases with more training data. The findings for the sentence-level tasks (Fig. 4b) are even more drastic, where, depending on the task and the available training data, as few as 300 to 1,000 sentences are sufficient to reach a similar performance as compared to using the entire training data.

Data	Embedding	Aggregation	k	F1
CoNLL-2003	RB	`SPS`	1	79.6
OntoNotes-v5	RB	`SPS`	9	65.9
SensEval 2	RB	`token`	8	78.1
SensEval 3	RB	`token`	15	73.3
SemEval '07 T7 (WNGT)	RB	`token`	1	69.7
SemEval '07 T17 (SemCor)	RB	`token`	7	63.6
TwitterAirline	RB	`BoW`	29	87.8
OffensEval'19	RB	`word-NS`	75	63.6
SE'07	w2v	`dep-path`	1	43.4
SE'10	RB	`dep-path`	5	78.7
SE'18	RB	`dep-path`	5	35.9
FN1.5	RB	`lexical-unit`	1	63.9
FN1.7	RB	`lexical-unit`	1	61.9

Table 6: Classification results using kNN for word-level tasks (upper part) and sentence-level tasks (lower part). k refers to the best identified validation k.

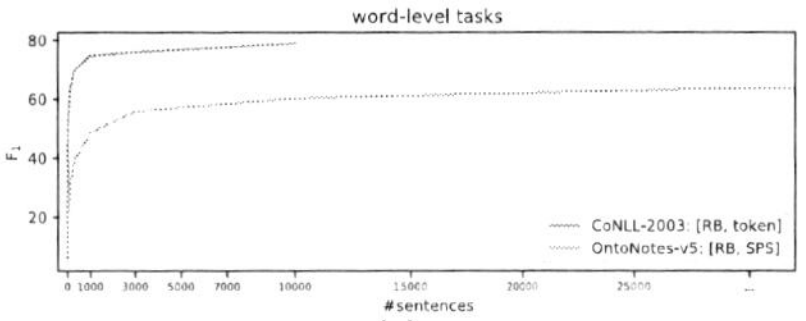

(a)

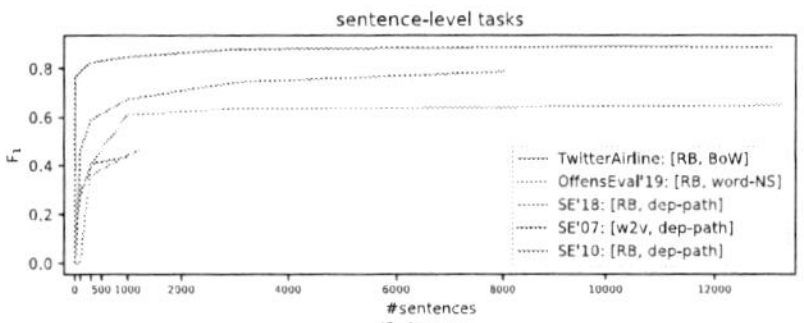

(b)

Figure 4: kNN performance for increasing training dataset sizes for the word-level task of NER (a) and the sentence-level tasks of short text classification and relation classification (b).

7 Conclusion

We presented an analysis of different linguistically informed aggregation strategies for word embeddings in an information retrieval setting to find semantic units of the same class for different NLP tasks. Our experiments show that more fine-grained label sets perform better with specifically designed task-dependent linguistic structures, whereas coarse-grained tasks such as short-text classification, work quite well with simple structures such as `chunk`, `word-NS`, or even the `BoW` baseline. We believe that particularly for the short-text classification tasks, certain keywords often are sufficient to trigger a certain class (e.g. offensive words). This can also be observed for word-level tasks. It is thus highly dependent on the task at hand if explicit structures based on external linguistic knowledge can be beneficial. We showed that more complex tasks benefit from both, linguistic structures and contextualized word embeddings. We also showed that for simple k nearest neighbor classification, only a certain amount of training data is sufficient to reach a decent performance. Use cases of this work include support for rapid training data collection, manual coding/annotation of datasets e.g. in social science and humanities applications, retrieval of similar language use in eDiscovery tasks, and many more.

References

Alan Akbik, Duncan Blythe, and Roland Vollgraf. 2018. Contextual string embeddings for sequence labeling. In *Proceedings of the 27th International Conference on Computational Linguistics*, pages 1638–1649, Santa Fe, NM, USA.

Collin F. Baker, Charles J. Fillmore, and John B. Lowe. 1998. The Berkeley FrameNet Project. In *Proceedings of the 36th Annual Meeting of the Association for Computational Linguistics and 17th International Conference on Computational Linguistics*, ACL '98, pages 86–90, Montréal, QC, Canada.

Kevin Clark, Urvashi Khandelwal, Omer Levy, and Christopher D. Manning. 2019. What does BERT look at? an analysis of BERT's attention. In *Proceedings of the 2019 ACL Workshop BlackboxNLP: Analyzing and Interpreting Neural Networks for NLP*, pages 276–286, Florence, Italy.

Dipanjan Das, Desai Chen, André F. T. Martins, Nathan Schneider, and Noah A. Smith. 2014. Frame-semantic parsing. *Computational Linguistics*, 40(1):9–56.

Jacob Devlin, Ming-Wei Chang, Kenton Lee, and Kristina Toutanova. 2019. BERT: Pre-training of deep bidirectional transformers for language understanding. In *Proceedings of the 2019 Conference of the North American Chapter of the Association for Computational Linguistics: Human Language Technologies*, pages 4171–4186, Minneapolis, MN, USA.

Philip Edmonds and Scott Cotton. 2001. SENSEVAL-2: Overview. In *Proceedings of SENSEVAL-2 Second International Workshop on Evaluating Word Sense Disambiguation Systems*, pages 1–5, Toulouse, France.

Jeffrey L. Elman. 1990. Finding structure in time. *Cognitive science*, 14(2):179–211.

Kata Gábor, Davide Buscaldi, Anne-Kathrin Schumann, Behrang QasemiZadeh, Haïfa Zargayouna, and Thierry Charnois. 2018. SemEval-2018 task 7: Semantic relation extraction and classification in scientific papers. In *Proceedings of The 12th International Workshop on Semantic Evaluation*, pages 679–688, New Orleans, LO, USA.

Roxana Girju, Preslav Nakov, Vivi Nastase, Stan Szpakowicz, Peter Turney, and Deniz Yuret. 2007. SemEval-2007 task 04: Classification of semantic relations between nominals. In *Proceedings of the Fourth International Workshop on Semantic Evaluations (SemEval-2007)*, pages 13–18, Prague, Czech Republic.

Iris Hendrickx, Su Nam Kim, Zornitsa Kozareva, Preslav Nakov, Diarmuid Ó. Séaghdha, Sebastian Padó, Marco Pennacchiotti, Lorenza Romano, and Stan Szpakowicz. 2010. SemEval-2010 task 8: Multi-way classification of semantic relations between pairs of nominals. In *Proceedings of the 5th International Workshop on Semantic Evaluation*, pages 33–38, Uppsala, Sweden.

Karl Moritz Hermann, Dipanjan Das, Jason Weston, and Kuzman Ganchev. 2014. Semantic frame identification with distributed word representations. In *Proceedings of the 52nd Annual Meeting of the Association for Computational Linguistics (Volume 1: Long Papers)*, pages 1448–1458, Baltimore, MD, USA.

Phu Mon Htut, Jason Phang, Shikha Bordia, and Samuel R. Bowman. 2019. Do attention heads in BERT track syntactic dependencies? In *Natural Language, Dialog and Speech (NDS) Symposium*, pages 1–7, New York, NY, USA.

Kenneth C. Litkowski. 2004. Senseval-3 task: Word sense disambiguation of WordNet glosses. In *Proceedings of SENSEVAL-3, the Third International Workshop on the Evaluation of Systems for the Semantic Analysis of Text*, pages 13–16, Barcelona, Spain.

Yinhan Liu, Myle Ott, Naman Goyal, Jingfei Du, Mandar Joshi, Danqi Chen, Omer Levy, Mike Lewis, Luke Zettlemoyer, and Veselin Stoyanov. 2019. RoBERTa: A robustly optimized BERT pretraining approach. *arXiv preprint arXiv:1907.11692*.

Tomas Mikolov, Kai Chen, Greg Corrado, and Jeffrey Dean. 2013. Efficient estimation of word representations in vector space. In *1st International Conference on Learning Representations, ICLR 2013*, Scottsdale, AZ, USA.

George A. Miller. 1995. WordNet: A lexical database for English. *Communications of the Association of Computing Machinery (ACM)*, 38(11):39–41.

George A. Miller, Claudia Leacock, Randee Tengi, and Ross T. Bunker. 1993. A semantic concordance. In *Proceedings of a Human Language Technology Workshop.*, pages 303–308, Plainsboro, NJ, USA.

Roberto Navigli, Kenneth C. Litkowski, and Orin Hargraves. 2007. SemEval-2007 task 07: Coarse-grained English all-words task. In *Proceedings of the Fourth International Workshop on Semantic Evaluations (SemEval-2007)*, pages 30–35, Prague, Czech Republic.

Martha Palmer, Daniel Gildea, and Paul Kingsbury. 2005. The Proposition Bank: An Annotated Corpus of Semantic Roles. *Computational Linguistics*, 31(1):71–106.

Hao Peng, Sam Thomson, Swabha Swayamdipta, and Noah A. Smith. 2018. Learning joint semantic parsers from disjoint data. In *Proceedings of the 2018 Conference of the North American Chapter of the Association for Computational Linguistics: Human Language Technologies*, pages 1492–1502, New Orleans, LA, USA.

Matthew Peters, Mark Neumann, Mohit Iyyer, Matt Gardner, Christopher Clark, Kenton Lee, and Luke Zettlemoyer. 2018. Deep contextualized word representations. In *Proceedings of the 2018 Conference of the North American Chapter of the Association for Computational Linguistics: Human Language Technologies*, pages 2227–2237, New Orleans, LA, USA.

Sameer Pradhan, Edward Loper, Dmitriy Dligach, and Martha Palmer. 2007. SemEval-2007 task-17: English lexical sample, SRL and all words. In *Proceedings of the Fourth International Workshop on Semantic Evaluations (SemEval-2007)*, pages 87–92, Prague, Czech Republic.

Sameer Pradhan, Alessandro Moschitti, Nianwen Xue, Hwee Tou Ng, Anders Björkelund, Olga Uryupina, Yuchen Zhang, and Zhi Zhong. 2013. Towards robust linguistic analysis using OntoNotes. In *Proceedings of the Seventeenth Conference on Computational Natural Language Learning*, pages 143–152, Sofia, Bulgaria.

Nils Reimers and Iryna Gurevych. 2019. Sentence-BERT: Sentence embeddings using Siamese BERT-networks. In *Proceedings of the 2019 Conference on Empirical Methods in Natural Language Processing and the 9th International Joint Conference on Natural Language Processing (EMNLP-IJCNLP)*, pages 3982–3992, Hong Kong.

Robert D. Rogers and Stephen Monsell. 1995. Costs of a predictible switch between simple cognitive tasks. *Journal of Experimental Psychology*, 124(2):207–231.

Livio Baldini Soares, Nicholas FitzGerald, Jeffrey Ling, and Tom Kwiatkowski. 2019. Matching the blanks: Distributional similarity for relation learning. In *Proceedings of the 57th Conference of the Association for Computational Linguistics*, pages 2895–2905, Florence, Italy.

Emma Strubell, Patrick Verga, Daniel Andor, David Weiss, and Andrew McCallum. 2018. Linguistically-informed self-attention for semantic role labeling. In *Proceedings of the 2018 Conference on Empirical Methods in Natural Language Processing*, pages 5027–5038, Brussels, Belgium.

Erik F. Tjong Kim Sang and Fien De Meulder. 2003. Introduction to the CoNLL-2003 Shared Task: Language-Independent Named Entity Recognition. In *Proceedings of the Seventh Conference on Natural Language Learning*, page 142–147, Edmonton, Canada.

Dmitry Ustalov, Alexander Panchenko, Andrei Kutuzov, Chris Biemann, and Simone Paolo Ponzetto. 2018. Unsupervised Semantic Frame Induction using Triclustering. In *Proceedings of the 56th Annual Meeting of the Association for Computational Linguistics*, pages 55–62, Melbourne, VIC, Australia.

Loïc Vial, Benjamin Lecouteux, and Didier Schwab. 2018. UFSAC: Unification of Sense Annotated Corpora and Tools. In *Proceedings of the Eleventh International Conference on Language Resources and Evaluation (LREC 2018)*, Miyazaki, Japan.

Wei Wang, Bin Bi, Ming Yan, Chen Wu, Zuyi Bao, Jiangnan Xia, Liwei Peng, and Luo Si. 2019. StructBERT: Incorporating language structures into pre-training for deep language understanding. *arXiv preprint arXiv:1908.04577*.

Ralph Weischedel, Martha Palmer, Mitchell Marcus, Eduard Hovy, Sameer Pradhan, Lance Ramshaw, Nianwen Xue, Ann Taylor, Jeff Kaufman, Michelle Franchini, et al. 2013. OntoNotes Release 5.0 LDC2013T19. *Philadelphia: Linguistic Data Consortium*.

Gregor Wiedemann, Steffen Remus, Avi Chawla, and Chris Biemann. 2019. Does BERT make any sense? Interpretable word sense disambiguation with contextualized embeddings. In *Proceedings of the 15th Conference on Natural Language Processing (KONVENS)*, pages 161–170, Erlangen, Germany.

Zhiyong Wu, Yun Chen, Ben Kao, and Qun Liu. 2020. Perturbed masking: Parameter-free probing for analyzing and interpreting BERT. In *Proceedings of the 58th Annual Meeting of the Association for Computational Linguistics*, pages 4166–4176, Online.

Marcos Zampieri, Shervin Malmasi, Preslav Nakov, Sara Rosenthal, Noura Farra, and Ritesh Kumar. 2019. SemEval-2019 task 6: Identifying and categorizing offensive language in social media (OffensEval). In *Proceedings of the 13th International Workshop on Semantic Evaluation*, pages 75–86, Minneapolis, MN, USA.

A KNN Results

Masking + Embedding	CoNLL-2003	OntoNotes-v5	SensEval 2	SensEval 3	SemEval '07 T7 (SemCor)	SemEval '07 T7 (WNGT)	SemEval '07 T17 (SemCor)	SemEval '07 T17 (WNGT)	
MFS	-	-	55.3	54.4	63.60	58.0	51.8	38.9	F1
token (w2v)	3	25	25	24	24	8	20	25	k
	64.5	44.9	54.8	51.8	62.9	58.5	50.7	43.9	F1
token (RB)	1	11	8	15	6	1	7	1	k
	79.4	65.6	78.1	73.3	69.6	69.7	63.6	60.7	F1
SPS (w2v)	3	16	-	-	-	-	-	-	k
	73.5	52.3	-	-	-	-	-	-	F1
SPS (RB)	3	9	-	-	-	-	-	-	k
	79.6	65.9	-	-	-	-	-	-	F1

Table 7: Word-level classification results using KNN. Showing the best identified hyperparameter k and the F1 score.

Data	CLS	BoW	token	word	word-NS	chunk	chunk-NS	dep-cat	dep-avg	dep-depavg	dep-path	lexical-unit	subj-v-object	
Twitter-Airline	-	9	22	5	133	113	31	194	200	194	-	-	-	k
(w2v)	-	83.3	62.8	68.0	75.3	77.0	73.7	78.9	79.9	78.5	-	-	-	F1
Twitter-Airline	42	29	24	17	14	58	21	89	141	29	-	-	-	k
(RB)	83.9	87.8	81.7	82.5	83.5	81.8	82.3	79.9	81.5	79.3	-	-	-	F1
Offens-Eval'19	-	16	160	180	164	154	84	30	67	39	-	-	-	k
w2v	-	42.2	56.4	59.5	59.3	56.9	55.1	51.3	56.0	54.4	-	-	-	F1
Offens-Eval'19	8	54	54	44	75	66	51	38	52	27	-	-	-	k
(RB)	33.4	46.1	61.7	60.0	63.6	56.9	60.0	56.7	61.1	55.5	-	-	-	F1
SE'18	-	6	4	13	4	26	6	8	2	9	3	-	-	k
(w2v)	-	27.9	15.8	14.4	16.5	15.6	22.4	19.8	15.7	19.7	27.9	-	-	F1
SE'18	10	4	14	15	18	38	27	25	2	20	5	-	-	k
(RB)	21.5	26.6	21.6	17.3	20.2	15.2	16.5	24.1	25.0	17.6	35.9	-	-	F1
SE'10	-	65	11	24	16	41	30	23	24	22	107	-	-	k
(w2v)	-	40.7	9.6	11.3	17.2	22.7	22.4	24.4	27.8	24.4	67.0	-	-	F1
SE'10	14	17	90	28	28	42	49	38	15	9	5	-	-	k
(RB)	33.9	50.5	24.8	29.0	30.0	34.8	34.1	31.2	40.2	41.7	78.7	-	-	F1
SE'07	-	1	16	6	10	2	7	2	1	16	1	-	-	k
(w2v)	-	22.3	8.6	7.0	8.6	12.6	12.6	14.7	16.5	11.3	43.4	-	-	F1
SE'07	6	2	5	4	10	3	3	11	3	1	12	-	-	k
(RB)	11.0	22.4	13.4	13.4	10.8	18.8	14.4	17.2	23.0	26.5	41.6	-	-	F1
FrameNet-1.5	-	24	42	44	41	79	92	79	27	25	-	1	1	k
(w2v)	-	1.5	0.2	0.4	1.1	2.6	1.7	1.8	2.1	1.9	-	58.8	55.1	F1
FrameNet-1.5	20	14	44	34	49	26	66	60	17	24	-	1	1	k
(RB)	0.8	1.4	1.6	2.2	2.9	3.1	3.0	1.8	2.9	3.4	-	63.9	54.3	F1
FrameNet-1.7	-	9	2	62	60	64	61	41	113	38	-	1	1	k
(w2v)	-	1.3	0.4	0.8	1.1	2.5	1.9	1.7	2.2	2.0	-	56.3	52.6	F1
FrameNet-1.7	2	13	76	38	36	49	65	83	41	69	-	1	1	k
(RB)	0.6	1.7	1.5	2.2	3.1	3.4	3.3	1.8	3.1	3.0	-	61.9	53.1	F1

Table 8: Sentence-level classification results using KNN. Showing the best identified hyperparameter k and the F1 score.

Proceedings of the 18th Conference on Natural Language Processing (KONVENS 2022)

TopicShoal: Scaling Partisanship Using Semantic Search

Sami Diaf , Ulrich Fritsche
Department of Socioeconomics
Universität Hamburg
[sami.diaf,ulrich.fritsche]@uni-hamburg.de

Abstract

Document scaling techniques have been widely used in political science to infer partisanship measures and to rank documents on a scale of ideal points, based on bag-of-word approaches. These approaches typically underestimate the semantic and syntactic patterns contained in the corpus. Recent advances in natural language processing, particularly semantic search models, offer an improved topic coherence due to a semantic space of embedded words and documents, whose structure is able to identify topics without setting their number as a hyperparameter. We propose a scaling technique, namely *TopicShoal*, that extracts meaningful topic vectors using a semantic search technique (*Top2Vec*) and scales partisanship among speakers or parties using a Bayesian factor analysis on the document-topic distances, thereby enabling a semantic explanation of the ideal points' variations. This novelty, suited for both monolingual and multilingual corpora, addresses the bag-of-word constraint by capturing the narrative signals in the corpus and exploiting a coherent and independent topic vector structure. Applied to a corpus of German party manifestos and *Deutsche Bundesbank* executive board members' speeches, *TopicShoal* successfully identifies discourse-level differences among parties and speakers via topic intensities, whose projection on the ideal points' scale reveals common debated themes and other sideline interests that differentiate parties and speakers.

1 Introduction

Text mining in political science comprises distinct families of methods usually applied to monolingual text data. Topic models define probabilistic models used to extract groups of words with a semantic meaning, referred to as topics based on a generative model of texts, while the document scaling family gathers probabilistic as well as non-probabilistic approaches used to infer a unidimensional scale assumed to be a proxy of ideal-points or (ideological) positions prevailing among speakers or parties.

Non-probabilistic scaling techniques are based on pre-established wordlists from *reference* texts (Laver et al., 2003) whose availability outside the English language is limited, while probabilistic techniques are mostly based on the assumption of a Poisson distribution for word frequencies, as for *Wordfish* (Slapin and Proksch, 2008) which infers a unidimensional, normally distributed $\mathcal{N}(0, 1)$ scale for document positions, or the Poisson reduced rank models which permit to endow a time-variability to the learned scale (Jentsch et al., 2020). *Wordshoal* (Lauderdale and Herzog, 2016) uses *Wordfish* estimates over distinct debates to aggregate the results at the level of speakers, where differences in document positions within debates approximate the ideological stance between speakers. Such schemes have been used in political sciences to measure polarization of political parties in the United Kingdom (Goet, 2019), investigate left-right differences (Däubler and Benoit, 2021), in Germany for parties' manifestos (Jentsch et al., 2021) or for economic institutions' forecasting reports (Diaf et al., 2022) and were found to have some drawbacks in applications with small corpora or limited vocabulary (Hjorth et al., 2015) and to text pre-processing choices (Denny and Spirling, 2018). Scaling speakers using topic variations (Vafa et al., 2020) was proposed as a generalization of *Wordshoal* where word contributions are allowed to differ among speakers using a hierarchical Poisson factorization, while Latent Semantic Scaling (Watanabe, 2021) is a semi-supervised approach to scale documents on a specific task, using Latent Semantic Analysis (Deerwester et al., 1990) over sentences or paragraphs, augmented with a wordlist for positive/negative terms. Another hybrid approach learns a *Wordfish* scale that serves as an explanatory variable to a supervised LDA (Diaf and Fritsche, 2021) with the aim of tracking topics' prevalence over time using dynamic word frequencies.

Latent Dirichlet Allocation (Blei et al., 2003) is still the workhorse for topic model applications, despite being a heuristic method yielding relatively unstable results and being highly dependent on the hyperparametrization chosen by practitioners (Airoldi et al., 2014). Further variants were proposed to adapt the algorithm to the corpus specifications' or to add prior information as a semi-supervised approach (Eshima et al., 2020).

The advent of distributional representations helped researchers exploring the field of semantics and overcoming the bag-of-word restrictions by adopting neural architectures able to capture word similarity in context (Mikolov et al., 2013) and facilitate document comparisons (Dieng et al., 2019) even for multilingual documents that require a Zero-shot learning strategy (Bianchi et al., 2021). *Semscale* (Nanni et al., 2019) was proposed as a scaling technique relying on word embedding models, aiming at uncovering party positions from political manifestos and able to capture differences in multilingual manifestos.

Top2Vec (Angelov, 2020) belongs to the semantic search class of topic models where the number of topics, usually set as a hyperparameter, is automatically learned as being equal to the clusters of document representations using UMAP (McInnes et al., 2018) as a non-linear dimensionality reduction technique. As a mixture of three unsupervised models, it uncovers coherent topics and set their hierarchies for a better document-word representation, that could be augmented with pre-trained word embedding models.

This article proposes a novel semantic, topic-based semi-supervised scaling approach that outperforms the existing document scaling techniques in terms of coherence and interpretability, combining topic vectors learned from a semantic space and an aggregation scheme to derive ideal points for an intuitive positional analysis, suited to monolingual and multilingual corpora. It consists, at the first stage, of a semantic search model (*Top2Vec*) that uncovers coherent topics, serving as an input for a Bayesian factor model (Lauderdale and Herzog, 2016) that yields a positional scale with semantic properties through topic intensities. We argue that the usual techniques are constrained by the bag-of-word hypothesis and cannot uncover semantic signals from the corpus, but just similarities in word counts, known as *lexical overlap* (Nanni et al., 2019), that overlook both semantic and syntactic features, in addition of rendering aggregate-level measures sensitive to word frequencies distributions. Moreover, recent applications built upon word embedding models are prone to an information bias transferred from large corpora to small and specific ones for monolingual documents (Papakyriakopoulos et al., 2020) or from one language to another (Bianchi et al., 2021), however, the use of multilingual pre-trained embedding models is mandatory to ensure a language-transferability of topics other than the training set (Bianchi et al., 2021) that requires setting the number of topics.

Two corpora were chosen to test *TopicShoal* at the monolingual and multilingual levels respectively. The corpus of Comparative Manifesto Project (CMP) (Volkens et al., 2021) was used to get the last three legislative elections' manifestos to scale the six main parties forming the current German political landscape, resulting in a scale that identifies partisanship of four parties (CDU/CSU, FDP, Grüne and SPD) in themes related to security, local affairs and economic concerns, in contrast of two parties (AFD, Linke) dominating the two ends of the scale as they have different priorities/focus, hence extending the partisanship spectrum. The corpus of executive members' speeches at the German Central Bank (*Bundesbank*) during the period 2012-2017 (Karim El-Ouaghlidi et al., 2019) is mainly bilingual (German-English) and cannot be analyzed using traditional text mining techniques, however, applying TopicShoal with the help of a multilingual embedding model uncovers a member-specialization strategy from the given addresses with specific interests given to Eurozone, financial stability and digitalization.

2 Methodology

2.1 Top2Vec

Aside from traditional topic models which use variational inference to uncover topics from word counts, *Top2Vec* augments the usual distributional representation methods, as for Word2Vec, by adding a paragraph vector to the neural network (Angelov, 2020) to create a joint word and document representations forming a semantic space able to uncover associations that helps learning coherent topic vectors from dense areas of document using *Hierarchical Density-Based Spatial Clustering of Applications with Noise* (HDBSCAN) (McInnes et al., 2017), under the hypothesis that the number of dense areas of documents is equal to the number of topics. Hence, the number of topics is no longer a hyperparameter as for most algorithms.

Top2Vec features a structure of independent, mostly low-correlated, topics because of the HDBSCAN application, ensuring a non-overlapping outcome often found in traditional topic models, hence enabling a robust Bayesian aggregation on independent topics, instead of a debate-structure that might have an intertwined topic prevalence.

2.2 Bayesian factor analysis

We use a modified version of the Bayesian aggregation used in *Wordshoal* (Lauderdale and Herzog, 2016) by setting the document positions as being drawn from a truncated normal distribution, instead of a normal distribution, as the document-topic coefficients are indeed distances mainly on the [0,1] interval.

Let ψ_{ij} defines the score of ith document in the jth topic learned via *Top2Vec*. The Bayesian aggregation used in *Wordshoal* to infer a latent scale, represented by a vector of speakers' positions θ_i is as follows:

TopicShoal

1st Stage: Apply *Top2Vec* and extract the inferred topics:
ψ_{ij} defines the distance between the ith document and the jth topic (based on cosine distance)
2st Stage: Each topic inferred is assumed to form a *debate*:
Inferring ideal points θ_i using the following factor analysis:
$\psi_{ij} \sim \mathcal{N}(\alpha_j + \beta_j\theta_i, \tau_i)$
$\theta_i \sim \mathcal{N}_{trunc}(0, 1)$
$\alpha_j, \beta_j \sim \mathcal{N}(0, 0.25)$
$\tau_i \sim \mathcal{G}(1, 1)$

---

where $\mathcal{N}_{trunc}$ denotes the truncated normal distribution as ψ_{ij} are represent document-topic distances. β_j is a topic polarization parameter.

Lauderdale and Herzog (2016) assumed debates being independent and serving as a basis to a multiple *Wordfish* scaling within each debate, that renders different word contribution for each scale. While this assumption allows a dynamic word contribution per debate, it ignores a potential topics' prevalence that might differentiate speakers or parties out of the debate dimension. Hence, building an Bayesian factor analysis on semantic topics makes it possible to track their prevalence in the unidimensional scale of positions, using the learned β_j.

In other terms, *TopicShoal* ensures a debate transfer from a time perspective to a topic structure for a better interpretability of the ideal positions. This is motivated by the fact that debates are defined by their occurrence, but usually discuss the same topics or concerns.

3 Application

3.1 German political manifestos

Manifestos of six main German parties (AFD, CDU/CSU, FDP, Grüne, Linke and SPD) for the last three legislative elections (2013, 2017 and 2021) were collected from the CMP (Volkens et al., 2021), consisting of 933 documents coded into 7 manually-annotated different categories (External Relations, Freedom and Democracy, Political System, Economy, Welfare and Quality of Life, Fabric of Society and Social groups).

The prevailing manifestos' interests appear to have a focus on the past and present rhetoric, inline with results found in international manifestos (Müller, 2022), with 20 topics learned, indicating a slight dominance of themes related to society and quality of life, as shown in Table 1.

Topics 14 and 9, respectively criminality and communes/municipalities, polarize the scale to the right-hand side (CDU and AfD) as indicated by positive β_i while most negative topic contributions are related to the left-hand side (Grüne and Linke, negative β_i) of the scale. The 95% confidence intervals offer an idea of parties' interest breadth that are captured by the topic intensities in Table 3. Noticeable are the close ideal points of three parties (Grüne, FDP and SPD), indicating similar interests displayed in their manifestos, and the contrary holds for the AfD, whose position dominates the right-hand scale and appears to be insulated from other parties.

Wordshoal estimation using the same corpus was not convergent [1] in addition of requiring setting an identification constraint[2]. Results do not render a clear partisanship scale, as demonstrated in Figure

[1] Tolerance level set to 10^{-10}

[2] We assumed $\theta_{Linke_{2013}} < \theta_{AFD_{2013}}$

Topic	Top 10 Words
1	fluchtlinge integration asyl bleiberecht gefluchteten asylbewerber antragstellerin optionszwang gefluchtete abschiebungen
2	schulden schuldenbremse eurozone stabilitats europaische eu wachstumspaktes ezb wachstumspakts maastricht
3	russland staaten frieden beziehungen internationale usa internationalen vereinten nationen multilateralen
4	demokratie parteien fußspur nebenverdienste abgeordneten vermengung demokratische transparenz parlamente mandats
5	leistungen versorgung pflege rente medizinische ambulante ambulanten alter medizinischen gesetzlichen
6	arbeitnehmer beschaftigten arbeit arbeitgeber beschaftigte beschaftigung arbeitsplatze tarifvertragen leiharbeit tarifvertrage
7	kultur gedenkkultur kulturelle kunst kulturforderung restitution kulturellen aufarbeitung filmerbe kulturpolitik
8	ehe ehen paare adoptionsrecht adoptionen patchwork fureinander familien verheiratet familie
9	kommunen gemeinden regionen landkreise stadte landlichen lander ort kommunale bund
10	nachhaltige okologische nachhaltigkeit energien nachhaltigen energie okologischen nachhaltiges wachstum erneuerbare
11	bundestagswahl politik merkel koalition steinbruck wahlerinnen marktkonforme koalieren wahlprogramm doch
12	bildung schulen lernen schuler schule schulerinnen lehrer hochschulen unterricht lehr
13	nato bundeswehr militarische abrustung atomwaffen rustung streitkrafte militarischen buchel nuklearen
14	straftaten polizei kriminalitat strafverfolgung tater organisierte fußballstadien aufzuklaren straftater gewalt
15	verbraucher produkte honorarberatung nahrwerte ampel markt wettbewerb finanzprodukten smiley finanzmarkte
16	infrastruktur technologien ausbau deutschlandtakt digitalisierung innovationen digitale anschlussen verkehrswege nutzen
17	wahlt zukunft starken starke grun bekampfen burgernahes schutzen statt stimmt
18	walder natur artenvielfalt tiere klima naturnahe lebensraume umwelt wald klimaschutz
19	engagement zusammenhalt ehrenamtliches feuerwehr ehrenamtlich ehrenamtliche ehrenamt ehrenamtes engagierte feuer
20	landwirtschaft landwirte landwirt ackerbau bauerliche kleinbauerliche landbau agrarbetriebe agrarzahlungen junglandwirte

Table 1: Top 10 words of the topics learned by *Top2Vec* on the German political manifesto corpus.

Topic	Top 10 words
1	eurosystems finanzpolitik eurosystem euroraums finanzkrisen eurozone bankensektors geldpolitik geldpolitischer finanzkrise
2	bargelds geldpolitik geldmarkt bankbilanzen currency monetaren bargeld monetaire wahrung eurosystem
3	bankensektors bankensektor innovationen innovations finanzbranche finanzsektors bankensystems innovation finanzsektor bankensystem
4	eurosystems eurosystem zahlungsverkehr euroraums eurozone zahlungsmittel euroraum kreditvergabe geldmarkt transaktionen
5	repercussions risikoteilung nachhaltig risques risks risiko nachhaltige krisenmaßnahmen risque risk
6	empirical data statistics analyses statistical trends informationen indicators analysen finanzsystems
7	digitalen verbraucher digitale digitalisation consumer digital consumers cyber technologien technologie
8	cyber security sicherheit threat sicherheiten sicherzustellen safeguarding vulnerable secure danger
9	blockchain bitcoins bitcoin geldmarkt currencies zentralbankgeld bankbilanzen bankensystem geldpolitik bankensystems
10	geldpolitik geldpolitischer geldmarkt renminbi geldpolitische geldpolitischen currencies currency zentralbankgeld staatsanleihen

Table 2: Top 10 words of the topics learned by *Top2Vec* on the Bundesbank speeches corpus.

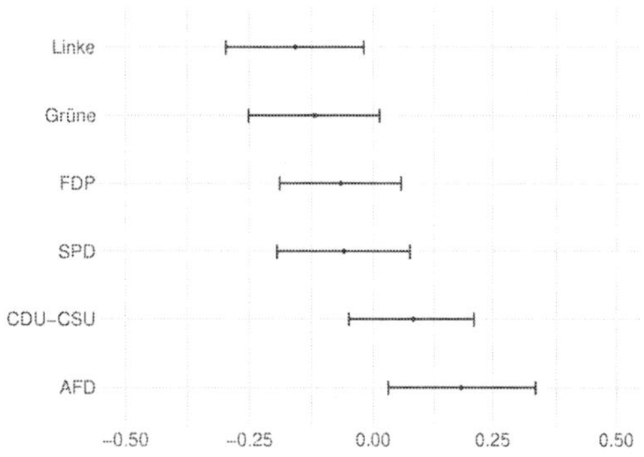

Figure 1: Estimated german parties' ideal points using *TopicShoal*.

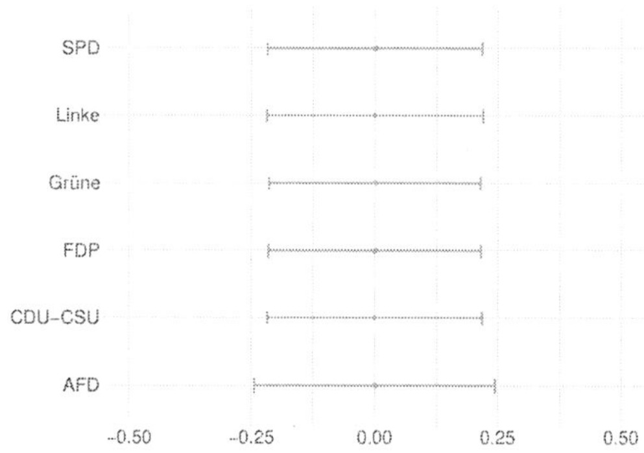

Figure 2: Estimated german parties' ideal points using *Wordshoal* (Lauderdale and Herzog, 2016).

	β_i
Topic 1	0.03
Topic 2	0.02
Topic 3	0.07
Topic 4	-0.16
Topic 5	-0.13
Topic 6	-0.23
Topic 7	-0.25
Topic 8	-0.33
Topic 9	0.15
Topic 10	-0.03
Topic 11	-0.08
Topic 12	-0.04
Topic 13	-0.30
Topic 14	0.30
Topic 15	-0.15
Topic 16	0.02
Topic 17	-0.31
Topic 18	-0.43
Topic 19	0.04
Topic 20	-0.05

Table 3: Estimated topic intensity β_i using *TopicShoal* on the German political manifesto corpus.

2, confirming that word counts are not always able to capture parties' partisanship.

3.2 *Bundesbank* speeches

Dataset of *Deutsche Bundesbank* executive board members' speeches (Karim El-Ouaghlidi et al., 2019) is used to test the multilingual version of *TopicShoal* with the help of a multilingual embedding model that ensures a topic-transferability between different languages used in the corpus. The dataset comprises 791 speeches given by nine different executive board members during the period 2012-2017 in four different languages (english, french, german and italian) although english and german share 98% of the corpus. *TopicShoal* is used to extract central bankers positions using multilingual embedding [3] (Reimers and Gurevych, 2019) given to *Top2Vec* that uncovered 10 different topics related to various aspects of monetary policy practices, as for risks and vulnerabilities (topic 5), European concerns (topic 1 and 4), financial innovation (topic 3), security and digitalization (topic 7, 8 and 9) and monetary policy (topic 10) as displayed in Table 2.

The positional analysis, as mentioned in Figures 4 and 5, helps classifying members into small groups of similar interests, given the learned topics, where topics related to classical monetary policy (topics 2 and 10) are polarizing positive members' positions, while risks and crisis-related concerns are mostly linked to negative positions, as reported in Table 4. Positions with wide confidence intervals (Beermann and Böhmler) could be explained by the variety of speeches, members gave during the period, while firm positions with relatively small confidence intervals (Dombret, Weidmann and Thiele) indicate a potential specialization or theme preferences of the members.

[3]paraphrase-multilingual-MiniLM-L12-v2

	β_i
Topic 1	-0.16
Topic 2	0.44
Topic 3	-0.15
Topic 4	0.22
Topic 5	-0.78
Topic 6	-0.22
Topic 7	0.30
Topic 8	-0.82
Topic 9	-0.01
Topic 10	0.53

Table 4: Estimated topic intensity β_i using TopicShoal on Bundesbank executive board members' corpus.

4 Conclusion

We presented a novel topic-based, scaling technique able to learn ideal points based on the corpus' semantic features and yielding an explanatory positional analysis, for both monolingual and multilingual corpora. It outperforms existing bag-of-word methods, which are not always convergent, and other semantic approaches that directly use bias-prone, pre-trained embedding models. Capturing meaningful topics, in addition to uncovering latent patterns within documents, helps building genuine unidimensional scales to rank speakers or parties without the need of taking the analysis to the multidimensional level or requiring further intervention on hyperparameters setting, though such efforts usually add a user-bias and are not time-efficient. *TopicShoal* demonstrated similar interests of four German political parties given to regular debated themes during the last three legislative campaigns, while scaling multilingual speeches at the *Bundesbank* proved to be effective in uncovering preferences and specialization of central bankers related

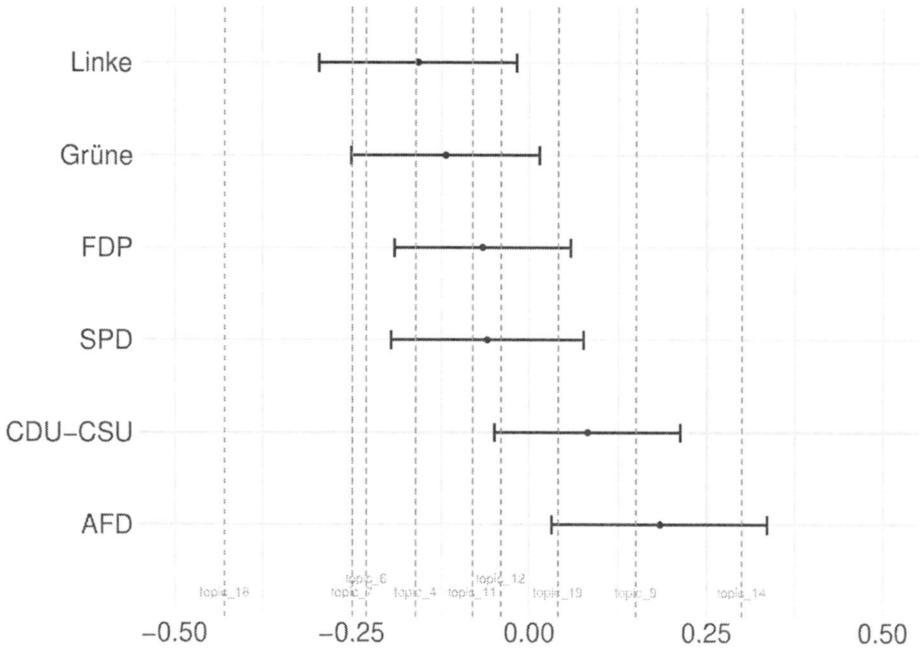

Figure 3: Estimated german parties' ideal points using *TopicShoal* with projected topic contributions.

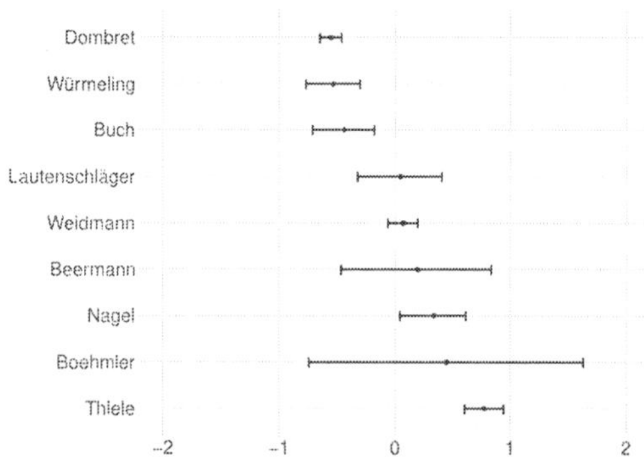

Figure 4: Estimated Bundesbank executive board members' ideal positions using *TopicShoal*.

to modern monetary policy practices and hot topics as for digitalization and financial innovation.

Acknowledgments

Financial support by the *Deutsche Forschungsgemeinschaft* (DFG) trough priority programme 1859, sub-project *Exploring the experience-expectation nexus in macroeconomic forecasting using computational text analysis and machine learning* is gratefully acknowledged.

References

Edoardo M. Airoldi, David Blei, Elena A. Erosheva, and Stephen E. Fienberg, editors. 2014. *Handbook of Mixed Membership Models and Their Applications*. Chapman & Hall / CRC Handbooks of Modern Statistical Methods. Taylor and Francis, Hoboken.

Dimo Angelov. 2020. Top2vec: Distributed representations of topics. *arXiv preprint arXiv:2008.09470*.

Federico Bianchi, Silvia Terragni, Dirk Hovy, Debora Nozza, and Elisabetta Fersini. 2021. Cross-lingual contextualized topic models with zero-shot learning. *Association for Computational Linguistics*, pages 1676–1683.

David M. Blei, Andrew Y. Ng, and Michael I. Jordan. 2003. Latent dirichlet allocation. *J. Mach. Learn. Res.*, 3(null):993–1022.

Scott Deerwester, Susan T. Dumais, George W. Furnas, Thomas K. Landauer, and Richard Harshman. 1990. Indexing by latent semantic analysis. *Journal of the American Society for Information Science*, 41(6):391–407.

Matthew J. Denny and Arthur Spirling. 2018. Text preprocessing for unsupervised learning: Why it matters when it misleads and what to do about it. *Political Analysis*, 26(2):168–189.

Sami Diaf, Jörg Döpke, Ulrich Fritsche, and Ida Rockenbach. 2022. Sharks and minnows in a shoal of words: Measuring latent ideological positions based

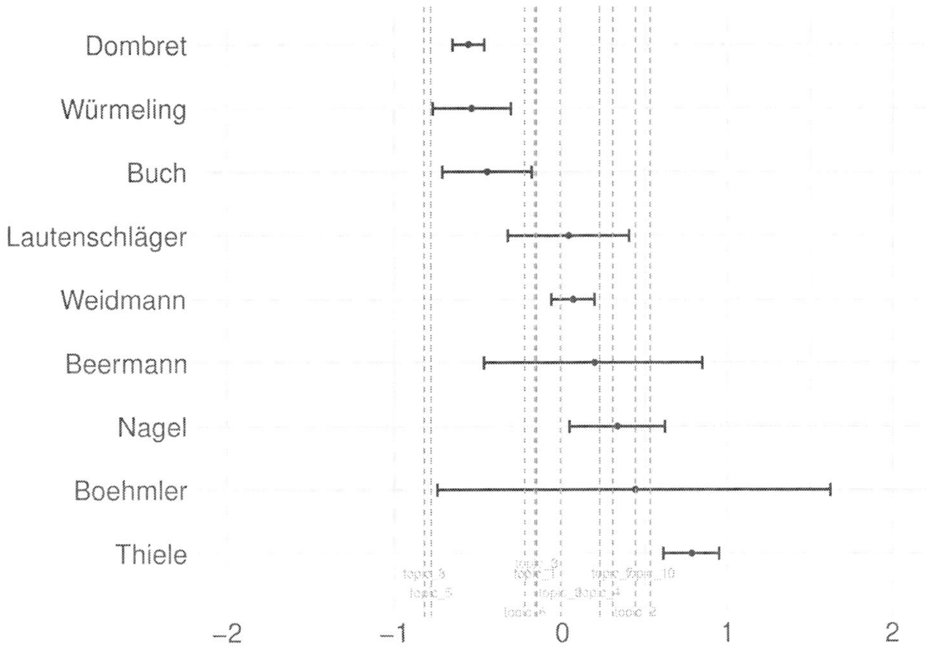

Figure 5: Estimated Bundesbank executive board members' ideal points using *TopicShoal* with projected topic contributions.

on text mining techniques. *European Journal of Political Economy*, page 102179.

Sami Diaf and Ulrich Fritsche. 2021. Topic scaling: A joint document scaling – topic model approach to learn time-specific topics. *arXiv preprint arXiv:2104.01117*, (2104.01117).

Adji B. Dieng, Francisco J. R. Ruiz, and David M. Blei. 2019. Topic modeling in embedding spaces. *arXiv preprint arXiv:1907.04907*.

Thomas Däubler and Kenneth Benoit. 2021. Scaling hand-coded political texts to learn more about left-right policy content. *Party Politics*, page 135406882110260.

Shusei Eshima, Kosuke Imai, and Tomoya Sasaki. 2020. Keyword assisted topic models. *arXiv preprint arXiv:2004.05964*.

Niels D. Goet. 2019. Measuring polarization with text analysis: Evidence from the uk house of commons, 1811–2015. *Political Analysis*, 27(4):518–539.

Frederik Hjorth, Robert Klemmensen, Sara Hobolt, Martin Ejnar Hansen, and Peter Kurrild-Klitgaard. 2015. Computers, coders, and voters: Comparing automated methods for estimating party positions. *Research & Politics*, 2(2):2053168015580476.

Carsten Jentsch, Eun Ryung Lee, and Enno Mammen. 2020. Time-dependent poisson reduced rank models for political text data analysis. *Computational Statistics & Data Analysis*, 142:106813.

Carsten Jentsch, Enno Mammen, Henrik Müller, Jonas Rieger, and Christof Schötz. 2021. Text mining methods for measuring the coherence of party manifestos for the german federal elections from 1990 to 2021. (8).

Karim El-Ouaghlidi, Matthias Gomolka, and Jens Orben. 2019. Bundesbank speeches: Data report 2019-12. (12).

Benjamin E. Lauderdale and Alexander Herzog. 2016. Measuring political positions from legislative speech. *Political Analysis*, 24(3):374–394.

Michael Laver, Kenneth Benoit, and John Garry. 2003. Extracting policy positions from political texts using words as data. *American Political Science Review*, 97(02).

Leland McInnes, John Healy, and Steve Astels. 2017. hdbscan: Hierarchical density based clustering. *The Journal of Open Source Software*, 2(11):205.

Leland McInnes, John Healy, Nathaniel Saul, and Lukas Großberger. 2018. Umap: Uniform manifold approximation and projection. *The Journal of Open Source Software*, 3(29):861.

Tomas Mikolov, Kai Chen, Greg Corrado, and Jeffrey Dean. 2013. Efficient estimation of word representations in vector space. *arXiv preprint arXiv:1301.3781*.

Stefan Müller. 2022. The temporal focus of campaign communication. *The Journal of Politics*, 84(1):585–590.

Federico Nanni, Goran Glavas, Ines Rehbein, Simone Paolo Ponzetto, and Heiner Stuckenschmidt. 2019. Political text scaling meets computational semantics. *arXiv preprint arXiv:1904.06217*.

Orestis Papakyriakopoulos, Simon Hegelich, Juan Carlos Medina Serrano, and Fabienne Marco. 2020. Bias in word embeddings. In *Proceedings of the 2020 Conference on Fairness, Accountability, and Transparency*, ACM Digital Library, pages 446–457, New York,NY,United States. Association for Computing Machinery.

Nils Reimers and Iryna Gurevych. 2019. Sentence-bert: Sentence embeddings using siamese bert-networks.

Jonathan B. Slapin and Sven-Oliver Proksch. 2008. A scaling model for estimating time-series party positions from texts. *American Journal of Political Science*, 52(3):705–722.

Keyon Vafa, Suresh Naidu, and David Blei. 2020. Text-based ideal points. *Association for Computational Linguistics*, 2020:5345–5357.

Andrea Volkens, Tobias Burst, Werner Krause, Pola Lehmann, Theres Matthieß, Sven Regel, Bernhard Weßels, Lisa Zehnter, and Wissenschaftszentrum Berlin für Sozialforschung. 2021. Manifesto project dataset.

Kohei Watanabe. 2021. Latent semantic scaling: A semisupervised text analysis technique for new domains and languages. *Communication Methods and Measures*, 15(2):81–102.

Proceedings of the 18th Conference on Natural Language Processing (KONVENS 2022)

Bye, Bye, Maintenance Work? Using Model Cloning to Approximate the Behavior of Legacy Tools

Piush Aggarwal **Torsten Zesch**
Computational Linguistics
CATALPA - Center for Advanced Technology-Assisted Learning and Predictive Analytics
FernUniversität in Hagen
{piush.aggarwal,torsten.zesch}@fernuni-hagen.de

Abstract

A lot of NLP tools are not maintained anymore, but might still provide some unique functionality. We investigate whether such legacy tools could be replaced by a neural network that closely imitates the original behavior. For this purpose, we propose *model cloning* that can be performed by solely looking at the output of the original model, which makes the cloning possible also for black-box systems. Using a single neural architecture for cloning legacy models, caries other benefits like ease-of-use, continued maintenance, and expected speed increase. As a proof-of-concept, we clone 9 models from 5 POS tagger implementations of different complexity. The cloned models all learn to perform POS tagging on par with the legacy models, but seem not to learn the specific tagging patterns of individual legacy models.

1 Introduction

End-to-end neural models are increasingly used to build NLP tools (Tao et al., 2022; Wolf et al., 2020; Qi et al., 2020; Akbik et al., 2019; Han et al., 2019) However, legacy tools are still being used in production and for research purposes, as they might provide a unique functionality that cannot be easily replaced. Such legacy tools are often not maintained anymore and increasingly hard to use. Or outright dangerous, as the Log4Shell vulnerability[1] has turned some legacy Java tools into unmanageable security risks. They might only work with a specific OS version or with an outdated version of the programming language. Or the required models have to be secretly traded between researchers, as the official download ceased to exist. For some very important tools, it might be possible to port them to the latest technology and keep them available, but the bulk of legacy tools will soon be gone.

[1] https://en.wikipedia.org/wiki/Log4Shell

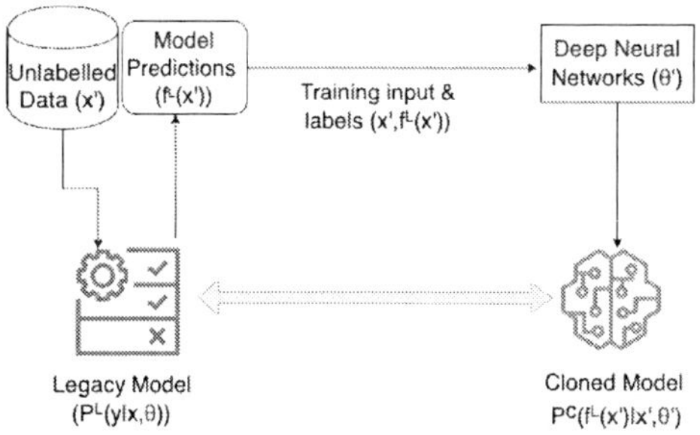

Figure 1: The model cloning process.

We argue that a possible solution is to clone the legacy models into a state-of-the-art neural model. We consider here a situation where the original training data is not available. Otherwise, we could simply retrain the model. The legacy models might also include hard-coded heuristics or dictionaries that are not reflected in the training data itself. We thus propose to apply the legacy model on plain text and then use the results to train a new model.[2]

In this paper, we choose POS tagging as a proof-of-concept use case to illustrate the potential properties of model cloning. We choose 9 different POS models from 5 legacy tools and clone their behavior into BiLSTM-CRF networks (Huang et al., 2015; Graves et al., 2013). We make all of the generated cloned models and our experimental code publicly available.[3]

2 Model Cloning

Under *model cloning*, we understand the process of copying the behavior of a legacy model by only looking at its output. Figure 1 gives an overview of the cloning process, where we select a *legacy model* ($P^L(y|x,\theta)$) which is trained on data (x,y) (unknown to us) is fed with unlabeled data (x'). To-

[2] Cloning might be restricted by the license of the legacy model.

[3] https://github.com/aggarwalpiush/model_cloning

gether with predictions ($f^L(x')$)) generated by the model these data-label pairs are use to train a deep neural network. After optimized training, the generated model ($P^c(f^L(x')|x', \theta')$) is called *cloned model*. Here θ and θ' represent model parameters.

3 Experimental Setup

To illustrate the potential properties of model cloning, we use *POS Tagging* as an example task. We apply the above mentioned model cloning architecture to classical POS taggers and evaluate how closely we can copy there behavior.

POS Taggers Table 1 lists the pre-neural legacy POS-taggers used in our experiments. We use the DKPro core framework (Eckart de Castilho and Gurevych, 2014) version of the following taggers: We use Java-based NLP4J (or ClearNLP) (Choi and Palmer, 2012), Hepple (Hepple, 2000), Mate tagger (Björkelund et al., 2010), OpenNLP[4] and Stanford (Toutanova et al., 2003).

Cloned Model Sequence labeling tasks such as POS-tagging are most promisingly taken care by linear statistical models (e.g. Conditional Random Fields (CRF) (Lafferty et al., 2001)) and neural network (NN) based models such as LSTM, BI-LSTM, etc. In our work, we use BILSTM-CRF based DNN architecture (Huang et al., 2015) for generating cloned models, where for a selected token in the text statement, a BILSTM layer carry the input text features from both direction of the sentence (Graves et al., 2013) as well as CRF layer provide sentence level tag information. We use a untrained embedding layer of 300 size input to 300 units of BILSTM cells followed by single layer of fully connected neural network having 13 units (number of classes). Model's raw predictions (pre-normalized) is used to generate CRF transition matrices which are input to a RNN cell to generate the final prediction. Negative log likelihood of CRF-layer output is used as loss function with Adam (Kingma and Ba, 2014) as an optimizer.

Note that for our proof-of-concept experiment, the actual architecture in the cloned model only needs to be powerful enough to simulate the original behavior. However, other architectures might be able to learn the same behavior from less data or reflect the behavior more closely.

[4] opennlp.apache.org

Tagger	Modelname	Domain	abbr.
Hepple	-	-	hp
Mate	Conll2009	mixed	mt
NLP4J	Ontonotes	news	on
	Mayo	medical	ma
OpenNLP	Maxent	unknown	mx
	Perceptron	unknown	pp
Stanford	csls-left3w	news	st1
	fast	unknown	st2
	wsj-0-18-csls	news	st3

Table 1: POS-taggers' models considered for cloning process.

Unlabelled Data Based on the model cloning process described in Figure 1, we use the known unlabeled data for training and labeled test data for evaluation. Note that all the labels are normalized and mapped to standard coarse grained universal tag-set (Das and Petrov, 2011). As an input to legacy models, we use web text of 1 Million sentences from news-wire platforms downloaded from the Leipzig Corpus Collection (Goldhahn et al., 2012). Before prediction, each sentence was tokenized using NLP4j's tokenizer (Choi and Palmer, 2012). We ignore the tags 'apos', '^' and 'X' in our experiments, as they are not easily mapped to coarse-grained labels for comparison.

Labeled Test Data As we also want to evaluate the objective tagging quality of the cloned models, we evaluate on a corpus with gold tags, following the setup in Horsmann et al. (2015). For evaluation, we consider formal writings, e.g. news articles, travel reports and how-to's which overlap the same domain with the known unlabeled data. We use three subsections of the GUM (Zeldes, 2017) and Brown (Francis and Kucera, 1964) corpus. Details of the corpora are provided in Table 3.

Model Training To generate the cloned models, we use the DELTA framework[5] (Han et al., 2019). We use a batch size of 36,864 for only single epoch cycle with a dropout rate of 0.5 and 0.001 as learning rate. Since our objective is to investigate how well we can learn the output of the taggers, we do not initialize the network with word embeddings to avoid any other external dependency than the training data. To generate the predictions labels, we use a 64 bit Intel(R) Xeon(R) Gold 5120 CPU @ 2.20GHz machine. For the training of cloned

[5] github.com/didi/delta

Tagger	Brown	GUM-News	ERROR GUM-Voyage	GUM-HowTo	tokens ($\times 10^3$ per sec) Cloned	Legacy	Δ
Mate (mt)	.05	.05	.05	.05	186.6	4.5	+182.1
Hepple (hp)	.04	.03	.03	.04	213.8	227.6	-13.8
OpenNLP (mx)	.04	.03	.04	.04	183.5	40.4	+143.1
OpenNLP (pp)	.06	.05	.07	.07	190.9	193.1	-2.2
Stanford (st3)	.04	.03	.04	.03	196.6	16.3	+180.3
Stanford (st1)	.04	.03	.04	.04	211.4	15.1	+196.3
Stanford (st2)	.04	.04	.04	.04	214.2	9.1	+205.1
NLP4J (ma)	.06	.04	.04	.05	208.2	26.7	+181.5
NLP4J (on)	.06	.03	.04	.04	198.9	14.9	+184.0
Average	.05	.04	.04	.04	200.5	60.9	+139.6

Table 2: The cloned models performance evaluated on labeled test data. ERROR is calculated by substracting Weighted F1 metric from 1. Δ provide tagging speed comparison with respect to legacy models.

Corpus	Tokens (x10^3)	Tagset	Sent Len ($\mu \pm \sigma$)
Brown	1,018	Brown	20.2 ± 13.1
GUM-News	8	PTB-TT	23.0 ± 12.5
GUM-Voyage	7	PTB-TT	22.0 ± 13.4
GUM-HowTo	11	PTB-TT	15.6 ± 9.9

Table 3: News domain labeled test data. Here, PTB-TT denotes penn tree bank with extended tree tagger tagset.

models, an additional 24 GB memory size Quadro RTX 6000 GPU is used.

4 Results

Table 2 shows how closely the cloned models were able to mirror the behavior of the legacy models. For that purpose, we treat the legacy results as the gold standard and report the ERROR, i.e. how much the cloned models deviates from it. We find that on average cloned models are able to approximate the behavior of legacy POS taggers with an error of 4 points. This value is statistically significant (based on McNemar Test (Dietterich, 1998) with $p < 0.05$), which means that our cloned models are significantly different from the legacy models.

Error Analysis The heatmap in Figure 2 shows where we find the major differences between legacy and cloned model. We only show results for the Stanford (st1) model, but the other models perform similarly. One source of mismatch are verb/noun and adj/noun confusions in both directions, which seems to indicate that the model has not learned the actual behavior of the legacy model. An error category that stands out is where the cloned model assigns a *NOUN* tag to what should have been *PUNCT* within the legacy model. For example in the sequence *Annapolis , Jan. 7 (special)*, the token the closing parenthesis is tagged as a noun by all cloned models.

Tagging Quality When the cloned model deviates from exactly mirroring the behavior of the legacy model, it could (i) assign a wrong tag when the legacy model was wrong, (ii) correct a mistake by the legacy model, or (iii) assign a wrong tag when also the legacy model was wrong (this last case would be neutral in term of tagging quality). To test what effect is dominating here, we also evaluate legacy models and their cloned versions on the gold labels of our evaluation corpus. We find that cloned models are either on par with legacy models or up to 2 percent points worse (in terms of average F_1). This shows that differences in behavior between legacy and cloned models are relevant for the task performance and result in worse tagging quality.

Tagging Speed To measure the tagging speed, we choose a single server setup for both legacy as well as cloned models. We only measure pure tagging speed and exclude model loading time, because when tagging a lot of text the one-time cost to load the model does not matter that much. Table 2 shows that cloned models are either much faster or on par with legacy tools. Projecting in the future, the neural models will get faster, while the legacy models are unlikely to benefit from using GPUs and improved library speed.

5 Related Work

Model cloning can be seen as a kind of *model extraction attack*, where copying a model has been investigated under the aspect of being a threat to a service's underlying business model (Yuan et al., 2022; Tramèr et al., 2016). In this scenario, an ad-

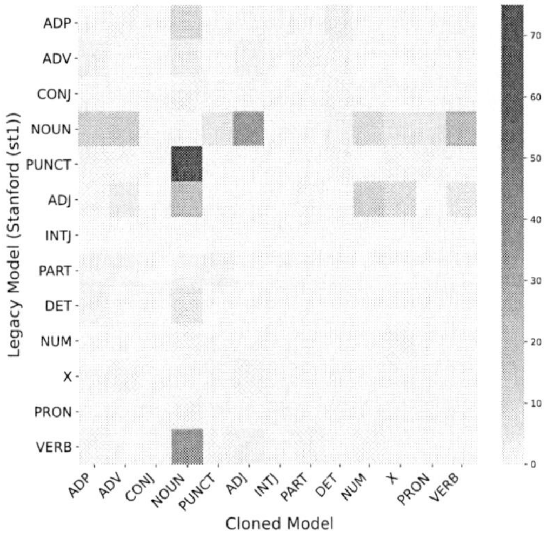

Figure 2: Heatmap illustrating failures of the cloned model to reproduce tags assigned by the Stanford legacy model (st1).

versary keeps using a model, which is offered via a paid or un-paid endpoint, until enough data has been gathered to train an own model. In particular, neural network-based model extraction is a powerful approach with their ability to approximate a function that maps an input on a certain output (Yi Shi et al., 2017). Adversaries can exploit the neural network to approximate the functionalities of endpoint services and become independent after successful cloning (Takemura et al., 2020; Atli et al., 2020). Extraction attacks are not only limited to attack model functionality, but also helps in stealing model hyper-parameters which are considered confidential specially for commercial and proprietary algorithms (Wang and Gong, 2018). Neural networks such as Knockoff Nets (Orekondy et al., 2019) are able to successfully by-pass the monetary and intellectual effort and create a reasonable cloned models as little as $30. Even cloning of real time systems such as artificial human voice synthesis (Arik et al., 2018) and autonomous driving (D'Este et al., 2003; Kuefler et al., 2017) are common practices nowadays.

Other related methods are distant (Mintz et al., 2009) and weak (Hoffmann et al., 2011) supervision which are used to build huge however relatively noisy labeled training data. They not only save time and money but are also less prone to induce human errors into the dataset. The algorithms which are used to generate the labels can be correlated with cloned model that approximate the behavioral mapping of available manually annotated data. Another area related to cloning is *Bootstrapping* (Goldman and Zhou, 2000), where machine-annotated raw data is generated as an attempt to overcome the lack of human-annotated gold data.

6 Summary

Model cloning is a potential solution to ensure the continued availability of legacy tools that are not maintained anymore. As a first experiment into model cloning, we have experimented with mirroring the behavior of 9 different pre-neural POS tagging models. We find that the cloned models come close in terms of POS tagging performance, but somewhat fail to closely resemble the specific behavior of individual taggers.

Our results are limited by only experimenting with POS tagging as one example task and by using only one neural architecture. Some NLP tasks might lend themselves more easily to cloning and some neural architecture might be better suited for cloning. In future work, we thus want to improve the cloning process to better capture the specific behavior of a given model the and to extend the paradigm to other tasks beyond POS tagging.

Acknowledgments

This work was conducted in the framework of CATALPA - Center for Advanced Technology-Assisted Learning and Predictive Analytics of the FernUniversität in Hagen, Germany.

References

Alan Akbik, Tanja Bergmann, Duncan Blythe, Kashif Rasul, Stefan Schweter, and Roland Vollgraf. 2019. Flair: An easy-to-use framework for state-of-the-art nlp. In *NAACL 2019, 2019 Annual Conference of the North American Chapter of the Association for Computational Linguistics (Demonstrations)*, pages 54–59.

Sercan Arik, Jitong Chen, Kainan Peng, Wei Ping, and Yanqi Zhou. 2018. Neural voice cloning with a few samples. In *Advances in Neural Information Processing Systems*, pages 10019–10029.

Buse Gul Atli, Sebastian Szyller, Mika Juuti, Samuel Marchal, and N. Asokan. 2020. Extraction of Complex DNN Models: Real Threat or Boogeyman? In *Engineering Dependable and Secure Machine Learning Systems*, pages 42–57, Cham. Springer International Publishing.

Anders Björkelund, Bernd Bohnet, Love Hafdell, and Pierre Nugues. 2010. A high-performance syntactic and semantic dependency parser. In *Proceedings of the 23rd International Conference on Computational Linguistics: Demonstrations*, COLING '10, page 33–36, USA. Association for Computational Linguistics.

Richard Eckart de Castilho and Iryna Gurevych. 2014. A broad-coverage collection of portable NLP components for building shareable analysis pipelines. In *Proceedings of the Workshop on Open Infrastructures and Analysis Frameworks for HLT*, pages 1–11, Dublin, Ireland. Association for Computational Linguistics and Dublin City University.

Jinho D. Choi and Martha Palmer. 2012. Fast and robust part-of-speech tagging using dynamic model selection. In *Proceedings of the 50th Annual Meeting of the Association for Computational Linguistics (Volume 2: Short Papers)*, pages 363–367, Jeju Island, Korea. Association for Computational Linguistics.

Dipanjan Das and Slav Petrov. 2011. Unsupervised part-of-speech tagging with bilingual graph-based projections. In *Proceedings of the 49th Annual Meeting of the Association for Computational Linguistics: Human Language Technologies*, pages 600–609, Portland, Oregon, USA. Association for Computational Linguistics.

Claire D'Este, Mark O'Sullivan, and Nicholas Hannah. 2003. Behavioural cloning and robot control. In *Robotics and Applications*, pages 179–182.

Thomas G. Dietterich. 1998. Approximate Statistical Tests for Comparing Supervised Classification Learning Algorithms. *Neural Computation*, 10(7):1895–1923.

W Nelson Francis and Henry Kucera. 1964. Brown corpus. *Department of Linguistics, Brown University, Providence, Rhode Island*, 1.

Dirk Goldhahn, Thomas Eckart, and Uwe Quasthoff. 2012. Building large monolingual dictionaries at the leipzig corpora collection: From 100 to 200 languages. In *Proceedings of the Eighth International Conference on Language Resources and Evaluation (LREC-2012)*, pages 759–765, Istanbul, Turkey. European Languages Resources Association (ELRA).

Sally A. Goldman and Yan Zhou. 2000. Enhancing supervised learning with unlabeled data. In *Proceedings of the Seventeenth International Conference on Machine Learning*, ICML '00, pages 327–334, San Francisco, CA, USA. Morgan Kaufmann Publishers Inc.

Alex Graves, Abdel-rahman Mohamed, and Geoffrey E. Hinton. 2013. Speech recognition with deep recurrent neural networks. *CoRR*, abs/1303.5778.

Kun Han, Junwen Chen, Hui Zhang, Haiyang Xu, Yiping Peng, Yun Wang, Ning Ding, Hui Deng, Yonghu Gao, Tingwei Guo, Yi Zhang, Yahao He, Baochang Ma, Yulong Zhou, Kangli Zhang, Chao Liu, Ying Lyu, Chenxi Wang, Cheng Gong, Yunbo Wang, Wei Zou, Hui Song, and Xiangang Li. 2019. DELTA: A DEep learning based Language Technology plAtform. *arXiv e-prints*.

Mark Hepple. 2000. Independence and Commitment: Assumptions for Rapid Training and Execution of Rule-based POS Taggers. In *Proceedings of the 38th Annual Meeting of the Association for Computational Linguistics*, pages 278–277, Hong Kong. Association for Computational Linguistics.

Raphael Hoffmann, Congle Zhang, Xiao Ling, Luke Zettlemoyer, and Daniel S Weld. 2011. Knowledge-based weak supervision for information extraction of overlapping relations. In *Proceedings of the 49th annual meeting of the association for computational linguistics: human language technologies*, pages 541–550.

Tobias Horsmann, Nicolai Erbs, and Torsten Zesch. 2015. Fast or Accurate ? – A Comparative Evaluation of PoS Tagging Models. In *Proceedings of the International Conference of the German Society for Computational Linguistics and Language Technology (GSCL-2015)*, pages 22–30, Essen, Germany.

Zhiheng Huang, Wei Xu, and Kai Yu. 2015. Bidirectional LSTM-CRF models for sequence tagging. *CoRR*, abs/1508.01991.

Diederik Kingma and Jimmy Ba. 2014. Adam: A method for stochastic optimization. *International Conference on Learning Representations*.

A. Kuefler, J. Morton, T. Wheeler, and M. Kochenderfer. 2017. Imitating driver behavior with generative adversarial networks. In *2017 IEEE Intelligent Vehicles Symposium (IV)*, pages 204–211.

John D. Lafferty, Andrew McCallum, and Fernando C. N. Pereira. 2001. Conditional random fields: Probabilistic models for segmenting and labeling sequence data. In *Proceedings of the Eighteenth International Conference on Machine Learning*, ICML '01, page 282–289, San Francisco, CA, USA. Morgan Kaufmann Publishers Inc.

Mike Mintz, Steven Bills, Rion Snow, and Dan Jurafsky. 2009. Distant supervision for relation extraction without labeled data. In *Proceedings of the Joint Conference of the 47th Annual Meeting of the ACL and the 4th International Joint Conference on Natural Language Processing of the AFNLP*, pages 1003–1011.

Tribhuvanesh Orekondy, Bernt Schiele, and Mario Fritz. 2019. Knockoff Nets: Stealing Functionality of Black-Box Models. In *CVPR*.

Peng Qi, Yuhao Zhang, Yuhui Zhang, Jason Bolton, and Christopher D. Manning. 2020. Stanza: A Python Natural Language Processing Toolkit for Many Human Languages. In *Proceedings of the 58th Annual Meeting of the Association for Computational Linguistics: System Demonstrations*.

Tatsuya Takemura, Naoto Yanai, and Toru Fujiwara. 2020. Model Extraction Attacks on Recurrent Neural Networks. *Journal of Information Processing*, 28:1010–1024.

Zhihua Tao, Chunping Ouyang, Yongbin Liu, Tonglee Chung, and Yixin Cao. 2022. Multi-head attention graph convolutional network model: End-to-end entity and relation joint extraction based on multi-head attention graph convolutional network. *CAAI Transactions on Intelligence Technology*.

Kristina Toutanova, Dan Klein, Christopher D. Manning, and Yoram Singer. 2003. Feature-rich Part-of-speech Tagging with a Cyclic Dependency Network. In *Proceedings of the 2003 Conference of the North American Chapter of the Association for Computational Linguistics on Human Language Technology - Volume 1*, NAACL '03, pages 173–180, Stroudsburg, PA, USA. Association for Computational Linguistics.

Florian Tramèr, Fan Zhang, Ari Juels, Michael K. Reiter, and Thomas Ristenpart. 2016. Stealing Machine Learning Models via Prediction APIs. In *Proceedings of the 25th USENIX Conference on Security Symposium*, SEC'16, pages 601–618, Berkeley, CA, USA. USENIX Association.

B. Wang and N. Gong. 2018. Stealing Hyperparameters in Machine Learning. In *2018 IEEE Symposium on Security and Privacy (SP)*, pages 36–52.

Thomas Wolf, Lysandre Debut, Victor Sanh, Julien Chaumond, Clement Delangue, Anthony Moi, Pierric Cistac, Tim Rault, Remi Louf, Morgan Funtowicz, Joe Davison, Sam Shleifer, Patrick von Platen, Clara Ma, Yacine Jernite, Julien Plu, Canwen Xu, Teven Le Scao, Sylvain Gugger, Mariama Drame, Quentin Lhoest, and Alexander Rush. 2020. Transformers: State-of-the-Art Natural Language Processing. In *Proceedings of the 2020 Conference on Empirical Methods in Natural Language Processing: System Demonstrations*, pages 38–45, Online. Association for Computational Linguistics.

Yi Shi, Y. Sagduyu, and A. Grushin. 2017. How to steal a machine learning classifier with deep learning. In *2017 IEEE International Symposium on Technologies for Homeland Security (HST)*, pages 1–5.

Xiaoyong Yuan, Leah Ding, Lan Zhang, Xiaolin Li, and Dapeng Oliver Wu. 2022. ES Attack: Model Stealing Against Deep Neural Networks Without Data Hurdles. *IEEE Transactions on Emerging Topics in Computational Intelligence*, pages 1–13.

Amir Zeldes. 2017. The GUM Corpus: Creating Multilayer Resources in the Classroom. *Lang. Resour. Eval.*, 51(3):581–612.

Association for Computational Linguistics
209 N. Eighth Street
Stroudsburg, Pennsylvania 18360

ISBN 978-1-7138-6763-0

CURRAN ASSOCIATES INC.
proceedings.com